MW00755168

INSPIRE / PLAN / DISCOVER / EXPERIENCE

MEXICO

DK EYEWITNESS

MEXICO

CONTENTS

DISCOVER 6

EXPERIENCE MEXICO CITY 64

EXPERIENCE MEXICO 134

NEED TO KNOW 310

Left: Ceramic skulls at a market stall

Previous page: Temple overlooking the beach, Tulum

Front cover: Colorful buildings in San Miguel de Allende

DISCOVER

The heart of San Miguel de Allende

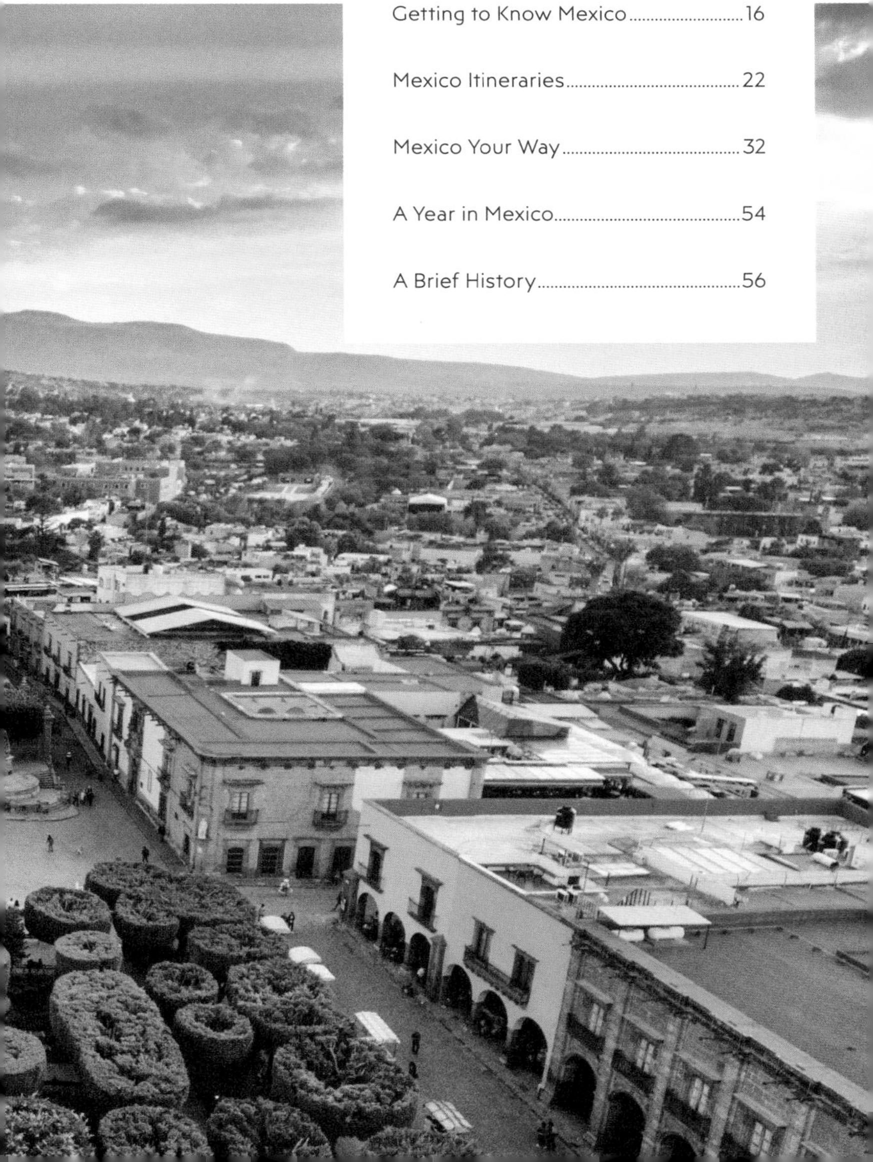

WELCOME TO
MEXICO

Bold Rivera murals in the city and ancient Maya ruins in the jungle. Tranquil deserts, pristine beaches, vast canyons, and snow-capped volcanoes. Spicy salsas followed up with fiery tequila. Whatever your dream trip to Mexico includes, this DK Eyewitness travel guide is the perfect companion.

1 Soft-tortilla tacos.

2 *Papel-picado* hanging over a street in San Miguel de Allende.

3 A mariachi musician.

4 Popocatépetl volcano and Cholula's hilltop Nuestra Señora de los Remedios.

Some people picture Mexico as a vast, cacti-studded desert – and while that reflects the landscape just south of the US border, a little exploring will turn up so much more. Farther inland, great mountains and volcanoes dominate the landscape, while the jungles of the south harbor tropical wildlife and the crumbling Mesoamerican ruins. All around the country, Mexico's beaches are a major draw, from the wildlife-rich waters of Baja California, to the wild, surf-rich stretches in the states of Chiapas and Oaxaca – not to mention the balmy, Caribbean coast of the Riviera Maya.

When it comes to urban pleasures, few places in the world can match Mexico City, with its teeming markets, vibrant galleries, and enthusiastic sports scene. Cities such as Guanajuato and San Miguel de Allende are beautiful bastions of old New Spain, while Monterrey and Tijuana are hubs of modern Mexican culture and entertainment. In the south, Oaxaca and San Cristóbal offer a very different vibe, immersed in rich Indigenous culture and culinary traditions.

From the western Baja California border to the curving Yucatán peninsula and everything in between, we've broken the country down into easily navigable chapters, with detailed itineraries, expert local knowledge, and comprehensive maps. So whether you're hunting down unique regional dishes, a fun local festival, or stunning views of weathered pyramids, this DK Eyewitness travel guide will ensure that you have everything you need to plan the perfect adventure. Enjoy the book, and enjoy Mexico.

REASONS TO LOVE
MEXICO

With such rich and varied cultural traditions, regional foods, and natural beauty, there's no such thing as "typical" here – instead you'll find hundreds of different things to discover and love. Here are just some of our favorites.

1 FIESTA CULTURE

From party-hard Carnival to the traditional Day of the Dead festivities – not to mention regional events up and down the country – there's always something going on (p54).

MESOAMERICAN CITIES 2

Mexico is studded with monumental pre-Hispanic remains. Scale the Pyramid of the Sun, hike the jungle paths of Palenque, and admire the murals at Bonampak.

3 MEXICAN FLAVORS

There's more to Mexican cuisine than its famous street food. Try the fragrant Veracruz-style red snapper, enjoy small-batch tequila, and indulge at gourmet restaurants (p52).

THE SILVER ROAD 4
Follow this old route *(p26)* that once linked the capital and the country's silver mines to discover all the beautifully preserved towns between Zacatecas and Mexico City.

VIBRANT ART 5
Folk-art-inspired paintings by Frida Kahlo and bold murals of Aztec serpents, the Day of the Dead, priests and revolutionaries all capture the spirit of Mexico *(p38)*.

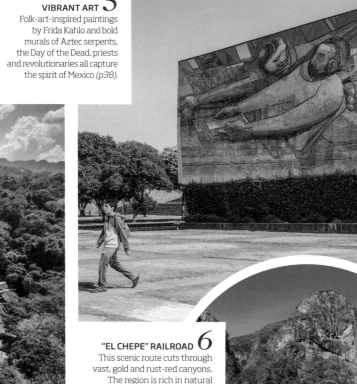

"EL CHEPE" RAILROAD 6
This scenic route cuts through vast, gold and rust-red canyons. The region is rich in natural beauty, making it perfect terrain for one of the world's great train journeys *(p180)*.

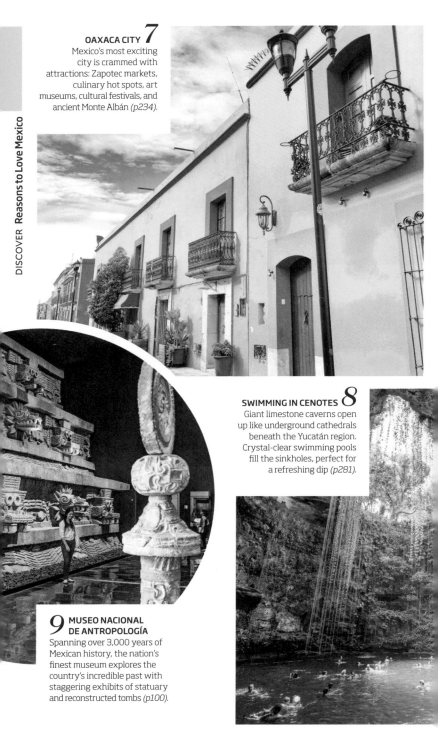

OAXACA CITY 7

Mexico's most exciting city is crammed with attractions: Zapotec markets, culinary hot spots, art museums, cultural festivals, and ancient Monte Albán *(p234)*.

SWIMMING IN CENOTES 8

Giant limestone caverns open up like underground cathedrals beneath the Yucatán region. Crystal-clear swimming pools fill the sinkholes, perfect for a refreshing dip *(p281)*.

9 MUSEO NACIONAL DE ANTROPOLOGÍA

Spanning over 3,000 years of Mexican history, the nation's finest museum explores the country's incredible past with staggering exhibits of statuary and reconstructed tombs *(p100)*.

10 BEAUTIFUL BEACHES

Mexico's beaches *(p44)* offer a bit of everything. Lounge on white-sand backed by desert mountains, surf on wild waters, or party all night on the golden coast with a margarita in hand.

TRADITIONAL CRAFTS *11*

Crafts in Mexico are an essential part of ceremonial and daily life. Head to a *mercado* (market) to hunt down local treasures like woven *huarache* sandals or Taxco silverwork.

MARIACHI MUSIC *12*

Beginning with guitars, trumpets, and a harmonized chorus, mariachi bands grow in number as the day goes on, enticing dancers to fill the city plazas *(p32)*.

BAJA CALIFORNIA
p164

NORTHERN MEXICO
p174

BAJÍO AND THE
CENTRAL COAST
p190

EXPLORE
MEXICO

This guide divides Mexico into eight color-coded sightseeing areas, as shown on this map. Find out more about each area on the following pages.

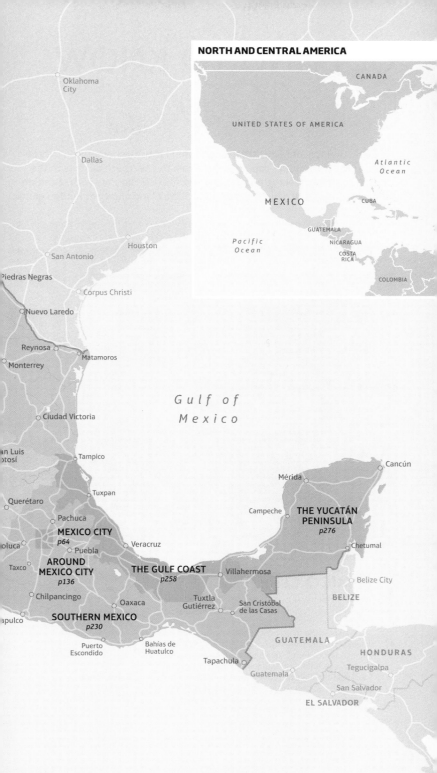

CANADA

UNITED STATES OF AMERICA

Atlantic Ocean

MEXICO

CUBA

GUATEMALA

NICARAGUA

Pacific Ocean

COSTA RICA

COLOMBIA

Oklahoma City

Dallas

San Antonio

Houston

Piedras Negras

Córpus Christi

Nuevo Laredo

Reynosa

Matamoros

Monterrey

Ciudad Victoria

Gulf of Mexico

an Luis otosí

Tampico

Cancún

Querétaro

Tuxpan

Mérida

Pachuca

Campeche

THE YUCATÁN PENINSULA
p276

oluca

MEXICO CITY
p64

Puebla

Veracruz

Chetumal

Taxco

AROUND MEXICO CITY
p136

THE GULF COAST
p258

Villahermosa

Belize City

Chilpancingo

Oaxaca

Tuxtla Gutiérrez

San Cristóbal de las Casas

BELIZE

apulco

SOUTHERN MEXICO
p230

Puerto Escondido

Bahías de Huatulco

Tapachula

GUATEMALA

HONDURAS

Tegucigalpa

Guatemala

San Salvador

EL SALVADOR

GETTING TO KNOW
MEXICO

Mexico is divided into 32 states, among them the autonomous district of Mexico City, the nation's capital *(p64)*. From the northern deserts to the tropical south and everything in between, Mexico abounds with stunning natural scenery, a rich history, delicious dishes, and plenty of hidden gems.

MEXICO CITY

PAGE 64

Teeming craft markets, massive Diego Rivera murals, the wafting aromas of street food, and the invigorating sounds of marimba and mariachi – Mexico City has it all. It's a sprawling metropolis of distinct neighborhoods, where you'll find high-end boutiques and hip bars in Polanco, colonial-era monasteries and Aztec ruins in the Historic Center, and tranquil suburban enclaves in San Ángel and Coyoacán. The city also boasts some of Latin America's best restaurants, museums, performing arts, and sporting events, so get ready for non-stop excitement in this high-energy capital.

Best for
Museums, art, architecture, dining, and nightlife

Home to
Catedral Metropolitana, Templo Mayor, Palacio de Bellas Artes, Palacio Nacional, Museo Nacional de Antropología, Museo Frida Kahlo, and Xochimilco

Experience
Listening to live mariachi bands in Plaza Garibaldi

PAGE 136

AROUND MEXICO CITY

The patchwork of small, densely populated mountain states around the capital are a treasure trove of Mexican history and culture. Indigenous civilizations created the pyramids of Tula and Teotihuacán, the latter being Mexico's most famous pre-Hispanic site. From the 16th century, the Spanish founded their own towns, such as Pachuca and Mineral del Monte, that are now picturesque spots full of pretty Spanish Colonial architecture. The western part of the region has cool forests and scenic lakes, while to the south, warmer weather attracts visitors to busy Cuernavaca and beautiful Taxco.

Best for
Ancient ruins and Spanish Colonial architecture

Home to
Teotihuacán, Museo Nacional del Virreinato, and Puebla

Experience
Scaling the Pyramid of the Sun to survey the ruins of the great Mesoamerican city of Teotihuacán

PAGE 164

BAJA CALIFORNIA

A long, thin peninsula surrounded by sub-tropical waters, Baja California is a land of giant cacti, golden deserts, and tranquil, untouched beaches. Sparsely populated, it's a favorite of North American snowbirds who migrate south on the Transpeninsular Highway every year. Its mix of wild landscapes, remote communities, and tourist fame means there's a diverse blend of experiences for travelers to discover here: the party-hard vibe of Tijuana, whale-watching at Guerrero Negro, ancient cave paintings in the wilderness, and pristine beaches enclaves of Los Cabos.

Best for
Beaches, nightlife, and watersports

Home to
Cabo San Lucas, Tijuana, and la Paz

Experience
Strolling along the seaside promenade in Ensenada then stopping for lunch to savor the town's famous fish tacos

$\rightarrow$

PAGE 174

NORTHERN MEXICO

This is the home of the cacti-strewn deserts that many people picture when they think of Mexico. Those who yearn for adventure will find the empty miles and wild landscapes that provide some of Mexico's most memorable moments. There are vast deserts, old-fashioned beach resorts, wild frontier towns, and modern cities – all inhabited by communities deeply rooted in tradition and ranching culture. Of course, there are plenty of great experiences that are easy to access without heading out by car: riding the magnificent Copper Canyon railroad, discovering energetic and cosmopolitan Monterrey, and walking the streets of western film sets near Durango.

Best for
Colonial-era history, culture, and natural beauty

Home to
Paquimé and the Copper Canyon

Experience
Riding on the El Chepe Railroad in Copper Canyon for incredible views of the Sierra Tarahumara

BAJÍO AND
THE CENTRAL COAST

Mexico's Pacific Coast is a sunseeker's paradise, dotted with beautiful resorts for those who want some serious leisure time. But most of the major highlights of the region are in the small states that make up Mexico's heartland – known as Bajío – which offers up a blend of colonial-era silver mining towns, rolling mountain scenery, and Indigenous cultures. The region has given the world quintessential Mexican exports such as tequila, mariachi music, and Diego Rivera, but it's also full of lesser-known Indigenous traditions – the colorful yarn paintings of the Wixáritari people, and the festivals of the Lake Pátzcuaro area, deeply rooted in the heartland's traditional cultures.

Best for
Beaches, Indigenous culture, architecture, and festivals

Home to
Guadalajara, Guanajuato, Zacatecas, Querétaro, and Morelia

Experience
Enjoying the concerts and art exhibitions at the Feria de San Marcos in Aguascalientes

$\rightarrow$

PAGE 230

SOUTHERN MEXICO

The southern states are blanketed with some of Mexico's most impressive backdrops, from spectacular mountain peaks to waterfall-streaked valleys. The Pacific coast is a major draw for many visitors, some of whom come for resorts such as Acapulco. Others seek the surfers' paradise of Puerto Escondido, or the wild beaches of Chiapas. One of the most fascinating things about the region, though, is that it's the meeting place of so many different cultures and communities, each of which has helped shape the way of life here. Even for Mexico, where several dozen Indigenous languages are still in use, this southern region is particularly diverse.

Best for
Indigenous culture, natural beauty, Mesoamerican ruins, and Mexican cuisine

Home to
Oaxaca, Monte Albán, Acapulco, and Palenque

Experience
Taking a foodie tour of Oaxaca city

PAGE 258

THE GULF COAST

While this region is little more than a thin slip of land, the Gulf Coast is still bursting with attractions both old and new. The cooler, mountainous interior is perfect for active travellers looking for some outdoor thrills, while El Tajín's ruins and Xalapa's anthropology museum offer up plenty of fun for history lovers. Meanwhile, the port of Veracruz is an interesting blend of cultures: traditional Mexican music drifts down streets lined with Spanish Colonial architecture, while the beach resort atmosphere and coffee culture are a taste of the ultra-modern.

Best for
History and outdoor adventures

Home to
El Tajín and the Museo de Antropología de Xalapa

Experience
Taking a temazcal in Catemaco – a sauna, followed by a massage or mud bath

THE YUCATÁN PENINSULA

The Yucatán Peninsula is Mexico's holiday haven. Visitors from around the world flock to the stunning Caribbean beaches and diving hotspots of the Riviera Maya, as well as the super-resort of Cancún and the Maya ruins of Chichén Itzá. Further inland, the peninsula is covered in a vast, flat swathe of jungle, its limestone surface riddled with cenotes (sinkholes), and sprinkled with pristine towns that look almost no different than they did in the days when Mexico was known as New Spain.

Best for
Beaches, diving, Mayan ruins, and nightlife

Home to
Riviera Maya, Uxmal, Tulum, Mérida, and Chichén Itzá

Experience
A refreshing dip in a crystal-clear cenote, keeping an eye out for the colorful marine life

1 Palacio de Bellas Artes.

2 A colorful *trajinera* on the canals of Xochimilco.

3 Sugar-dusted churros with chocolate sauce.

4 A performance of the Ballet Folklórico de México.

Mexico is bursting at the seams with unique cultural experiences, diverse cuisines, and truly magnificent natural scenery. These itineraries will help you make the most of your visit to this fascinating country.

3 DAYS
in Mexico City

Day 1

Morning Start with an indulgent breakfast of churros and chocolate at El Moro *(www. elmoro.mx)*. After, stroll north up Cárdenas to the Torre Latinoamericana *(p88)* which has a spectacular observation deck.

Afternoon Walk along pedestrianized Madero, the city center's premier shopping strip, and you'll reach the city's traditional heart: the grand plaza known as the Zócalo *(p92)*. Sit back and relax with lunch on the plaza – a perfect spot to people watch – then tour the famous sights on the plaza, including the Palacio Nacional *(p82)* and the Catedral Metropolitana *(p76)*.

Evening Enjoy a dinner of fajitas at the elegant La Ópera Bar *(p87)* then head to Plaza Garibaldi *(p83)*, where you'll be serenaded by mariachi bands over cocktails in one of the plaza's many bars.

Day 2

Morning Start the day at Museo Frida Kahlo *(p116)*. Here you'll find artwork by Kahlo and mementos of her turbulent life.

Afternoon For lunch, head to Plaza Hidalgo in the tranquil Coyoacán district and choose from street food such as sizzling quesadillas or bubbling *pozole* (stew) at the stalls in Mercado de Antojitos *(Higuera 10)*. Next stop is a visit to the

canal-side neighborhood of Xochimilco *(p128)* to hire a traditional boat for a cruise through the famous floating gardens.

Evening Linger in Xochimilco to experience one of its many *pulquerias* (traditional bars). Pulqueria El Templo de Diana *(Av. 5 de Mayo 17)* is one of the oldest, evocative of the 1950s.

Day 3

Morning Journey out of the city to see the spellbinding Mesoamerican ruins at Teotihuacán *(p140)*. From the Pyramid of the Sun, head down the main avenue to the Citadel, where the Temple of Quetzalcoatl is the star attraction. Stop off at the on-site museum before heading back to Mexico City for lunch.

Afternoon Make for the Museo Nacional de Antropología *(p98)*, Mexico's greatest museum. With such an abundance of fascinating exhibits, such as giant Olmec heads and replicas of ancient tombs, you can spend the whole afternoon here.

Evening Book dinner at Pujol *(www.pujol. com.mx)*, a swanky restaurant from celebrity chef Enrique Olvera in the upscale Polanco district. For a spectacular finale to your Mexico City stay, reserve tickets to see the Ballet Folklórico de México at the Palacio de Bellas Artes *(p78)*.

6 DAYS
in Baja California

Day 1

The western peninsula of Baja California is the perfect place for a road trip. Long stretches of highway wind through wild desert or stretch out beside vivid blue coastlines, all broken up with interesting towns, hidden gems, and tasty regional dishes to discover along the way. Begin your journey in the northern town of Ensenada *(p168)*. Take in the scene along the seafront promenade then peruse the exhibits on the peoples and cultures of Baja California at the Museo de Historia *(www.museoens.com)*. Sample Ensenada's famed fish tacos at the Mercado de Mariscos, then get a taste of Baja's famous wines at the Bodegas de Santo Tomás *(www.santo-tomas.com)*. End the day at Hussong's *(www.cantinahussongs.com/inicio. html)*, which serves tasty tacos and what many claim to be the original margarita.

Day 2

South of Ensenada, the Transpeninsular Highway cuts through arid mountain chains and heavily farmed plains. On the three-and-a-half hour journey from Ensenada to El Rosario, stop and take a break at San Quintín to sample the local oysters served at La Ostionera de Bahía Falsa *(www.laostionera.com)*. Finish up the drive in El Rosario, a quintessential rural Baja California town. Have dinner at Mama Espinoza's *(616 165 87 70)* in the middle of town, famed for its lobster burritos.

Day 3

Get an early start for the 575 km (360 mile) journey to Santa Rosalía. Allow nine hours for the drive, plus time for breaks, such as a seafood lunch at Malarrimo *(www.malarrimo. com)* in Guerrero Negro. Stop for a while in San Ignacio *(p170)* in the late afternoon to stretch your legs on a walk to the pretty central plaza. If you have time to spare, head to the Museo de las Pinturas Rupestres de San Ignacio to learn more about the ancient artwork that has been discovered in Baja California *(p170)*. Reaching Santa Rosalía *(p170)* before dark, take an early evening ramble to view the Iglesia de Santa Bárbara, built entirely of steel.

① Museo de Historia, Ensenada.

② Freshly baked treats at Panaderia El Boleo, Santa Rosalía.

③ The Transpeninsular Highway.

④ Nuestra Señora de Loreto, Baja California's first mission church.

⑤ Waterfront in Cabo San Lucas.

Day 4

Try the French-style pastries at Panadería El Boleo (Obregón 30), before a short drive to Mulegé (p171). Visit the hilltop church and see prehistoric artifacts in the Museo Mulegé, before lunch at Los Equipales (Moctezuma 70). Loreto (p171) is two-and-a-half hours south, but you'll want to pause at one or two of Bahía Concepción's mesmerizing beaches en route for some sunbathing and a dip in the beautiful waters of this inland bay. Tonight, enjoy more of Baja's exquisite seafood at El Calorón (López Mateos 2), which has stellar views across the Gulf of California.

Day 5

Spend the morning taking a walk to explore Loreto's enigmatic mission church, the first to be established in Baja. Have an early lunch at Mi Loreto (Salvatierra 50), a colorful local restaurant known for its mole sauces, then continue your road trip with about a four-hour drive to La Paz (p172). Enjoy a leisurely promenade along the city's famously scenic malecón, then indulge in a dinner of lobster and tacos

at Mariscos Bismarkcito (Paseo Álvaro Obregón), finishing up with cocktails at Cervecería La México (Obregón 1665).

Day 6

Start with artisanal coffee and pastries at Doce Cuarenta (Madero 1240) near the central Plaza Constitución. View the local history exhibits at the Museo Regional de Antropología e Historia before lunch at Rancho Viejo (Márquez de León 228) – a popular spot renowned for its steak tacos. Hop back in the car for an hour's drive to Todos Santos (p173), where you can easily spend a couple of hours wandering the town's charming streets. Stop for a coffee at the Hotel California (www.hotelcalifornia baja.com), then take a stroll to the lovely, palm-fringed plaza in the heart of town, surrounded by the humble church and elegant theater. One last hour on the road will get you to your final destination: Cabo San Lucas (p172). Embrace the town's free-wheeling spirit at one of the bars on Playa El Médano and enjoy the views of the stone arch known as El Arco, a jagged rocky archway, on Lover's Beach.

6 DAYS
on the Ruta de Plata

Day 1

The silver route takes in several of Mexico's iconic colonial-era towns, following the former silver transport trails used by the Spanish. This tour begins in the elegant city of Querétaro *(p206)*. For an idea of what life was like for local elites in the 18th century, amble south to the Museo Casa de la Zacatecana, which is decorated with original furnishings. At lunchtime, try a *torta* (Mexican sandwich) at Las Tortugas *(Andador 5 de Mayo 27a)*. After, take a stroll through town to the Mirador de los Arcos, which provides spellbinding views of the city's historic aqueduct. Sample the creative Mexican dishes at Tikua *(Ignacio Allende Sur 13)*, then head to Alquimia *(5 de Mayo 71)* – a sophisticated, dimly lit bodega – for cocktails.

Day 2

A couple of hours by bus will take you to Dolores Hidalgo *(p220)*. The town's top sights are clustered around Plaza Principal, beginning with the church where Father Hidalgo issued the declaration that started Mexico's War of Independence in 1810.

Make sure you stop and sample the town's famously inventive ice-cream flavors, such as cactus and shrimp, that are sold around the main plaza. After a 45-minute bus ride, finish the day at San Miguel de Allende *(p224)*, and while away the evening at La Azotea *(Umarán 6)*, the town's coolest rooftop bar.

Day 3

Stay in San Miguel Allende and spend the whole day exploring this beautifully preserved colonial-era town. Start with a stroll around El Jardín Principal, admiring the sights on this charming plaza. Follow this up with lunch at La Alborada *(Sollano 11)*, famed for its traditional soups and stews. Stop at Plaza Cívica to see its two colonial-era churches – Templo de Nuestra Señora de la Salud with its unusual concave facade, and San Felipe Neri for its stunning oil paintings. Afterward, peruse Mexican folk art, pottery, and souvenirs at the Mercado de Artesanías. For dinner, try the excellent Peruvian restaurant La Parada *(www.laparadasma.com)*.

1 Statue overlooking the aqueduct in Querétaro City.

2 A colorful street in Guanajuato.

3 Cable car in Zacatecas.

4 A *gordita*, a popular appetizer.

5 Ice-cream vendor in the town of Dolores Hidalgo.

Day 4

An hour and a half by bus will take you to the city of Guanajuato *(p196)*. Start by taking the funicular up to the Monumento al Pipila – a statue of a local key figure in the Mexican War of Independence – where you can enjoy spectacular views of the city. Descend on foot to Jardín de la Unión, the main plaza, then treat yourself to a delicious lunch of Mexican street food from Mercado Hidalgo. Head north to Museo Regional de Guanajuato and spend the afternoon learning more about Mexico's War of Independence *(p59)*. Enjoy a dinner of classic Spanish dishes at Tasca de la Paz *(Plaza de la Paz 28)*, before joining a traditional *callejoneada*, a street tour conducted in Spanish by students dressed as medieval minstrels *(p198)*.

Day 5

Take the bus to Aguascalientes *(p224)*, and spend the late morning wandering around Plaza de la Patria. Have lunch at Mercado Juárez, where stalls serve *birria* (goat or mutton stew). It's a short stroll to the fascinating Museo Nacional de la Muerte, which examines Mexico's preoccupation with images of death. This evening, take a taxi to experience the hot springs that gave Aguascalientes its name – the Baños Termales de Ojocaliente *(Av. Tecnologico 102, Héroes)*. For dinner, sample traditional Mexican dishes at Restaurante Mitla's buffet *(Madero 220)*.

Day 6

After the two-hour bus ride to Zacatecas *(p202)*, head straight to the cathedral in Plaza de Armas. From here you can make a loop through the heart of the old city, exploring its narrow, arcaded streets and grand churches and mansions. Head over to Gorditas Doña Julia *(Hidalgo 409)* for lunch at this locally famous chain known for its *gorditas* (stuffed corn pastries). Take a guided tour of Mina El Edén, a preserved silver mine deep in the hillside. For dinner, splurge on the restaurant inside the fabulous Quinta Real hotel *(www.quintareal.com)*, before heading to La Mina Club *(www.minaeleden.com.mx)*, a dance club and bar inside the Edén mine.

1 Mole ingredients for sale in Mercado Benito Juárez.

2 A craftsman weaving in Teotitlàn del Valle.

3 Ruins at Monte Albán.

4 Paper in Taller Leñateros, San Cristóbal de las Casas.

5 DAYS
in Southern Mexico

Day 1

Starting in the city of Oaxaca *(p234)*, wander north on Macedonio Alcalá, browsing the craft shops along this pedestrianized shopping street. For lunch, visit Casa Oaxaca *(www.casa oaxacaelrestaurante.com)* to try mole – a traditional marinade and sauce dish that comes in many varieties and flavors. In the afternoon, explore the Museo de las Culturas de Oaxaca, a regional history museum with a fine collection of Mixtec jewelry and gold. For dinner, Los Danzantes *(www.losdanzantes.com)* offers innovative Oaxacan dishes such as barbecue chicken with fried cactus and chocolate.

Day 2

There are enough fascinating markets in Oaxaca to take up the whole morning. The vast food market of Mercado Benito Juárez is filled with the wafting scent of fresh produce, mole powder, and chilli peppers, while Mercado de Artesanías is the place for Zapotec handicrafts. Make sure you end at the sprawling Mercado de Abastos, where there are plenty of choices for lunch. After, admire Mesoamerican art at Museo de Arte Prehispánico de México. For dinner, splurge at Zandunga *(www. zandungasabor.com)*, which serves 60 types of mezcal plus regional specialties.

Day 3

You'll need to rent a car for some adventures farther afield today. Leave early and spend the morning at the famously scenic ruins at Monte Albán *(p240)*. Head to Santa María del Tule for lunch at the food stalls at Mercado el Tule, then drive to Teotitlán del Valle, home to more ancient ruins and Zapotec arts-and-crafts stalls, famous for their fine rugs. Enjoy some tasty moles, tamales, and enchiladas at Teotitlán's Comedor Conchita's *(Juárez 104)* before driving back to Oaxaca. Here you'll need to switch to a bus for the overnight trip to San Cristóbal de las Casas *(p249)*.

Day 4

Ease into San Cristóbal life with coffee at El Kiosko *(Plaza 31 de Marzo)*. Afterwards, check out Museo de San Cristóbal, the stately former city hall converted into a local history museum. After lunch, walk north up Andador Eclesiástico to Santo Domingo. The plaza here, filled with craft stalls, is the best place to buy souvenirs. Next door is the fascinating Museo Centro Cultural de los Altos, which focuses on local Indigenous cultures, with an especially rich textile display. For dinner, try Spanish tapas at La Viña de Bacco *(Real de Guadalupe 7)*.

Day 5

Take a guided tour of the contemporary Tzotzil Maya villages of San Juan Chamula and San Lorenzo de Zinacantán, where the people are known for maintaining their cultural traditions. You can book through your hotel, or via Jalapeño Tours *(www.jalapenotours.com)*. Afterward, make for Taller Leñateros *(www.tallerlenateros. com)*, a paper-making shop that uses traditional Maya techniques. For a dinner of innovative, contemporary Chiapas food, snag a table at El Secreto *(16 de Septiembre 24)*.

1

5 DAYS

in the Yucatán Peninsula

Day 1

Start your tour of the peninsula in Campeche *(p300)* with a hearty breakfast at El Bastión *(Calle 57, Entre 8–10)*, which overlooks the central plaza. Check out the grand cathedral followed by the Museo de la Arquitectura Maya, which contains Maya monuments and sculpture, and also provides access to the old city walls. Just beyond the walls, the city market is worth a browse for its stalls of colorful fruit and produce. It's also sur-rounded by restaurants where you can stop for lunch. Drive out to the archaeo-logical museum in Fuerte de San Miguel, home to an impressive cache of pre-Hispanic gold and the first mummified body to be found in Mesoamerica. The *paradores de cocteleros* (seafood cocktail stalls) on the coast are perfect for dinner as you watch the sun go down.

Day 2

It's just over two hours by car to the ancient Maya city of Uxmal *(p284)*, famed for its elaborately decorated buildings. After a couple of hours exploring the site,

drive on to Mérida *(p290)*. Grab a seafood lunch at El Marlin Azul *(Calle 62 No. 488)*, before setting off to explore the town. Check out the beautifully restored Museo Casa Montejo – a 16th-century palace – as well as the vast murals by Fernando Castro Pacheco in the Palacio de Gobierno. You can then spend several happy hours admiring the handicrafts in the Casa de las Artesanías *(Calle 63)* which sells traditional products made by local artisans; the hammocks you'll see here are a particular specialty. Sample the innovative Mexican fusion cuisine at Rosas and Xocolate *(www.rosasandxocolate.com)* for dinner, and then catch a classical performance at the Teatro Peón.

Day 3

Drive to the iconic Maya ruins at Chichén Itzá *(p294)*, aiming to arrive early so you can miss the busy late morning rush. Allow about three hours to explore; start with the pyramids in the area known as Chichén Nuevo on the north side of the site, then tackle the Chichén Viejo ruins to the south, where fewer visitors go. For

1 The Baroque cathedral on Plaza de la Independencia, Campeche.

2 Uxmal's Pyramid of the Magician.

3 Climbing the ruins of Cobá.

4 Archaeological site of Tulum overlooking the sandy beach.

5 A diver in Gran Cenote.

lunch, try the excellent Yucatecan buffet (roast pork to fresh seafood) at Hacienda Selva Maya (www.mesondelmarques.com/hacienda-selva-maya), a short drive away in Valladolid (p306). One hour's drive from here is the Maya city of Cobá (p304), where you can spend a couple of hours exploring huge pyramids soaring high above the jungle. In the evening, have a modern Mexican dinner at Hartwood (www.hartwoodtulum.com) on Tulum beach, where all the cooking is done by open fire.

Day 4

The collection of Maya pyramids and structures sitting above the Caribbean in Tulum (p288) takes only an hour or so to explore but it's best to arrive early to avoid the crowds. After Tulum, head to Gran Cenote, one of the area's best cenotes – a naturally forming sinkhole in the limestone, filled with crystal-clear water. Lucky visitors may even spot turtles here – make sure to keep your distance if you do. After a swim, head back into Tulum town for lunch; try the tasty tacos and moles at El Tacoqueto (Av. Tulum at Acuario). Decamp to the beach – Tulum has one of the best in the area. There are several public access points, but you can also try one of the beach clubs where you pay for lounge chairs and drinks (your hotel may have its own operation). If you're in town on Friday, Saturday, or Sunday, check the events schedule at the Papaya Playa Project hotel complex (www.papayaplaya project.com), which hosts regular parties and brunches.

Day 5

Drive north up the stunning Riviera Maya (p282), stopping at Akumal (p283) for a refreshing swim in Cenote Azul. Aim to reach the Cancún (p282) beach strip for a late seafood lunch at El Fish Fritanga (p283). The best thing about Cancún is the beach, so dedicate a whole afternoon to enjoying the sun, sea, and sand. For a tranquil spot away from the busy Hotel Zone, head to the north-facing beaches on Boulevard Kukulcan. Finish the day with a lavish meal at Restaurante Careyes (www. oasishoteles.com/es/restaurantes/careyes).

The Fiesta Sound

Mexico's rich music and dance culture is the focal point of several major festivals, giving you a great chance to immerse yourself in the sights and sounds of lively musical traditions. Some of the best options are Día del Músico on November 22nd - when the patron saint of musicians is feted with gusto across the country - or Guadalajara's Encuentro Internacional del Mariachi y la Charrería in late August to early September, celebrating both mariachi music and *charrería*, the Mexican art of horsemanship. Many other fiestas include music and dance as part of their festivities, such as Guelaguetza *(p48)* and Vive Latino *(p55)*.

→
Dancers performing at the Encuentro Internacional del Mariachi y la Charrería

MEXICO FOR
MUSIC
AND DANCE

Fed by its cultural diversity, Mexico's traditional music and dance scene is fantastically rich and exciting, and with so many street performers and fiestas around, it's easy to lose yourself to the country's rhythms.

Regional Traditions

Mexico has a vast range of dances performed only by specific communities or in certain regions. Some hark back to pre-Hispanic times and ancient rituals, while others were introduced by Spanish friars and show European influences. During Carnival in Tlaxcala *(p159)*, for example, dancers wear elaborate, sequined garments and carved wooden masks with pale skin tones, to parody their ancient oppressors. In Mexico City, the *concheros* dance has evolved over the centuries from different spiritual traditions, both Indigenous and Spanish. You can find performers at the main plaza *(p94)* - just keep your ears out for the tell-tale rattle that comes from the seed pods worn on the dancers' ankles.

←
Conchero dancers performing for a crowd in Mexico City

African Roots

The Afro-Mexican community has had a big influence on the country's music and dance scene. The Gulf and Pacific coasts, with their large Afro-Mexican populations, are particularly rich in dance: look out for the *danza de los diablos* (dance of the devils), for example, which is often performed in Oaxaca and Guerrero states during the Day of the Dead and other festivities. The city of Veracruz *(p268)*, meanwhile, is a great place to hear the Afro-Mexican branch of *son mexicano* folk music known as *son jarocho*, with performances on Friday and Saturday nights in the Plazuela de la Campana.

← *Danza de los diablos* dancers wearing suits and masks for an event

Mariachi Beats

Mariachi music boomed in the 1950s with a string of films that made stars of Mariachi Vargas – considered the best mariachi band of all time. Today, you'll hear it all over Mexico, especially in its birthplace of Guadalajara *(p194)*. Typical bands comprise guitars, violin, trumpet, and singer, but drummers and other musicians may join in to create bigger, more complex bands, especially around popular spots like Plaza Garibaldi *(p85)*, where a band can grow as the night goes on and create an impromptu party atmosphere that lasts until the early hours.

549

The number of musicians in the largest mariachi band ever.

Mariachis in traditional attire playing at Plaza Garibaldi, Mexico City ↑

▷ Tropic Jungles

A rich array of wildlife roams through the jungles in the south of Mexico. All kinds of magical sights are hidden away amid the lush growth, so a trip out to these verdant landscapes is worth it not just for the beautiful scenery but also to stumble on enigmatic sights like The Bamboo Palace at Las Pozas *(p218)* or the ruins of the Maya site of Palenque *(p244)*.

◁ Mexico from the Movies

Deserts really do smother northern Mexico and Baja California, with the vast Chihuahuan hot desert being the largest in North America. To see this stunning landscape of cacti-studded hills, bright sunshine, and dried riverbeds, hit the Transpeninsular Highway for a road trip *(p24)*, or stay in a Baja oasis town such as Mulegé *(p171)*.

MEXICO FOR
NATURAL
BEAUTY

Beyond the dusty deserts of Mexico's northern border, an incredible mixture of landscapes decorate the country, from soaring, snow-fringed volcanoes to golden coastlines hugging sapphire blue oceans.

◁ Snorkeling the Cenotes

Some of the most enticing snorkeling spots in Mexico are actually found inland, across the Yucatán Peninsula. Thanks to the Yucatán's unique geology – riddled with limestone caverns and underground rivers – giant sinkholes known as cenotes pockmark the peninsula *(p281)*. The natural holes are filled with crystal-clear water, and many – such as the beautiful Cenote Azul (p300) – provide great opportunities for cave diving, snorkeling, or just a leisurely dip.

△ Mountains and Canyons

More than half the country is over 1,000 m (3,200 ft) above sea level, making Mexico a true land of mountains. See the soaring heights and plunging depths at the epic, lake-filled Sumidero Canyon *(p252)*, and the stunning gorges of the Copper Canyon system *(p180)*, which dwarfs the Grand Canyon in the US.

▷ Rich Wetlands

Birdwatchers should always have their binoculars at the ready in the Yucatán. Mangroves along the coastline provide a habitat for a plethora of wading birds, while the marshlands of the Sian Ka'an Biosphere Reserve *(p309)* attract even rarer birds. But the highlight of the region is the phenomenal sight of vast colonies of coral pink flamingos that inhabit the lagoons *(p303)*.

◁ Smoking Giants

Central Mexico is peppered with volcanic mountains, from the mighty Pico de Orizaba *(p270)* – the nation's highest peak – to the more humble cinder cone volcano of Paricutín *(p214)*. There are also some active volcanoes, such as the Volcán de Fuego; hike up to the summit of nearby Nevado de Colima *(p216)* to see its smoky top from a safe distance.

Did You Know?

Popocatépetl volcano became active again in 1994 and has been erupting at irregular intervals ever since.

Magnificent Muralists

Mexican artists have been creating colorful murals since pre-Hispanic times, as seen in the vibrant friezes found in Teotihuacán *(p140)* and Bonampak *(p248)*. The art form exploded onto the scene again after the 1910 Mexican Revolution, with huge murals promoting a sense of national identity. Visit universities and city halls across the country to get a look at these dramatic tableaux, proudly preserved as national cultural treasures. Of course, Mexico City has a plethora of examples, by leading artists of the mural movement such as José Clemente Orozco, David Alfaro Siqueiros, and Diego Rivera.

MEXICO FOR
ART LOVERS

From mysterious Maya glyphs to modern murals emblazoned with symbolism, Mexican art is at once familiar and yet startling. Day of the Dead skulls and Frida Kahlo's self-portraits have become global pop icons, but there are plenty of lesser-known works just waiting to be discovered.

Folk Crafts

The unique vitality of Mexican folk art is a result of the fusion of traditional Mexican arts and crafts with technologies and themes introduced after the Spanish colonization. See the evolution of folk art at the Museo de Arte Popular *(p87)*, where curated collections trace its development throughout history. Better yet, see traditional arts and crafts in person while wandering through a market like Mercado de Abastos *(p237)* where you can pick something up as an authentic souvenir.

Vochol by Bautista and Ortiz families, Museo de Arte Popular, Mexico City ↑

Did You Know?

On the last Wednesday of each month, many museums stay open till late in the evening.

INSIDER TIP
ArtWalk

The city of Puerto Vallarta *(p225)* is a major arts center. Get a taste of its flourishing contemporary art scene on the weekly Wednesday ArtWalk, held from late October to late May *(www. puertovallartaart walk.com)*. During the event, over half a dozen galleries open their doors until 10pm.

←

Rivera's *The History of Mexico* (1935) in the Palacio Nacional, Mexico City

A Mexican Icon

Known for her bold, Surrealist self-portraits, Frida Kahlo is one of the most instantly recognizable artists in the world. Kahlo didn't start painting seriously until she was 18, inspired by folk art, politics, and even the chronic pain she suffered throughout her life. Kahlo's paintings can be seen in galleries all over Mexico but the best place to start is her former home, the Casa Azul in Mexico City *(p116)*.

←

A photograph of iconic Mexican artist Frida Kahlo

Modern Mexico

Today, murals and folk art have been exchanged for digital works and urban street art. At the same time, many Mexican artists are rediscovering their Indigenous roots, freeing themselves from European and US influences. Discover Mexico's latest artistic movements in modern galleries such as the Museo Jumex *(www.fundacionjumex.org)* and the Museo de Arte Indígena Contemporáneo *(p157),* which explores contemporary Indigenous art.

→

Museo Jumex on Plaza Carso, Mexico City, surrounded by modern architecture

Sun, Sea, and Sand

Mexico's coasts offer plenty of ways to enjoy some quality family time, whether you're playing on the sandy beach, snorkeling among tropical fish, or chowing down on freshly cut coconuts. Isla Mujeres (p280) features the most kid-friendly beaches in Mexico, while older children can try surfing in Oaxaca or exploring the wilder beaches in Baja California.

$\rightarrow$

Surfing practice in the tropical waters of the Riviera Maya

MEXICO FOR
FAMILIES

With so many colorful fiestas, fascinating facts, and amazing flavors, Mexico is a big hit with the kids. Family is central to Mexican society and traveling with children is common practice, so you'll find plenty to occupy excited kids wherever you go, as well as the facilities to make it easy.

SHOP

Mercado De Artesanías La Ciudadela

This market is full of colorful handicrafts, jewelry, hammocks, and traditional artwork. It's a great spot for the whole family: an exciting place for the kids to explore, and full of authentic Mexican souvenirs for adults to peruse.

🅐H4 🅐Avenida Balderas and Plaza de la Ciudadela, Mexico City
🕙10am-6pm daily
🆆laciudadela.com.mx

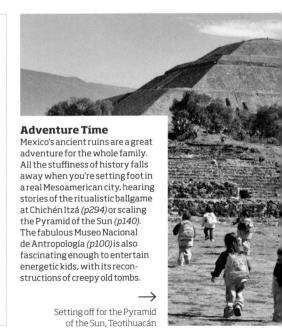

Adventure Time

Mexico's ancient ruins are a great adventure for the whole family. All the stuffiness of history falls away when you're setting foot in a real Mesoamerican city, hearing stories of the ritualistic ballgame at Chichén Itzá (p294) or scaling the Pyramid of the Sun (p140). The fabulous Museo Nacional de Antropología (p100) is also fascinating enough to entertain energetic kids, with its recon-structions of creepy old tombs.

$\rightarrow$

Setting off for the Pyramid of the Sun, Teotihuacán

Theme-Park Fun

When it comes to letting off steam (and cooling down), resorts like Cancún (p283) and Acapulco (p242) boast numerous water parks. And just outside Mexico City, serious thrills are delivered at the Six Flags México theme park - Latin America's most popular - where you can tackle the world's first boomerang coaster and rides themed around DC superheroes.

INSIDER TIP
Ice Cream for the Bold

In Dolores Hidalgo (p220) ice cream has evolved into something extra special. Come here to brave bizarre flavors such as mole, avocado, and even shrimp.

↑ A kid-friendly roller-coaster at the popular Six Flags México

Fiesta Fever

Raucous parades, vibrant costumes, pounding drums, and folk dancers - Mexican festivals are sure to be a thrill for young visitors (p54). Fiestas almost always include special events to get children involved and active, as well as temporary funfairs. For sheer spectacle, it's hard to beat the Guelaguetza cultural festival, or Carnival, which is at its most flamboyant in La Paz (p172) and Veracruz (p268).

←

Dressing up at Oaxaca's Guelaguetza, a festival celebrating Indigenous culture

Wild Mexico

You don't need zoos to get a glimpse of the wildlife in Mexico. Whale-watching is common all along the Pacific coast, but especially in Baja California (p173). Bring your binoculars to spy the animals out at sea, or take a boat tour with Baja Expeditions (www.bajaex.com) to catch a closer look. The Yucatán is also home to the awesome sight of a flamboyance of flamingos at Celestún (p303) and Río Lagartos (p307).

→

A whale leaping up from the inland Sea of Cortez in Baja California

Lace Up Your Boots

The national parks, mountain ranges, and snow-capped volcanoes of Mexico are all laced with fantastic hiking trails, so whether you're looking for a casual walk or an epic challenge, there's plenty to enjoy. Grades of difficulty vary as much as the landscapes, from the gentle lakeside walks of Valle de Bravo *(p155)*, to the climb up Pico de Orizaba *(p270)*, which requires crampons and an ice axe. The awe-inspiring Copper Canyon *(p180)* is a popular hiking area, with trekking trails plus dramatic gorges for more adrenaline-fueled activities like abseiling.

$\longrightarrow$

Mountain climbers resting atop Pico de Orizaba, the highest peak in Mexico

MEXICO FOR
OUTDOOR ADVENTURES

Rafting the white-water rapids of the Río Filobobos, horseback riding in the rugged homeland of the Rarámuri, hiking the blackened slopes of dormant volcanoes – Mexico's enormously varied landscapes provide enticing settings for all kinds of action-packed adventures.

Annual Adventures

The Mexican calendar is peppered with events that make the perfect focal point for an adrenaline-fueled trip. For the Baja 1000 *(p168)*, hundreds of vehicles compete in a grueling off-road race in Baja California. For sports-fishing fans, there's a cash prize to be won at the Black and Blue Marlin Tournament in Cabo San Lucas *(p172)*.

$\longleftarrow$

Racing in the Baja 1000, held every November

TOP 4 **GOLF COURSES IN MEXICO**

Cabo del Sol
🔲 cabodelsol.com
Luxury resort in Cabo San Lucas.

One & Only Palmilla
🔲 oneandonlyresorts.com
Designed by retired pro golfer Jack Nicklaus.

El Camaléon
🔲 mayakoba.com
Home of the World Wide Technology Championship since 2007.

Riviera Maya Golf Club
🔲 pgarivieramaya.com
Incorporating jungle, cenotes, and lakes.

Roving Riders

Mexico is a land of cowboys, which makes a tour on horseback a truly traditional way to experience the country's exciting landscapes. Ride the flower-filled trails of Valle de Bravo *(p155)*, the volcanic slopes of Paricutín *(p214)*, or the rustic byways of the Sierra Chincua Monarch Butterfly Sanctuary. Always be sure to find a reputable company for your tour and don't ride in the midday sun, for the safety of yourself and the horses.

←
Horseback riders exploring the area around Cabo San Lucas

Mexico's Waterways

Expert thrill-seekers and casual explorers alike can enjoy seeing Mexico by boat. Mountain torrents tumble out of the Sierras, offering thrilling adventures like rafting the rapids on the Río Filobobos *(p265)*. For more tranquil exploration, many hotels on the Riviera Maya *(p280)* offer kayaks for trips through the mangroves toward Ascension Bay, or around the exquisite lake at Bacalar. There are also plenty of ways to get out and enjoy Mexico's fabulous coastal waters *(p44)*.

→
Whitewater rafting near Huasteca in San Luis Potosí

◁ The Colonial Era

From tiny hamlets to the biggest cities, colonial-era churches abound in Mexico. With missionaries as architects and Indigenous craftsmen adding the details, the result was a blend of styles that add unique and eclectic facades to the nation's townscapes. Follow the Convent Route from Maní *(p307)* for a string of examples.

▷ Modernist Marvels

The functional, clean lines of Modernism transformed the Mexican architectural scene after World War II. Luis Barragán (1902–88) designed everything from urban sculptures – such as the Torres de Satélite in Mexico City – to housing projects and gardens. A tall, slim skyscraper, the Torre Latinoamericana *(p90)*, was the pinnacle of the 1950s Modernist style in Mexico.

MEXICO FOR
ARCHITECTURE

From towering Maya pyramids to Modernist innovations, Mexico is crammed with architectural wonders. Today, a new generation of Mexican architects continues to transform the country with exciting, contemporary designs.

▷ Mesoamerican Masterpieces

The distinctive pyramids and geometric designs of Mexico's early civilizations are not just ruins – they've influenced modern architects such as Frank Lloyd Wright and the whole Art Deco movement. The Zapotec site of Mitla *(p252)* is especially well known for its intricate mosaic fretwork .

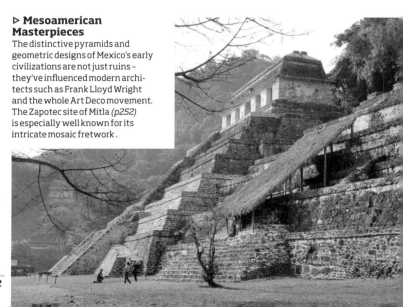

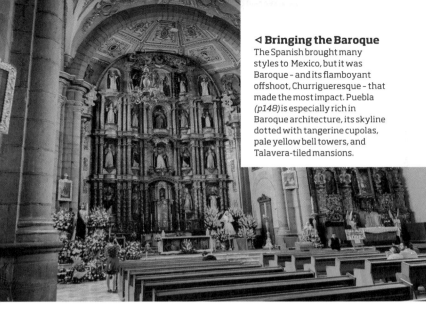

◁ Bringing the Baroque

The Spanish brought many styles to Mexico, but it was Baroque – and its flamboyant offshoot, Churrigueresque – that made the most impact. Puebla (p148) is especially rich in Baroque architecture, its skyline dotted with tangerine cupolas, pale yellow bell towers, and Talavera-tiled mansions.

◁ The Porfiriato

In the 19th century, a newly independent Mexico was eager to impress the world, and President Porfirio Díaz did it with buildings. There's the wonderful Art Nouveau Palacio de Bellas Artes (p78), and the Teatro Juárez (p196), which combines Neo-Classicism with lavish French styles of decoration. Much of the investment went into public buildings; Mexico City's Correo Mayor (Main Post Office) is a particularly grand example.

TOP 3 MODERN MEXICAN ARCHITECTS

Tatiana Bilbao (b. 1972)
An architect with a diverse range of projects from gardens to sustainable housing.

Frida Escobedo (b. 1979)
A Mexican artist who specializes in designing and restoring different urban spaces.

Michel Rojkind (b. 1969)
Responsible for innovative designs such as the Nestlé Chocolate Museum.

△ Contemporary Mexico

While historic highlights dominate the average sightseeing checklist, there's nothing quite like taking a stroll in the city and stumbling upon an extravagant 21st-century masterpiece. There are magical modern wonders to discover everywhere, such as the snake-like Nestlé Chocolate Museum near Toluca (p160) or the fabulous, glittering Museo Soumaya (p133).

Beach Life

Sure, Mexico's coastlines provide plenty of adventures – but there's nothing quite like lazing in a deck chair, sipping margaritas under the palm trees while you watch jewel-blue waves lapping at the sand. Whether you're looking for a secluded spot or a luxury resort, sunseekers will be spoiled for choice all across Mexico. For some serious R&R, head to one of the big resort beaches around Cancún (p282), Cabo San Lucas (p172), or Acapulco (p242). Each one offers watersports and swimming for when you're feeling active, as well as cocktails on the sand or spa facilities when you need a break.

→

Puerto Vallarta, a port city on the popular Pacific resort of Banderas Bay

MEXICO FOR
INCREDIBLE
COASTS

Mexico has an epic 9,330 km (5,800 miles) of coastline, so whether you're after a quiet place to relax and sunbathe, some prime coral reefs for scuba diving, or serious surf spots, you'll find the perfect niche carved out for you somewhere on the country's coast.

Eco-Friendly Wildlife Tours

Baja California is famous for the rare marine animals that can be seen here, in the Sea of Cortez to the east and the tranquil lagoons dotting the west coasts. Baja Expeditions (www.bajaex.com) and Cabo Expeditions (www.caboexpeditions.com.mx) are two reputable tour operators, both of which visit Isla Espíritu Santo – a protected reserve where the number of visitors is carefully managed at all times to enforce sustainable wildlife tourism.

←

The tail of a humpback whale off Baja California

STAY

**The Beach
Tulum Hotel**
This luxurious hotel
has rooms that open up
right on the beach.
Enjoy lavish four-poster
beds, outdoor tubs, a
stylish pool, and free
yoga classes.

🅰G4 🅰Carr. Tulum-
Boca Paila Km 7, Tulum
Beach Ⓦthebeach-
tulum.com

$$$

Under the Sea

The Great Maya Reef is one of the world's largest coral
reef systems. The reef is an endangered ecosystem,
so it's best to book a trip to a protected area, such as
the Sian Ka'an Biosphere Reserve *(p309)*, which
can help to regulate guests and their impact on
the reef. Snorkeling is an easy alternative, and
off Cozumel *(p280)* – where reefs come close
inshore – you can often see as much with a
snorkel as with scuba tanks.

A scuba diver observing a French
Angelfish in the waters off Cozumel

Surf's Up

A perfect match to all Mexico's
inland action *(p40)*, the Pacific
coast is prime surf territory
for travelers looking for a
fun-fueled day at the beach.
Puerto Escondido *(p254)* is the
most popular surfing hotspot,
with many local operators
offering lessons and board
rentals for first-timers and
casual surfers. Those with
more experience can head for
the wild, undeveloped
beaches of Baja California.

Surfing in Puerto Escondido,
in the state of Oaxaca

¡Viva la Revolución!

Bring history to life by following the life and times of some of the best-known figures in Mexican history – radical revolutionaries Emiliano Zapata *(p62)* and Pancho Villa *(p184)*. Trace Zapata's footsteps along the Ruta Zapata – a network of historic towns in the state of Morelos. For the life of Pancho Villa, visit Museo Histórico de la Revolución *(p184)*, his former house in Chihuahua.

←

A mural depicting Pancho Villa, in the Museo de la Revolución

MEXICO FOR
HISTORY BUFFS

With its roots in ancient civilizations stretching back over 20,000 years, Mexico draws on a long and rich cultural heritage. From majestic ancient pyramids to dazzling futuristic museums and galleries, it's easy to immerse yourself in the history that echoes all around you.

The Time of New Spain

The legacy of the Spanish rule is best seen through a stroll in one of the well-preserved towns that date from this period (1521–1821). Urban planning was strictly controlled, and towns were modeled on the capital. Straight streets led to a large *plaza mayor* (main plaza) with civic buildings and churches, plus *portales* (arcades) for the merchants. Mérida *(p290)* and San Cristóbal de las Casas *(p249)* are perfect examples, with fine central plazas that reflect the old colonial era.

→

Church towers rising above the trees on Mérida's *plaza mayor*

Did You Know?

The town of Valladolid was renamed Morelia in 1828 in honor of its most famous citizen.

The Mexican War of Independence

No history tour would be complete without discovering the stories of Miguel Hidalgo and José María Morelos: two of Mexico's most famous figures in the Mexican War of Independence (p59). There are museums in each of their birthplaces, Guanajuato (p196) and Morelia (p208) respectively, but the best way to experience their legacy is to join the crowds celebrating Independence Day on September 16.

→

A parade commemorating Independence Day

Archaeological Wonders

Some of Mexico's ancient cities and enigmatic pyramids are world-famous sights, such as Teotihuacán (p140) and Chichén Itzá (p294). Other lesser-known spots, however, reveal unique art and majestic architecture of their own. The walls of Mitla (p252) are covered with magnificent geometric mosaics; the vibrant Maya murals at Bonampak (p248) are amazingly preserved; and excavations at Sayil (p302) uncovered intriguing details of how ordinary Maya once lived in a sacred ceremonial center.

←

The incredible Maya murals at Bonampak dating from around AD 790

Remains to be Seen

Despite the ravages of time and forces of nature, Mexico has preserved an incredible archive of archaeological treasures. While many sites have kept their most precious artifacts in situ at on-site museums, there are also some magnificent collections to visit, particularly Xalapa's Museo de Antropología (p264), one of the country's finest.

→

A reconstructed facade at the Museo Nacional de Antropología

Cultural Festivals

There's no better place to immerse yourself in Mexican culture than one of its fantastic fiestas, where you can often see performers from local communities displaying their traditional dances and attire. Oaxaca's Guelaguetza in July is the perfect choice, a dedicated Indigenous cultural festival with dances, food stands, and crafts by communities from around Oaxaca. Be aware that some locals don't appreciate having tourists at this festival, so be respectful and considerate if attending.

A folk dance group at Oaxaca's Guelaguetza cultural festival

MEXICO FOR
INDIGENOUS CULTURE

Descendants of Mexico's ancient civilizations and a number of other Indigenous peoples still live all over the country, preserving their heritage in contemporary Mexico through traditional customs and creative works.

Trading Places

Markets are part of everyday life for Mexico's Indigenous peoples, as much a social hub as a place to sell their produce. For visitors, these markets are a fantastic cultural showcase of food, arts, and crafts. Some of the best markets are the Mercado de Abastos (p236) and Tlacolula Sunday market in Oaxaca state, and Mexico City's sprawling Mercado de La Merced (p132), on the site of an old Aztec market.

Fresh produce on sale at the food stalls in Tlacolula's Sunday market

Learning Firsthand

Organizations and activities run by Indigenous peoples help to share the history, customs, and daily life of the communities. The Na Bolom foundation *(p249)* has a museum and guesthouse and plans expeditions with the Lacandón Maya, while Kiichpam Kaax, north of Chetumal, shows visitors traditional activities, such as beekeeping and rubber-tree tapping.

$\longrightarrow$
The Na Bolom headquarters in San Cristóbal de las Casas

Artisan Crafts

Indigenous handicrafts range from delicate jewelry to massive sculptures. This rich artistic heritage dates back to the earliest civilizations, with modern artisans often adapting to today's changing fashions. The best place to see modern crafts is in markets, like those in Tequisquiapan *(p216)* and Izamal *(p305),* where you can buy items from the makers.

$\longleftarrow$
Embroidering a *huipil,* a common style of traditional dress from the Yucatán Peninsula

Timeless Towns

Sleepy plazas shaded by palms. Shoe-shine stalls and sugarcane juice sellers. Cobbled streets and weathered Baroque churches built by the Spanish. Mexico is rich with lesser-known towns and villages dripping with charm and history. Santa Rosalía's *(p170)* mining roots are clear from the old installations still scattered around, while Batopilas *(p183)* is so remote it feels untouched by the modern world.

→

The colorful veranda of the Riverside Lodge, in Batopilas

MEXICO
OFF THE BEATEN PATH

Step off the regular tourist trail and you'll discover intriguing surprises all across Mexico. You might stumble upon isolated jungle ruins, a colonial-era town seemingly frozen in time, or a trendy new winery.

Quirky Festivals

While it's no secret that the Mexican calendar is full of great events, even well-known dates can offer up surprises, like the fascinating regional variations you'll see at Easter *(p185)*. Sometimes, you may even stumble on a truly unique event, like Oaxaca's *Noche de los Rábanos* (Night of the Radishes) in December *(p254)*.

↑ Night of the Radishes, when locals compete in radish carving

Lost Missions of Mexico

Some of the most haunting sights in Mexico are its isolated mission churches from the time of New Spain. The Misión San Francisco Javier de Viggé-Biaundó *(p171)* is an enigmatic memorial to the Cochimí people, while the "lost" Satevo Mission *(p182)* lies in a remote valley in the Copper Canyon.

$\longrightarrow$

A Franciscan mission built by the local Xi'iuy people in the Sierra Gorda

Craft Beer and Boutique Wine

Large breweries have dominated production for years in Mexico, but times are changing. The craft beer scene is growing steadily, with companies like Baja Brewing *(www.baja brewingcompany.com)* creating high-quality beers you can try at its own tap rooms. Meanwhile, the wines of Valle de Guadalupe *(p168)* continue to gain international renown, led by the likes of Casa de Piedra winery.

$\longleftarrow$

Wine tasting in Mexico's finest wine region, Guadalupe Valley in Baja California

TOP 4 BAJA VINEYARDS

Adobe Guadalupe
🖸 adobeguadalupe.com
Famous for its Cabernet Sauvignon, Merlot, and Malbec blend, Gabriel.

Monte Xanic
🖸 montexanic.com.mx
Try its exquisite Gran Ricardo Bordeaux blend.

Château Camou
🖸 chateaucamou.com.mx
Its specialty is the multi-award-winning Gran Vino Tinto.

L.A. Cetto
🖸 lacetto.mx
Known for its Nebbiolo, made from an Italian red grape.

Trees growing up the sides of an ancient pyramid at Calakmul, a Classic Maya city

Mighty Mesoamerica

Mexico is dotted with the ruins of historic Mesoamerican civilizations, and while there are plenty on the tourist map, others are empty, remote spots perfect for adventurous travelers. The Río Bec sites *(p308)*, for example, are extremely isolated and rarely visited. Deep in the jungle, the once great city of Calakmul *(p309)* is rarely busy, despite boasting one of the largest Maya pyramids.

Street Food

The Mexican foods most foreigners are familiar with are known as *antojitos* (light bites or appetizers), best experienced at street stalls and food markets in places like Oaxaca *(p234)*, Ensenada *(p168)*, and Mexico City. Tortillas are a staple element of *antojitos*, used for tacos (filled with meat or veggies), enchiladas (similar to tacos but rolled), chilaquiles (chopped up tortillas served with red or green salsas), and *gorditas* (fried and stuffed corn pockets).

$\rightarrow$

A street food stall in Oaxaca, one of Mexico's greatest foodie spots

MEXICO FOR
FOODIES

The dishes you'll find here bear little resemblance to the typical meals made elsewhere in the world in the name of Mexico. The country's real cuisine blends ingredients and recipes that have developed through Aztec, Spanish and modern eras, creating a sophisticated menu of delicious flavors.

Spicy Salsas

The spicy heat of Mexican dishes comes from red and green salsas. From celebrity chefs to street stall owners, everyone takes pride in their recipes, though all use the same basic ingredients, incuding tomato, onion, and chili. Taquería Hermanos González in La Paz *(p172)*, offers some tasty examples.

Did You Know?

There are over 60 varieties of chili pepper grown in Mexico.

Making *salsa roja* $\uparrow$ (red salsa) with chopped tomatoes

THE SPIRIT OF MEXICO

A potent distilled spirit made from the agave plant, mezcal has been made in Mexico since roughly the 16th century. Tequila is a type of mezcal, albeit one that must use only blue agave and is produced mainly in the state of Jalisco. Aficionados usually sip tequila straight, never in cocktails.

Celebrity Chefs

Mexico has some innovative chefs leading the way in fine cuisine. Norma Listman and Saqib Keval blend South Asian, East African, and Mexican flavors at Masala y Maiz (www. masalamaiz.com) in Mexico City. In Ensenada, Benito Molina cooks up fresh seafood at Manzanilla (www.rmanzanilla.com), while Josefina Santacruz serves Pan-Asian cuisine at Sesame (Colima 183, Cuauhtemoc) in Mexico City.

Camarón y jícama, a shrimp and root vegetable dish made by Estanis Carenzo, a visiting chef at Pujol

Taste the Regions

Across Mexico you'll discover regional dishes that take pride of place on the menu in each state. Baja California is famous for fish tacos, while Central Mexico is considered the home of guacamole. Some towns even have their own specialty, so keep an eye out for local favorites or ask for recommendations. In Monterrey (p187) they'll suggest the cabrito asado (roast goat), while Puebla (p148) is known for mole poblano, a blend of chilis and chocolate.

A chef from Oaxaca state's El Sabor Zapoteco Cooking School making tamales

A YEAR IN
MEXICO

JANUARY

△ **Día de Reyes** *(Jan 6)*. Throughout Mexico, street stalls, parties, and gift exchanges are held in honor of the biblical Three Wise Men.

Mérida Fest *(from 6 Jan for three weeks)*. The city celebrates the anniversary of its founding with folk dance, music, and cultural events.

FEBRUARY

Día de la Bandera *(Feb 24)*. Day of tribute to the Mexican national flag, celebrated with military parades, patriotic songs, and speeches.

△ **Carnival** *(Feb/Mar)*. Colorful parades, gigs, and dances are held over five days leading up to Ash Wednesday, with particularly lively celebrations in Veracruz and Mazatlán.

MAY

Día del Trabajo *(May 1)*. Labor Day public holiday with parades held in Mexico City and other large cities.

△ **Corpus Christi** *(May/Jun)*. Masses are held across the country on this important date in the Catholic calendar, 60 days after Easter.

JUNE

Día de la Marina *(Jun 1)*. Battle reenacts and torchlit processions honoring the navy and fishing industry, particularly popular in Guaymas, Sonora.

△ **Mexico City Gay Pride** *(late Jun)*. Around one million people attend this Pride parade from the city's main LGBTQ+ district, Zona Rosa.

SEPTEMBER

Día del Charro *(Sep 14)*. This hugely popular event is held nationwide in tribute to Mexico's cowboys and cowgirls – *los charros* – with horseback displays, rodeos, and parades.

△ **Día de la Independencia** *(Sep 16)*. The most patriotic event in the Mexican calendar, particularly important in Dolores Hidalgo where independence was proclaimed.

OCTOBER

△ **Festival Internacional Cervantino** *(throughout)*. A diverse arts festival, with performances of Cervantes plays on the streets of Guanajuato.

Día de la Raza *(Oct 12)*. Originally the celebration of Christopher Columbus's arrival in the Americas, this day now focuses on celebrating Mexico's ethnic diversity.

MARCH

△ **Vive Latino** *(mid-Mar)*. A huge Latin American rock festival in Mexico City, attracting top international stars.

Natalicio de Benito Juárez *(Mar 21)*. The revered 19th-century president is celebrated with flag displays and floral tributes, notably in his birthplace of San Pablo Guelatao, in Oaxaca state.

APRIL

△ **Semana Santa** *(Easter)*. Starting on Palm Sunday, a week of parades and passion plays, with some regions such as the Copper Canyon blending Catholic and Indigenous rituals.

Regata del Sol al Sol *(late Apr)*. Fireworks, a basketball match, and parties mark the end of this international yacht race from St. Petersburg, Florida, to Isla Mujeres off the coast near Cancún.

JULY

△ **Festival Internacional de Guitarra de México** *(mid-Jul)*. Celebrating string instrument music of all kinds – from Baroque lute to tango guitar – Saltillo hosts orchestral concerts and recitals across the city, with leading international musicians.

Guelaguetza *(late Jul)*. A riot of color, traditional dance, and local cuisine, this week-long celebration of Indigenous cultures is held in Oaxaca city.

AUGUST

△ **Festival Zacatecas del Folclor Internacional** *(late Jul/early Aug)*. This festival of traditional music and dance in Zacatecas is one of the best of its kind in the country.

Dia de la Asunción *(Aug 15)*. Parades and processions commemorating the Virgin Mary's ascent to heaven, with some of the most famous celebrations held in the states of Aguascalientes, Jalisco, and Tabasco.

NOVEMBER

△ **Día de Muertos** *(Nov 1–2)*. Mexico's most famous festival, when families commemorate their deceased loved ones. Celebrated with multicolored papier-mâché skeletons, food, and drink. Pátzcuaro has particularly atmospheric festivities.

Día Internacional del Músico *(Nov 22)*. Concerts throughout the country to honor the patron saint of music; particularly popular with mariachi bands in Mexico City and Guanajuato.

DECEMBER

△ **Día de la Virgen de Guadalupe** *(Dec 12)*. Millions of devotees of Mexico's patron saint join an annual pilgrimage to the Basilica of Guadalupe in Mexico City.

Dia de la Navidad *(Dec 25)*. Mexicans celebrate Christmas Day with particular zeal and elaborate Nativity scenes.

1

A BRIEF
HISTORY

Mexico's history spans the rise and fall of ancient civilizations, the Spanish crown, short-lived emperors, famous revolutionaries, and political leaders. Today, Mexico continues to forge its own modern identity while still bearing the influence of these historic eras and cultures.

Earliest Settlers

By 8000 BC, Mexico's early hunter-gatherer population had begun settling in villages and farming the land. Around 1500 BC, the Olmec culture arose on the Gulf Coast, resulting in great ceremonial centers – but during the first millennium BC, the Olmecs declined, for reasons unknown.

Classic Cultures

One of Central America's most advanced civilizations – the Maya – originated in southern Mexico. The Maya Classic Period peaked from roughly AD 200 to 800, with many city-states based around

Did You Know?

The name Mexico is thought to be derived from the alternative word for the Toltec culture: the Mexica.

Timeline of events

20000 BC

Hunter-gatherer migrants cross from Asia into the Americas and gradually spread south to the Valley of Mexico.

c 8000 BC

Development of agriculture, with the cultivation of corn, chili peppers, and beans.

c 1500 BC

First Olmec settlements established on the Gulf Coast.

c 200 BC

Founding of the city of Teotihuacán.

c AD 800

Collapse of the Classic Maya civilization. Monte Albán abandoned at around the same time.

elaborate temples. The Classic Maya were sophisticated artists and their complex "Long Count" calendar showed remarkable mathematical and astronomical knowledge. Nevertheless, by around AD 900, the Maya Classic culture had collapsed, unable to sustain its growing population. Further north, meanwhile, a great city-state was emerging in the Valley of Mexico. Teotihuacán was built and abandoned by unknown founders before rising once again from c AD 100 to 650. During the 7th century, however, it waned, weakened by attacks, poverty, and internal dissent.

Warring Rivals and Invaders

Teotihuacán's fall led to the rise of militarized successor states, most notably the Toltecs, who settled in the Valley of Mexico prior to the 10th century. After their capital at Tula was overrun by rival groups, the Aztecs emerged as Central America's last great empire. When Spanish conquistador Hernán Cortés landed in Mexico in 1519, he and his men marched on the Aztec capital, Tenochtitlán. By now, the Aztecs faced overpopulation, internal dissidence, and resistance from outlying states. Joining forces with one such state, Cortés took on the Aztec army and, after a destructive siege, Tenochtitlán was defeated.

1 A map of Nueva Galicia, a kingdom of New Spain on Mexico's central coast. ↑

2 A giant Olmec head at the Parque-Museo de la Venta, in Villahermosa.

3 Detailed stonework in the Hall of the Columns, in the Zapotec city of Mitla.

4 A meeting between Cortés and Moctezuma II, the Aztec ruler.

909
Last recorded inscriptions of the Classic Maya, found at Toniná in Chiapas state.

c 1325
The Aztecs establish their capital Tenochtitlán (modern Mexico City) on an island in Lake Texcoco.

1519
Cortés lands on the coast of Veracruz, with a hundreds-strong force of colonizers.

1521
The Aztecs surrender to the Spanish at Tenochtitlán and the Aztec Empire falls.

Colonial-Era Mexico

Within three years of the Aztecs' defeat, the Spanish had subjugated most of present-day Mexico, which was renamed "New Spain." Huge quantities of bullion were remitted to its European ruler, and as the colonial economy grew, New Spain relied heavily upon the free labor of enslaved African peoples. By the early 1600s, Mexico had the largest population of enslaved African peoples in the Americas. Meanwhile, the mixing of Spanish-born settlers with other ethnic groups led to intermediate castes and a new Creole elite in addition to the wealthy, white European immigrants, who spent their time financing grandiose residences and lavish churches. A huge number of Indigenous peoples died from diseases introduced by European colonizers, who also seized their lands and banished them to less hospitable areas.

Rising Discontent

Being a vast colony far away from the seat of the Spanish crown, and with a new elite growing rich and powerful from the treasures and land of New Spain, Mexico enjoyed partial autonomy

ENCOMIENDAS

The Spanish Crown granted conquistadors *encomiendas*: parcels of land with their own Indigenous workers. *Encomendero* landlords were expected to protect and convert their charges who, in return, provided tribute with labor, produce, and resources such as metals. In practice, the *encomienda* system became a brutal form of slavery, and it was abolished in 1542.

Timeline of events

1531

An apparition in Tepeyac, in the north of Mexico City, initiates the cult of the Virgin of Guadalupe, the patron saint of Mexico.

1546

Zacatecas city is founded, following the discovery of silver deposits.

1692

Anti-government riots by Indigenous protestors in Mexico City, triggered by food shortages and ethnic tensions.

1765

Bourbon reforms tighten Spain's hold on Mexico.

compared to other colonies. In the 18th century, however, the new Bourbon dynasty in Spain sought to claw back control. Royal power was centralized, weakening the Church, and relations between Spain and Mexico worsened as the Creole community resented the interference of Spanish officials, while the lower castes suffered from rising taxes and shortages of basic goods. The old alliance between Crown and Church was further undermined when, in 1767, the Jesuits were expelled for their perceived excessive power and influence.

The War of Independence

Responding to the tensions, and exploiting Spain's distraction with the Napoleonic Wars, Mexican independence campaigners acted. On September 16, 1810, a parish priest, Miguel Hidalgo, gave his famous call to arms, *El Grito* (The Cry). The revolt failed, however, and Hidalgo was executed. Another revolt in 1814, led by priest José María Morelos, was also crushed. Guerrilla resistance continued and, in 1821, Mexico's Creole elite proclaimed independence. Spain lacked the ability to fight on, and its main American colony became the independent nation of Mexico.

① Zacatecas, a silver-mining town. ↑

② A hacienda built by Spanish colonizers.

③ Plaza Mayor, Mexico City, in 1692.

④ José María Morelos.

Did You Know?

There are thought to be about 1.5 million self-identified Afro-Mexicans in Mexico today.

1810

Miguel Hidalgo launches a popular revolt against Spanish rule, sparking the War of Independence.

1821

The War of Independence ends; Agustín de Iturbide becomes president of the Regency of Mexico.

1767

Expulsion of the Jesuits from Mexico, in a purge in Europe and its colonies.

1813

Leona Vicario, a key member of the insurgents fighting in the Mexican War of Independence, is imprisoned but manages to escape.

The New Nation

After a brief imperial interlude – when Agustín de Iturbide made himself emperor (1822–3) – Mexico became a republic. The newly independent country was split between Liberals and Conservatives. Liberal intellectuals, supported by Indigenous workers, favored a progressive, free-trading secular society. Elite Conservatives preferred a centralized state, backed by Church and army. Administrations came and went: 30 presidents governed in the 50 years following Mexican independence. The army also generated a host of *caudillos* (military leaders) who built up their retinues and contested for political power.

Disastrous Wars

The most prominent *caudillo* was Antonio López de Santa Anna. He attained the presidency 11 times, but led the country to a crushing defeat in the 1836 war with Texas – then part of Mexico, but home to a large population of US immigrants. Ten years later, Texas joined the US, sparking a war between the two countries. Mexico's defeat resulted in the loss of nearly half its territory to the US, in the Treaty of Guadalupe.

1 Emperor Agustín I.

2 Monument honoring participants of the Mexican-American War.

3 The death of Emperor Maximilian I.

4 Castillo de Chapultepec.

Did You Know?

The era under president Porfirio Díaz is known as the *Porfiriato*.

Timeline of events

1824
Mexico becomes a federal republic.

1836
Texas Revolution; General Santa Anna is victorious at the Alamo but defeated at San Jacinto.

1846
The start of the Mexican-American War.

1848
The war ends; Mexico loses much of its territory to the US.

1857–60
War of the Reform; Liberal victory under Benito Juárez.

4

The Reform

Provoked by its defeat, Mexico's Liberal government, led by Benito Juárez, advocated radical reforms. Its 1854 program known as *La Reforma* (The Reform) would separate Church and State, and make all citizens equal. The Church and the army resisted, but in the ensuing War of the Reform (1857–60) the Liberals were victorious. In 1864, however, the Conservatives sought support from Napoleon III, and declared Maximilian of Habsburg the Emperor of Mexico. The Liberals fought back and Maximilian was executed. Mexico's last monarchy had fallen, and the republic, under Juárez, was restored.

From Dictatorship to Revolution

Four years after the death of Juárez in 1872, general Porfirio Díaz seized power, ruling as an authoritarian president for over three decades. During this time, cities expanded and communications improved but, by the 1900s, Díaz had impoverished the rural workers and exasperated the middle classes with his authoritarian control. Mexico yearned for real democracy, setting the scene for revolution.

> **VICENTE GUERRERO**
>
> Mexico's second president, Vicente Guerrero, was of Afro-Mestizo descent, according to the colonial caste system - making him North America's first Black president. Guerrero became president after serving as a general in the War of Independence. Among other liberal orders, he called for the immediate abolition of slavery on September 16, 1829.

1862
Mexican forces defeat French invaders at Puebla.

1863
French forces enter and successfully capture Mexico City.

1864–7
French occupation under Emperor Maximilian.

1867
On June 19, Maximilian is executed by firing squad in Querétaro.

1876–1911
Porfirio Díaz serves as president of Mexico seven times.

A Decade of Revolution

The Mexican Revolution began in 1910, initially in opposition to Diaz's dictatorial regime. Although Diaz was succeeded by Francisco Madero, Madero failed to unify the country and was assassinated by the military. Another war broke out when revolutionary leaders Emiliano Zapata and Pancho Villa joined together against the subsequent regime of General Victoriano Huerta. Despite their victory against Huerta, disagreements over authority broke out between opposing revolutionary groups, prompting a final civil war. Venustiano Carranza's defeat of Villa in 1917 led to a radical new constitution and Carranza's rise to presidency. By the end of the revolution, violent conflict had touched almost every part of Mexico. Over a million people had died or left the country, the currency had collapsed, and Mexico's infrastructure was in tatters.

The Aftermath

Carranza was eventually ousted by his former general, Álvaro Obregón, in 1920. In the following years, the new regime battled to appease the Church and the US, which disapproved of its

↑ Venustiano Carranza, a key leader of the Mexican Revolution

Timeline of events

1910
The Mexican Revolution is launched by Francisco Madero.

1917
Mexico's liberal, revolutionary constitution is passed.

1929
Partido Nacional Revolucionario (PNR) is formed.

1941–5
Mexico joins with the Allies during World War II.

1957
Death of Diego Rivera, one of the founding members of Mexican mural movement.

expropriation of foreign-owned businesses and land. In 1928, Obregón was assassinated, causing further instability.

Toward the New Millennium

The 1950s and 1960s saw an "economic miracle," powered by the private sector. Later, the discovery of offshore oil led the government to borrow and spend extravagantly. Inflation rose, the economy slumped, and recession continued despite the 1993 North American Free Trade Agreement. However, social reform was on the rise. In 1992, Mexico launched the Third Root Project, acknowledging African presence and influence in Mexico. And in 1994, Indigenous peoples in Chiapas united in rebellion against the government, demanding political representation.

Mexico Today

The early 21st century has been turbulent for Mexico: the distribution of wealth remains imbalanced and drug gang violence, corruption, and migration are concerns for the government. The building of factories in a few rural areas is helping redistribute the wealth by drawing people away from Mexico City.

1. Pancho Villa in 1914.
2. Chihuahua in the 1960s.
3. Leaders gather in 1993.
4. Ancient sights such as Teotihuacán draw visitors to present-day Mexico.

Did You Know?

Mexico City is the most populous urban area in North America.

1985
An earthquake hits Mexico City, killing an estimated 9,000 people.

2007
Chichén Itzá is named one of the New Seven Wonders of the World.

2021
Abortion is legalized in Mexico.

1979
Rosario Ibarra de Piedra founds Eureka, an organization fighting political oppression.

2018
Andrés Manuel López Obrador, from the Party of the Democratic Revolution, is elected president of Mexico.

EXPERIENCE
MEXICO CITY

Shops and cafés in the Coyoacán district

FOTO MEXICO
5658 1125
Café del Barrio Viejo
Coca-Cola
TAQUERIA "LA FE"

EXPLORE
MEXICO
CITY

This section divides Mexico City into three sightseeing areas, as shown on this map, plus an area beyond the city center. Find out more about each area on the following pages.

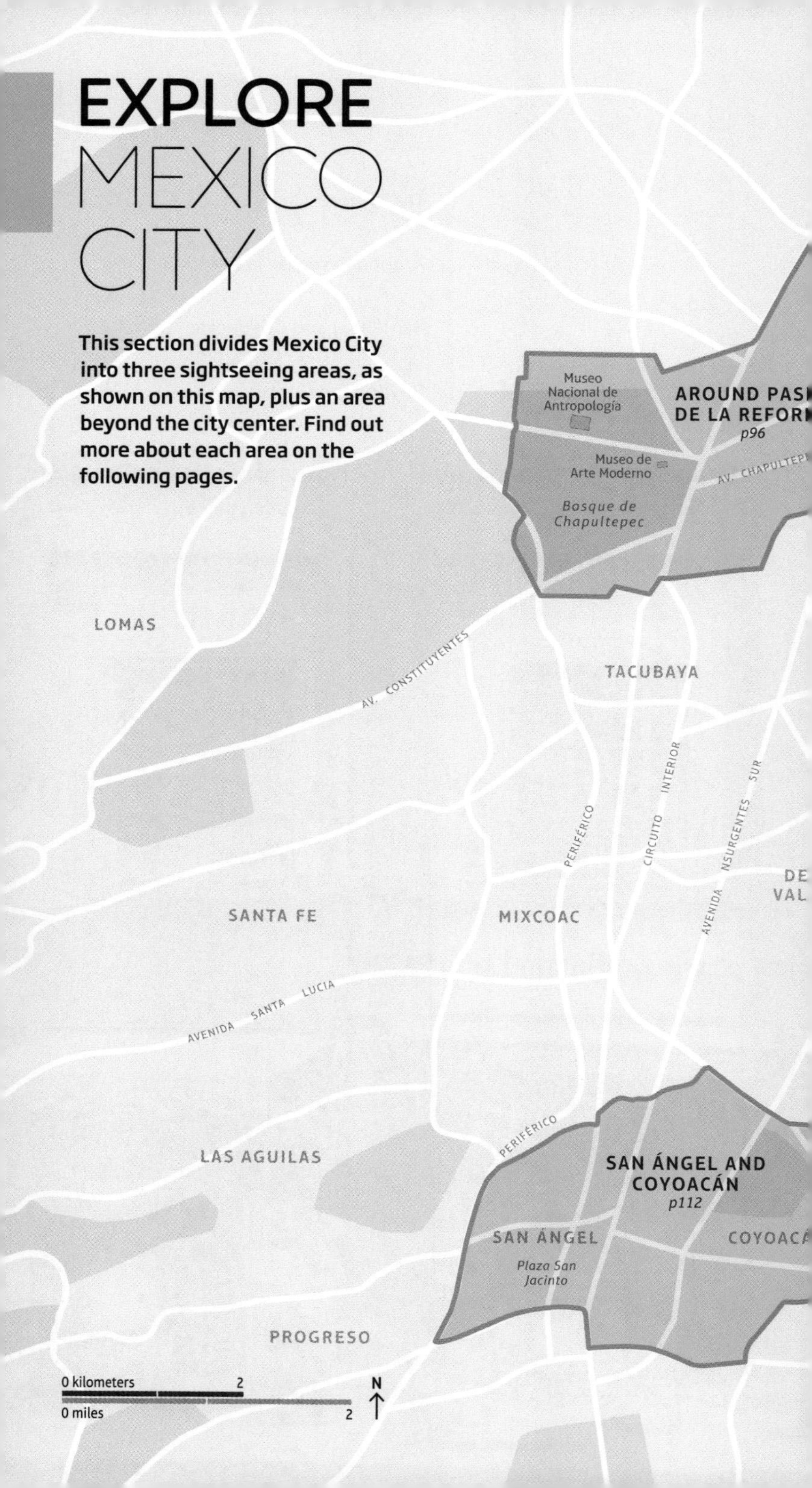

Museo Nacional de Antropología

AROUND PASE DE LA REFORM
p96

Museo de Arte Moderno

AV. CHAPULTEPE

Bosque de Chapultepec

LOMAS

AV. CONSTITUYENTES

TACUBAYA

PERIFÉRICO

CIRCUITO INTERIOR

AVENIDA NSURGENTES SUR

DE VAL

SANTA FE

MIXCOAC

AVENIDA SANTA LUCIA

PERIFÉRICO

LAS AGUILAS

SAN ÁNGEL AND COYOACÁN
p112

SAN ÁNGEL

COYOACÁ

Plaza San Jacinto

PROGRESO

0 kilometers 2

0 miles 2

N ↑

GETTING TO KNOW
MEXICO CITY

Surrounded by mountains and volcanoes, Mexico City is situated in the Valley of Mexico on what used to be Lake Texcoco. The sprawling metropolis, with its 350 neighborhoods *(colonias)*, is the fiesta-fueled, football-loving, political, economic, and cultural heart of the nation.

THE HISTORIC CENTER

PAGE 72

The Aztec Empire may be long gone, but its former capital, Tenochtitlán, is now the beating heart of Mexico City. The Spanish colonizers began building their own city over the remains of Tenochtitlan in the 16th century, and now the Historic Center is so named for the many important buildings that stand here. Today the area is one of the best places to see the many faces of Mexico all in one place: priests and nuns mingle with shoe-shiners and taco-vendors, and mariachi blares from shop windows while patrons linger over *café de olla* in cool cafés.

Best for
Architecture, history, and culture

Home to
Catedral Metropolitana, Palacio de Bellas Artes, Templo Mayor, and Palacio Nacional

Experience
Catching a live performance of Mexican folk dances at the Ballet Folklórico

AROUND PASEO DE LA REFORMA

Running through the heart of the city, the Paseo de la Reforma is a magnificent avenue modeled after those in European capitals. Clustered along the edges are the skyscrapers of the nation's financial center, and on the outskirts there are plenty of cool districts to discover. The Zona Rosa is Mexico's most popular LGBTQ+ scene, while affluent Polanco is home to posh boutiques, superb restaurants, and the e-scooters favored by young professionals. At the southern end of the Paseo lies Mexico's most beautiful urban park, Bosque de Chapultepec, replete with bike trails, gardens, and a castle.

Best for
Museums, nightlife, and parks

Home to
Museo Nacional de Antropología

Experience
Staying up all night in the Zona Rosa, hopping between its many restaurants, bars, and nightclubs

SAN ÁNGEL AND COYOACÁN

In this sprawling metropolis, San Ángel and Coyoacán stand out as especially enticing suburbs, perfect for those seeking out an authentic local atmosphere. Stroll the tranquil, cobbled streets and you'll be rewarded with chic cafés, interesting boutiques, aging churches, picturesque canals, and the vestiges of the old Aztec city. This is also where you'll find the homes and studios of Frida Kahlo and Diego Rivera, as well as the last home of Leon Trotsky – all of which are now fascinating museums.

Best for
Art, history, and strolling

Home to
Museo Frida Kahlo

Experience
Having brunch at the San Ángel Inn before perusing the local Saturday craft market

BEYOND THE CENTER

Mexico City has expanded into the valleys and high plateaus far beyond its traditional center, and is full of diverse neighborhoods, from residential areas to swanky suburbs filled with skyscrapers. Dotted all around are interesting spots that are well worth the trip beyond the more famous central districts. Tour the canals of Xochimilco, join the locals at the home of Mexican soccer, wander through the city's biggest market, and visit exciting art museums and modern architectural marvels.

Best for
Traditional culture and modern architecture

Home to
Xochimilco

Experience
Hopping aboard a boat in Xochimilco for a cruise through its ancient waterways and floating gardens

An imposing entrance to the Metropolitan Cathedral

THE HISTORIC CENTER

Mexico City's Historic Center lies on what was once the ceremonial heart of Tenochtitlán, the Aztec capital. When Hernán Cortés led his army into the city in 1521, it stood on an island in Lake Texcoco. After the Spanish conquered the city, the Aztec empire crumbled rapidly, smallpox wiped through much of the Indigenous population (hindering resistance opportunities), and eventually the Aztecs were subjugated or killed. The Spanish razed the city to the ground, reusing much of the stonework in their own constructions, and gradually filling in the lake.

Today the historic center of Mexico city has narrow streets lined with old-fashioned cafés and shops, and its elegant mansions have been converted into offices, banks, and museums.

THE HISTORIC CENTER

Must Sees

1. Catedral Metropolitana
2. Palacio de Bellas Artes
3. Templo Mayor
4. Palacio Nacional

Experience More

5. Secretaría de Educación Pública
6. Antiguo Colegio de San Ildefonso
7. Templo de la Enseñanza
8. Plaza Garibaldi
9. Iglesia de la Santísima Trinidad
10. Museo José Luis Cuevas
11. Museo de la Ciudad de México
12. Museo de Arte Popular
13. Museo Mural Diego Rivera
14. Laboratorio Arte Alameda
15. Casa de los Azulejos
16. Museo Nacional de Arte
17. Palacio de Cultura Citibanamex
18. Museo de la Caricatura
19. Museo Nacional de la Estampa
20. Torre Latinoamericana
21. Plaza de Santo Domingo
22. Museo Franz Mayer
23. Palacio de la Escuela de Medicina

Eat

1. Café de Bellas Artes
2. El Caguamo
3. Tortas Been
4. Tacos El Huequito

Drink

5. La Ópera Bar
6. Café de Tacuba
7. Terazza Gran Hotel

❶

CATEDRAL METROPOLITANA

📍 K3 🚇 Zócalo Ⓜ Zócalo 🕐 8am-6pm daily 🌐 catedralmetropolitana.mx

Dominating the Zócalo plaza, the Metropolitan Cathedral is built atop the ruins of a former Aztec ceremonial center. The ornate facade bristles with Churrigueresque sculptures, while its interior dazzles with gilded altars, and unadorned white columns supporting a soaring ceiling.

One of the biggest churches in Latin America, Mexico City's cathedral is at the heart of the world's largest Catholic diocese. It took over two centuries – from 1573 to 1813 – to complete. This long period is reflected in the multiple styles of its architecture and internal decoration, ranging from Classical through Baroque and Churrigueresque to Neo-Classical. It has five principal altars, and 16 side chapels containing a valuable collection of paintings, sculpture, and church furniture.

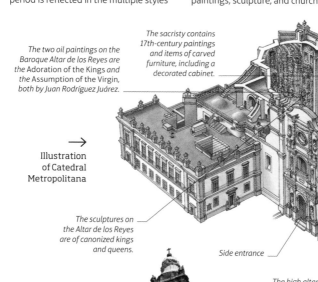

The sacristy contains 17th-century paintings and items of carved furniture, including a decorated cabinet.

The two oil paintings on the Baroque Altar de los Reyes are the Adoration of the Kings and the Assumption of the Virgin, both by Juan Rodríguez Juárez.

→
Illustration of Catedral Metropolitana

The sculptures on the Altar de los Reyes are of canonized kings and queens.

Side entrance

The high altar is a block of white marble carved with images of saints.

Capilla de San José is one of 16 dedicated to saints and manifestations of the Virgin, all exquisitely decorated.

←
The imposing facade of the massive Catedral Metropolitana

Spanish Colonial

Work began in 1573. The basic plan of three huge vaulted naves was the work of Claudio de Arciniega. Much of the first walls were built by Juan Miguel de Agüero.

Churrigueresque

▽ Built between 1710 and 1737, the *estípites* (square-sided relief columns) are a hallmark of the Churrigueresque style. The foremost example is the Sagrario Metropolitano's facade, built by Lorenzo Rodríguez.

Baroque

△ Most of the cathedral was built in the mid-17th century, the oldest sections in the Spanish Baroque style known as Plateresque. The three portals of the main facade, from the late 1600s, are grander.

Neo-Classical

The bell towers and upper stories were added in the 1780s. Manuel Tolsá added the clock tower and rebuilt the dome in an austere Neo-Classical style.

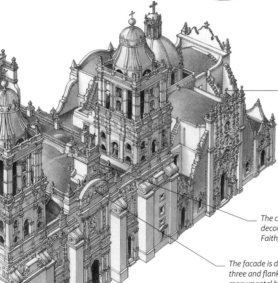

Attached to the east side of the cathedral is the Sagrario, built in the mid-18th century as the parish church. It has a high Baroque facade adorned with sculpted saints.

The clock tower is decorated with statues of Faith, Hope, and Charity.

The facade is divided into three and flanked by monumental bell towers.

Main entrance

With its gold-alloy choir-rail imported from Macao, superbly carved stalls, and two magnificent organs, the choir is one of the highlights of the cathedral.

> **INSIDER TIP**
> **Subsidence**
>
> Over time, the cathedral began sinking into the soft clay on which it was built, causing its floor to slope. After a devastating earthquake in 1985, the structure was stabilized.

2 ⟨⟩ Ⓜ ▭ 🏛

PALACIO DE BELLAS ARTES

📍 J3 🏛 Eje Central & Avenida Juárez Ⓜ Bellas Artes 🕐 11am-5pm Tue-Sun
🌐 museopalaciodebellasartes.gob.mx

This magnificent monument houses a prestigious collection of Mexican muralist art, and its theater hosts traditional folk-dance performances and live classical concerts by world-leading orchestras and artists.

Arguably the most beautiful building in the Historic Center, the Palacio de Bellas Artes was conceived in 1904 as a new national theater. Italian architect Adamo Boari designed an innovative building around a steel frame, incorporating Neo-Classical and Art Nouveau elements together with pre-Hispanic decorative details. The exterior of the building is clad in Italian marble and its cupolas are covered in tiles. The largest, central dome is surmounted by a Mexican eagle surrounded by figures representing the dramatic arts. Interrupted by the revolution, the work was completed by Federico Mariscal in 1934. This accounts for the contrasting Art Deco interior, with its geometric shapes in colored marble and eye-catching illumination, especially the vertical lamps flanking the entrance to the auditorium.

Outside the Palacio de Bellas Artes, its dome a major landmark in the Historic Center ↑

→ The Art Deco entrance hall, clad in cream and gold-colored marble

EAT

Café de Bellas Artes
Whether you're seeking a mid-concert cocktail, or a hearty meal after browsing the galleries, this little café is the ideal place for a break, with a great menu and a convenient location inside the Palacio. Dishes include Mexican classics such as *chiles en nogada* (stuffed chiles in walnut sauce).

 Eje Central and Avenida Juárez (inside the Palacio de Bellas Artes) **℡** 5512-2593

$$⑤

↑ A stunning glass mosaic curtain, which was made by Tiffany Studios of New York

TOP 4 HIGHLIGHTS OF THE PALACIO

Murals
17 artworks by Mexico's foremost muralists, including Rivera, Orozco, and Siqueiros.

Theater Curtain
Made of more than a million pieces of glass by Tiffany Studios, the curtain depicts the iconic Popocatépetl and Iztaccíhuatl volcanoes.

Museo Nacional de Arquitectura
Contemporary architecture from around the world is displayed.

Facade
The Art Nouveau exterior features Carrara Italian marble columns, topped by golden domes of Marotti glass and ironwork.

③ ⌖ ⌖ ⌖

TEMPLO MAYOR

**◉K3 ◪Seminario Ⓜ Zócalo ◷9am-5pm Tue-Sun
ⓦtemplomayor.inah.gob.mx**

Although in ruins and surrounded by modern buildings, the remains of the Great Temple still convey the grandeur of the former Aztec city, Tenochtitlán. The museum houses a scale model of the original complex and the giant carved monolith of the goddess Coyolxauhqui.

This temple once stood at the heart of the Aztec city of Tenochtitlán. The Aztecs chose this spot for their most important religious building to fulfil a prophecy, having been advised by their god, Huitzilopochtli, to pitch their tents where they saw an eagle perched on a cactus devouring a snake.

The first temple was built some time after 1325, but it was enlarged many times over the course of the next two centuries. The complex was almost completely destroyed by the Spanish after their conquest of the Aztec capital in the early 1500s. The chance discovery of the extraordinary Coyolxauhqui carving in 1978 prompted excavations that uncovered the remains of superimposed temples denoted by their stages of construction.

A museum attached to the archaeological site contains eight rooms of impressive Aztec exhibits, with some of the items having been discovered here at Templo Mayor. These include the Eagle Knights, two identical life-size clay statues of elite Aztec warriors in feathered costumes.

The layout of the ruin complex can be confusing. Authorized tours are recommended, as are audio guides, both of which are available from the museum.

↑ Stones carved by the Aztecs uncovered at the site, now displayed in the museum

Did You Know?

The snake is a powerful component of the temple's rich symbolism.

↑ The complex, showing the successive pyramids built one on top of the other

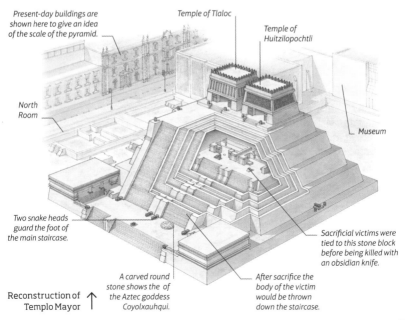

Present-day buildings are shown here to give an idea of the scale of the pyramid.

Temple of Tlaloc

Temple of Huitzilopochtli

North Room

Museum

Two snake heads guard the foot of the main staircase.

Sacrificial victims were tied to this stone block before being killed with an obsidian knife.

A carved round stone shows the of the Aztec goddess Coyolxauhqui.

After sacrifice the body of the victim would be thrown down the staircase.

Reconstruction of ↑ Templo Mayor

PALACIO NACIONAL

📍 K3 🏛 Plaza de la Constitución s/n 📞 (55) 36 88 12 55
Ⓜ Zócalo 🕘 9am-5pm Tue-Sun

The National Palace has been the seat of government since 1562. Its distinguished facade reflects the history of the presidents who have lived and worked here, as depicted by Rivera's murals.

Filling the east side of the Zócalo, this imposing building occupies the former site of the palace of Aztec emperor Moctezuma, and later the home of the conquistador Hernán Cortés. The present palace was begun in 1562 in an austere Baroque style typical of Spanish architecture of the time. It has had an eventful history, and was attacked by rebels in 1624 and 1692. After independence in 1821, it became the residence of the presidents of Mexico, and the offices used by President Juárez in the 1860s are open to the public. In the 1920s a third story was added, in harmony with the original style. While Rivera's murals are the undoubted highlight of the palace, the former Chamber of Deputies, Benito Juarez's rooms, and the history museum are all worth seeing.

Rivera Murals

These extraordinary murals around the staircase and the main patio were painted by Diego Rivera from 1929 to 1951. The main murals above the great staircase present a dynamic panorama of Mexican history. On the right-hand wall is an idealized vision of ancient Mexico before the arrival of the Spanish. Filling the bottom of the central panel are the bloody battles of the Conquest, while independence forms the centerpiece of the main panel. Foreign invasions – by the United States in 1847 and France in the 1860s – are shown in the far right and left panels of the main wall. The inner right panel refers to Juárez's Reform Laws of 1857, and the 1910 revolution appears on the upper left. On the left wall is the astonishing *Mexico Today and Tomorrow*, an exuberant portrayal of the promise of the revolution.

> **Filling the east side of the Zócalo, this imposing building occupies the former site of the palace of Aztec emperor Moctezuma.**

↑ Interior detail show-casing the building's Spanish Baroque style

←

Exterior of the Palacio Nacional, beguiling when illuminated at night

↑ Visitors pausing on the staircase to admire the Rivera murals

Murals

Wrapped around the staircase of the main patio, Rivera's murals depict Mexican history, enlivened by the artist's distinctive characterization.

Botanical Garden

▽ These little gardens of Mexican flora occupy a tranquil courtyard next to the Royal Chapel. They contain hundreds of native species.

Juárez Museum

▲ Benito Juárez spent the last five years of his life in the palace. This museum has his possessions, including personal letters and effects.

History Museum

The six rooms of this museum cover some 600 years of Mexican history, including Hernán Cortés, the Spanish viceroys, and the Bourbon era.

Main Balcony

▲ Home of the bell rung by Miguel Hidalgo in 1810, and where the president makes the "Grito" on the night of September 15 before Independence Day.

EXPERIENCE MORE

5

Secretaría de Educación Pública

📍 K3 🏛 República de Argentina 28 Ⓜ Zócalo, Allende 🕐 9am–5pm Mon–Fri 🌐 sep.gob.mx

This former convent building, dating from 1594, is renowned for its large series of murals by prominent Mexican painter Diego Rivera. Painted between 1923 and 1928, they reflect Rivera's diverse influences: Italian frescoes, French Cubists, and pre-Hispanic Mexico. Visitors will need to bring photo ID to enter the site.

The ground floor of the first patio is dedicated to the glorification of labor. On the staircase is a series of Mexican landscapes, while on the third floor, in a panel called *The Painter, The Sculptor and the Architect*, is a well-known self-portrait. The first-floor walls contain *grisailles* (monochromatic paintings) depicting scientific, artistic, and intellectual labor, and on the top floor are portraits of the leaders of the Mexican Revolution, such as Zapata *(p62)*. The second patio, on the ground floor, features panels

of fiestas. The third floor draws on revolutionary songs *(corridos)* for its subject matter and includes a panel, *The Arsenal*, in which the artist Frida Kahlo *(p116)* hands out guns to gathered revolutionaries.

In stark contrast to the style of Rivera is a striking mural by David Alfaro Siqueiros, *Patriots and Parricides*. This is located on the staircase in a part of the building which used to be a customs house (the Ex-Aduana), near the República de Brasil entrance.

6

Antiguo Colegio de San Ildefonso

📍 K3 🏛 Justo Sierra 16 Ⓜ Zócalo, Allende 🕐 11:30am–5pm Thu–Sun 🌐 sanildefonso.org.mx

This 16th-century building, originally a Jesuit seminary, is an outstanding example of Mexican civil architecture from the colonial era. It was remodeled in the 18th century, but the Baroque- and Neo-Classical-inspired facade on Calle San Ildefonso is original.

Today the building belongs to the national university and

🔍 HIDDEN GEM
Palacio Postal

A 15-minute walk from the Antiguo Colegio, the Main Post Office reveals a fabulously ornate wrought-iron and marble interior behind its somber stone facade. It still functions as a post office and has a small postal museum.

serves as a museum. Its star attraction is the collection of murals from the earliest years of the Mexican muralist movement (1920s–70s) – in fact, San Ildefonso is considered to be the birth-place of the movement.

The first murals commissioned included those of Siqueiros, who, in 1922–4, painted four works around the stairwell of the Colegio Chico, the oldest of the three patios which make up the San Ildefonso complex. At around the same time, Orozco was painting a series of murals on the north wall of the Patio Grande with equally universal themes – among them motherhood, freedom, and justice and the law. These

↑ Mariachi musicians playing for diners seated outside on Plaza Garibaldi

include *Revolutionary Trinity* and *The Strike*. Arguably the most dramatic piece, however, is *The Trench*.

The Orozco works to be found on the staircase – including a nude study of Cortés and his mistress La Malinche – relate mostly to the theme of *mestizaje*, or the mixing of the races that formed the Mexican nation. The Anfiteatro Simón Bolívar contains an early work by Diego Rivera, *The Creation*. Another mural in this hall was painted by Fernando Leal between 1930 and 1933.

The conference room to the north of the Patio Grande, known as El Generalito, is furnished with 17th-century carved wooden choir stalls.

Templo de la Enseñanza

📍 K3 ⬛ Donceles 102
☎ (55) 57 02 18 43
Ⓜ Allende, Zócalo
🕙 9:30am–6pm Mon–Sat, 11am–2pm Sun

One of the most remarkable churches in Mexico City, the Templo de la Enseñanza has

← Diego Rivera murals at the Secretaría de Educación Pública

an extremely narrow and ornate facade sloping backward slightly from ground level. The atrium is tiny and the interior decoration the height of late-18th-century "ultra-Baroque."

Built as a convent church, La Enseñanza was vacated by the nuns as a result of the anti-clerical Reform laws of the 19th-century. It was later used by various government bodies, including the Ministry of Education.

The dazzling gold main altarpiece is studded with the sculpted figures of saints. It rises up to the roof of the church, flanked by huge paintings, its height enhancing its vertical dimensions. The vault above is adorned with a fresco of the Virgin of El Pilar, to whom the church is dedicated.

In the lower choir, situated to either side of the altar, are lattice work screens intended to hide the nuns from the gaze of other worshippers in the church.

Plaza Garibaldi

📍 J2 ⬛ N of the Alameda, off Eje Central Lázaro Cárdenas

Plaza Garibaldi is the home of mariachi music in Mexico City. Dressed in their iconic outfits, the musicians can be seen scouting for work along the nearby Avenida Lázaro Cárdenas.

Mariachi music was born in the area around Guadalajara in Jalisco (p194). In the early 20th century there was heavy migration from Jalisco to the capital, and Plaza Garibaldi became the mariachis' home.

Today the area abounds with bars and restaurants serving a staple fare of tacos and tequila. Mariachi bands can be hired per song or by the hour, and rates vary depending on the size of the band and its musical prowess.

The plaza also has a modern cultural space, MUTEM Garibaldi, which houses **El Museo del Tequila y el Mezcal**, where visitors can learn about the two spirits and have a taste.

El Museo del Tequila y el Mezcal

⬛ Plaza Garibaldi s/n
🕙 11am–10pm daily (to midnight Thu–Sat)
🌐 mutemgaribaldi.mx

> ### LUCHA LIBRE IN THE CAPITAL
>
> *Lucha libre* (wrestling) is massively popular in Mexico City. In the freestyle acrobatic bouts, competing *luchadores* (wrestlers) often wear masks and costumes to create superhero-like personalities. Bouts take place several times a week at the two wrestling arenas close to the historic center: Arena México (*Dr Lavista 189*) and Arena Coliseo (*República de Perú 77*).

The intricate facade of the Iglesia de la Santísima Trinidad

INSIDER TIP
Late-Night Museums

Museums in Mexico City stay open until late on the last Wednesday of the month, and some also offer guided tours, concerts, workshops, film screenings, and other activities.

19th century and declared a national monument in 1932. Since 1988 it has housed an art gallery reflecting the personal tastes of Mexican painter and sculptor José Luis Cuevas (1934–2017).

The exquisite patio is dominated by the massive bronze sculpture of *La Giganta (The Giantess)*, which Cuevas created specifically for this space. A number of smaller bronzes by the artist are dotted around the ground floor. The galleries contain paintings by Cuevas and other Mexican artists, including a number of portraits of him and his wife Bertha. There are also temporary exhibits by international artists.

At the entrance to a small "dark room" dedicated to Cuevas' works of erotica, visitors are warned, tongue-in-cheek, of the dangers they

⑨ Iglesia de la Santísima Trinidad

📍 L3 🏠 Santísima 12
📞 (55) 55 22 22 15 Ⓜ Zócalo
🕐 8am–8pm daily

Formerly a hospice, the 18th-century Church of the Holy Trinity is only a few blocks from the Zócalo *(p94)* but is easily overlooked amid the bustle of the surrounding streets. It has an intricate Churrigueresque facade, with finely worked tapered columns and sculpted figures.

The interior is simpler, but it's still worth entering the church to see the paintings of the martyrs in the nave, the two wooden sculptures representing the Trinity, and the crucifix inlaid with bone and precious woods. The wooden screen in the entrance to the church and the choir balustrade is also impressively carved.

---

⑩ Museo José Luis Cuevas

📍 L3 🏠 Academia 13
Ⓜ Zócalo 🕐 10am–5pm
Mon–Fri 🌐 museo
joseluiscuevas.com.mx

Formerly the cloisters of the Santa Inés convent, this 17th-century jewel was converted to private dwellings in the

→

Jose Louis Cuevas' *La Giganta* (1991) at the Museo José Luis Cuevas

pose to those who have had a puritan upbringing.

On your way out of the museum, take a moment to admire the entrance of the church of Santa Inés next door. The doors are carved with reliefs showing scenes from the life of St. Inés, and portraits of the founders of the convent kneeling in prayer.

Museo de la Ciudad de México

Q K4 **Q** Pino Suárez 30, corner of República del Salvador **C** (55) 55 22 99 36 **M** Zócalo **Q** 10am-6pm Tue-Sun

The palace of the counts of Santiago de Calimaya, long renowned for their ostentatious lifestyle, is regarded as one of the most outstanding 18th-century buildings in the city. Built in 1776, the palace is faced with red volcanic *tezontle* stone. Its Baroque portal and magnificent carved wooden doors convey the social standing of its former inhabitants. At the foot of the southwest corner, the builders incorporated a stone serpent's head, which was taken from a wall made up of similar heads that surrounded the Aztecs' ceremonial center.

The first courtyard is noteworthy for the fountain with its carving of a mermaid holding a guitar, and for the trilobate arches near the staircase. Also outstanding is the richly carved stone doorway to the first-floor chapel.

In the early 20th century, the building was home to the painter and political activist Joaquín Clausell (1866–1935). The walls of his studio, on the third floor, are covered with an unusual mural, consisting

of a collage-like set of scenes influenced by the Impressionists that Clausell met when he was in France.

The building has been occupied by the Museum of Mexico City since the 1960s. The collection displays furniture and carriages associated with the house, as well as temporary exhibits.

Museo de Arte Popular

Q H3 **Q** Revillagigedo 11 **M** Juárez **Q** 10am-6pm Tue-Sun (to 9pm Wed) **W** map. cdmx.gob.mx

Located inside an Art Deco building, the Museum of Folk Art brings together traditional works from all over Mexico. Its collection of more than 3,000 objects includes contemporary and traditional pieces made from many different materials, such as wood, ceramics, glass, metal, paper, and textiles. Indigenous costumes and religious art are especially well represented.

→

A boy studies folk art exhibits at the Museo de Arte Popular

EAT

El Caguamo
One of the city's most famous seafood stalls.

Q J4 **Q** Corner of Ayuntamiento 18 and López Ayuntamiento 18

Tortas Been
This tiny joint is worth tracking down for its amazing *torta* sandwiches.

Q L4 **Q** Off República del Salvador 152 **C** (55) 55 22 46 18

$ $ $

Tacos El Huequito
Superb tacos are served at this hole-in-the-wall, no-frills takeaway.

Q J3 **Q** Ayuntamiento 21

Museo Mural Diego Rivera

⊠H3 ⌂Corner of Colón and Balderas Ⓜ Hidalgo, Juárez ⓒ10am-6pm Tue-Sun ⓦmuseo muraldiegorivera.bellas artes.gob.mx

This gallery is built around one of muralist Diego Rivera's masterpieces: *Dream of a Sunday Afternoon in Alameda Park*. Painted in 1947 for the dining room of the Hotel Prado, it combines Mexico's history with the dreams of its protagonists and the recollections of the artist. He includes two self-portraits, and an image of his wife, the famous artist Frida Kahlo *(p116)*.

> **Did You Know?**
>
> One of the Historic Center's subway stations, Pino Suárez, contains an Aztec pyramid.

The three-sectioned painting caused a stir when first unveiled. The phrase "God does not exist" was removed by Rivera after a Christian group defaced the mural.

Laboratorio Arte Alameda

⊠H3 ⌂Doctor Mora 7 Ⓜ Hidalgo ⓒ9am-5pm Tue-Sun ⓦartealameda. bellasartes.gob.mx

This museum of contemporary art is located in the former convent and church of San Diego de Alcalá, built in the 16th century. From 1964 to 1999, the building housed the Pinacoteca Virreinal, a collection of religious art now displayed in the Museo Nacional de Arte. In 2000 the doors opened to the Laboratorio Arte Alameda. This art space is dedicated to showing major works by Mexican and international artists, and focusing on trans-disciplinary, temporary exhibits and events. With its cutting-edge shows, it hopes

to interest new audiences in contemporary art and to raise the profile of Mexican artists.

Casa de los Azulejos

⊠J3 ⌂Francisco I Madero 4 ⓒ(55) 55 12 13 31 Ⓜ Bellas Artes, Allende ⓒ7-1am daily

The 16th-century "House of Tiles" was originally the palace of the counts of Orizaba. The blue-and-white tiled exterior is attributed to a 1737 remodeling by the 5th countess, who is said to have imported the style from the city of Puebla, where she had been living previously. Now occupied by the Sanborns store and restaurant chain, the lovingly restored building conserves much of its original Mudéjar interior. The main staircase is decorated with waist-high tiling, and there is a mural on the first floor landing by José Clemente Orozco, entitled *Omniscience*, which was painted in 1925. On the upper floor it is worth taking note of the

Diego Rivera's *Dream of a Sunday Afternoon in Alameda Park* (1947) ↑

↑ The restaurant at the Casa de los Azulejos, or "House of the Tiles"

mirrors surrounded by elaborate gold frames that contain the figures of angels and cherubs.

Museo Nacional de Arte

◯ J3 ◯ Tacuba 8 Ⓜ Allende ◯ 11am–5pm Tue–Sun Ⓦ munal.mx

Created in 1982, the National Art Museum is worth a visit for the building alone. An imposing, Neo-Classical piece of architecture, it was completed in 1911 as the Ministry of Communications and Public Works. Its double staircase, in bronze and marble, is enclosed by a semi-circular window three stories high. The interior, with its intricate ironwork and many candelabra, is sumptuous.

The museum's galleries encompass Mexican art from the 16th century to 1954. The collection includes commercial engravings, political cartoons, and folk art, as well as paintings. Much of the collection of religious art from the 16th to early 19th century resulted from confiscations following anti-clerical Reform laws in the 1800s. As well as works by the great muralists – Rivera, David Alfaro Siqueiros, and Orozco – the outstanding pieces include a series of landscapes by 19th-century painter José María Velasco. One room is devoted to portraits, including a depiction of the art-lover María Asúnsolo by Siqueiros.

Right in front of the museum is the Plaza Manuel Tolsá, centering on one of the city's favorite monuments – *El Caballito* (The Little Horse), which is a massive equestrian statue of Carlos IV of Spain by Manuel Tolsá (1803).

Palacio de Cultura Citibanamex

◯ J3 ◯ Madero 17 Ⓜ Allende ◯ 10am–7pm Mon–Sun Ⓦ fomento culturalbanamex.org

This magnificent 18th-century residence was the home of Agustín de Itúrbide during his reign as the first Emperor of Mexico (1821–23). The elaborate, Churrigueresque facade had wrought-iron balconies and fortified towers. It now houses a cultural center with a museum of antiquities and an art gallery that displays temporary exhibitions in its spectacular central courtyard.

Museo de la Caricatura

◯ K3 ◯ Donceles 99 Ⓜ Zócalo ◯ 10am–6pm daily Ⓦ museodela caricatura.org

With its intricate and finely preserved Baroque facade, the former Colegio de Cristo is one of the best examples in Mexico City of an upper-class 18th-century dwelling. Originally conceived in 1610 as an educational foundation for poor students, it was rebuilt in the 1740s, and later became a private house. The tiny patio and the broad staircase with its low, stone archway are some of the architectural highlights.

In the 1980s, the building was restored to house the collection of the Mexican Society of Cartoonists. This includes contemporary cartoons and works by the influential political satirist and engraver José Guadalupe Posada (1852–1913).

DRINK

La Ópera Bar
This historic bar oozes old-world charm, and the mixologists make some of the best cocktails in the city.

◯ J3 ◯ Calle 5 de Mayo 10 Ⓒ (55) 55 12 89 59

Café de Tacuba
Set in a beautiful 16th-century mansion, the bar in this elegant restaurant is famous for its namesake cocktail.

◯ J3 ◯ Calle de Tacuba 28 Ⓦ cafedetacuba. com.mx

Terazza Gran Hotel
One of the capital's swankiest addresses, the fifth-floor terrace bar at this venerable old hotel makes an ideal choice for a special occasion, or even just an indulgent evening out.

◯ K3 ◯ Avenida 16 de Septiembre 82 Ⓦ granhotelciudad demexico.com.mx

19

Museo Nacional de la Estampa

📍J3 🏛 Avenida Hidalgo 39 Ⓜ Bellas Artes 🕐10am-6pm Tue-Sun 🌐museo nacionaldelaestampa. inba.gob.mx

The Museum of Graphic Arts (also known as MUNAE) has an extensive collection of pre-colonial and contemporary prints, only part of which is on show at any one time.

Probably the best-known artist on display is José Guadalupe Posada (1852–1913). Posada's work featured in the satirical newspapers of his day, and his enduring image of *La Calavera Catrina* – a well-dressed skeleton woman – is among the most familiar symbols of the nation's fascination with death.

In the Sala de Técnicas is a range of works illustrating different techniques used by print artists. The building itself has a 1986 stained-glass skylight by Salvador Pinoncelly.

20

Torre Latinoamericana

📍J3 🏛 Eje Central Lázaro Cárdenas and Francisco I Madero Ⓜ Bellas Artes 🕐Viewing platform: 10am-9pm Mon-Thu, 9am-10pm Fri-Sun; restaurant: 10am-10pm daily (to 9pm Mon & Sun) 🌐torrelatino.com

This skyscraper rises 44 floors and has the best view of the city – weather permitting. Completed in 1956, it has survived many earthquakes, notably that of 1985. In 30 seconds, its elevators whisk visitors to the 37th floor. On the 38th floor is an exhibition devoted to the history of the tower. Two floors down, the Museo del Bicentenario covers the history of Mexico after its independence in 1821. A second elevator rises to a 44th-floor viewing platform and a bar-restaurant.

21

Plaza de Santo Domingo

📍K3 Ⓜ Allende

Second only in importance to the Zócalo (p94), the Plaza de Santo Domingo (just south of Plaza 23 de Mayo) is steeped in history. The Dominicans built a convent here – the first in New Spain – in 1527, of which all that remains today is a restored chapel, the Capilla de la Expiación. Most of the other buildings that flank the square date from the 18th century. The church of Santo Domingo, with its sober facade partly covered in red volcanic *tezontle* stone, was completed in 1737.

Its tower is capped by a pyramidal pinnacle covered with Talavera tiles (p131). The interior of the church contains statues of saints thought to date from the 16th century, as well as oil paintings by Juan Correa and Alonso López de Herrera. The side altars, antique organ, and the cedarwood choir stalls with carved images of the saints are among the treasures.

The subsidence that led to the demolition of previous churches on this site is widely evident in the square. From the door of the church, the

←

The Torre Latinoamericana skyscraper and *(inset)* its observation deck, with views over the city

↑ The tranquil courtyard of the Museo Franz Mayer, a former hospital turned art museum

INSIDER TIP
On Your Bike

On Plaza de Santo Domingo you'll spot one of the city's nearly 500 EcoBici stations, the capital's popular public bike-sharing scheme. It's a great way to explore the city (www. ecobici.cdmx.gob.mx).

undulation of the Tuscan-style *portales* (arcade) which runs down the west side of the square, is noticeable. Under the arcade sit scribes, who, for a small fee, will fill out official documents using old manual typewriters; the remaining few of a centuries-old tradition.

22

Museo Franz Mayer

📍 H3 🏛 Avenida Hidalgo 45
Ⓜ Hidalgo, Bellas Artes
🕐 11am-5pm Tue-Fri (to 6pm Sat & Sun)
🌐 franzmayer.org.mx

This is the richest collection of applied art in Mexico City. Assembled by German financier and art collector Franz Mayer (1882–1975), it is housed in a 16th-century former hospital. The museum has possibly the most beautiful courtyard in the Historic Center, featuring a delightful fountain.

The collection contains more than 10,000 pieces from Europe, the Far East and colonial-era Mexico. Exhibits include tapestries, furniture, carvings of religious scenes, ceramics, 20,000 antique tiles, and over 1,000 pieces of silverwork. Among the most exquisite objects are a number of inlaid wooden chests. There are also some impressive wooden screens, one of which has a rendering of the conquest of Mexico City on one side and a partial view of the city in the colonial period on the reverse.

23

Palacio de la Escuela de Medicina

📍 K2 🏛 Brasil 33 Ⓜ Zócalo, Allende 🕐 9am-6pm daily
🌐 pem.facmed.unam.mx

Now home to the Museum of Mexican Medicine, the Palace of the School of Medicine stands on the site of the building in which the Holy Inquisition carried out its fearsome interrogations from the late 16th to early 19th centuries.

The current building dates from the 18th century, and underwent restoration in the 1970s. The architecture is notable for its Baroque facade – unusually set on the corner of the building – and graceful main courtyard. There are "hanging" arches in each corner of the courtyard, with the supporting pillars set into the wall behind.

A typical 19th-century apothecary's store, transferred in its entirety from Oaxaca (p234), is one of the museum's more unusual features. It has displays on the history of Mexican medicine from pre-Hispanic times, including sacred and medicinal plants.

> **The Palacio de la Escuela de Medecina features a typical 19th-century apothecary's store, transferred in its entirety from Oaxaca.**

A SHORT WALK
THE ALAMEDA CENTRAL

Distance 1 mile (2 km) **Time** 20 minutes
Nearest metro Bellas Artes

This peaceful oasis amid the surrounding bustle offers shady paths lined with jacaranda trees, decorative fountains and statues, and elegant architecture – a great introduction to the best of the Historic Center. The Alameda takes its name from the *álamos* (poplar trees) planted here in the late 16th century. Its many statues date mainly from the 1900s, although the central Baroque fountain has been there since the mid-18th century. The most imposing monument is the *Hemiciclo a Juárez*, a marble monument with Doric pillars.

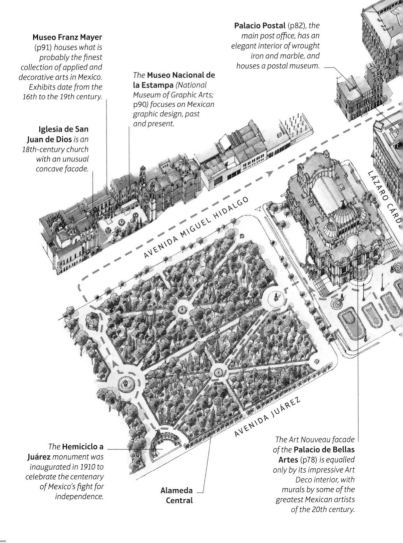

Museo Franz Mayer (p91) *houses what is probably the finest collection of applied and decorative arts in Mexico. Exhibits date from the 16th to the 19th century.*

The **Museo Nacional de la Estampa** *(National Museum of Graphic Arts; p90) focuses on Mexican graphic design, past and present.*

Iglesia de San Juan de Dios *is an 18th-century church with an unusual concave facade.*

Palacio Postal (p82), *the main post office, has an elegant interior of wrought iron and marble, and houses a postal museum.*

LÁZARO CÁRD

AVENIDA MIGUEL HIDALGO

AVENIDA JUÁREZ

The **Hemiciclo a Juárez** *monument was inaugurated in 1910 to celebrate the centenary of Mexico's fight for independence.*

Alameda Central

The Art Nouveau facade of the **Palacio de Bellas Artes** *(p78) is equalled only by its impressive Art Deco interior, with murals by some of the greatest Mexican artists of the 20th century.*

Museo Nacional de Arte (p89) *is a gallery dedicated to modern Mexican art. The building was constructed between 1904 and 1911.*

Café Tacuba (p89)

Locator Map
For more detail see p74

The **Museo del Ejército y Fuerza Aérea Mexicanos** *(Museum of the Mexican Army and Air Force) has a collection of weaponry and military memorabilia dating from the Spanish conquest to the 21st century.*

Palacio de Minería *is one of the city's finest 19th-century Neo-Classical buildings.*

La Ópera Bar (p87) *is an old-fashioned restaurant on 5 de Mayo. A bullet hole in the ceiling is said to have been made by famous revolutionary Pancho Villa (p184).*

TACUBA

FILOMENO MATA

START

FINISH

FRANCISCO I MADERO

Palacio de Iturbide, *named after the Emperor Agustín de Iturbide (ruled 1821–3), is a superb example of Spanish Colonial architecture.*

GANTE

0 meters	100	N
0 yards	100	

Talavera tiles cover the outside of **Casa de los Azulejos** (p88), *an 18th-century mansion. Inside is a mural by José Clemente Orozco.*

One of Mexico City's first skyscrapers, **Torre Latinoamericana** (p91) *was completed in the 1950s and has survived many earthquakes.*

→ The blue-tiled facade of the Casa de los Azulejos

A SHORT WALK
ZÓCALO

Distance 1.5 miles (2 km) **Time** 25 minutes
Nearest metro Zócalo

The Plaza de la Constitución, invariably known as the Zócalo, is one of the biggest public squares in the world. Walking through this vast open space, visitors can relive history, with the remains of Aztec temples revealed beneath the Spanish Colonial architecture. A giant national flag flies in the middle of this vast paved space, which is dominated by two buildings, the cathedral and the Palacio Nacional. On the square stand other public buildings, restaurants, shops, and hotels.

A dazzling gold altarpiece is the main feature of the **Templo de la Enseñanza**, *a late 18th-century Baroque church, which was originally designed as a convent chapel.*

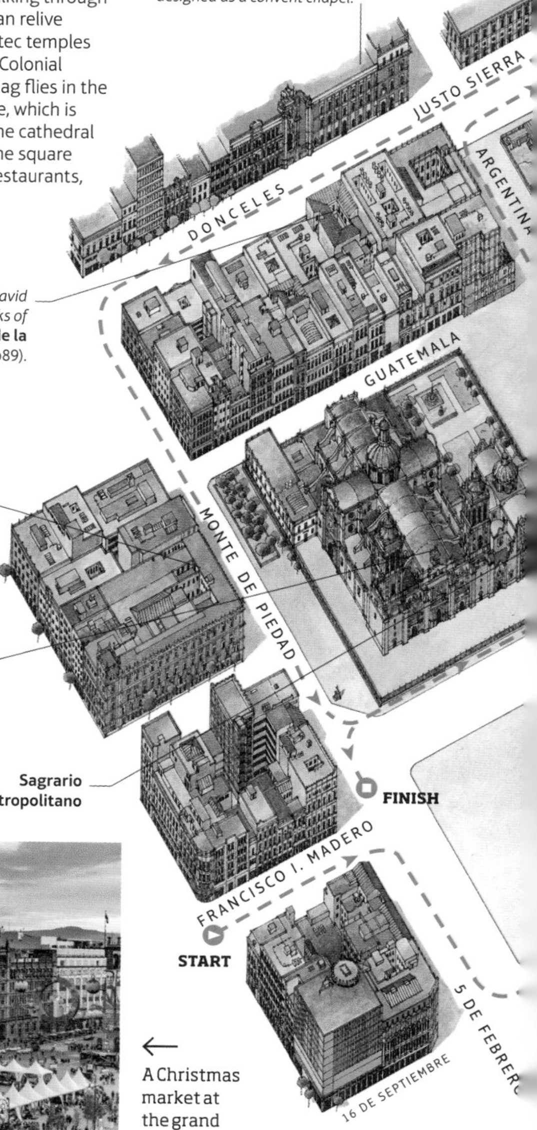

A caricature of singer David Bowie is among the works of cartoon art in the **Museo de la Caricatura** *(p89).*

Nacional Monte de Piedad, *a government-run pawn shop, occupies a historic building dating from the 16th century.*

Although damaged by the subsidence affecting the center of Mexico City, the **Catedral Metropolitana** *(p76) is still one of the greatest religious buildings in Latin America.*

Sagrario Metropolitano

FINISH

JUSTO SIERRA

ARGENTINA

DONCELES

GUATEMALA

MONTE DE PIEDAD

FRANCISCO I. MADERO

START

5 DE FEBRERO

16 DE SEPTIEMBRE

← A Christmas market at the grand Zócalo plaza

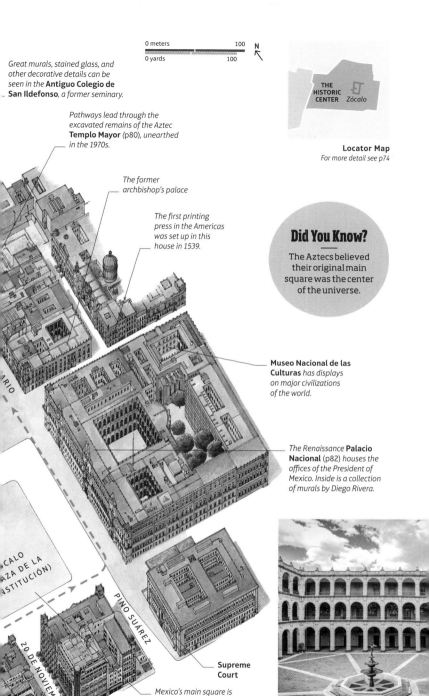

Great murals, stained glass, and other decorative details can be seen in the **Antiguo Colegio de San Ildefonso**, a former seminary.

Pathways lead through the excavated remains of the Aztec **Templo Mayor** (p80), unearthed in the 1970s.

The former archbishop's palace

The first printing press in the Americas was set up in this house in 1539.

Locator Map
For more detail see p74

Did You Know?

The Aztecs believed their original main square was the center of the universe.

Museo Nacional de las Culturas has displays on major civilizations of the world.

The Renaissance **Palacio Nacional** (p82) houses the offices of the President of Mexico. Inside is a collection of murals by Diego Rivera.

Supreme Court

Mexico's main square is used as a venue for state ceremonial occasions and military parades.

Former city hall

↑ A fountain in the inner courtyard of the Palacio Nacional

The striking Angel of Independence statue

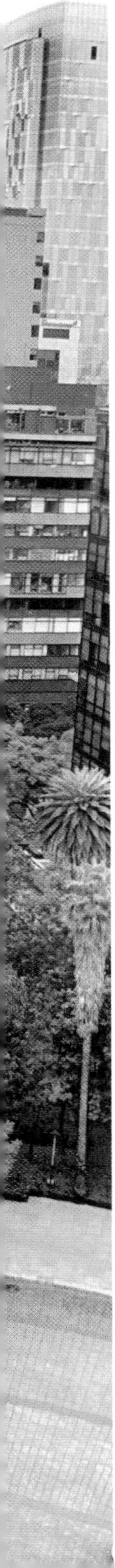

AROUND PASEO DE LA REFORMA

Commissioned in the 1860s, by Emperor Maximilian, the Paseo de la Reforma is a grand boulevard linking the Historic Center and the Bosque de Chapultepec (Chapultepec Park). Though it is flanked by tall, modern office buildings today, monumental statues and fountains still adorn the avenue, including the golden Angel of Independence, the symbol of Mexico City.

Until the 1980s this was the city's high-end shopping district, but the fancy boutiques have since migrated to the chic neighborhood of Polanco on the northern edge of Bosque de Chapultepec. The park itself, once the residence of the Aztec emperors, has been a public park since 1530. The castle on the top of the hill at its northeastern end was also Maximilian's home.

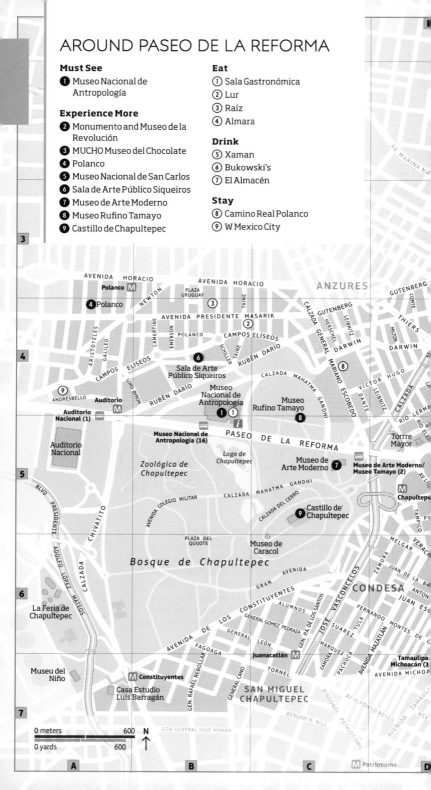

AROUND PASEO DE LA REFORMA

Must See

1. Museo Nacional de Antropología

Experience More

2. Monumento and Museo de la Revolución
3. MUCHO Museo del Chocolate
4. Polanco
5. Museo Nacional de San Carlos
6. Sala de Arte Público Siqueiros
7. Museo de Arte Moderno
8. Museo Rufino Tamayo
9. Castillo de Chapultepec

Eat

1. Sala Gastronómica
2. Lur
3. Raíz
4. Almara

Drink

5. Xaman
6. Bukowski's
7. El Almacén

Stay

8. Camino Real Polanco
9. W Mexico City

0 meters 600
0 yards 600
N

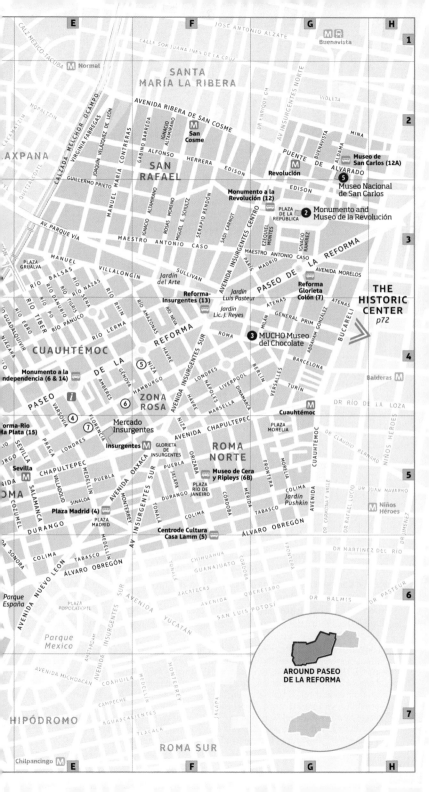

Did You Know?

The Museo Nacional de Antropología ranks as Mexico's most visited museum most years.

The museum's entrance hall, providing an insight into the fascinating galleries beyond ↑

MUSEO NACIONAL DE ANTROPOLOGÍA

📍B4 🏠 Corner of Gandhi and Paseo de la Reforma Ⓜ Auditorio, Chapultepec
🕙10am–7pm Tue–Sun 🌐 mna.inah.gob.mx

Mexico's ancient civilizations are brought to life through this collection, one of the greatest archaeological museums in the Americas. Entering beneath its huge, hovering canopy, visitors are met by the array of priceless treasures, from the huge Aztec Piedra del Sol to a reproduction of Moctezuma's feather headdress.

Inaugurated in 1964, the National Museum of Anthropology was designed by Pedro Ramírez Vázquez. The vast and airy space creates a just setting for a world-renowned collection of finds from Mexico's pre-Hispanic cultures. The museum's large, central patio is almost entirely covered by a 275-ft (84-m) long canopy, balanced on a 36-ft (11-m) pillar decorated with bas-reliefs. This canopy is considered to

be the largest concrete structure in the world supported by a single pillar. In the entrance hall is a space that is dedicated to temporary exhibitions, which have previously covered themes such as Maya art techniques and desert cultures. There is also an audio-visual display here giving useful background context about Mexico's ancient Mesoamerican eras, civilizations, and cultures *(p144)*.

↑ The main entrance to
   the Museo Nacional
   de Antropología

PICTURE PERFECT
**The Symbol
of Mexico**

In front of the museum's
entrance is a sculpture
of the national symbol:
an eagle locked in
combat with a serpent.
The hot pink bird and
lime green reptile are a
perfect pop of color for
Instagram lovers.

Upper Floor

▽ The interconnected
galleries on the upper
floor of the museum
contain the ethnology
collection. Grouped
roughly in regions,
exhibits showcase the
traditional lifestyle of
the major Indigenous
groups of Mexico.

Museum Guide

Ground Floor

△ Laid out around a
central patio, the twelve
galleries on the ground
floor are dedicated to
archaeological finds
from ancient Mexico.
Each room deals with
a particular civilization
or region of the country.

Outside

△ Doors lead out to structures
built within the grounds of
the museum, including
reconstructions of Maya
temples, a Monte Albán
tomb, and a Trascan house.
A giant statue of a rain deity,
either Chalchiuhtlicue or
Tlaloc, stands near the
museum's entrance.

101

ARCHAEOLOGY COLLECTION

Preclassic Era

Beginning with the earliest agricultural settlements in the central plateau around 1700 BC, the Preclassic gallery illustrates the rise of more complex cultures, shown in particular detail through the development of the ceramic arts. Outstanding among the collection are a number of figures influenced by the Olmecs (p272) from the Gulf of Mexico, including the "jaguar-boy" found at Tlapacoya in Mexico State.

Teotihuacán

Centered on the mysterious, ancient city that the Aztecs dubbed "the place where humans became gods," the culture of Teotihuacán (p140) was among the most important of the Classic era in Mesoamerica. The gallery is dominated by the huge stone statue of the water-goddess, Chalchiuhtlicue. Along one wall a reconstruction of the facade of the Temple of Quetzalcoatl reproduces the original blues and reds with which it was painted. Colorful murals of Teotihuacán life adorn the gallery's side walls. Some of the finest pieces include a variety of pottery vessels, such as grain and water storage urns, figurines, and funerary masks showing a talent for lapidary, and obsidian carvings.

Toltecs

As Teotihuacán declined, other cities of the central plateau, Tula in particular, rose to prominence. The founders of Tula (p154) were the Chichimecas from the north, who adopted the name Toltecs, meaning

Did You Know?

The inhabitants of Teotihuacán were experts in fashioning obsidian knives.

artisans. They soon acquired a reputation as specialists in the military arts. The most noticeable exhibit is a gigantic stone warrior figure known as an Atlante, with which the Toltecs are most commonly associated. These figures were used as pillars in their temples. The Toltec gallery also includes items from other cities of the Postclassic period, including Xochicalco in Morelos. Notable among these exhibits are stone carvings dedicated to the god Quetzalcoatl, and the stylized head of a macaw, which was perhaps used as a ballcourt marker. Xochicalco's most famous monument, the serpent frieze around the base of the temple of Quetzalcoatl, is beautifully illustrated with a photographic mural.

Oaxaca

Following on from the Aztec Hall (p102), this is the first gallery dedicated to the regions of Mexico. It presents the artifacts of the two great peoples of Oaxaca: the Zapotecs (also known as Ben'Zaa), builders of the hilltop city of Monte Albán, and their neighbors and successors the Mixtecs, who created Mitla, with its stone friezes. On display are polychrome ceramic pieces from both cultures.

 A sculpture of the Aztec water-goddess Chalchiuhtlicue

↑ A family looking at vivid Cacaxtla frescoes, displayed in the museum

Gulf of Mexico

Among the most spectacular, of all the museum's exhibits are the extraordinary colossal stone heads from the Pre-classic Olmec culture, which flourished from 1200 to 400 BC. The Olmecs also produced smaller, equally remarkable, sculptures of heads and figures in a variety of stone, most of them with the characteristic Olmec features of broad, flat-nosed faces and thick lips, curled downward. The Olmecs share this gallery with the Totonacs from central Veracruz and the Huastecs from the northern shores of the Gulf.

The Maya

There is no doubting the special hold of the Maya on the imagination of visitors to Mexico, whether because of the intricate beauty of their great stone cities in the jungle, such as Palenque in Chiapas (p244), or the continuing mystery of their sudden collapse, before the arrival of the Spanish colonizers. Among the highlights of the Maya gallery are carved stelae, such as the one from Yaxchilán, lintels from the Classic period, and a particularly outstanding carved head of a young man, found at Palenque. A small, underground gallery contains a reconstruction of the royal tomb of Pakal found beneath Palenque's Temple of the Inscriptions. It also displays artifacts from the site, such as high-quality stucco heads.

Northern and Western Mexico

The sparsely inhabited northern deserts never produced the great civilizations traits of central and southern Mexico. Nonetheless, the ceramic art from Paquimé (p178) – the most notable of the so-called Oasis cultures – has a distinctive elegance, with its geometric patterns, smooth-polished surfaces and adornments such as copper or turquoise. The gallery also contains examples of metalwork, and models of the unique multi-story adobe houses of Casas Grandes. At the height of the Aztec (Mexica) empire, the Tarascans (Purépechas), the dominant culture of the Pacific coast, retained their independence, and with it a distinctive artistic tradition. This gallery provides evidence of their skill in metalworking (they were among the first in the region to use gold, silver, and copper for jewelry and utensils), and in pottery. Other items of particular note include the polished earthenware from Classic-era Colima, and the ceramics of the cloisonné technique using different colored clays, which is thought to have originated there.

> ### EXPLORING THE MUSEUM
>
> The galleries on the ground floor are all accessible from the central patio, so your tour of the museum can begin anywhere. The first seven galleries are in chronological order, covering the history of the central plateau. The next five galleries visit the various regions of Mexico, including one dedicated to the great civilization of the Maya. The upper floor is devoted to costumes, houses, and artifacts of the 68 surviving Indigenous cultures in Mexico, and explores their religions, social organization, and festivals.

↑ The intricately carved Sun Stone, a highlight of the Aztec Hall

THE AZTEC HALL

The Aztecs

The largest gallery in the museum displays the treasures of the Mexica culture – better known as the Aztecs. When Hernán Cortés and his conquistadors arrived in 1519 *(p56)*, the Aztecs ruled most of what is now Mexico, either directly or indirectly. This gallery gives the visitor a strong sense of the everyday culture of the Aztec people, the power and wealth of their theocratic rulers, and their enormous appetite for blood, sacrifice, war, and conquest.

Large Sculptures

The entrance landing and central section of the gallery are devoted to large stone sculptures. Near the entrance is the Ocelotl-Cuauhxicalli, a 3-ft- (94-cm-) high stone vessel in the form of a jaguar-eagle. It was used as a receptacle to hold the hearts of human sacrificial victims. A statue of Coatlicue, the mother of Coyolxauhqui and later of Huitzilopochtli, is one of the few representations of the goddess in Aztec art. This statue shows her with eagle's claws, a dress made of snakes, and a necklace of hearts and hands. She has been decapitated, and two serpents emanate from her neck to symbolize blood. Other large sculptures are of the goddesses Coyolxauhqui and Cihuateteo, small-scale representation of a teocalli or temple, and a *tzompantli*, an altar of skulls from the Templo Mayor. On the wall opposite the door, dominating the gallery, is the Sun Stone.

 PICTURE PERFECT
The Umbrella

Among all the photos of old artifacts, make sure to snap a shot of the central courtyard, dominated by José Chávez Morado's *El Paraguas* (The Umbrella), an inverted fountain. Its massive canopy is balanced on a carved 36-ft (11-m) bronze pillar.

The Aztec People and their History

The section to the right of the entrance describes the Aztec people, their physical appearance and their history. The most conspicuous piece here is a carved round stone, known as the Stone of Tizoc, which records the victories of Tizoc, the seventh ruler of the Aztecs (1481–6). This trachyte stone was found in the Zócalo. Another object of interest is a stone head with inset teeth and eyes to add to its realism. It is thought to represent the common man. Other sculptures represent everyday Aztec people, including a statue of a Mexica noble dressed in robes appropriate to his rank. This part of the museum includes a model of the temple complex that stood at the center of

→ Giant sculpture of the goddess Coyolxauhqui

Tenochtitlán. Surrounded by a wall, it focused upon the Templo Mayor topped by its twin shrines. The rounded temple in front of the Templo Mayor was dedicated to the god Quetzalcoatl.

Sacred Objects

The display cases to the left of the entrance show items used for religious purposes by the Aztecs. One of the most notable is a vase in the form of a pregnant monkey, carved out of obsidian, a hard black, volcanic stone akin to glass. This vase symbolizes the wind loaded with black rain clouds, which will engender growth and fertility. Also on display here is the stone altar on which human sacrificial victims were stretched in order to remove their hearts.

Other Exhibits

Aspects of Aztec daily life are described in other parts of the hall. Notable collections include decorative ceramics, Aztec jewelry made out of bone, gold, wood, crystal, and shells, and clothing that includes animal skins and feathers. The musicality of the Aztecs is shown with a range of instruments, such as flutes and whistles. Along the back wall are documents and drawings explaining the system of tribute that sustained the Aztec economy.

ETHNOLOGY COLLECTION

Contemporary Cultures

The ten galleries on the top floor of the museum are devoted to all aspects of Mexico's various Indigenous cultures, and include displays dedicated to housing, costumes, religious artifacts, social structures, and festivals. The exhibits focus on the period after the colonial era (*p58*), showcasing how the dozens of different Indigenous cultures in Mexico have both preserved and developed their traditions over the centuries.

Starting with an introductory gallery on the north wing, the rooms are divided loosely by region, beginning with Gran Nayar. This covers the cultures of the Náayerite (also known as the Cora), Huichol (Wixáritari), Tepehuan, Nahua, and Mestizos (those of mixed Indigenous and European descent) from Nayarit, Jalisco, and Zacatecas states.

Other highlights include the Oaxaca exhibit in the south wing, displaying Mixtec and Zapotec handicrafts from wicker-work and ceramics to jewelry and textiles. In The Northwest: Sierras, Deserts and Valleys gallery, the agricultural rituals, basketry, and the Deer Dance of groups such as the Comcáac (Seri), Cochimí, Yaqui (Yoeme), Rarámuri (Tarahumara), and Tepehua are showcased.

68

The number of Indigenous languages spoken in Mexico.

EAT

Sala Gastronómica

This modern restaurant has a menu inspired by the regions of Mexico. Try Veracruz-style eggs for breakfast or classic Oaxacan *mole negro* (dark mole) for lunch.

🖪Mon

$ $ $

↑ An exhibit of festival costumes, found among the ethnology collection

EXPERIENCE MORE

2

Monumento and Museo de la Revolución

📍G3 ⌂Plaza de la República Ⓜ Revolución ⏰Noon–8pm Mon–Sat (to 9pm Fri & Sat), 11am–8pm Sun 🌐mrm.mx

This striking dome-topped monument was designed as part of a parliament building under the dictator Porfirio Díaz (*p61*). Due to unanticipated problems with the marshy ground, it was never finished.

Then, in 1933, as an alternative to demolishing it, the architect Carlos Obregón Santacilia proposed that it be converted into a monument celebrating the 1910 revolution that put an end to the *Porfiriato*. Stone cladding and sculptures were added, and the remains of revolutionary figures such as Francisco Villa were interred at the base of the columns. The austerity of the monument's functional and Art Deco styling is relieved by details in bronze. The statues, sculpted by Oliverio Martínez de Hoyos, represent independence, the 19th-century liberal reform, and the post-revolutionary agrarian and labor laws.

At the base of the monument is the Museo de la Revolución, which covers a 63-year period from the founding of the liberal Federal Constitution of the United Mexican States in 1857 to the installation of the post-revolutionary government in 1920. The exhibits include photos, documents, reproductions of period newspapers, carriages, and contemporary clothing.

3

MUCHO Museo del Chocolate

📍G4 ⌂Calle Milan 45 Ⓜ Cuauhtémoc ⏰11am–5pm daily 🌐mucho.org.mx

Housed in a restored 20th-century residence, the tooth-tingling Chocolate Museum is dedicated to chocolate. Its collection contains artifacts from the Americas, Europe, and

Did You Know?

The Aztecs considered chocolate to be a gift from the gods.

Asia, and the production process is explained from the cultivation of cacao to the making of chocolate. (Note that most exhibits are in Spanish only.)

Temporary exhibitions cover an eclectic range of topics, such as cacao-loving insects and chocolate's aphrodisiac qualities. Workshops and courses are also available, and the shop offers tasting samples.

4

Polanco

📍A4

Developed in the 1940s and 50s as a residential neighborhood for the well-to-do

middle classes wanting to escape the busy center, Polanco is today one of Mexico City's most chic areas. Its streets are lined with upscale cocktail bars, clubs, hotels, and famous fine-dining restaurants, while Avenida Presidente Masarik has Mexico's highest concentration of luxury stores.

5

Museo Nacional de San Carlos

G2 **Avenida México-Tenochtitlán 50** **Hidalgo, Revolución** **11am–5pm Tue–Sun** **mnsancarlos. inba.gob.mx**

Occupying an imposing Neo-Classical building, this museum has the oldest and most important collection of European art in Latin America. The bulk of the collection consists of paintings spanning the 14th to the early 20th century, including notable examples of the Flemish, French, Italian, and Spanish schools. Among the highlights are paintings by Rubens and sculptures by Rodin.

Galleries on the upper floor house the permanent collection. Pride of place at the entrance is given to *La Encarnación*, a stunning gilded altarpiece dating from 1465, by the Aragonian painter Pere Espallargues.

At one time the building was home to a "museum of strange objects," but this was later moved to the nearby **Museo Universitario del Chopo** (Chopo University Museum). This fabulous twin-towered Art Nouveau structure, nicknamed "the Crystal Palace," focuses on contemporary art and performing arts.

←

Fountains in front of the Monumento a la Revolución on Plaza de la República

↑ Exploring the artwork on display at the Museo Nacional de San Carlos

Museo Universitario del Chopo

 Calle Dr. Enrique González Martínez 10 **11:30am–7pm Wed–Sun** **chopo.unam.mx**

6

Sala de Arte Público Siqueiros

B4 **Tres Picos 29** **Auditorio, Polanco** **11am–5pm Tue–Sun** **saps-latallera.org**

This was the home and studio of the celebrated Mexican muralist David Alfaro Siqueiros (1896–1974). The painter's life and work are represented here by a collection that includes finished pieces, as well as drawings, plans, models, and photo-montages of his many murals. There are also photos and documents charting Siqueiros's life, which was singularly eventful. It included two prison terms, one of which was for his part in a plot to kill Leon Trotsky (p121).

The ground-floor gallery is the site of the mural *Maternity*, which was originally designed for a school. The upper floor galleries contain paintings by Siqueiros. The second-floor gallery has works of other artists, both contemporary Mexican and international.

DRINK

Xaman
This cozy cocktail bar makes an ideal spot for a quiet drink, with an unusual shaman-themed decor.

F4 **Copenhague 6** **Mon & Sun** **xaman.bar**

Bukowski's
Named after the notoriously booze-fueled American writer, this bohemian bar is appropriately sited above a bookshop. Live jazz nights are regularly held here.

E4 **Hamburgo 126** **pendulo.com/ especial/bukowski-bar**

El Almacén
One of the city's oldest LGBTQ+-friendly bars, this unpretentious club is famous for its good-humored drag shows.

E5 **Florencia 37-B** **(55) 4857 0359** **Mon**

↑ A visitor photographing Frida Kahlo's *Las Dos Fridas* at the Museo de Arte Moderno

Museo de Arte Moderno

📍 C5 📌 Corner of Paseo de la Reforma and Gandhi Ⓜ Chapultepec 🕐 10:15am–5:30pm Tue–Sun 🌐 mam.inba.gob.mx

A wide range of 20th- and 21st-century Mexican painting and sculpture is housed in the Museum of Modern Art. The collection includes works by all the well-known figures – Rufino Tamayo, Diego Rivera, David Alfaro Siqueiros, and Frida Kahlo – as well as artists who do not belong to the mainstream established by the muralists and others since the revolution. International artists who have worked in Mexico are also represented.

The museum has a fine array of oils by Tamayo and several works by Francisco Toledo, his fellow Oaxacan. Among the other highlights are Frida Kahlo's *The Two Fridas*, Diego Rivera's portrait of Lupe Marín, and José Clemente Orozco's *Las Soldaderas*. Contemporary artists displayed include Alberto Castro Leñero, Irma Palacios, and Emilio Ortiz.

Sculptures are exhibited in the gardens, and the adjacent circular gallery has temporary exhibitions of modern Mexican and international art.

Museo Rufino Tamayo

📍 C5 📌 Corner of Paseo de la Reforma and Gandhi Ⓜ Chapultepec 🕐 10am–6pm Tue–Sun 🌐 museotamayo.org

This outstanding collection of modern painting and sculpture was assembled by one of Mexico's foremost 20th-century artists, Rufino Tamayo, and his wife Olga. It occupies a stunning, futuristic, concrete-and-glass building which is set among the trees of Bosque de Chapultepec (p110). The building was designed by renowned Mexican architects Teodoro González de León and Abraham Zabludovsky, and was awarded the National Prize for Arts and Sciences in 1982.

Housed within this light and airy gallery are some 800 paintings in all, as well as drawings, sculptures, and graphic art. There are a number of paintings by Rufino Tamayo himself, and many modern artists, including international names such as Andy Warhol, Salvador Dalí, and René Magritte.

 HIDDEN GEM

Casa Estudio Luis Barragán

On the southwest corner of Bosque de Chapultepec (p110) is the home of Pritzker-Prize-winning Luis Barragán (1902–88). Visit by booking a guided tour (www.casaluisbarragan.org).

9

Castillo de Chapultepec

C5 **Bosque de Chapultepec** **Chapultepec**

The hill that forms the highest point of Bosque de Chapultepec once stood on the lakeshore across the water from Tenochtitlán, the Aztec's capital city. On its summit is the 18th-century Chapultepec Castle, begun in the late 1700s and completed in the 1900s.

A crucial battle was fought here in 1847, when young army cadets died trying to defend the fortress against invading US troops. In the 1860s, the castle became the palace of Emperor Maximilian. Subsequently it was an official residence for the president.

Today the castle houses the **Museo Nacional de Historia** (National History Museum), which covers Mexican history from the Conquest to the revolution. Exhibits include items relating to historical figures, such as the glasses worn by former president Benito Juárez (p61). The walls of the museum are decorated with large murals showing historical events.

In the castle's grounds is the Galería de Historia, known as the Museo del Caracol (Snail Museum) because of its shape. Here visitors are guided through a series of dioramas that illustrate scenes from the struggle for independence up to the 1917 Constitution.

Museo Nacional de Historia

Bosque de Chapultepec **9am–5pm Tue–Sun** **mnh.inah. gob.mx**

Stained glass in the Castillo de Chapultepec; *(inset)* the castle's grand facade

EAT

Lur
This stylish restaurant specializes in Basque cuisine, mixing old and new influences.

B4 **Presidente Masaryk 86** **restaurantelur.mx**

$$$

Raíz
One of the city's leading gourmet restaurants, Raiz bases its contemporary Mexican cuisine on local ingredients.

B4 **Schiller 331** **restauranteraiz.com**

$$$

Almara
This restaurant fuses Mediterranean and modern Mexican cuisines, plus an extensive wine list.

E4 **Corner of Varsovia and Hamburgo** **almara.rest**

$$$

STAY

Camino Real Polanco
A chic, colorful hotel opposite the Bosque de Chapultepec.

C4 **Calz General Mariano Escobedo 700** **caminoreal.com**

$$$

W Mexico City
An ultramodern, luxury hotel with a cool and quirky style.

A4 **Campos Elíseos 252** **marriott.com**

$$$

A LONG WALK
BOSQUE DE CHAPULTEPEC

Distance 5.5 miles (9 km) **Time** 2 hours **Terrain** An easy walk on well-kept footpaths **Nearest metro** Chapultepec

The city's biggest park provides plenty of footpaths and shady lawns where you can escape the noise of traffic and city bustle. A favorite weekend recreational spot for residents of Mexico City, Chapultepec has been a public park since the 16th century. Its attractions include a zoo, a boating lake, a number of museums and galleries, and occasionally live, open-air entertainment. It is well worth making the climb up to the castle terrace, which offers stunning views across the city.

↑ Diego Rivera's Fuente de Tláloc fountain in the western half of the park

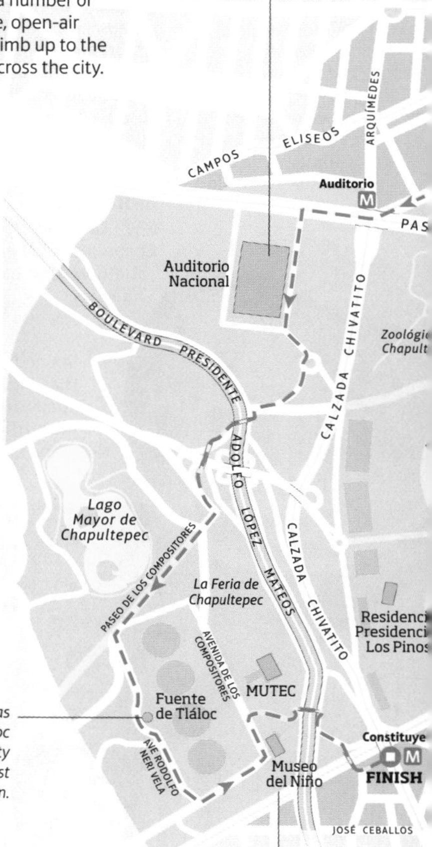

The **Fuente de Tláloc** fountain was designed by artist Diego Rivera. Tlaloc was the central Mexican rain deity (p287), and one of the most important gods in the pantheon.

Mexico's national concert hall, **Auditorio Nacional**, is considered one of the best in the world.

Auditorio Nacional

CAMPOS ELISEOS ARQUIMEDES

Auditorio Ⓜ

PAS

BOULEVARD PRESIDENTE

CALZADA CHIVATITO

Zoológic Chapult

ADOLFO LOPEZ MATEOS

Lago Mayor de Chapultepec

PASEO DE LOS COMPOSITORES

La Feria de Chapultepec

AVENIDA DE LOS COMPOSITORES

CALZADA CHIVATITO

Residenci Presidenci Los Pinos

Fuente de Tláloc

MUTEC

AVE RODOLFO NERI VELA

Museo del Niño

Constituye Ⓜ Ⓜ
FINISH

JOSÉ CEBALLOS

The **"Papalote" Museo del Niño** children's museum has over 400 interactive exhibits, organized into five themes: the human body, expression, the world, "Conscience," and communication. A giant video screen shows educational movies.

0 meters 600
0 yards 600

N ↑

AROUND
PASEO DE LA
REFORMA

*Bosque de
Chapultepec*

Locator Map
For more details see p98

*The house of muralist
David Alfaro Siqueiros
is now a museum,*
**Sala de Arte Público
Siqueiros,** *displaying
his paintings and
documents relating
to his life (p107).*

*One of the city's highlights,
the* **Museo Nacional de
Antropología** *(p100) has
a world-famous collection
of ancient relics.*

*Works by Tamayo himself and
other painters are on show in*
Museo Rufino Tamayo *(p109).*

Opened in 1964, the
**Museo de Arte
Moderno** *(p109) has a
collection of works by
modern Mexican artists.*

AV. PRESIDENTE
MASARIK

DARÍO

DARWIN

PLAZA
MELCHOR
OCAMPO

Sala de Arte
Público Siqueiros

RUBÉN

CALZADA MAHATMA

LEIBNITZ

VICTOR HUGO

LEIBNITZ

CIRCUITO INTERIOR

Museo Rufino
Tamayo

CALZADA GEN.
M. ESCOBEDO

GANDHI

RÍO LERMA

PASEO DE
LA REFORMA

Museo
Nacional de
Antropología

LA   REFORMA

SEVILLA

*Lago de
Chapultepec*

Museo de Arte
Moderno

Torre
Mayor

HAMBURGO

Sevilla Ⓜ

SALAMANCA

START ▶ Ⓜ Chapultepec

GIO MILITAR   CALZADA MAHATMA GANDHI

Monumento
a los Niños Héroes

AV. SONORA

PUEBLA

SALAMANCA

CALZADA DEL CERRO

Castillo de
Chapultepec

TAMPICO

VERACRUZ

DURANGO

Museo del
Caracol

MELGAR

*Bosque de
Chapultepec*

GRAN   AVENIDA

The **Monumento a los Niños
Héroes** *(Monument to the Boy
Heroes) honors the army cadets
who died defending Chapultepec
castle from the US in 1847.*

JUAN ESCUTIA

ENIDA   DE   LOS   CONSTITUYENTES

GEN. RAFAEL REBOLLAR

*Once the residence of
Mexican rulers,* **Castillo
de Chapultepec**
*(p109) offers views of
the park and of the
Paseo de la Reforma.*

→ Visitors to Bosque de
Chapultepec enjoying the
deckchairs and boats

Museo Frida Kahlo, also known as Casa Azul (the Blue House)

SAN ÁNGEL
AND COYOACÁN

At the time of the Spanish conquest, Coyoacán was a small town on the shore of Lake Texcoco. Hernán Cortés set up his headquarters here in 1521 while the former Aztec capital of Tenochtitlán nearby was rebuilt. Nearby San Ángel was then a village called Tenanitla – it became known as San Ángel in the 17th century, after the foundation of the convent-school of San Ángelo Mártir.

Until the 20th century both San Ángel and Coyoacán were rural communities outside Mexico City. The growth of the metropolis has since swallowed them up, but both retain most of their Spanish Colonial architecture. Much favored as a place of residence by artists and writers, the area has been the home of several famous people, including Diego Rivera, Frida Kahlo, and Russian revolutionary Leon Trotsky.

SAN ÁNGEL AND COYOACÁN

Must See
1. Museo Frida Kahlo

Experience More
2. Plaza San Jacinto
3. Museo de El Carmen
4. Museo de Arte Carrillo Gil
5. Museo Casa Estudio Diego Rivera y Frida Kahlo
6. Avenida Francisco Sosa
7. Museo Nacional de la Acuarela
8. Museo Nacional de las Intervenciones
9. Museo Casa de León Trotsky

Eat
1. San Angel Inn
2. Ruta de la Seda
3. Churrería General de la República

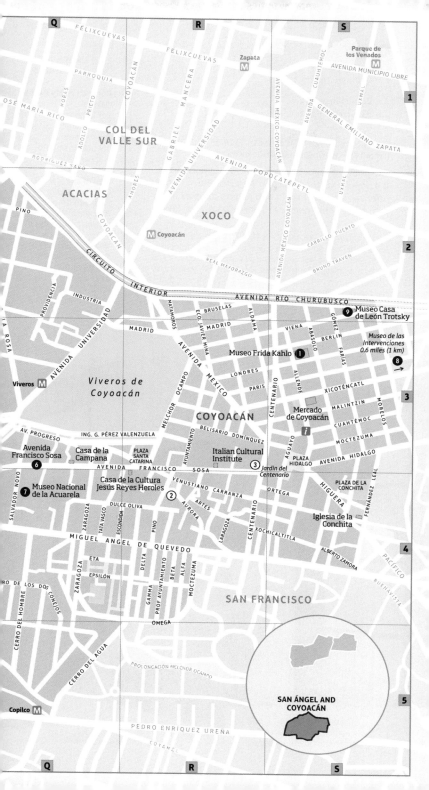

❶

MUSEO FRIDA KAHLO

📍 S3 🏠 Londres 247 Ⓜ Coyoacán ⏰ 10am–6pm Tue–Sun (from 11am Wed) 🌐 museofridakahlo.org.mx

The home of arguably Mexico's most famous artist is a popular visitor attraction. A tour of the museum offers an intimate insight into Kahlo's complex life, with many of her personal belongings on display.

Better known as Casa Azul (Blue House), this is where painter Frida Kahlo was born and died. She painted some famous works here, many inspired by the pain she suffered as a result of her multiple crippling injuries. This house is a treasure trove of paintings and artifacts associated with her life and that of her husband Diego Rivera, with whom she shared the house. On display are letters and diaries as well as ceramics and other everyday items. Frida's wheelchair and one of the corsets she had to wear because of her disability are also on display. Book in advance as there are long lines to purchase tickets on the day.

TOP 3 UNMISSABLE ARTWORKS

Portrait of My Father (1952)
Kahlo painted this with hints of brown to recall the sepia-toned images her father, a photographer, used to take.

My Family (1949)
One of several unfinished pieces in the house, this shows Kahlo's family tree.

Viva la Vida (1954)
Kahlo's last finished piece, painted just days before her death, is full of life and joy in the shapes, colors, and words in the watermelon.

The brightly colored dining room with Frida Kahlo's personal artifacts on display ↑

↑ The iconic blue exterior of the museum, from which the building takes its name

↑ An exhibition dedicated to the artist's wardrobe on display at Casa Azul

6 Jul, 1907

▷ Frida is born Magdalena Carmen Frida Kahlo Calderón in the Casa Azul. She often told people she was born in 1910, to coincide with the revolution.

17 Sep, 1925

Frida's back is broken in a streetcar accident. During her convalescence she begins to paint seriously.

21 Aug, 1929

▷ Frida marries artist Diego Rivera. It is Rivera's third marriage; he is 20 years older than his bride.

1929–1930

Kahlo begins wearing traditional clothing, especially that of matriarchal Indigenous cultures, to express her anti-colonial and feminist beliefs.

1931–4

Frida and Rivera live in the United States while Rivera works on several commissions.

Nov, 1938

◁ Frida's first solo exhibition is held in New York City. She becomes a sensation for her unique look as much as her art.

Nov, 1939

Frida and Rivera divorce, both having had affairs over the years. The couple remarry the following year.

1940s

▷ Frida's lifelong health problems worsen, but she still paints, teaches, is politically active, and attends exhibitions at home and abroad.

Apr, 1953

Frida's first solo exhibition in Mexico. Her health is so bad that she arrives in an ambulance and is carried to a bed where she remains throughout the event.

13 Jul, 1954

Frida dies in Casa Azul. The same day, her body is taken to lie in state at the Palacio de Bellas Artes.

↑ Handicraft and art market at the Plaza San Jacinto

EXPERIENCE MORE

② Plaza San Jacinto

 N4 ⬛ San Ángel
Ⓜ Miguel Ángel de Quevedo

On Saturdays this square, which forms the center of San Ángel, is an excellent place to shop for Mexican handicrafts, either at the outdoor stalls or in El Bazaar Sábado, which is located in a 16th-century house in the northwest corner.

The 16th-century Iglesia de San Jacinto, just off the square, was originally annexed to a Dominican monastery of the same name. The church has a

---

PICTURE PERFECT
San Ángel in Bloom

Just north of Plaza San Jacinto is the Mercado de las Flores de San Ángel (flower market). The stalls are lit up in the evening, making it a great time to take photos of the beautiful flowers on display.

---

fine dome. Inside, the carved wooden screen and the onyx font are both worth seeing.

The most impressive building on the north side of the square is the Casa del Risco (also known as the Casa del Mirador), a well-preserved, 18th-century house built for the Marqués de San Miguel de Aguayo and donated to the nation in 1963. Built around an inner courtyard with an grand fountain, the house features a wealth of colonial-era furniture and decor.

---

③ Museo de El Carmen

 N4 ⬛ Avenida Revolución 4-6 Ⓜ Miguel Ángel de Quevedo ⏰ Noon-2pm Wed-Fri, 11am-2pm Sat & Sun 🌐 elcarmen.inah.gob.mx

The Carmelite monastery-school of San Angelo Mártir, built in 1615, gave its name to the San Ángel district. The three beautiful domes that rise above it, elaborately

decorated with colorful tiles, are still a symbol of the area. Later the monastery and its church became known as El Carmen. Since 1929 it has served as a museum of furniture, paintings, and other artistic and historical objects from the colonial period.

Much of the original interior is preserved, including the monks' cells. In crypt 11, mummified bodies, which were disinterred by troops during the revolution, are displayed in glass-topped coffins. The chapel on the first floor contains an 18th-century gold-painted altarpiece.

---

④ Museo de Arte Carrillo Gil

 N3 ⬛ Avenida Revolución 1608 Ⓜ Miguel Ángel de Quevedo ⏰ 11am-5pm Tue-Sun 🌐 museodearte carrillogil.com

This light and airy gallery on three floors has temporary exhibitions and sometimes shows the collection of art that embraces some of the finest 20th-century Mexican artists. The collection was assembled by Dr. Álvar Carrillo Gil and his wife, Carmen. It includes works by Diego Rivera, José Clemente Orozco, and David Alfaro Siqueiros. Among the Rivera canvases are a number of works from the artist's Cubist period. Less well-known, but equally interesting, are paintings by Austrian Wolfgang Paalen (1905–59) and Gunther Gerzso (1915–2000).

Dr. Carrillo, who studied medicine in Paris, was himself a painter of some note, and a close friend of Orozco.

Museo Casa Estudio Diego Rivera y Frida Kahlo

Ⓜ M3 **Ⓐ Corner of Calle Diego Rivera and Altavista** **Ⓜ Viveros, Barranca del Muerto** **Ⓞ 11am–5pm Tue–Sun** **Ⓦ inba.gob.mx/ recinto/51**

One of the most outstanding 20th-century architects of Mexico, Juan O'Gorman, built these twin houses in 1931–2 for two of the country's most distinguished painters, Diego Rivera and Frida Kahlo. Surrounded by a cactus hedge, the houses are connected by a rooftop bridge, over which Frida used to take Diego his meals. *The Two Fridas* and

Inside the Museo Casa Estudio Diego Rivera y Frida Kahlo and *(inset)* the museum's exterior ↓

several other of her works were painted here. Behind the house is a building her father used as a studio.

The large living room/ studio in Rivera's house contains an assortment of his personal belongings, from paintbrushes to huge, papier-mâché skeletons and pre-Hispanic pottery. Other rooms are devoted to temporary exhibitions.

EAT

San Angel Inn
Housed in a 17th-century hacienda, this elegant restaurant is renowned for its Mexican cuisine and live music, and has been attracting famous patrons since the mid-20th-century.

Ⓜ M4 **Ⓐ Calle Diego Rivera 50** **Ⓦ san angelinn.com**

$⑤$⑤

Ruta de la Seda
A café-patisserie with beautifully presented homemade cakes make it a local favorite. It has a focus on organic and fair-trade produce.

Ⓠ R4 **Ⓐ Aurora 1** **Ⓦ caferutadelaseda. com**

$⑤$⑤

Churrería General de la República
This bustling café offers dozens of varieties of churros, stuffed with all sorts of sweet treats, or dusted with spices, all freshly made to order.

Ⓠ R3 **Ⓐ Francisco Sosa 1** **Ⓦ chgr.com.mx**

$⑤$⑤

⑥
Avenida Francisco Sosa

📍 Q3 🏠 Between San Ángel and Coyoacán Ⓜ Miguel Ángel de Quevedo

Coyoacán's most attractive street is also one of the oldest streets in Latin America, dating back more than 500 years when it was originally part of an Indigenous road network. Running roughly a mile (1.5 km) between Avenida Universidad and the Jardín Centenario in Coyoacán (p122), it is lined with handsome residences.

At the beginning of it stands the quaint, 17th-century chapel of San Antonio Panzacola. Continuing down the street there are a number of very attractive residences, such as the Casa de la Campana (No 303) and No 319, which has a replica of one of the Atlante towering statues from the Toltec site of Tula (p154). No 383 is another interesting house, alleged to have been constructed in the 18th century by Pedro de Alvarado, the Spanish conqueror of Mexico and Guatemala. The house next door belonged to his son. About halfway along the avenue is the pleasant Plaza Santa Catarina. On this

square stand a church and the Casa de la Cultura Jesús Reyes Heroles, an impressive building with patios and well-tended gardens. It houses a cultural center for art and literary events. A short way farther along the avenida, at No 77, is the Italian Cultural Institute.

---

⑦
Museo Nacional de la Acuarela

📍 Q4 🏠 Salvador Novo 88 Ⓜ Miguel Ángel de Quevedo 🕐 11am–4pm daily 🌐 acuarela.org.mx

Dedicated primarily to some of the finest works by Mexican watercolor artists from the 19th century to the present day, this museum is located in a small, two-story house set in a pretty garden.

The larger part of the collection consists of works by contemporary artists, including many winners of the Salón Nacional de la Acuarela annual prize for watercolors. Embracing a wide range of styles and subject matter, it may surprise those who think of watercolors primarily in terms of delicate landscapes.

Two outstanding canvases are *La Carrera del Fuego* and

The inner courtyard of Museo Casa de León Trotsky ↑

Jazz, both by Ángel Mauro Rodríguez, on display on the ground floor.

There is an international room containing a selection of paintings by artists from all over the Americas, as well as Spain and Italy, including Australian artists Robert Wade and Janet Walsh.

A separate gallery in the garden outside houses temporary exhibitions.

---

⑧
Museo Nacional de las Intervenciones

📍 S3 🏠 Calle 20 de Agosto Ⓜ General Anaya 🕐 10am–6pm Tue-Sat 🌐 intervenciones.inah.gob.mx

This former convent still bears the bullet holes from a battle that took place here between US and Mexican forces in 1847. Today it is a museum dedicated to the foreign invasions of Mexico since its

←

The Casa de la Cultura Jesús Reyes Heroles on Avenida Francisco Sosa

independence in 1821. The collection consists of weapons, flags, and other artifacts, including a throne and saber belonging to Emperor Agustín (ruled 1821–3) and a death mask of the Emperor Maximilian (p61), as well as paintings, maps, and models.

Adjoining the museum is the former convent church, which houses religious paintings dating from the 16th to the 18th centuries. These include *La Asunción* by the 16th-century painter Luis Juárez and the 17th-century work *La Virgen y San Ildefonso* by Manuel de Echave.

Museo Casa de León Trotsky

S2 Avenida Río Churubusco 410 Coyoacán
10am–5pm Tue–Sun
museotrotsky.com

Leon Trotsky, the Russian revolutionary, lived in this house from 1939 until his assassination in 1940. Before moving here he lived with the artists Diego Rivera and Frida Kahlo (p116).

To frustrate would-be assassins, Trotsky fitted the windows and doors with armor-plating, raised the height of the surrounding wall, and blocked off most of the windows that overlooked the street, among other things. All this foiled one attempt on his life: about 80 bullet holes can still be seen in the outer walls.

However, these precautions did not stop Ramón Mercader, a regular visitor to the house, who had won his victim's confidence. The room where the murder took place is just as it was at the time, complete with the chair and table where Trotsky was sitting when he died. Trotsky's typewriter, books, and other possessions can be seen where he left them. One of the photographs on display shows him on his arrival in Mexico in 1937, standing on the quay in Tampico with his wife Natalia and Frida Kahlo.

THE ASSASSINATION OF TROTSKY

The intellectual Leon Trotsky was born Lev Davidovich Bronstein, in Russia, in 1879. He played a leading role in the Bolshevik seizure of power in 1917 and in forming the Red Army to fight the Russian Civil War of 1918–20. But Lenin's death in 1924 led to a power struggle within the ranks of the victorious revolutionaries, and in 1927 Trotsky was forced into exile by his rival, Joseph Stalin. He was granted asylum in Mexico in 1937 but even across the Atlantic he was not safe from Stalin's purge of all his opponents. On August 20, 1940, he was fatally wounded by Ramón Mercader, who pierced his skull with an ice-pick.

A SHORT WALK
COYOACÁN

Distance 1.5 miles (2 km) **Time** 25 minutes
Nearest metro Coyoacán

The lovely suburb of Coyoacán has been a favorite area for many famous Mexicans, from Hernán Cortés to Frida Kahlo. The area is an ideal place for a stroll, packed with cafés, restaurants, and *cantinas*. Calle Felipe Carrillo Puerto, heading south out of the plaza, is a good place to shop for souvenirs. Coyoacán is also known in Mexico City for its delicious ice-cream. The weekend is a particularly great time to explore the area, as a lively craft fair operates in its two main squares, Jardín Centenario and Plaza Hidalgo.

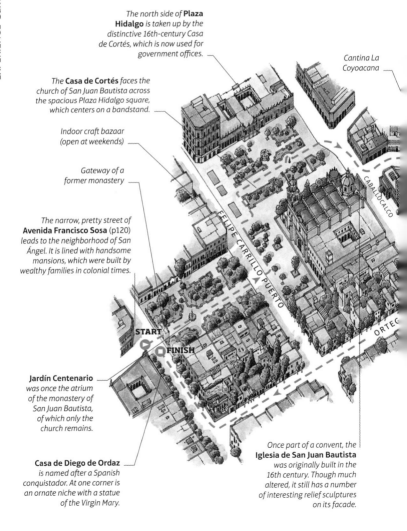

The north side of **Plaza Hidalgo** is taken up by the distinctive 16th-century Casa de Cortés, which is now used for government offices.

Cantina La Coyoacana

The **Casa de Cortés** faces the church of San Juan Bautista across the spacious Plaza Hidalgo square, which centers on a bandstand.

Indoor craft bazaar (open at weekends)

Gateway of a former monastery

The narrow, pretty street of **Avenida Francisco Sosa** (p120) leads to the neighborhood of San Ángel. It is lined with handsome mansions, which were built by wealthy families in colonial times.

CABALLOCALCO

FELIPE CARRILLO PUERTO

ORTEG

START

FINISH

Jardín Centenario was once the atrium of the monastery of San Juan Bautista, of which only the church remains.

Casa de Diego de Ordaz is named after a Spanish conquistador. At one corner is an ornate niche with a statue of the Virgin Mary.

Once part of a convent, the **Iglesia de San Juan Bautista** was originally built in the 16th century. Though much altered, it still has a number of interesting relief sculptures on its facade.

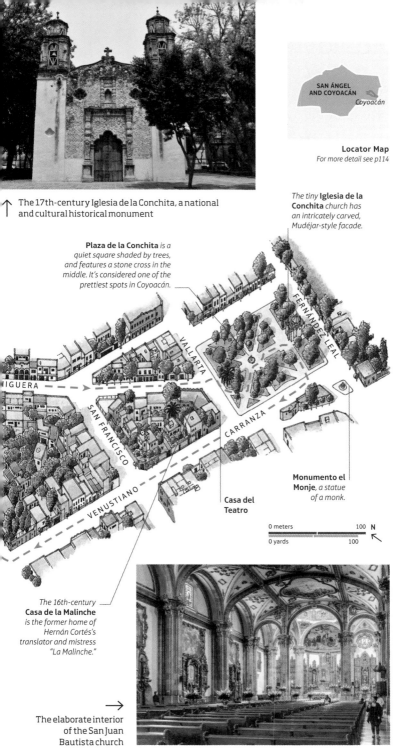

The 17th-century Iglesia de la Conchita, a national and cultural historical monument

The tiny **Iglesia de la Conchita** church has an intricately carved, Mudéjar-style facade.

Locator Map
For more detail see p114

SAN ÁNGEL AND COYOACÁN
Coyoacán

Plaza de la Conchita *is a quiet square shaded by trees, and features a stone cross in the middle. It's considered one of the prettiest spots in Coyoacán.*

FERNÁNDEZ LEAL

VALLARTA

IGUERA

SAN FRANCISCO

CARRANZA

VENUSTIANO

Casa del Teatro

Monumento el Monje, *a statue of a monk.*

0 meters 100
0 yards 100
N

The 16th-century **Casa de la Malinche** *is the former home of Hernán Cortés's translator and mistress "La Malinche."*

→ The elaborate interior of the San Juan Bautista church

A LONG WALK
SAN ÁNGEL
TO COYOACÁN

Distance 2.5 miles (4 km) **Time** 50 minutes
Terrain An easy walk on well-kept footpaths
Nearest metro Miguel Ángel de Quevedo

Few parts of Mexico City can boast a domestic architecture of the colonial and pre-revolutionary eras as well-preserved as that of Coyoacán and San Ángel. This walk connects the two squares at the heart of these districts, both of which are well-known in the city for their weekend craft fairs. The walk often follows tree-lined, cobbled streets. Along the way are churches, museums, art galleries, and monuments, as well as some picturesque places to stop for a meal.

*Nex to San Antonio Panzacola is an old stone bridge over a tributary of the Río Magdalena. Cross this and you come to one of the prettiest streets in the city, **Avenida Francisco Sosa** (p120).*

*Cross Avenida Insurgentes and you will come to the **Parque de la Bombilla**, the small, wooded park that surrounds the monument to General Álvaro Obregón (p63), assassinated nearby in July 1928.*

*Leave Plaza San Jacinto (p118) via Calle Madero. At the end of this road you will pass the **Centro Cultural San Ángel** on the right.*

*At Avenida Revolución, cross over to the **Museo de El Carmen**, which contains some fine religious paintings and colonial-era furniture. Afterwards, head to the cobbled street of Avenida La Paz where there are some good restaurants to stop for a break.*

*Continue on through the tranquil, green oases of **Plaza Frederico Gamb** and **Parque Tagle**.*

0 meters		600	N
0 yards		600	↑

Did You Know?

General Obregón's arm, lost in battle, used to be kept in the monument in Parque de la Bombilla.

SAN ÁNGEL
AND COYOACÁN

*San Ángel
to Coyoacán*

Locator Map
For more detail see p114

Cafés and shops lining the borders of the Plaza del Centenario

Halfway along Francisco Sosa you come to the enchanting **Plaza Santa Catarina** *where story-tellers gather on Sunday lunchtimes.*

HORTENSIA

MINERVA

AVENIDA UNIVERSIDAD

M Viveros

Viveros de Coyoacán

ING. G. PÉREZ VALENZUELA

AVENIDA PROGRESO

Casa de la Campana

PLAZA SANTA CATARINA

AVENIDA FRANCISCO SOSA

Museo Nacional de la Acuarela

SALVADOR NOVO

Casa de la Cultura Jesús Reyes Heroles

ZARAGOZA

TATA VASCO

DULCE OLIVA

MIGUEL

PINO

ANGEL

DE

QUEVEDO

AVENIDA MEXICO

MELCHOR OCAMPO

AVENIDA MÉXICO

COYOACÁN

BELISARIO DOMÍNGUEZ

AYUNTAMIENTO

Italian Cultural Institute

FINISH

VENUSTIANO CARRANZA

ARTES

AURORA

Mercado de Coyoacán

MALINTZIN

CENTENARIO

AGUAYO

CUAUHTÉMOC

MOCTEZUMA

PLAZA HIDALGO

AVENIDA HIDALGO

Jardín Centenario

HIGUERA

CENTENARIO

VENUSTIANO CARRANZA

Turn down Calle Salvador Novo for a short detour to visit a gallery of watercolor paintings, the **Museo Nacional de la Acuarela**.

At the end of Francisco Sosa you arrive at the twin arches of what was once the gateway into the convent of **San Juan Bautista**. *This then leads into the pleasant square of* **Jardín Centenario** *at the heart of Coyoacán (p122).*

The charming Iglesia de Santa Catarina on the square of the same name

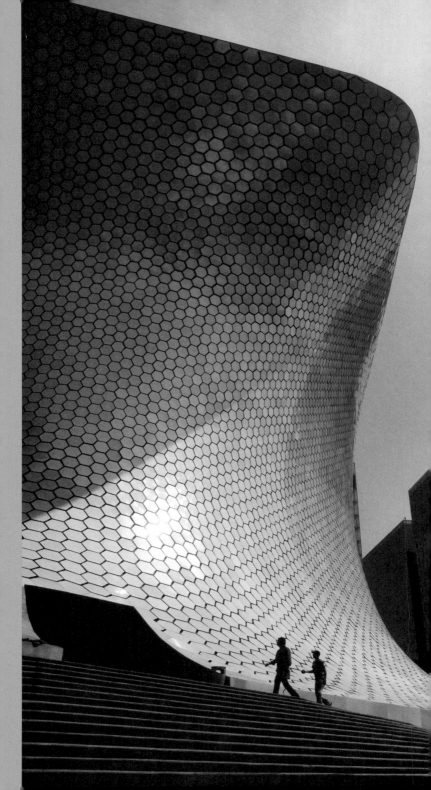

BEYOND THE CENTER

In the 1870s, Porfirio Díaz presided over a massive extension of the city's infrastructure, and its rapid growth continued into the 20th century. While the outer edges of the city comprise shantytowns and workaday suburbs, hidden among them are a number of gems such as the floating gardens of Xochimilco and the magnificent murals around the university campus. It's easy to zip between the neighborhoods by bus and taxi, so don't miss the chance to step outside the bounds of the city center and explore the lesser-known highlights.

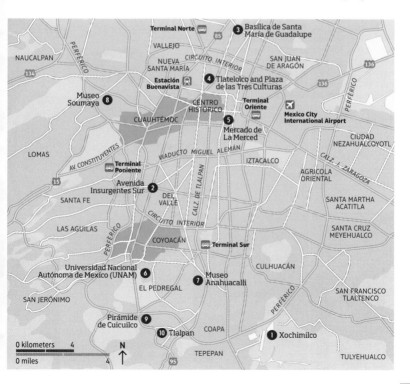

❶
XOCHIMILCO

🛈 Avenida Guadalupe I Ramírez s/n, San Juan Ⓜ Xochimilco

This network of canals and vegetable plots was created by the Aztecs, and is still in use today. Families flock here on Sundays, hiring colorfully decorated boats to explore the waterways, accompanied by mariachi bands that create a uniquely Mexican party atmosphere.

The History of Xochimilco

Known as "the place of the flower fields" in Nahuatl, the language spoken by the Aztecs, Xochimilco was once a lakeside village connected by a causeway to Tenochtitlán, the Aztec city where the Historic Center of Mexico City now stands. Today it is the only part of Mexico City still to have the canals and semi-floating flower and vegetable gardens, or *chinampas*, built by the Aztecs. The *chinampas* were originally created on a base of aquatic roots that were then covered with soil. They remain an important source of flowers and vegetables to Mexico City even today.

Xochimilco Today

A favorite weekend pastime – popular with tourists as well as the city's inhabitants – is to rent one of the many brightly decorated *trajineras* (punts), which have roofs and a table down the middle. A local boatman poles the punt along between banks shaded by willows. Waterborne mariachis will provide entertainment while smaller boats sell typical Mexican snacks and drinks, such as *pulque*, a slightly sour drink made from fermented agave sap, often flavored with fruit and nuts.

The northern part of Xochimilco's wetlands has been preserved as the Parque Ecológico de Xochimilco, and serves as an important habitat for birds such as storks, hummingbirds, eagles, and egrets. Since 2019, the park has been undergoing a long-needed rehabilitation, but the Cuemanco Plant Market is still worth a visit (open 9am–6pm daily). It lies on the edge of the park, and its alleys are crammed with flower and plant stalls.

→
Mexican fare being served from a smaller boat to visitors abroad a *trajinera* (punt)

←
A mariachi band providing musical entertainment to a waterborne audience

INSIDER TIP
Trajinera Tours

Hire a *trajinera* (punt) from the canal-side piers, to tour the Aztec canals. Prices are set at a standard rate of around $25 per hour. *Trajineras* operate daily with a roof to protect against the elements.

↑ Rows of colorful *trajineras* stacked up on the canals at Xochimilco

EXPERIENCE MORE

2

Avenida Insurgentes

◩ South and North from
Glorieta de Insurgentes
Ⓜ Insurgentes, Insurgentes
Sur, Chilpancingo

The Avenida Insurgentes runs
just over 18 miles (30 km)
from the capital's border with
Mexico state in the north to
the start of the highway to
Cuernavaca in the south, and
is said to be the longest street
in Latin America.

Its southern *(Sur)* stretch
has several sights of interest.
Just a few blocks south of its
junction with the Viaducto
Miguel Alemán stands the
World Trade Center, formerly
the Hotel de México. This
is one of the most prominent
buildings on the Avenida. Its
slim, glass tower is surmounted
by a huge circular section that
has a revolving floor.

The Polyforum Siqueiros,
one of Mexico City's most
audacious works of modern
architecture, is next door

> **The Polyforum
> Siqueiros on Avenida
> Insurgentes Sur is
> one of Mexico City's
> most audacious
> works of modern
> architecture.**

to the World Trade Center.
Its upper floor, which is
reached by twin, circular
staircases, is topped by
an octagonal dome. This
is decorated by one of the
largest murals in the world:
March of Humanity, by David
Alfaro Siqueiros (1896–1974).

At Eje 6 Sur and Insurgentes
is the Ciudad de los Deportes,
which includes a soccer
stadium and the Plaza México
arena. Reputedly the world's
largest bullring by seating
capacity, it holds up to 50,000
people and is surrounded
by statues commemorating
famous bullfighters, including
Manuel Rodríguez ("Manolete"),
who was in the arena's
inaugural program in 1946.

Just before the junction with
Barranca del Muerto is the
Teatro de los Insurgentes,
built in the early 1950s by
architect Alejandro Prieto.
The curved facade is adorned
with an allegorical mural by
artist Diego Rivera. Completed
in 1953, the mural centers on
a huge pair of hands holding
a mask, around which are
gathered key revolutionary
and independence figures.

3

Basílica de Santa María de Guadalupe

◩ Plaza de las Américas 1
Ⓜ La Villa Ⓣ 7am–7pm
daily Ⓦ virgende
guadalupe.org.mx

The richest and most visited
Catholic shrine in the Americas
is a complex of buildings at
the foot of Cerro del Tepeyac
hill. Legend says it was here
that a dark-skinned Virgin
Mary miraculously appeared
to a shepherd, Juan Diego, in
1531. She is named after the
Virgin of Guadalupe in
Extremadura, Spain.

The Antigua Basílica was
built in the early 1700s. Twin
towers flank its Baroque

THE VIRGIN OF GUADALUPE

Every year on December 12, thousands of pilgrims flock to the Basílica de Santa María de Guadalupe to commemorate the apparition of Mexico's patron saint on the Cerro del Tepeyac. Birthday songs *(las mañanitas)* are sung at dawn, followed by special church services, then dancing and music in town squares. As often in Mexico, Catholic tradition has merged with pre-Hispanic influence: the cult of the Virgin of Guadalupe has distinct parallels with that of Tonantzin, a Mesoamerican goddess.

facade, which features relief carvings of the Virgin. It is overshadowed by the circular, modern church that now stands beside it, which can hold up to 10,000 worshippers. An object of veneration inside it is Diego's tunic on which the image of the Virgin is said to have been imprinted as proof of the miracle.

The Virgin is supposed to have appeared five times in all. The impressive Capilla del Pocito – a chapel regarded as one of the finest achievements of Mexican Baroque architecture – was constructed on the site of her fourth appearance. It is roughly elliptical in shape and its domed roof is faced with dazzling blue and white Talavera tiles, a style brought to Mexico in the 16th century by Dominican monks from Talavera de la Reina, Spain.

Also in the complex is the Capilla de Indios, the house in which Juan Diego is said to

The modern church of the Basílica de Santa María de Guadalupe

have lived after the Virgin's first appearance until his death in 1548.

Tlatelolco and Plaza de las Tres Culturas

🚇 Eje Central & Ricardo Flores Magón Ⓜ Tlatelolco, Garibaldi 🕐 8am–6pm daily 🌐 tlatelolco.inah.gob.mx

The remains of the ceremonial center of Tlatelolco form a major part of the Plaza de las Tres Culturas. The square gets its name (The Three Cultures) from the mix of modern, colonial, and pre-Hispanic architecture that has developed around it. A powerful earthquake in 2017 caused some damage, but even so this centuries-old site is still standing.

Tlatelolco, the "twin city" of the Aztec capital, Tenochtitlán *(p78)*, was the most important commercial center of its day. The site here has a *templo mayor* (main temple) similar to that of Tenochtitlán. There are also smaller temples including the "calendar temple," which

owes its name to the glyphs adorning three of its sides, representing dates in the Aztecs' ritual calendar. In the northwest corner of the complex are the remains of the carved "wall of serpents," which marked the boundary of the ceremonial center.

The Spanish erected their own temples and shrines on the site, including the Templo de Santiago – a Catholic church in an almost militaristic style. In front of the Templo de Santiago is a plaque that reads: "On 13 August 1521, heroically defended by Cuauhtémoc, Tlatelolco fell to the power of Hernán Cortés. It was neither triumph nor defeat, but the painful birth of the *mestizo* nation that is Mexico today."

The modern era is represented by several buildings, particularly the concrete-and-glass foreign ministry tower. Scattered around the plaza are sculptures by artist Federico Silva. Between the monastery and the nearby residential tower block is a 1944 mural by David Alfaro Siqueiros. Entitled *Cuauhtémoc Against the Myth*, it combines sculpture with alfresco painting, and represents Cuauhtémoc, the last Aztec emperor, who was killed by the Spanish.

EAT

Bellini
Soak up the stunning views of Mexico City from this revolving restaurant on the 45th floor of the World Trade Center while enjoying classic Mexican and international cuisine.

🏢 Torre WTC Piso 45, Montecito 38, Nápoles 🌐 bellini. com.mx
💲💲💲

Jardín Botánico

 Cto. Zona Deportiva s/n
9am-3pm & 4-5pm daily
ib.unam.mx

7

Museo Anahuacalli

Museo 150 11am-
5:30pm Tue-Sun museo
anahuacalli.org.mx

This museum was conceived
and created by muralist Diego
Rivera to house his collection
of pre-Hispanic art, and was
completed after his death by
multiple artists, including
Rivera's daughter. Built of
black volcanic stone, it takes
the form of a pyramid. The
collection consists of around
2,000 pieces that represent
most of the Indigenous
civilizations of Mexico. There
are funerary urns, masks, and
sculptures from the ancient
culture of Teotihuacán *(p140)*.

The studio, although
never actually used by Rivera,
has been set up as if it were,
with his materials and half-
finished works on display.
A smaller gallery next to the
pyramid contains an exhi-
bition of papier-mâché
sculptures relating to the
Day of the Dead, cele-
brated on November 1
and 2 *(p221)*.

5

Mercado de La Merced

Anillo de Circunvalación
& Calle Callejón de
Carretones Merced
6am-7pm daily

Said to be one of the biggest
markets in the Americas, La
Merced has over 5,000 stalls.
It occupies the spot on which
an Aztec market stood prior
to the conquest by the
Spanish *(p57)*.

La Merced is divided into
seven sections, six of which
specialize in different types
of merchandise, while the
last is a traditional market.

The Mercado area is well
known for sex work, and can
be dangerous at night.

6

Universidad Nacional
Autónoma de México
(UNAM)

Ciudad Universitaria
Universidad, Ciudad
Universitaria 7am-
9:30pm daily unam.mx

The largest university
in Latin America is also a
UNESCO World Heritage Site.
It occupies a vast campus
in the south of the city.
Many of the most interesting
buildings are decorated with
incredible murals. Over the
entrance of the striking

↑ The colorful food
market of the Mercado
de La Merced

stadium – the symbol of the
1968 Mexico Olympics – is a
high-relief mural by Diego
Rivera, while the rectory tower
is adorned with dramatic
designs by David Alfaro
Siqueiros. Nearby is the
Biblioteca Central (Central
Library), whose tower is
covered with mosaics of
colored tiles, made by Juan
O'Gorman from 1950 to 1956.
Each wall illustrates a period
of Mexican history and its
scientific achievements.

A separate complex of
buildings farther south
includes one of the city's
major performing arts centers:
the Sala Nezahualcóyotl *(www.
musica.unam.mx)*. The **Museo
Universitario de Arte
Contemporáneo (MUAC)**,
housed in an angular, modern
building flooded with light,
exhibits the largest collection
of contemporary art in Mexico.
Close to the Olympic stadium
is the **Jardín Botánico**. The
garden has a cactus collection,
an arboretum, and a section
devoted to jungle plants.

**Museo Universitario de
Arte Contemporáneo
(MUAC)**
 Insurgentes 3000
11am-5pm Fri-Sun
muac.unam.mx

Museo Soumaya

📍 Blvd Miguel de Cervantes Saavedra & Presa Falcón
🕐 10:30am-6:30pm daily
🌐 soumaya.com.mx

This curvaceous modern building, designed by Mexican architect Fernando Romero, houses one of the country's most outstanding collections of European, Mexican, and pre-Colombian art. The stunning gallery has more than 65,000 pieces spanning three millennia, including European masterpieces by da Vinci, Rodin, and Rubens.

The Mexican collection includes murals by Rivera, Tamayo, and Siqueiros, as well as pre-Hispanic artifacts and religious icons.

Pirámide de Cuicuilco

📍 Avenida Insurgentes Sur & Periférico 📞 (55) 56 06 97 58 🕐 10am-4pm Wed-Fri

This pyramid belongs to the earliest known urban civilization in the Valley of Mexico, founded around 700 BC. It is all that is left of the ceremonial center of a settlement thought to have comprised as many as 20,000 inhabitants at its peak.

The surviving structure is a truncated, layered cone, just 82 ft (25 m) high but roughly 328 ft (100 m) across. The eruption of a nearby volcano, Xitle, forced the inhabitants of the area to flee around AD 100. The solidified lava, which can be as much as 26 ft (8 m) deep, makes excavation of the area difficult. However, a museum on the site exhibits the pottery, tools, and spearheads that have been found.

Tlalpan

📍 Mex 95, 15 miles (25 km) S of city center

In the age of the Spanish viceroys, Tlalpan was a favorite country retreat for both ordinary Mexicans and the nobility. As a result, a large number of elegant mansions and haciendas were built here from the early 18th century onward.

Visitors to the old town, now the seat of Mexico City's largest *delegación* (suburban area), can stroll along narrow streets and admire the beautiful architecture, which dates from the 17th to the 20th centuries.

 INSIDER TIP
Gooooal!

Catch a soccer match at Estadio Azteca *(www. estadioazteca.com.mx)*, east of Pirámide de Cuicuilco. The season's highlight is the Súper Clásico between Chivas de Guadalajara and Club América.

The 18th-century Casa Chata, the Casa del Marqués de Vivanco, and the Casa del Conde de Regla are among some of the outstanding buildings here.

In the central Plaza de la Constitución, with its *Porfiriato*-era bandstand and busts of national leading figures scattered around, is the Capilla del Rosario, an 18th-century chapel with a Baroque facade. In the same square stands the tree from which 11 patriots, who rebelled against the French occupation under Emperor Maximilian I, were hanged in 1866.

The former country house of General Antonio López de Santa Anna, the victor of the Battle of the Alamo *(p60)*, stands at the corner of San Fernando and Madero. He was named president of Mexico 11 times.

← The striking architecture of the Museo Soumaya, and *(inset)* visitors studying the art on display

EXPERIENCE MEXICO

A boat trip on the river in the Sumidero Canyon

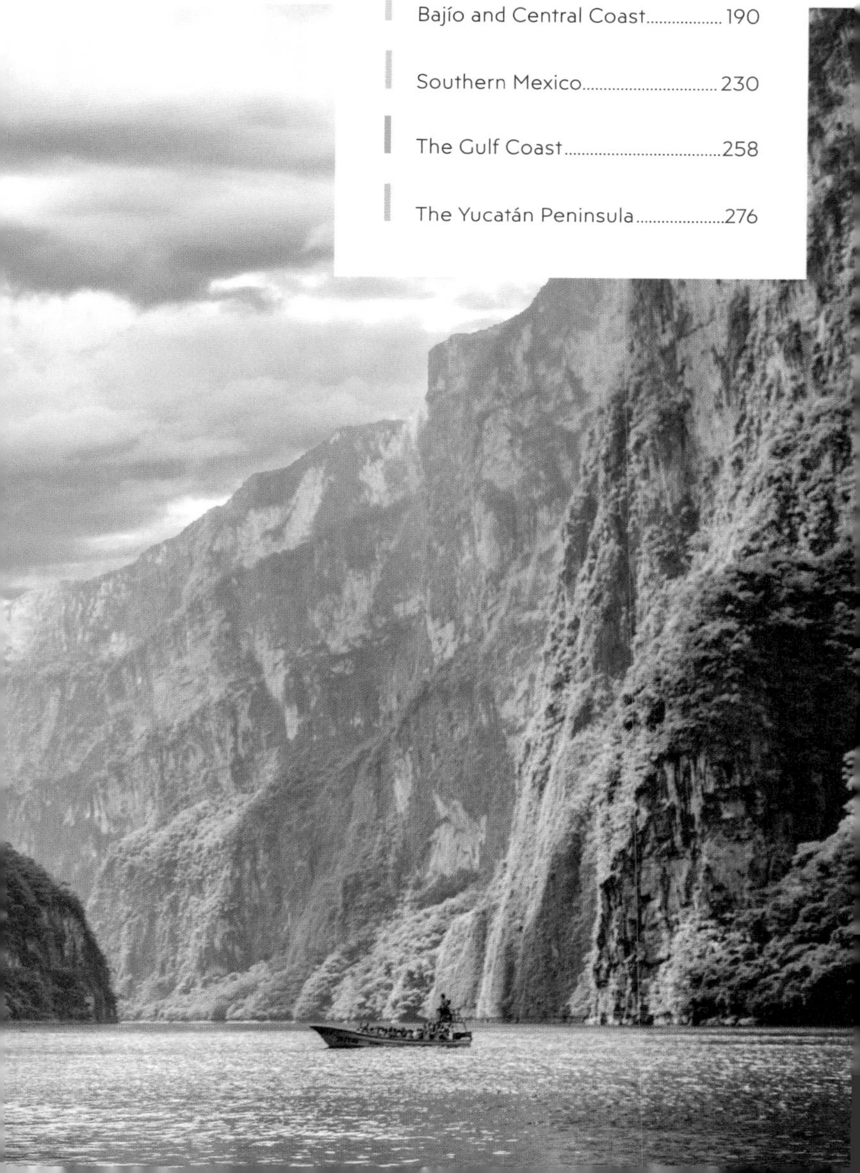

Hot-air balloons over the ancient city of Teotihuacán

AROUND MEXICO CITY

Snowcapped volcanoes tower over the country's central plateau – a series of vast plains and broad valleys. Great Indigenous civilizations flourished here and built extensive cities and awesome ceremonial sites such as Tula and Teotihuacán. After the arrival of the Spanish in the early 16th century, missionaries fanned out from these sites to explore and colonize the vast territories later consolidated as New Spain. As they spread out, they dotted the region with fortress-like convents and opulent churches, taking possession of Indigenous lands and bringing with them new diseases, which ravaged the native peoples. The discovery of precious metals by the colonizers sparked the development of mining towns, and the rich volcanic soil led to endless fields of crops that belonged to huge estates, run from haciendas.

Today busy highways radiate from Mexico City to burgeoning cities in the neighboring states. So far, however, the incursions of modern Mexico into the region have not significantly disturbed the area's natural beauty, protected in part by a series of national parks.

AROUND MEXICO CITY

Must Sees

1. Teotihuacán
2. Museo Nacional del Virreinato
3. Puebla

Experience More

4. Pachuca
5. San Agustín Acolman
6. Huasca
7. Mineral del Monte
8. Tula
9. Cholula
10. Valle de Bravo
11. Xochicalco
12. Cuernavaca
13. Malinalco
14. Tepoztlán
15. Popocatépetl and Iztaccíhuatl
16. Cacaxtla and Xochitécatl
17. Tlaxcala
18. Toluca
19. Cantona
20. Convento de San Nicolás de Tolentino de Actopan
21. Taxco

Tanquián

105

Tempoal

180

Tantoyuca

127

Naranjos

132

Tuxpán

102

Huejutla

105

Río Tempoal

Chicontepec de Tejeda

180

130

Metlaltoyuca

Molango

Tlacuilotepec

Poza Rica

Gutiérrez Zamora

Zacualtipán

130

Villa Lazaro

THE GULF COAST
p258

Metztitlán

Xicotepec

Nautla

Metzquititlán

105

Atotonilco el Grande

Huauchinango

Tenampulco

Martínez de La Torre

180

6 HUASCA

7 MINERAL DEL MONTE

4 PACHUCA

Tulancingo

Zacatlán

Tlapacoyán

129

Misantla

132

Chignahuapan

Teziutlán

VERACRUZ

40

Sahagún

119

129

140

EOTIHUACÁN

Apan

Xalapa

N AGUSTÍN OLMAN

Calpulalpan

Tlaxco

Ciudad de Libres

129

19 CANTONA

Coatepec

Texcoco

40

136

TLAXCALA

Apizaco

Tepeyahualco

140

125

apaluca

150

TLAXCALA **17**

136

Oriental

Tequixquitla

alco

16 CACAXTLA AND XOCHITÉCATL

Huamantla

140

Puebla International Airport ✈

meca

15 **CHOLULA** **9**

3 PUEBLA

S. Salvador el Seco

150

Córdoba

POPOCATÉPETL AND IZTACCÍHUATL

Tepeaca

140

Ciudad Serdian

Orizaba

150

utla

438

190

Atlixco

Presa Valsequillo

Tecamachalco

RELOS

160

Izúcar

Tepeonjuma

Tlacotepec

150

135

Chapulco

Río Atoyac

PUEBLA

Atencingo

Tehuacán

Axochiapan

190

S. Juan Ixacaquixtla

S. Gabriel Chilac

Ajalpán

Chiautla

Coxcatlán

Huautla

Acatlán

182

Teotitlán del Camino

135

OAXACA

SOUTHERN MEXICO
p230

San Juan Bautista

Gulf of Mexico

AROUND MEXICO CITY

Looking down on the Teotihuacán site and *(inset)* a feathered serpent's head on the temple of Quetzalcóatl ↑

❶ 🗺️ 🅼 🍴

TEOTIHUACÁN

🅐 B6 **🅐 Mex 132D, 29 miles (47 km) NE of Mexico City, Mexico State** **🕐 9am–3pm daily; Museum: 8am–5pm daily** **🆆 teotihuacan.inah.gob.mx**

Walking down Teotihuacán's Avenue of the Dead, with one vast pyramid in front and another behind, is one of the most awe-inspiring experiences in the Americas. The magnificent monuments of this ancient site bear witness to a mysterious culture that dominated the region for five centuries.

Teotihuacán is one of the most impressive cities of the ancient world. Founded before the Christian era, this colossal urban center once housed up to 125,000 people and covered over 8 sq miles (20 sq km). It dominated life in the region for 500 years before being destroyed (possibly by its own people) and abandoned, around AD 650. Later, the site was held sacred by the Aztecs, who believed it had been built by giants. The ceremonial center, with its temples, palaces, and pyramids, bears witness to the city's splendor. However, the first inhabitants' origin, way of life, and even demise remain a mystery. Teotihuacán is an active archaeological site, with new discoveries made regularly. Today, it's still not known who built Teotihuacán.

↑ Exploring the remarkable ruins, with the Pyramid of the Sun rising behind

PICTURE PERFECT
Time it Right

Teotihuacán is a very popular day trip from Mexico City. Its best to arrive early if you want the opportunity to take some photos of the empty enigmatic ruins before the midday crowds start to arrive.

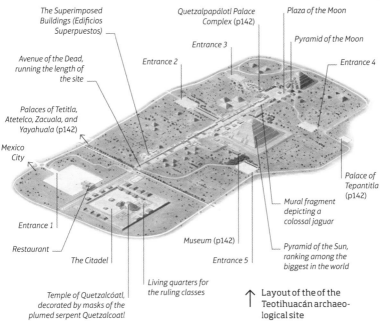

The Superimposed Buildings (Edificios Superpuestos)

Quetzalpapálotl Palace Complex (p142)

Plaza of the Moon

Entrance 3

Pyramid of the Moon

Avenue of the Dead, running the length of the site

Entrance 2

Entrance 4

Palaces of Tetitla, Atetelco, Zacuala, and Yayahuala (p142)

Mexico City

Entrance 1

Palace of Tepantitla (p142)

Mural fragment depicting a colossal jaguar

Restaurant

Museum (p142)

The Citadel

Entrance 5

Pyramid of the Sun, ranking among the biggest in the world

Temple of Quetzalcóatl, decorated by masks of the plumed serpent Quetzalcoatl

Living quarters for the ruling classes

↑ Layout of the of the Teotihuacán archaeological site

EXPLORING TEOTIHUACÁN

To fully explore this colossal and awesome site, visitors should be prepared for long walks over uneven ground and stiff climbs up steep stairways – all at an altitude of 7,550 ft (2,300 m) and often under a hot tropical sun. Comfortable shoes, a hat, and sunblock are a must, plus rain gear in summer.

The Museum

The on-site museum is just south of the Pyramid of the Sun. It displays artifacts that were found at Teotihuacán, explanatory maps and diagrams, and, beneath the glass floor of its main hall, a scale model of the city.

The shady gardens outside are a good place to rest during a tour of the site. They are planted with botanical species native to the area and decorated with an original, partially restored, mural depicting feathered Teotihuacán sculptures.

Outlying Palaces

Several impressive ancient dwelling complexes are situated beyond the fence and road that ring the site.

Just east of the Pyramid of the Sun lies the Palace of Tepantitla, which contains the most important and colorful murals discovered so far at Teotihuacán. These include representations of elaborately dressed priests, the rain god Tlaloc, and his carefree paradise, known as Tlalocan, where miniature human figures frolic in an Eden-like setting. West of the site, and best reached by car, are four other palaces – Tetitla, Atetelco, Zacuala, and Yayahuala – which have great examples of frescoes, murals, and wall paintings.

Quetzalpapálotl Palace Complex

This maze of residential and temple structures grew slowly over several centuries. The last part to be built was probably the elegant Palace of Quetzalpapálotl, uncovered in 1962 and reconstructed with mostly original materials. It sits atop the now buried Temple of the Feathered Conches (2nd–3rd century AD). The Jaguar Palace, just to the west, has a large courtyard faced by a portico and a stepped temple base.

THE UNEARTHING OF TEOTIHUACÁN

For over 1,000 years after its decline, the crumbled ruins of Teotihuacán remained hidden below a layer of earth and vegetation. There was unofficial digging and looting in the late 19th century, but official excavations started only in 1906. Underground tunnels and chambers (as well as statues, jade, and even conch shells) have been unearthed but one thing archaeologists have yet to discover is a tomb.

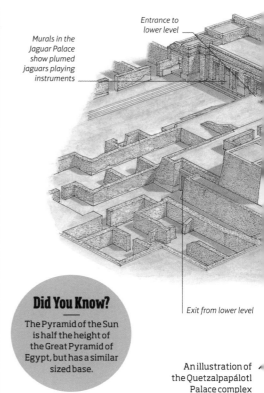

Murals in the Jaguar Palace show plumed jaguars playing instruments

Entrance to lower level

Exit from lower level

Did You Know?

The Pyramid of the Sun is half the height of the Great Pyramid of Egypt, but has a similar sized base.

An illustration of the Quetzalpapálotl Palace complex

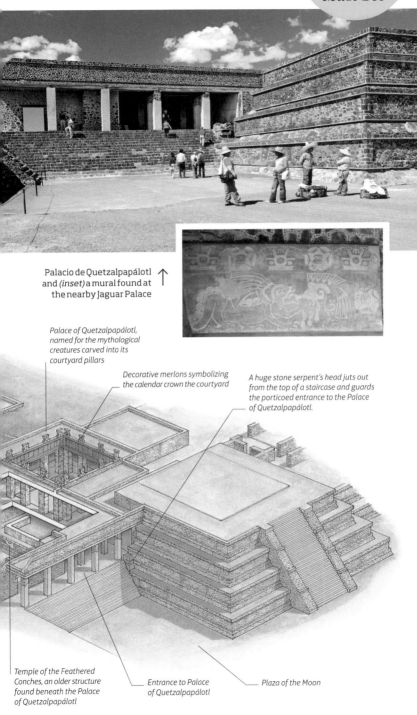

Palacio de Quetzalpapálotl and *(inset)* a mural found at the nearby Jaguar Palace ↑

Palace of Quetzalpapálotl, named for the mythological creatures carved into its courtyard pillars

Decorative merlons symbolizing the calendar crown the courtyard

A huge stone serpent's head juts out from the top of a staircase and guards the porticoed entrance to the Palace of Quetzalpapálotl.

Temple of the Feathered Conches, an older structure found beneath the Palace of Quetzalpapálotl

Entrance to Palace of Quetzalpapálotl

Plaza of the Moon

MESOAMERICA

Mexico is strewn with many incredible reminders of the Mesoamerican civilizations that once lived here. The term Mesoamerica refers to a geographical region whose people shared a broadly similar culture before the arrival of the Spanish. It covers what is now central and southern Mexico, and parts of Central America.

ANCIENT CIVILIZATIONS

The civilizations of Mesoamerica are normally divided into "highland" (especially the Valley of Mexico) and "lowland," such as the Maya in the Yucatán Peninsula. Despite the distances between them, the various cultures had many things in common, including gods, a calendar, and building practices, but they had different languages and customs.

↑ A clay doll made by an Olmec artisan

Some cultures existed concurrently, but often - as in the case of the Mixtecs and the Zapotecs - one group would take over the territories of its predecessors. In some cases, the rise and fall of cultures - like the one based at Teotihuacán *(p140)* - is still a mystery to this day.

PRECLASSIC AND CLASSIC PERIODS

The first era of Mesoamerica, known as the Preclassic period, lasted from around 1500 BC to AD 0. Its most notable culture is that of the Olmecs (1200-400 BC), who are often called the *cultura madre* (mother culture) because of their influence on later civilizations. Their main sites, at San Lorenzo and La Venta, wielded political, economic, and religious authority over big regions and a large population - but even so, the civilzation eventually faded into obscurity.

The Maya *(p298)* were the longest surviving Mesoamerican civilization (c 1000 BC-AD 1500),

and their descendents *(p238)* still live in Mexico. The powerful Maya Empire spread from southern Mexico into Central America, building extensive ceremonial centers.

The Zapotecs were another long-lasting Mesoamerican culture, rising to prominence around 500 BC. They produced some of the earliest forms of writing in ancient Mexico. The Zapotec civilization ended around AD 900, coinciding with the end of the Classic period, but, as with the Maya, their culture carries on in present-day Mexico.

THE POSTCLASSIC ERA

This period (AD 900–1500) gave rise to multiple cultures that existed at the same time across Mexico. The militarized and artistic Toltecs (900–1200) were based in Tula *(p154)*. Successors of the nearby Zapotecs, the Mixtecs (1100–1450) built the ceremonial center Mitla *(p252)*, and produced detailed codices, picture histories. The Tarascans (1350–1529) formed a formidable empire in central Mexico, rivalling the Aztecs (1300–1520), whose vast empire was overthrown by the Spanish. Beginning in the 1520s, Spain rapidly conquered Mexico and systemically destroyed its remaining civilizations, and by the 17th century only ruins remained.

↑ The ruins of a pyramid at Mayapán, a Maya site in the Yucatán Peninsula

MESOAMERICAN RELICS

Chacmool
These carved figures can be seen at many archaeological sites. The stone dishes placed on their stomachs are thought to have held sacrificial offerings.

Pyramids
Stepped and then crowned with a temple, Meso-american pyramids had different uses in different cultures, from human sacrifice to funerary rites.

Food
Many foods that are now eaten all over the world originated in Mesoamerica. They include tomatoes, chilies, and corn (maize).

The Wheel
Although the wheel was known, it was used only for nonfunctional objects such as toys. Most burdens were carried by porters or by canoe.

Jade
This green stone was more highly prized than gold in Mesoamerica. It was used for art and jewelry as well as being a key material for religious items.

Obsidian
A hard, glassy stone, obsidian was used instead of metals, which were not used until the 6th century, and never for functional objects.

② ⊗ ⊗ ⊕ ⊕

MUSEO NACIONAL DEL VIRREINATO

🗺 A6 📍 Plaza Hidalgo 99, Tepotzotlán, 27 miles (44 km)
N of Mexico City, Mexico State ⏰ 9am–4:45pm Tue–Sun
🌐 virreinato.inah.gob.mx

Within the Iglesia de San Francisco Javier and its cloisters, school rooms, and gardens, splendid art, furniture, and reliquaries recreate the daily life of the former Jesuit college.

Mexico's most complete collection of colonial-era art and artifacts, one of its finest Baroque churches, and a splendid former Jesuit college built in the 17th and 18th centuries together make up this stunning museum covering Mexico's viceregal era. The church and college buildings, a vast complex with courtyards and gardens in the village of Tepotzotlán, were nearly complete when the Jesuits were expelled from New Spain in 1767. Restored and opened as a museum in 1964, exhibits include treasures preserved in situ as well as pieces from collections around the country.

Iglesia de San Francisco Javier

Built in the late 1600s, this majestic Baroque church is famous for its elegant 18th-century additions: the richly decorated Churrigueresque facade and tower, the exuberant gold altars, a trio of unusual chapels on one side, and the Miguel Cabrera murals in the chancel and cross vaults. The facade and interior are both prime examples of Mexican High Baroque. Together they form a harmonious whole equaled only by Santa Prisca in Taxco *(p161)* and San Cayetano near Guanajuato *(p199)*.

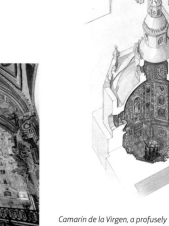

The main altar is dedicated to St. Francis Xavier, co-founder of the Jesuit college.

Entrance from museum

The altar to the Virgin of Guadalupe centers on a Miguel Cabrera painting of the patron saint of Mexico.

Camarín de la Virgen, a profusely decorated octagonal chamber, once served as a dressing room for the Virgin of Loreto – the statue's vestments and jewels were changed regularly.

↑ The Capilla de los Novicios, once used by college residents, now part of the museum

GALLERY GUIDE

Most of the collection is displayed on the entrance level of the former college building. The upper floor contains exhibits on artisan guilds, convent workshops, and female religious orders, while the lower level houses the old kitchen, rare stone sculptures, temporary exhibits, and the museum store.

The altar to St. Stanislaus Kostka honors a Polish Jesuit who served as a model to the students of the institution.

The dome rising above the intersection of the Latin Cross nave is best seen from a viewpoint in the museum.

The altar to St. Ignatius Loyola shows the founder of the Jesuits with a book displaying the order's motto.

The bell tower has 13 bells hanging on three levels under a tiled dome topped by a filigreed iron cross.

Pulpit

The Altar to the Virgen de la Luz is adorned with a multitude of cherubs and angels, which surrounds the central image of the Virgin and Child.

The imagery and style of the frontispiece echoes that of the altars inside, while the abundance of finely carved limestone hints at the brilliant interior.

So-called estípite pilasters form the verticals of the altars. Inspired by the proportions of the human figure, estípites taper off at the base, thus appearing to be upside down.

Corridor

The Casa de Loreto is said to be a replica of the Virgin Mary's Nazareth home, which angels moved to Loreto in Italy when the Muslims invaded the Holy Land.

Relicario de San José was built to house relics revered by the Jesuits – resembling the inside of a treasure chest.

↑ Illustration of Iglesia de San Francisco Javier, part of the Museo Nacional del Virreinato

3

PUEBLA

 C7 🏛 Puebla 🚇🚌 ℹ️ Avenida Palafox y Mendoza;
www.turismopuebla.gob.mx

Founded in 1531, Puebla combines Spanish Colonial
architecture with the vibrant buzz of a cosmopolitan
city. Its rich Spanish heritage is still evident today
in the finely preserved old center, with sumptuous
palaces, churches, and museums.

①

Estrella de Puebla

🏛 Osa Mayor 2520 🕐 3:30-
10pm Mon–Fri, 11am–10pm
Sat & Sun 🌐 estrella
depuebla.com

Puebla's Big-Wheel stands
tall in the Angelópolis district
and is one of the city's most
popular modern attractions.

From the top, which is
more than 260 ft (80 m) above
the ground, passengers are
rewarded with breathtaking
views over the charming city
of Puebla and, on a clear day,
may even be able to glimpse
the volcanoes of Popocatépetl
and Iztaccíhuatl *(p158)* west
of the city.

②

Catedral de Puebla

🏛 5 Oriente & 16 de
Septiembre 🌐 arquidio
cesisdepuebla.mx

The second largest cathedral
in Mexico, after the one in the
capital, Catedral de Puebla
was built in a mix of Renaissance and Baroque styles.
The pillars around the large
atrium – the plaza in front of
the building – are surmounted
by statues of angels, symbols
of the town whose full name
is Puebla de los Ángeles ("City
of Angels").

Inside there are five naves
and 14 side chapels. The main
altar, known as the *ciprés*, was

designed by Manuel Tolsá in
1797. Standing on an octagonal
base, it has two superimposed
"temples" supported by
Corinthian columns, crowned
by a tiled dome in imitation
of that of St. Peter's in Rome.
Behind the *ciprés* is the Altar
de los Reyes whose dome
was painted by Cristóbal de
Villalpando in 1688.

③

Teleférico de
Puebla

🏛 Calzada Ignacio Zaragoza
🕐 2–10pm Mon, 10am–10pm
Tue–Sun 🌐 visitpuebla.mx

Puebla's cable car quickly
become one of the city's top

🔍 HIDDEN GEM
**Alley of
the Frogs**

Near the Zócalo (main
square), *Callejón de los
Sapos* is in the Artists'
Quarter, which hosts an
arts and crafts market
on Sunday mornings. Its
name comes from floods
that drew many frogs.

The impressive City Hall standing on Puebla's main square (Zócalo)

attractions after opening in 2016. The two-minute journey zips across the Xanenetla neighborhood and offers a chance to admire the largest urban mural in the world, as well as stunning views over the city and volcanoes beyond.

---

④

Secret Tunnels of Puebla

🏠 Bulevar 5 de Mayo 208, Barrio de Xanenetla
🕑 10am–4pm Tue–Sun
🌐 viajapopuebla.mx

Discovered in 2015, a 6-mile (10-km) network of tunnels runs beneath the center of Puebla, thought to have been constructed up to 500 years ago. Some of the tunnels are still in a state of disrepair and not easy to find. The best part to explore is the Pasaje Histórico 5 de Mayo, which is well-lit and has historical artifacts on display.

---

⑤

Museo de los Hermanos

🏠 6 Oriente No. 206
📞 (222) 242 10 76
🕑 10am–6pm Tue–Sun

This museum of revolutionary memorabilia is housed in the same building where the event said to have sparked the Mexican Revolution *(p60)* took place. On November 19, 1910, Aquiles Serdán – a shoemaker and political activist – resisted arrest for his revolutionary activities, and he and around a dozen others, including his family, were killed by the police.

---

⑥

Taller Uriarte Talavera

🏠 4 Poniente No 911
🕑 10am–3pm Mon–Fri
🌐 uriartetalavera.com.mx

Guided tours of this Talavera pottery workshop show the production process from the early purifying of the clay, to the painting, glazing, and final firing of the piece.

TOP 4 **ART MUSEUMS**

Museo Internacional del Barroco
🏠 Atlixcáyotl 2501
📞 (222) 326 71 30
Imaginative displays around Puebla's Baroque heritage.

Museo Amparo
🏠 2 Sur No 708
🌐 museoamparo.com
A collection of Meso-american, colonial-era, and modern art.

Centro Cultural Ex-Convento de Santa Rosa
🏠 3 Norte No. 1210
📞 (222) 232 77 92
A former convent, displaying crafts produced in Puebla.

Museo de Arte Religi-oso de Santa Mónica
🏠 18 Poniente No 103
📞 (222) 232 01 78
Ecclesiastical artifacts, art, and sculpture.

Must See

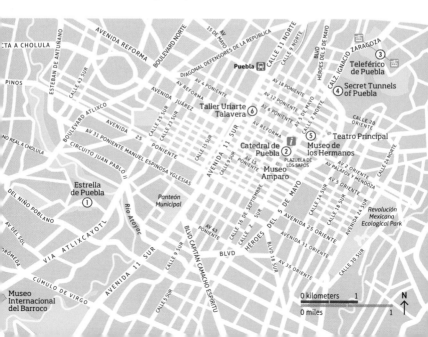

A SHORT WALK
PUEBLA

Distance 1.5 miles (2.5 km) **Time** 30 minutes
Nearest bus stop 8 Poniente - 2 Norte

Puebla is best known for the beautiful Talavera tiles that adorn its walls, domes, and interiors; for *mole poblano*, the thick sauce enriched with chocolate that originated here; and for being the site of an important battle against the French on May 5, 1862. The streets of the compact city center are lined with churches, mansions, and handsome old buildings, and are a delight to stroll around.

Built in the 17th century as part of an orphanage, the **Templo de San Cristóbal** *is noted for its collection of sculptures.*

Calle 6 Oriente *is known for its shops selling handmade candies, crystallized fruits, and rompope (eggnog).*

The Revolution of 1910 supposedly began in this house, which is now a museum: the **Museo de los Hermanos** *(p149).*

START

FINISH

Iglesia de Santa Clara

The 18th-century **Casa del Alfeñique** *is so named because its delicate white ornamental plasterwork resembles alfeñique, a sugar and almond paste. It now houses the state museum.*

VIPS *restaurant occupies this metal-framed building dating from the early 1900s.*

Diners at the arcade opposite the leafy Plaza Principal ↓

The facade of **Casa de los Muñecos** – *now a restaurant – is covered with decorative red tiles.*

Teatro Principal

6 ORIENTE

4 NORTE

6 ORIENTE

2 NORTE

City Hall

Plaza Principal
(Zócalo)

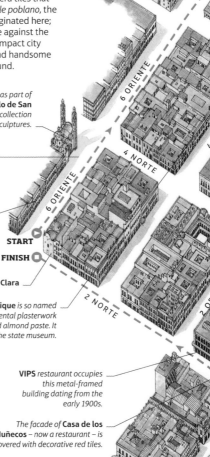

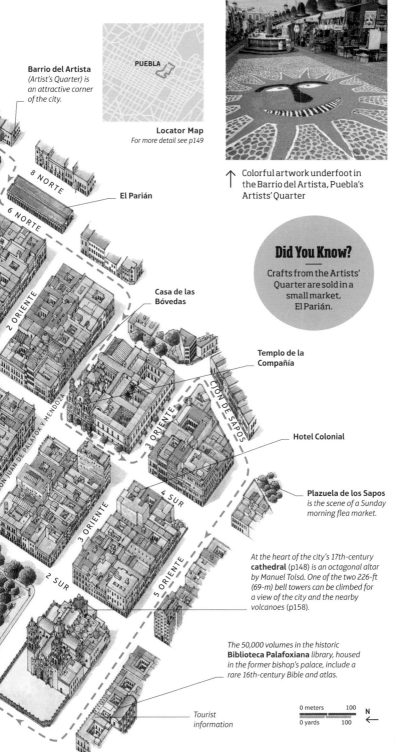

Barrio del Artista
(Artist's Quarter) is an attractive corner of the city.

PUEBLA

Locator Map
For more detail see p149

↑ Colorful artwork underfoot in the Barrio del Artista, Puebla's Artists' Quarter

Did You Know?

Crafts from the Artists' Quarter are sold in a small market, El Parián.

8 NORTE

El Parián

6 NORTE

2 ORIENTE

Casa de las Bóvedas

Templo de la Compañía

3 ORIENTE

CIÓN DE SAPOS

Hotel Colonial

4 SUR

Plazuela de los Sapos
is the scene of a Sunday morning flea market.

3 ORIENTE

2 SUR

DON JUAN DE PALAFOX Y MENDOZA

5 ORIENTE

At the heart of the city's 17th-century **cathedral** *(p148) is an octagonal altar by Manuel Tolsá. One of the two 226-ft (69-m) bell towers can be climbed for a view of the city and the nearby volcanoes (p158).*

The 50,000 volumes in the historic **Biblioteca Palafoxiana** *library, housed in the former bishop's palace, include a rare 16th-century Bible and atlas.*

Tourist information

| 0 meters | 100 |
| 0 yards | 100 |

N ←

EXPERIENCE MORE

❹
Pachuca

 C4 **Hidalgo** 🚌 **ℹ️ Camino Real de La Plata 340; (771) 718 44 89**

Pachuca, capital of Hidalgo state, lies in the heart of a rich mining area. The center of town, with its steep, narrow lanes and small squares, retains some buildings from the two mining booms of the 16th and 18th centuries.

The tower in Plaza de la Independencia, the 130-ft (40-m) Neo-Classical Reloj Monumental (Monumental Clock), has an eight-bell carillon made by the creators of the Big Ben bell in London.

The late-16th-century Ex-Convento de San Francisco and its adjoining church form a large complex in the town center. The church contains the remains of the 3rd-century martyr St. Columba, whose mummified body was brought here in the 18th century. Part of the massive former monastery building houses the **Fototeca Nacional** and **Museo de la Fotografía**. The latter has exhibits on the history of photography and shows selections from the one million photos on file at the former (the National Photographic Archive). One section is dedicated to the Casasola Archive, an outstanding chronicle of the Mexican Revolution and post-revolutionary daily life. It is also worth seeing the photographs and mining equipment at the **Archivo Histórico y Museo de Minería**.

On the southern outskirts of Pachuca is the Parque David Ben Gurión, featuring a huge, stunning mosaic made from around seven million tiles by Hidalgo-born artist Byron Gálvez Avilés. The park was founded in 2005 by the city's Jewish community as a tribute to David Ben Gurion, Israel's first prime minister.

On the other side of town, the Santa Apolonia hill provides amazing views.

Fototeca Nacional and Museo de la Fotografía
🕐 **Casasola** ℂ (771) 714 36 53 🕐 10am–6pm Tue–Sun

HIDDEN GEM
Pachuca Football Club

The soccer-obsessed town of Pachuca is home to Mexico's oldest club, as well as the Centro Interactivo Mundo Fútbol, a fun interactive soccer museum *(www.mundofutbol.com)*.

Archivo Histórico y Museo de Minería
🕐 **Javier Mina 110** ℂ (771) 715 09 76 🕐 10am–6pm Tue–Sun

❺
San Agustín Acolman

 B6 **Calzada De Los Agustinos, Acolman, Mexico State** 🕐 9am–5:30pm daily 🌐 inah.gob.mx/paseos/exacolman

One of Mexico's oldest monasteries, San Agustín Acolman was founded in 1539 by Augustinian monks who came here to convert the local indigenous people. It is notable for its atrium, a Christian version of the pre-Hispanic ceremonial plaza, where crowds of Indigenous disciples would gather to hear the new religion preached from a

The imposing Reloj Monumental, in Plaza de la Independencia, and *(inset)* brightly colored houses on ↓ Pachuca's hillside

→ A bridge over the canyon of Prismas Basálticos, near Huasca

chapel balcony above. The fortress-like building now houses colonial-era artwork.

The forbidding aspect of the monastery is softened, however, by the adjoining church's beautiful Plateresque facade, which is characterized by classic Italian Renaissance columns, richly decorated door arches, and a choir window replicating the portal below. The sparse interior of the nave is notable for its Gothic fan vaulting adorned with rich frescoes.

___

6 Huasca

⚑C4 **⚐Hidalgo** **🛈Plaza Principal; (771) 792 07 47**

The picturesque village of Huasca is best known for its *haciendas de beneficio*, where mineral ores were refined. San Miguel Regla 2 miles (3 km) northeast of town, is a particularly popular spot with visitors, and is now a hotel. More impressive is **Hacienda Santa María Regla**, which has vaulted cellars, and patios with stone drag mills and melting ovens. From here visitors can access the spectacular 9-mile (15-km) canyon Prismas Basálticos, whose walls are made up of red and ocher basalt hexagons.

Hacienda Santa María Regla

⊛ ⚐4.5 miles (7 km) NE of Huasca ⚐Daily ⬜hacienda deregla.com.mx

___

7 Mineral del Monte

⚑C4 **⚐Hidalgo** **🚌** **🛈Rubén Licona Ruiz 1; (771) 797 05 10**

Also known as Real del Monte, this mining town used to be the richest in the area. Gold and silver were discovered here after the Conquest *(p57)*, and the Spanish started mining in the mid-1500s.

The town's steep streets, stairways, and small squares are lined with low buildings. The houses with high sloping roofs and chimneys indicate a Cornish influence, the legacy left by the 350 Cornishmen employed by the English company that ran the mines between 1824 and 1848. They are also responsible for *pastes*, a local specialty based on the Cornish pasty, as well as for introducing soccer to Mexico.

The town has several museums dedicated to its British industrial heritage, such as the Museo Casa Grande, the Museo de Sitio Mina de Acosta, and the **Museo del Paste**, dedicated to the Cornish pasty.

Museo del Paste

⊛⊚ ⚐Av Juaréz 114 ⬛(771) 797 15 48 ⚐10am–5pm Wed–Mon

EAT

The British miners who worked in Mineral del Monte are responsible for the area's popular pastes. Pachuca is home to some of the best places to try them.

Pastes Kikos
⚑C4 ⚐Guanajuato & Blvd del Minero, Pachuca ⬛(771) 380 74 45

⑤⑤⑤

___

Pastes El Billar
⚑C4 ⚐Avenida Revolución 507-A, Pachuca ⬛(771) 713 37 38

⑤⑤⑤

___

Restaurante La Blanca
⚑C4 ⚐Calle Mariano Matamoros 201, Pachuca ⬛(771) 715 18 96

⑤⑤⑤

↑ The giant Atlantes warrior statues at the Toltec site of Tula

Tula

⬛ C4 ◻ Off Mex 57, 53 miles (85 km) N of Mexico City, Hidalgo ☎ (773) 100 36 54 ◷ 9am–5pm daily

The most important Toltec site in Mexico, Tula flourished as a great urban center from AD 900 to 1100, after the decline of Teotihuacán (*p140*) and prior to the rise of Tenochtitlán (*p78*). At its peak, the city covered up to 6 sq miles (16 sq km) and had an estimated population of around 30,000. Then inner strife, invasions, and fire destroyed the Toltec empire and this, its capital. Only remnants of the main palaces, temples, and ballcourts survive on a windswept hill overlooking the small town of Tula de Allende.

The site is most famous for its giant stone sculptures, the Atlantes, some of which are reproductions. At a height of 15 ft (4.6 m), these four figures in battle gear crown the Pyramid of Tlahuizcalpantecuhtli, or the Morning Star. Together with a massive serpent and other pillars, they probably once supported an ornately carved roof.

Certain stylistic elements at Tula – such as the column-filled Palacio Quemado (Burnt Palace), the *chacmool* sculptures, and the huge size of Ballcourt No 2 – underline the site's similarity to the Maya city of Chichén Itzá (*p294*). It was once thought that Toltec king Topiltzín was driven out of Tula and fled to the Yucatán Peninsula (*p276*) where he ushered in a cultural renaissance. However, recent theories suggest that the similarities are a result of Maya influence on Tula, and not vice versa.

Cholula

⬛ C7 ◻ Puebla 🚌 ℹ Portal Guerrero 3, 4 Norte; (222) 261 23 93

In pre-Hispanic times, Cholula was a sacred city and a large and important commercial center. Before subjecting it to one of the bloodiest massacres of the Spanish Conquest,

THE TOLTECS

The Toltecs settled in central Mexico in around AD 900. At the site of their magnificent capital, Tula, carved warrior and sacrificial stones discovered in excavations indicate a society based on military might and ritual sacrifice. The Toltecs were also superb artists, influencing other Mesoamerican cultures, including the Aztecs. When Tula was overthrown in around 1100, some Toltecs moved to the Yucatán Peninsula (*p276*), where one of their leaders may have been Quetzalcóatl (*p287*), who purportedly transformed into a god.

REGIONAL FIESTAS

Chalma Pilgrimages
Pilgrims make their way to the El Señor de Chalma shrine at Easter.

Fiesta de los Tiznados
A festival held on January 21 in Tepoztlán, in remembrance of the ancient Tepoztec king.

El Día de la Batalla de Puebla
Commemorating the Battle of Puebla, military parades take place on May 5.

Fiesta de la Virgen de la Caridad
An image of the Virgin is carried for 3 miles (5 km) through Huamantla in mid-August.

Reto al Tepozteco
Villagers race up Tepozteco Hill in early September.

Cortés allegedly described it as "the most beautiful city outside Spain."

The arcade on the west side of Cholula's large *zócalo* (main square) shelters restaurants and cafés. Opposite is the fortified, Franciscan **Convento de San Gabriel**. Founded in 1528 on the site of a temple to Quetzalcóatl, the main church has a single nave with rib vaulting and Gothic tracery. On the left of the atrium is the Capilla Real, which was built for Indigenous converts. It acquired its 49 mosque-like domes in the early part of the 18th century.

To the east is the **Zona Arqueológica**, a site which is dominated by the remains of the largest pyramid ever built

→

The beautiful tile-covered church of San Francisco Acatepec

in Mesoamerica, at 213 ft (65 m) high. Since the 1930s, archaeologists have dug 5 miles (8 km) of tunnels through this Great Pyramid, identifying at least four stages of construction between 200 BC and AD 800.

Opposite the entrance to the tunnel is a museum with a large cutaway model of the pyramid, as well as artifacts from the site. Atop the pyramid is the 16th-century church of Nuestra Señora de los Remedios. The view from the atrium takes in Puebla (p148), the volcanoes, and Cholula's many other churches.

The extraordinary folk-Baroque church of Santa María Tonantzintla, 3 miles (5 km) south of Cholula, has an interior that is bursting with colorful saints, fruit, angels, and cherubs. Begun in the 16th century, it took its craftsmen 200 years to complete. A farther 1 mile (1.5 km) south, the church of San Francisco Acatepec has a facade entirely covered in colorful Talavera tiles (p131).

Convento de San Gabriel
🏠 Corner of Calle 2 Norte and Avenida Morelos ⏰ 9am–5pm daily

Zona Arqueológica
 🏠 Calle 14 Poniente
📞 (222) 247 90 81
⏰ 10am–5pm Tue–Sat

↑ View over Valle de Bravo and its lake, a popular spot for hang gliding

⑩

Valle de Bravo

🅰 C5 🏠 Mexico State 🚌
ℹ Rincón de San Vicente; www.turismovalledebravo.gob.mx

Set among pine-covered volcanic mountains, this pretty colonial-era town achieved popularity in the 1950s after the construction of an artificial lake. Easy access from Mexico City makes the town a favorite weekend destination for the capital's elite, but during the week peace returns to the cobbled streets.

Local attractions such as the waterfalls of Cascadas Velo de Novia, the **Santuario Piedra Herrada** butterfly reserve, and the peaceful

Carmel Maranathá temple all make the most of the beautiful natural scenery. The area is also a popular place to enjoy activities, with lots of opportunities for hang gliding, hiking, horseback riding, and waterskiing.

Santuario Piedra Herrada
 🏠 San Mateo Almomoloa
⏰ 9am–4pm daily

Carmel Maranathá
🏠 Carretera México Valle de Bravo ⏰ 10am–2pm & 4–7pm Mon–Fri 🅆 carmelmaranatha.wixsite.com/ocd-en-valle

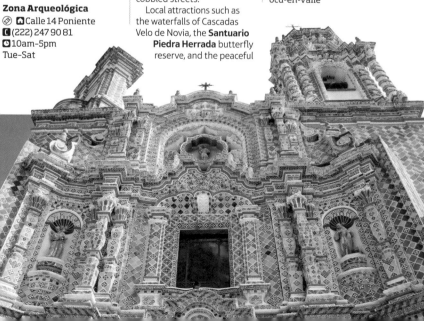

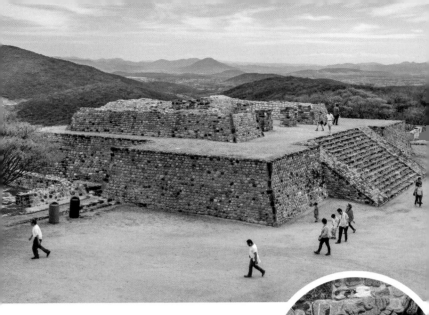

❶ ✍

Xochicalco

🅰 A7 🅰 Off Mex 95, 25 miles (40 km) SW of Cuernavaca 🅲 9am–6pm daily (Museum: to 5pm) 🆆 inah.gob.mx

The ruins of Xochicalco Archaeological Zone are all that remains of an important city-state that rose to prominence after the decline of Teotihuacán (p140). The city flourished from AD 700 to 900, before being eclipsed by the rise of the Toltecs (p144).

About 30 per cent of the site has been unearthed, including three ballcourts and the remains of several pyramidal structures. An on-site museum displays artifacts found during archaeological work. The site, situated on a plateau, offers incredible views of the surrounding area.

The Temple of the Feathered Serpent, excavated in the early 20th century, is

The pyramidal ruins ↑ at Xochicalco and (inset) a bas-relief carving on the Temple of the Feathered Serpent

considered one of the nation's most beautiful monuments. It features remarkably well-preserved bas-reliefs of serpents, glyphs, and Maya-style figures.

---

❷

Cuernavaca

🅰 A7 🅰 Morelos 🚌 🅸 Avenida Motolinía 2; www.cuernavaca.gob mx

Inhabited since 1200 BC, Cuernavaca is one of the oldest cities in Mexico. Today it is a popular weekend destination from Mexico City, and full of history and culture for visitors to discover.

The **Palacio de Cortés** was built by the Spanish on the site of Aztec pyramids they had destroyed. It served as Cortés's residence until his return to Spain in 1541. Known for a series of Diego Rivera murals depicting Mexico's history, it also contains the Museo Regional Cuauhnáhuac, which has a fine collection of historical artifacts.

The fortress-like Catedral de la Asunción, dating from the 1520s, has murals thought to have been painted by Indigenous artists, who were likely inspired by murals they had seen or encountered in Southeast Asia. The **Museo Robert Brady**, situated in a former cloister, holds the art and craft collection of this American artist. **La Tallera** is the former studio of the great

> Xochicalco's Temple of the Feathered Serpent, excavated in the early 20th century, is considered one of the nation's most beautiful monuments.

muralist David Alfaro Siqueiros (1896–1974). Revolutionary politics shaped his life and work, and inspired the aesthetic behind his projects.

A few blocks from the main *zócalo* (square) is the **Museo de Arte Indígena Contemporáneo**, which focuses on works by contemporary Indigenous artists.

Palacio de Cortés

⊗⊗⊚ 🔲 Avenida Leyva 100 🔲 (777) 312 69 96 🔲 9am–6pm Tue–Sun

Museo Robert Brady

⊗⊚ 🔲 Netzahualcóyotl 4 🔲 10am–6pm Tue–Sun 🔲 museorobertbrady.com

La Tallera

⊗⊗ 🔲 Venus 52, Jardines de Cuernavaca 🔲 10am–6pm Tue–Sun 🔲 saps-latallera.org

Museo de Arte Indígena Contemporáneo

⊗⊚ 🔲 Avenida Morelos 275 🔲 (777) 310 57 00 🔲 10am–5pm Tue–Sun

---

⑬

Malinalco

🔺 A7 🔲 Mexico State 🚌 🔳 Rincón de San Vicente; www.malinalco.gob.mx

This charming town is nestled in a valley, surrounded by steep volcanic hills. An Aztec

ceremonial center sits on a narrow ledge 20 minutes' climb above town.

Its main structure, the House of the Eagle (Cuauhcalli), is carved entirely out of the rock. The building is thought to have been used for initiation ceremonies of high-ranking Aztec knights. Behind it stand the remains of the Temple of the Sun and the Tzinacalli Edifice, where the bodies of knights killed in combat were deified.

A reproduction of the temple facade and the inner chamber can be seen in the **Museo Universitario Dr. Luis Mario Schneider**.

Museo Universitario Dr. Luis Mario Schneider

⊗ 🔲 Calle Amajac 🔲 (714) 147 12 88 🔲 10am–6pm Tue–Sun

---

⑭

Tepoztlán

🔺 A7 🔲 Morelos 🚌 🔳 22 Avenida Revolución de 1910; www.info tepoz.com

Lying in a lush green valley, Tepoztlán is surrounded by spectacular volcanic rock formations. The town's main landmark is the massive, fortified Ex-Convento Dominico de la Natividad, although the building is in

a state of disrepair. The market on Plaza Santo Domingo, meanwhile, is a great place to browse. You'll find everything from fresh fruit to Mexican handicrafts.

A tiring but worthwhile climb above the town stands the Santuario del Cerro Tepozteco, a shrine dedicated to Tepoztécatl, the ancient god of pulque – an alcoholic beverage made from the agave plant.

For lovers of pre-Hispanic art, the **Museo Carlos Pellicer** holds a small but interesting collection, the legacy of the Tabascan poet and anthropologist Carlos Pellicer, who lived in Tepoztlán.

Museo Carlos Pellicer

⊗⊗ 🔲 González 🔲 (739) 395 10 98 🔲 10am–6pm Tue–Sun

EAT

Tepoznieves

This is the original branch of a local chain that offers more than 100 delicious flavors of ice cream and sorbet.

🔺 A7 🔲 Avenida 5 de Mayo No 21, Tepoztlán 🔲 nieves-tepoznieves.com

⑤⑤⑤

STAY

Hostería Las Quintas

Spacious rooms in a hotel surrounded by botanical gardens.

🔺 C5 🔲 Blvd Gustavo Díaz Ordaz No 9, Cuernavaca 🔲 hosteria lasquintas.com.mx

⑤⑤⑤

↑ Visitors exploring the Aztec ruins above the town of Malinalco

15

Popocatépetl and Iztaccíhuatl

B7 Mexico State

The snow-capped volcanoes of Popocatépetl, or Popo, ("Smoking Mountain") and Iztaccíhuatl ("Sleeping Lady") are the second and third highest peaks in Mexico. On a clear day, they are two of Mexico's most awesome sights.

According to legend, the warrior Popocatépetl fell in love with Iztaccíhuatl, an Aztec princess. To win her hand, he defeated a great rival in battle. Wrongly believing him to be dead, the princess herself then died of a broken heart. In his grief, Popocatépetl turned himself and his princess into these two adjacent mountains. The outline of Iztaccíhuatl bears a resemblance to that of a sleeping woman.

The Paso de Cortés, a saddle between the two peaks accessible by car, is an ideal base for walks on Iztaccíhuatl, but ascents of the peak itself should be left to experienced climbers and those who have hired a guide. Such services are offered by the park.

Access to the area around Popocatépetl volcano is restricted because of seismic activity. If you plan to hike, check posted warnings and contact your embassy or SECTUR (Secretaría de Turismo) for the latest information.

16

Cacaxtla and Xochitécatl

C7 Off Mex 119, 19 miles (30 km) NW of Puebla, Tlaxcala (246) 416 00 00 9am–5:30pm daily

Cacaxtla was the capital of the Olmeca-Xicalanca, a Gulf Coast group who dominated this area from the 7th to 10th centuries AD. Some of Mexico's best-preserved murals, probably painted by Maya artists, were discovered here in 1975.

The 72-ft- (22-m-) high *Mural de la Batalla* depicts a violent battle between jaguar and eagle warriors, with no fewer than 48 human figures in vibrant colors.

Two other extraordinary murals are in Edificio A. The *Hombre-jaguar* represents a lord dressed in a jaguar skin, surrounded by a border of sea creatures. The *Hombre-ave* is a "bird-man" painted in black with an eagle headdress. He holds a blue serpent staff and stands on a plumed snake. Heads of corn around the edge have small human faces.

Perched on a neighboring peak just 1.5 miles (2 km) away is another Olmeca-Xicalanca site, Xochitécatl. Situated atop an extinct volcano overlooking the surrounding valley, Xochitécatl is thought to have been used as a ritual ceremonial center in conjunction with Cacaxtla. Dating from about 800 BC, its pyramids and other main buildings flank two plazas.

DRINK

La Vista Café Bar
Sip a cool cocktail on the roof terrace of this hugely popular local café-bar, with great views over the city rooftops. It also has games rooms and a decent menu of snacks and pasta dishes.

D5 San Gabriel 22, Tlaxcala (246) 466 62 60

→

The lavish exterior of the Basílica de Ocotlán, situated above Tlaxcala

⑰
Tlaxcala

🅰 C6 🏠 Tlaxcala 🚌
ℹ️ Corner of Avenida Juárez and Lardizábal; www.turismotlaxcala.com

Often seen as a provincial backwater, the city of Tlaxcala is, in fact, one of the country's early 16th-century treasures. Its seclusion is partly due to the historical independence of the local people, the Tlaxcaltecas. During the Conquest they took up arms against their old enemy, the Aztecs, joining Cortés to conquer Tenochtitlán.

The so-called Ciudad Roja (Red City) is dominated by earthy tones of terracotta and ocher. In the center is the spacious tree-filled *zócalo* (main plaza). The colorful and richly decorated brick, tile, and stucco facade of the Parroquia de San José dominates the northwest corner of the square. At the entrance to this church two fonts have pedestals depict-

←

A hiker climbing to the snowy peak of Popocatépetl volcano

ing Camaxtli, the ancient Tlaxcalan god of war and hunting, and the Spanish imperial coat of arms.

Across Plaza Xicohténcatl to the south, a path leads uphill to the cathedral, which has a stunning Moorish-style coffered ceiling and contains the font used to baptize the four local chiefs who allied with Cortés. The **Museo Regional**, in the cloisters next door, has a collection of pre-Hispanic pieces, including a large stone figure of Camaxtli, the god of war. The two rooms upstairs are dedicated to colonial-era art.

The **Museo Vivo de Artes y Tradiciones Populares de Tlaxcala** is a fascinating living museum where artisans demonstrate their techniques.

Housed in a 19th-century former hospital, the **Museo de Arte de Tlaxcala** contains some of artist Frida Kahlo's early works. Around the corner is the fascinating **Museo de la Memoria de Tlaxcala**, focused on the town's history.

On a hill above the city, the twin-towered Basílica de Ocotlán is one of the most lavish Churrigueresque churches in Mexico. The

> 🔍 HIDDEN GEM
> ### Puppet Story
> The town of Huamantla, east of Tlaxcala, is famous for its puppetry, as the Rosete Aranda puppet company was founded here in 1850. Learn more at the National Puppet Museum *(Parque Juárez 50).*

18th-century facade combines hexagonal brick and white stucco decoration, and the interior features Baroque giltwork.

Museo Regional

⌖ 🏠 Ex-Convento de San Francisco, off Plaza Xicoténcatl ☎ (246) 462 02 62 🕙 10am–6pm Tue–Sun

Museo Vivo de Artes y Tradiciones Populares de Tlaxcala

⌖ 🕙 🏠 Blvd Emilio Sánchez Piedras 1 ☎ (246) 462 57 04 🕙 10am–6pm Tue–Sun

Museo de Arte de Tlaxcala

⌖ 🏠 Plaza de la Constitución 21 ☎ (246) 466 03 52 🕙 10am–6pm Tue–Sun

Museo de la Memoria de Tlaxcala

⌖ 🕙 🏠 Avenida Independencia 3 ☎ (246) 466 07 92 🕙 10am–5pm daily

↑ Striking stained glass by Leopoldo Flores, at Toluca's Cosmovitral Jardín Botánico

Toluca

**⚑A7 ⌂Mexico State ✈🚌
ℹ Plaza Fray Andrés de
Castro; www2.toluca.
gob.mx**

At 8,727 ft (2,660 m) above
sea level, Toluca is the highest
state capital in the country.

Founded by the Spanish
in the late 17th century, Toluca
is full of fine buildings. The
Neo-Classical cathedral, a
massive late-19th-century
pile, dominates the main
square, Plaza de los Mártires.
Nearby are the 18th-century
Templo de la Santa Veracruz
and the 19th-century Portales,
a series of walkways lined with
cafés and shops. To the north

**PICTURE PERFECT
Rare Pyramid**

A photo of the
rounded pyramid
of Calixtlahuaca, 25
minutes north of Toluca,
makes a great contrast
to Mexico's other ruins.
It was built in the 7th
century BC as a site of
pilgrimage for the Otomi.

---

is the **Museo de Bellas Artes**,
which exhibits Mexican art
from the last four centuries.
Nearby, the **Cosmovitral
Jardín Botánico** shows
botanical specimens in the
beautiful old market, its walls
and ceiling ablaze with colorful stained glass. The **Central
de Abastos** food market, with
around 2,000 stalls, is one of
the largest in Mexico.

To the southeast, the
suburb of Metepec is famous
for its brightly colored,
ceramic *árboles de la vida*
(trees of life), loosely based on
the story of Adam and Eve.

There's also plenty more
to see in the surrounding area,
making Toluca a great base for
exploring the region. To the
west is the **Centro Cultural
Mexiquense**, a complex of
museums devoted to modern
art, local history, and regional
crafts. A short drive southwest
is the extinct, snow-capped
Nevado de Toluca volcano. A
dirt road leads almost to the
top, and hikers can descend
into the crater. The hilltop ceremonial center of Teotenango is
south of Toluca. Dating from
AD 900, the site features
restored pyramids, plazas,
a ballcourt, and a museum.

500,000

The number of pieces
of stained glass in
Toluca's Cosmovitral
Jardín Botánico

**Museo de
Bellas Artes**

⊗ ⌂Santos Degollado
102, Poniente ☎(722)
215 53 29 ⌚10am-6pm
Tue-Sat (to 3pm Sun)

**Cosmovitral
Jardín Botánico**

⊗⊗ ⌂Juárez & Lerdo
s/n ☎(722) 214 67 85
⌚10am-6pm Tue-Sun

**Central de
Abastos**

⌂José López Portillo
Km 4.5 ☎(722) 210 26 29
⌚7am-8:30pm daily

**Centro Cultural
Mexiquense**

⌂Blvd Jesús Reyes
Heroles 302 ☎(722) 274
12 00 ⌚10am-6pm Tue-
Sat (to 3pm Sun)

Cantona

🄰D5 **🄰19 miles (30 km) NE of Oriental, Puebla** **🕒9am-6pm daily** **🌐inah. gob.mx**

The remains of a once major city occupy a vast area of low hills beside a lava field. Little is known about the history of Cantona but it was probably inhabited from about AD 700 to 950. One of the most built-up of all Mesoamerican cities, it may have supported a population of 80,000.

A full visit will take at least two hours. A signposted route from the parking lot sets off on one of the *calzadas*, or cobbled streets, which connect the various parts of Cantona. This leads past the ruins of houses and patios before climbing to the Acrópolis, the cluster of public buildings at the heart of the city. Soon the route reaches the first of 27 ballcourts excavated here – more than at any other site in Mexico. Of these, 12 are unusual in that they form parts of complexes with a pyramid at one end and the playing area at the other.

Convento de San Nicolás de Tolentino de Actopan

🄰C4 **🄰Lerdo de Tejada, Actopan, Hidalgo** **☎(772) 728 35 80** **🕒9am-5pm Tue-Sun**

Built in the 1550s, the imposing Convent of San Nicolás de Tolentino de Actopan is one of Mexico's most remarkable and best-preserved 16th-century fortress-monasteries. Even more spectacular than its Plateresque facade, square Moorish tower, and vaulted open chapel are its frescoes, which are considered the most beautiful and extensive from this era in Mexico.

Taxco

🄰C5 **🄰Guerrero** **🚌** **🛈Avenida de los Plateros 126; (762) 622 07 98**

Set against a spectacular rugged mountainside, Taxco is one of the least spoiled early 16th-century towns in Mexico. Its history is inextricably tied to the local silver boom, and today many of its attractions focus on the industry. Housed in the main handicrafts center, the **Museo de la Platería** offers an immersive experience of the silver production process. The **Mina Prehispánica de Taxco** runs tours exploring historic mine shafts. Taxco's silver market, **Mercado de Plata**, is a great place to buy silver at reasonable prices.

The success of those who grew rich from the silver mines have also left their mark on the town, such as with the grand **Iglesia De Santa Prisca**. It is a fantastic exmple of the Churrigueresque style of Mexican architecture.

Museo de la Platería

🄰🄰 🄰Patio de las Artesanías, Plaza Borda 1 ☎(762) 622 06 58 🕒10am-6pm Tue-Sun

Mina Prehispánica de Taxco

🄰🄰🄰 🄰Cerro de la Misión 32 ☎(762) 622 82 86 🕒9am-6pm daily

Mercado de Plata

🄰Calle de Fundiciones y de Mora 🕒9am-4pm Sat

Iglesia De Santa Prisca

🄰Plaza Borda 1 ☎(762) 622 01 83 🕒9am-7pm Mon-Sat, 10am-8:15pm Sun

↑ Rooftops of Taxco, a town famous for its silver mining

A SHORT WALK
TAXCO

Distance 0.5 miles (1 km) **Time** 15 minutes **Nearest bus stop** Central de Autobuses Estrella Blanca

Exploring Taxco on foot takes you along steep cobble-stoned streets and narrow alleys lined with laid-back cafés and restaurants. In the historic center is the magnificent, Baroque Iglesia de Santa Prisca, a testament to the wealth brought into this silver boom town during the colonial era. The town's fortunes were revived with the arrival of silver designer William Spratling in 1929, who established Taxco as a center for silversmiths.

Overlooking the main square, **Casa Borda** *was built by the Borda family in 1759 for the parish priest. Today, it holds exhibitions by local artists.*

An intimate and lively square, **Plaza Borda** *is lined with charming old buildings. There are numerous restaurants and bars nearby. In addition, the area abounds with silver shops, filled with the high-quality pieces for which Taxco's many silversmiths are famous.*

Casa Figueroa *was built for the Count of Cadena. It has a dark and interesting history involving subterfuge and murder.*

PLAZUELA DE BERNAL

FINISH

START

PLAZA BORDA

OJEDA

← The cathedral towers rising above the old buildings of Taxco's old town

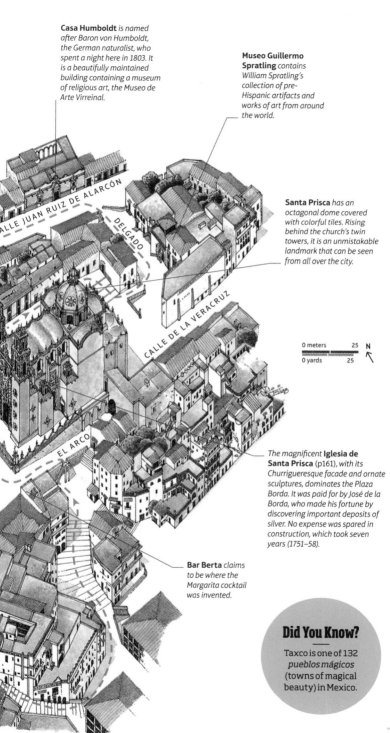

Casa Humboldt is named after Baron von Humboldt, the German naturalist, who spent a night here in 1803. It is a beautifully maintained building containing a museum of religious art, the Museo de Arte Virreinal.

Museo Guillermo Spratling contains William Spratling's collection of pre-Hispanic artifacts and works of art from around the world.

Santa Prisca has an octagonal dome covered with colorful tiles. Rising behind the church's twin towers, it is an unmistakable landmark that can be seen from all over the city.

CALLE JUAN RUIZ DE ALARCÓN

DELGADO

CALLE DE LA VERACRUZ

EL ARCO

| 0 meters | 25 |
| 0 yards | 25 |

N

The magnificent **Iglesia de Santa Prisca** (p161), with its Churrigueresque facade and ornate sculptures, dominates the Plaza Borda. It was paid for by José de la Borda, who made his fortune by discovering important deposits of silver. No expense was spared in construction, which took seven years (1751–58).

Bar Berta claims to be where the Margarita cocktail was invented.

Did You Know?

Taxco is one of 132 *pueblos mágicos* (towns of magical beauty) in Mexico.

Cactus plant, an iconic symbol of Baja California

BAJA CALIFORNIA

Indigenous peoples such as the Cochimí, Kiliwa, Kumeyaay, and Guaycura have inhabited the Baja peninsula for over 10,000 years. Baja was virtually ignored by European explorers until 1697, when Jesuit missionaries began establishing isolated churches across the peninsula. The Europeans brought diseases to the area, which turned into epidemics that decimated the region's population – by the early 1800s the Indigenous population was virtually extinct, and Baja remained a desolate place well into the 20th century. The border city of Tijuana began to flourish after US Prohibition in the 1920s turned it into a party town for citizens of neighboring California, a reputation it retains today. In 1930 the peninsula was divided in two: Baja California in the north, and Baja California Sur in the south. Though it became popular with US fishermen and adventurers such as John Steinbeck, growth in the rest of Baja was sluggish until the completion of the Transpeninsular Highway (Hwy 1) in 1973.

Today Baja California is a major holiday destination, particularly the southern resort towns such as Cabo San Lucas. Even the parts of the peninsula that remain swathed in isolated desert or crisscrossed by arid mountain chains exude a charm for more adventurous travelers looking for an epic road trip.

0 kilometers 150

0 miles 150

N ↑

Salton
Sea

San Diego

Mexic
Internat
Airpo

TIJUANA ❹ ✈ Tijuana
International
Airport

Rosarito

Mexicali ✈

VALLE DE GUADALUPE ❶

ENSENADA ❷

Santo Tomás

El Chinero

Colonet

San Feli

Camalú

Parque Natura
San Pedro Márt

BAJA CALIFORN
NORTE

El Rosarito

San Fernando

Cataviñ

Parque Natur
del Desierto Centr

Isla
Cedros

Ba
Seba
Vizc

Isla Natividad

Bahía Tortugas

Pacific
Ocean

BAJA CALIFORNIA

Experience

EXPERIENCE

❶
Valle de Guadalupe

 D1 🏛 Baja California
🛈 Paseo de los Héroes 10289, Tijuana; www.bajacalifornia.travel

The vineyards of Guadalupe Valley have received international acclaim since the 1990s. The villages of Francisco Zarco in the north and San Antonio de las Minas in the south anchor the valley's more than 100 vineyards. The **Museo de la Vid y el Vino** provides an introduction to the region, and most wineries offer tours and tastings.

Museo de la Vid y el Vino

⊛ 🏛 Carretera Federal Tecate-Ensenada Km. 81.33 📞 (646) 156 81 65 ⏰ 9am–5pm Tue–Sun

❷
Ensenada

 D1 🏛 Baja California
❌🚌 🛈 Blvd Lázaro Cárdenas 609; www.bajacalifornia.travel

This busy port and cruise-ship destination is popular with sportfishing fans, surfers, and divers, as well as foodies who come here for the town's famous fish tacos.

The city's landmarks include the twin-towered church of Nuestra Señora de Guadalupe and the giant sculpted heads of three national revolutionary leaders – Juárez, Hidalgo, and Carranza – on the Plaza Cívica.

Several old buildings have been repurposed and are now dedicated to preserving local history. Just inland, the **Museo Histórico Regional de Ensenada** was built in 1886 as a military barracks; today its cells are galleries chronicling the history of the town. The **Riviera de Ensenada**, near the waterfront, was a hotel in the 1930s but now houses exhibitions and a history museum. In the lobby is a remarkable 3D mural showing the 18th-century Jesuit missions of the Californias.

The huge complex opposite the Riviera is the Caracol (Museo de Ciencas), an interactive science museum showcasing Baja California's geology and environments. **Bodegas de Santo Tomás** makes some of Baja's finest wine from grapes grown in vineyards near town; it offers daily tours and wine tasting. Ensenada's small but lively "party district" clusters around the old-fashioned Hussong's Cantina on Avenida Ruíz, founded in the 19th century by the German Hussong family, still a powerful force in the city.

Museo Histórico Regional de Ensenada

🏛 Gastélum 56 📞 (646) 178 36 92 ⏰ 9am–5pm Tue–Sun

Riviera de Ensenada

🏛 Blvd Lázaro Cárdenas 1421 📞 (646) 176 43 10 ⏰ 8am–10pm daily

Bodegas de Santo Tomás

⊛⊛⊛⊛ 🏛 Av Miramar 666 📞 (646) 178 33 33 ⏰ Daily 🌐 santo-tomas.com

TOP 3
REGIONAL FIESTAS

Carnival
One of Mexico's best Pre-Lent Carnivals is held in La Paz.

Vendimia Wine Festival
In August, growers and producers show off their wares in Ensenada.

Baja 1000
A grueling off-road race Ensenada to La Paz held annually over several days in November.

❸
Bahía de los Ángeles

 E2 🏛 Baja California
🌐 bajacalifornia.travel

Located on the beautiful bay of the same name, the town of Bahía de los Ángeles is a tranquil spot, even by Baja standards. Popular with

↑ Visitor photographing a vineyard in the Valle de Guadalupe

The Millennial Arch on the busy Avenida Revolución in Tijuana

sportfishing enthusiasts, it also offers opportunities for diving and kayaking around the numerous islands in the bay. Other attractions include trips across a spectacular desert landscape to see prehistoric rock paintings (p170), and the well-preserved San Borja mission.

Boats are available to visit various offshore islands, but visiting or camping on the islands requires a permit. You can obtain one from the reserve office in town.

④

Tijuana

🅰 D1 🅰 Baja California
📧 ➡ *i* HSBC Centro, Av Revolución 791; www. tijuana.gob.mx

A well-known party town, Tijuana is one of the world's busiest border cities, just 20 miles (32 km) from the US city of San Diego, California.

Towering skyscrapers and massive shopping malls are a measure of its modernity, but Tijuana's focus is the cluster of bars, clubs, and souvenir stalls on Avenida Revolución. Even in this busy leisure district, however, you'll find

history close by – two blocks west of Revolución, the elegant Catedral de Nuestra Señora de Guadalupe, built in 1909 was designated a cathedral in 1964.

Tijuana also has a few cultural attractions, the main one being the **Centro Cultural Tijuana** where concerts and art exhibitions are held. At the same location is the illuminating **Museo de las Californias**, which chronicles the history of Baja California.

Centro Cultural Tijuana

⊛ ⊜ ⊛ 🅰 Paseo de los Héroes 9350 🕙 10am-7pm daily 🖿 cecut.gob.mx

Museo de las Californias

⊛ 🅰 Paseo de los Héroes 9350 📞 (664) 687 96 36 🕙 Noon-7pm Wed-Sun

> ### Did You Know?
>
> César salad was invented in Tijuana by Caesar Cardini at Hotel Caesars (*Av Revolución 1079*).

THE MEXICO-US BORDER

The US and Mexico are separated by a heavily guarded land border that runs for 1,950 miles (3,140 km). A large number of people cross every year at Tijuana alone. When crossing from the US into Mexico there are no customs checks, and only casual checks for pedestrians. Stop at the *migración* office for a Mexican entry form, or "FMM" (these are not handed out automatically).

Always allow more time heading into the US, and be prepared for a line - crossing the border at Tijuana can take up to three hours. For Tijuana Airport, use the CBX skybridge, which connects to the San Diego side (*www. crossborderexpress.com*).

5

Misión San Ignacio de Kadakaamán

🅰E2 🏠Hidalgo 1916, Juan Batista, San Ignacio, Baja California Sur

Standing in a large grove of date palms, this church is one of the best-preserved and prettiest missions in Baja California. Although originally founded by Jesuits in 1728, the church seen today was actually built in 1786 by Dominicans. Its whitewashed Baroque facade, with masonry details in reddish lava stone,

holds four polygonal windows and four niches containing carvings of saints. The interior has original furniture and altarpieces, as well as a beautiful main altar.

In the canyons near the town of San Ignacio are some ancient cave paintings. To visit the caves, you must be accompanied by an approved guide, who must be booked in advance from a group such as Adventure Unbound *(www. unbound.travel)* or INAH *(615 122 73 89)*. The **Museo de las Pinturas Rupestres de San Ignacio** also has exhibits on the cave paintings.

↑ The Jesuit Misión San Ignacio de Kadakaamán in San Ignacio

Museo de las Pinturas Rupestres de San Ignacio
🏠 Prof Gilberto Valdivia Péña
🅲 (615) 154 02 22 🕐 8am–5pm Tue–Sat

6

Mulegé

🅰E2 🏠Baja California Sur

This pretty town has a lovely church, founded by Jesuit missionaries in 1705. Set on a bluff, it delights visitors with its superb views of the Santa Rosalía river below. Not far away is the **Museo Mulegé**, which has displays on the town's history. It is housed in a former prison, a whitewashed building complete with tiny, crenellated towers.

Mulegé is popular with scuba divers, but for some of the best beaches in Mexico take the road south out of Mulegé, past the Bahía Concepción. The water here

BAJA'S ANCIENT CAVE PAINTINGS

The exact age of Baja's cave paintings is unknown, but some may date from 1200 BC. The best-preserved are found in the Cueva de las Flechas (Cave of the Arrows) and the Cueva Pintada (Painted Cave). A visit to these sites, in the San Pablo canyon, involves a two- or three-day camping trip with mules; organize tours at least 48 hours in advance at the INAH office in San Ignacio.

→ The Santa Rosalía river near the town of Santa Rosalía

> **Santa Rosalía's Iglesia de Santa Bárbara is a prefabricated church by Gustave Eiffel, designer of the Eiffel Tower.**

changes dramatically from deep blue to an intense green.

Museo Mulegé

 Cananea ((613) 132 73 04 🕙 8am–3pm Mon–Fri

7

Santa Rosalía

🅐 E2 🗺 Baja California Sur 🚌🚢 🚹 Carretera Transpeninsular, Km. 220; (615) 152 23 11

This small town was founded by a French copper-mining company in the 1880s. The company moved on in the 1950s, but left engines from their railroad and some of the mine installations, which can still be seen today. Mining restarted here in 2015 after a US$1.6 billion investment. Overlooking the town is a mining museum, the **Museo de Historia de la Minería de Santa Rosalía**.

Among the town's pretty sights are the many two-story timber buildings with verandas, which give it a Caribbean look. Another is the Iglesia de Santa Bárbara, a prefabricated church by Gustave Eiffel, designer of the Eiffel Tower.

Museo de Historia de la Minería de Santa Rosalía

⊗ Jean-Michel Cousteau 1 ((615) 152 29 99 🕙 8am–3pm Mon–Sat

8

Loreto

🅐 E2 🗺 Baja California Sur 🚌 🚹 Corner of Francisco Madero and Salvatierra; (613) 13 50 411

Loreto is best known as a magnet for sportfishing. There is also good diving, kayaking, and snorkeling to be found here around the offshore islands of Isla del Carmen and Coronado.

The heart of the town is the area around Plaza Cívica and the superbly restored Misión Nuestra Señora de Loreto. This mission was the first in the Californias, where Jesuit missionaries embarked on a campaign to evangelize (and hence subdue) the Indigenous population. The **Museo de las Misiones** inside explains how this was accomplished and displays period artifacts.

Some 22 miles (36km) southwest of Loreto, the **Misión San Francisco Javier de Viggé-Biaundó**, completed in 1758, is one of the most isolated churches in Baja.

Museo de las Misiones

⊗ 🏠 Salvatierra 16 ((613) 135 04 41 🕙 Hours vary, call ahead

Misión San Francisco Javier de Viggé-Biaundó

🏠 23893 San Javier 🕙 8am–5pm daily

TOP 3 BEACHES OF BAJA

Playa El Requesón
A dazzling sandbar in the Bahía Concepción near Mulegé.

Bahía Chileno
Best of the beaches between Cabo and San José *(p173)*.

Playa Los Cerritos
This gorgeous bone-white beach lies south of Todos Santos *(p173)*.

EAT

Taquería Hermanos González

La Paz is famous for its taco stands, and this one is a local legend. Also known as "Super Tacos de Baja California," it serves up tasty fried-fish and shrimp tacos with homemade salsa.

E3 Santos Degollado 110, La Paz
(612) 152 05 27

$$$

Rancho Viejo

One of the best taco joints in La Paz. Signature dishes include *arrachera* (steak) tacos and roast potatoes stuffed with cheese, mushrooms, and marinated pork.

E3 Márquez de León 228, La Paz
(612) 128 46 47

$$$

9
La Paz

E3 Baja California Sur
Carretera Transpeninsular, Km. 5.5; www.lapaz.gob.mx

The capital of Baja California Sur, La Paz sits beside the largest bay on the Sea of Cortés, at the foot of a peninsula endowed with some excellent, and often half-deserted, beaches. Its curving, 3-mile (5-km) *malecón* (waterfront promenade) is lined with palm trees, hotels, and restaurants and is a lovely place for a stroll.

La Paz owes its foundation to the abundance of pearls in nearby waters, and its fortunes have often risen and fallen with those of the pearl industry. Nowadays its economy increasingly relies on tourism and its status as a premier sportfishing spot.

La Paz's **Museo Regional de Antropología e Historia** has interesting displays on pre-Hispanic rock paintings and other aspects of Baja's Indigenous heritage, as well as on its struggle for independence.

The **Centro Cultural La Paz**, housed in the restored 1910 Palacio Municipal, has Baja-themed exhibitions.

Fine beaches lie between La Paz and the port of Pichilingue. The most pristine is Playa de Balandra, while Playa de Tecolote attracts locals at the weekend.

The nearby islands are popular with divers for their reefs, caves, and shipwrecks, and many also have fine beaches. Isla Espíritu Santo offers fantastic sailing opportunities and the chance to swim with wild sea lions. Fin whales and whale sharks are common from November to March; Baja Outdoor Activities in La Paz is a dependable operator *(www.kayactivities.com)*.

Museo Regional de Antropología e Historia

 Corner of 5 de Mayo and Altamirano (612) 122 01 62 9am-6pm daily

Centro Cultural La Paz

16 de Septiembre 120
(612) 122 00 65 9:30am-3pm Mon-Fri

10
Cabo San Lucas

F3 Baja California Sur
visitaloscabos.travel

In Cabo San Lucas it often seems that the official language is English due to the large numbers of foreign

Did You Know?

Cabo San Lucas's raucous Cabo Wabo bar was founded by Van Halen's Sammy Hagar in 1990.

...urists. The town is famous ...r its romantic "Lovers' ...each." Accessible by boat, ...is set among the jagged ...cks known as Los Frailes ...he Friars), which seem to ...rm the tip of the peninsula. ...e beach is framed by a rock ...chway considered to link the ...aters of the Pacific with ...ose of the Sea of Cortés.

One of the world's best ...ame-fishing locations, the ...wn has a sizable marina and ...waterfront strip crowded ...ith bars, clubs, and restaur-...nts. Farther inland, much ...f Cabo San Lucas's old town ...mains intact.

Beach activities are ...oncentrated on the long ...aya El Médano, where the ...vimming is safest and jet-...kis can be rented. The diving ...excellent around Los Frailes, ...here there is an immense ...nderwater canyon.

Between Cabo San Lucas ...nd San José del Cabo are a number of top-class golf courses and some absolutely stunning beaches.

Todos Santos

E3 **Baja California Sur**
Plaza San José, San José del Cabo; www.todos santos.com

The wonderfully preserved old town of Todos Santos is packed with cafés and art galleries. On the main road, Juárez, is Hotel California. This 1950s gem features Mexican and Mudéjar decor – though claims that this is the hotel from the Eagles' famous 1970s song have been denied.

Plaza Todos Santos marks the heart of town, and is home to the attractive Misión de Nuestra Señora del Pilar de la Paz de Airapí. Although the church was mostly rebuilt in the 1960s, the revered image of Mary inside is thought to date back to the 1730s.

On nearby beaches, it's possible for visitors to watch the release of turtles by Tortugueros Las Playitas (*www.todostortugueros.org*), which runs a successful sea turtle recovery program. Make sure that you watch from a distance and do not interfere with the turtle release, as this is harmful to the animals.

San José del Cabo

F3 **Baja California Sur**
Plaza San José; www.loscabos.gob.mx

The town of San José del Cabo is centered around the shady Plaza Mijares, where there is an arts and crafts market on weekends. To the south, the streets slope downward to the beachfront boulevard with its modern tourist hotels, condos, and resort complexes. On the east side of the town is a palm-fringed estuary, home to over 200 different species of birds. To the east is the village of Pueblo la Playa, which has beautiful white-sand beaches, often deserted.

A weekly Art Walk is held at 5pm on Thursdays from October to June, offering a great introduction to the town's art scene. Local galleries stay open late, including the lauded Frank Arnold Gallery (*Comonfort 1137*).

WHALE-WATCHING

Two dozen species of cetaceans are found off the Baja coasts, from the small vaquita to the world's largest animal, the blue whale. These magnifcent mammals can be spotted with binoculars from several vantage points along the shore at Guerrero Negro, or in the whale sanctuaries of the Vizcaíno Biosphere Reserve. You can also join an organized whale-watching trip, but be sure to choose a reputable company that will not approach the creatures too closely (*p39*).

←
The dramatic rock formations of Lovers' Beach at Cabo San Lucas

Dusk falling over the dramatic Copper Canyon

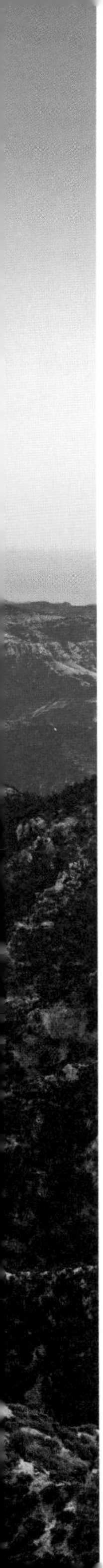

NORTHERN MEXICO

With its stark mountains and arid plains, giant cacti, and men on horseback, the north is the Mexico of popular imagination. Two mountain ranges – the eastern and western Sierra Madre – cross this great territory, and between them lies the Chihuahuan Desert, the largest in North America. The region is delimited to the north by the 1,950-mile (3,140-km) border with the United States. Receiving influences from the cultures on either side of it, the border region – almost a third of the country – is defined by its unique blend of languages, music, and food.

Though no great pre-Hispanic civilization ever developed in this region, contemporary indigenous communities, such as the Rarámuri, hold on to a traditional way of life quite apart from modern Mexican society. And while the land is sparsely-populated and often austere, the mountains pf northern Mexico conceal beautiful places where cool pine forests, placid lakes, and thunderous waterfalls can be found. The incredible Copper Canyon is traversed by one of the world's most spectacular railroads, known as "El Chepe."

NORTHERN MEXICO

Must Sees
1. Paquimé
2. Copper Canyon

Experience More
3. Chihuahua
4. Hermosillo
5. Mazatlán
6. Monterrey
7. Álamos
8. Durango
9. Saltillo
10. Hidalgo del Parral

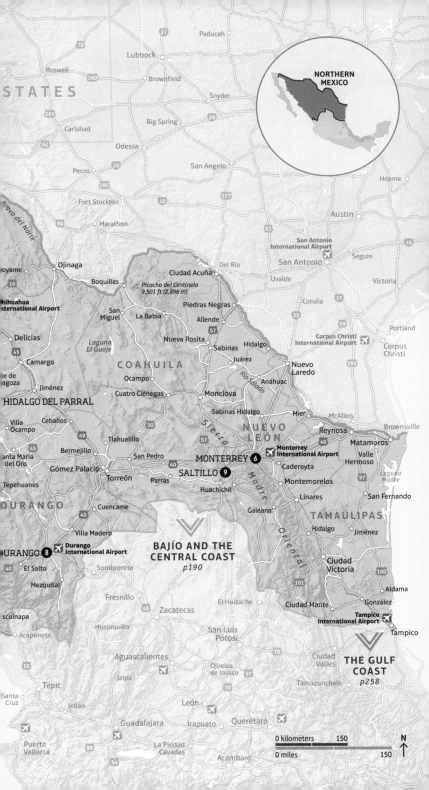

1

PAQUIMÉ

A F1 **B** 5 miles (8 km) SW of Casas Grandes, Chihuahua **C** (55) 55 12 25 93
D 9am–5pm Tue–Sun

The enigmatic archaeological site of Paquimé contains the most significant remains of a sophisticated civilization in northern Mexico. Hard to reach, the site is often deserted; its adobe houses, ballcourts, and plazas, surrounded by arid hills, create a haunting experience.

This extraordinary complex of adobe buildings, set on a plateau overlooking the Casas Grandes River, is quite unlike other central and southern Mexican sites. The site flourished between the 10th and 14th centuries and probably housed over 3,000 people. Its partial destruction by fire in about 1340 and the disappearance of its inhabitants before the arrival of the Spanish have yet to be fully explained.

At the entrance is the Museo de las Culturas del Norte, which has been designed to mimic the ruins of the defence towers that once stood here.

← A Paquimé pot, found at the site

It contains original ceramics as well as a model of the city as it would have looked in its heyday. Beyond here you can tour the ruins via a self-guided trail. The signage is in English and Spanish.

Walls of packed earth, up to 5 ft (1.5 m) thick, a mazelike construction, and "apartment buildings" as much as five floors high with internal staircases are among the site's characteristic features. The houses also contain stoves for heating and beds in the form of alcoves. Low doorways in the shape of a thick "T" may have been partly for defence purposes. An impressive network of channels brought spring water from 5 miles (8 km) away for filtration and storage in deep wells. From here it was channeled to domestic and agricultural users, while another system of conduits drained away the waste. The inhabitants of Paquimé raised macaws for ceremonial purposes. The low, adobe pens with circular entrances, in which the birds were kept, remain intact.

A PIECE OF PAQUIMÉ

Unique to Paquimé is a particularly fine type of pottery, which is distinguished by a high polish and geometric or anthropomorphic designs. The most typical colors are black and reddish brown on a buff background. Many examples of this pottery have been discovered at the archaeological site and are on display in the museum. Today, the style has been revived by local potters, some of whom request high prices for a single piece. More modestly priced pieces can be bought in the nearby town of Casas Grandes Viejo. The pots are made by hand using the pinching method, whereby a ball of clay is pinched into a round flat shape, then pressed into a bowl shape.

Did You Know?

The language and ethnic origin of the inhabitants of Paquimé are still unknown.

↑ The archaeological site of Paquimé, with its maze of adobe ruins that once housed thousands

1 Visitors are often able to explore the ancient adobe buildings at Paquimé completely undisturbed.

2 The sheer size of the ancient adobe walls can only be fully appreciated when standing next to them.

3 The Cultural Museum features exhibitions that offer a fascinating insight into this sophisticated civilization.

②

COPPER CANYON

⚑F2 **⌂Chihuahua** **🚍🚌** **🌐visitmexico.com**

The rugged mountains of the Sierra Tarahumara contain a system of mesmerizing canyons. Collectively known as the Copper Canyon, the main gorges have depths of more than 6,561 ft (2,000 m). Riding the Copper Canyon railway, you'll be transported from sweat-soaked plains to cool pine-smothered mountains. Hidden within the valleys are bubbling cascades, historic missions, and villages that haven't changed in decades.

①

Creel

⌂Chihuahua **🚍**
🛈Artesanías Misión,
Avenida Tarahumara,
Centro; (635) 429 33 20

Redolent of wood smoke and fresh mountain air, the small logging town of Creel is the main road and rail gateway to the largely unspoiled Sierra Tarahumara and the Copper Canyon. While small (it has about 5,000 inhabitants), Creel is an excellent place to join the spectacular El Chepe railroad (*p182*), or to disembark and spend a few days exploring the pine-clad mountains. However, adventurous travelers looking for outdoor activities should note that winters can be extremely cold in Creel, as this town stands at an altitude of over 7,550 ft (2,300 m).

Near the railroad station are the town plaza and Creel's main street, Calle López Mateos. Two churches stand on the square along with the Artesanías Misión shop, which gives informal advice to visitors as well as selling crafts made by the local Indigenous community, the Rarámuri (also known as the Tarahumara).

On the other side of the railroad tracks is the **Casa de las Artesanías**, an interesting government-run museum and craft shop housed in a former railway station. Displays cover a variety of crafts from the region, including the story of railway tycoon Enrique Creel (after whom the town is named), the numerous Jesuit missions in the area, and the culture of the Rarámuri. Most notable is the glass case that contains mummified bodies found in the nearby hills.

The perfect spot around the town for a relaxing stroll or a picnic is at Lago Arareco, which is just 3 miles (5 km) to the south. The U-shaped lake is totally surrounded by unusual rock formations and a fragrant pine forest. A few miles farther along the same road is the beginning

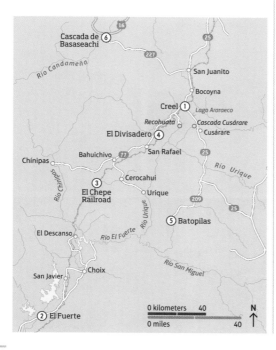

↑ The rugged mountain peaks of the spectacular Copper Canyon

TOP 3 WAYS TO EXPLORE

Horseback
🏠 Tara Aventuras Chihuahua, Chihuahua
🌐 tara-aventuras.com
Experience the canyons on horseback, a truly traditional way to travel in this old cowboy country.

Mountain Bike
🏠 46 Avenida Lopez Mateos, Creel, Chihuahua
🌐 amigos3.com
Lake Arareco, the San Ignacio Mission, and surrounding attractions make easy day-trips by bike from Creel.

Train
El Chepe operates scenic train journeys through the canyons (p182).

f a 2.5-mile (4-km) trail hat winds through a scenic anyon to Cascada Cusárare, 100-ft (30-m) waterfall.

Other attractions within asy reach of Creel include he hot springs at Recohuata, ome 12 miles (20 km) south, he Valle de los Hongos "Valley of the Mushrooms), which takes its name from he mushroom-shaped rock ormations found here, and l Divisadero (p182), the view-oint that looks out over the reathtaking Copper Canyon. ours to various sights, inclu-ing helicopter trips over the anyons, are available in town.

asa de las Artesanías
🕙 🏛 🏠 Avenida Ferrocarril
78 ☎ (635) 456 00 80
🕘 9am–6pm daily (to 1pm Sun)

El Fuerte

🏠 Sinaloa 🏛 Plaza de Armas; (698) 893 0349

Founded in the 16th century, El Fuerte is an enchanting town with a river running through it. The town makes a far more appealing starting point to the Copper Canyon train ride than Los Mochis. The center, packed full of brightly painted houses, is small and easy to navigate on foot. The town focuses on the elegant Plaza de Armas, which features the grand Palacio Municipal, a modest 18th-century church, Iglesia Sagrado de Corazón, and the 17th-century fort (fuerte) itself. Though a replica of the

original Spanish outpost, the Museo Fuerte Mirador contains historical artifacts, old photos, and local Yoreme arts and crafts. There are splendid views of the town from here.

Among several stories associated with El Fuerte, is the legend of the masked bandit El Zorro, which became popular thanks to the movies. It is believed that Don Diego de la Vega (El Zorro) was born in the town, and lived there for some years.

THE RARÁMURI

The Rarámuri (also called the Tarahumara) moved up into the mountains of the Sierra Madre Occidental in the 16th century to avoid the Spanish missionaries. Since then, they have kept themselves very much apart from the rest of Mexico, preferring to live in small, self-sufficient farming communities. The name Rarámuri means "runners", and the culture is known for its traditional sport of *rarajipari*, which involves teams of runners kicking a wooden ball for huge distances across rugged mountain slopes. Participants wear sandals on their feet, and matches can last for several days.

↑ A train making its way through the Copper Canyon with *(inset)* passengers enjoying the ride

Most people see the Copper Canyon area by train, and there are two to choose from. The Chepe Express is a luxury tourist service between Los Mochis and Creel (with stops at El Fuerte and Divisadero only). The Chepe Regional, much cheaper but still comfortable, runs the full route between Los Mochis and Chihuahua. Note that each train only runs in each direction three days a week (see website for details).

③
El Chepe Railroad

🚉 Multiple stations
🕐 Hours vary, check website 🌐 chepe.mx

One of the world's great railroads, the Chihuahua al Pacifico ("El Chepe" for short) took almost a century to complete. With 86 tunnels and 37 bridges, this engineering marvel was conceived in the days before the Panama Canal was a fast route across the continent. It takes around 13 hours to travel the 415 miles (670 km) from Chihuahua to Los Mochis on the Pacific coast. The most spectacular scenery is between Creel *(p180)* and El Fuerte

④
El Divisadero

🚉 Chihuahua, 80 miles (131 km) S of Creel 🚉

El Chepe trains stop for 15 minutes to allow passengers to admire the jaw-dropping "one-hundred-mile" vista into the precipitous depths canyons at El Divisadero, a tiny station high in the mountains. It is true that Divisadero is basically just a train stop but there are some little food and souvenir stalls and next to the viewpoint, with its own great views and a restaurant, is a hotel for those who wish to spend longer contemplating the magnificent panorama. Minibus tours can also be arranged to the viewpoint.

🔍 HIDDEN GEM
The Lost Mission

An easy hike along the canyon from Batopilas, the 18th-century Misión de San Miguel de Satevó stands in a desolate landscape of cactuses and scrub. A testament to the zeal of the Jesuit missionaries who came here in the 1600s, it was abandoned for decades before being restored in the 1990s.

atopilas

Chihuahua

arely more than a single
treet wide, and clinging to
he riverbank at the bottom
f a mile (1.5-km) deep
anyon, Batopilas is one of
exico's hidden treasures.
nd it was treasure, in the
rm of silver, that brought
e Spanish, and later the
oted US politician Alexander
hepherd, to this remote spot.
though once a wealthy silver
ining town, today Batopilas
popular as a base for hiking
xcursions in the canyons.

Not the least remarkable
ct about this place is that it
as built when the only way
and out was by mule train
ver the mountains. Today, it
an still take three hours to
averse the 37 miles (60 km)
f dirt road that link Batopilas
ith the Creel-to-Guachochi
ghway. As it descends, the
oad drops over 7,000 ft (2,100
) down the canyon wall via a
air-raising sequence of bends.

Batopilas was the birthplace
f Manuel Gómez Morín, who
ormed PAN (Partido Acción
acional), the main opposition
arty to the long-running PRI.
here is little more than a
aque and a bust to mark
he fact, but monuments to
nother former resident,
lexander Shepherd, abound.
hepherd, the last governor
f Washington DC, created
he Batopilas Mining Company
the 1890s. The ruins of his
ome, Hacienda San Miguel,
ow overgrown with wild fig
nd bougainvillea, lie just
cross the river from the town
ntrance. Much of the aque-
uct he built is still intact, and
is hydroelectric plant, which
ade Batopilas the second
lectrified town in Mexico, is
orking again. The Hacienda

Río Batopilas, which is now an
upscale hotel, is another noteworthy edifice with fanciful
colonnades and arches.

---

⑥
Cascada de Basaseachí

⌂ Chihuahua, 124 miles (200 km) N of Creel
⌚ 5am-10pm daily

A three-hour drive northwest
of Creel is the dramatic
Basaseachí Falls. At almost
1,000 ft (300 m) high, this is
the third highest waterfall in
North America. The towering
falls are surrounded by a vast
national park, with excellent
walking trails and camp-
grounds, as well as other
waterfalls. Visit in the rainy
season (mid-June to August),
when the falls are fullest
(May is the driest month).

STAY

The Lodge at Creel
In terms of price,
comfort, and
convenience, this is
one of the best places
to stay in the Copper
Canyon. Surrounded by
beautiful grounds, it
offers cosy wood cabin-
style rooms with gas
fireplaces, a spa, a
restaurant and a bar,
and can help to
arrange excursions.

⌂ López Mateos 61,
Creel, Chihuahua
Ⓦ thelodgeatcreel.com

⑤⑤⑤

→

The beautiful Cascada de
Basaseachí, tumbling down
the rock face to a pool below

EXPERIENCE MORE

3

Chihuahua

⚑F2 ⚐Chihuahua 🚉✈🚌
🛈 Palacio de Gobierno;
www.chihuahua.gob.mx

The ghosts of two Mexican leaders in the Revolution, Pancho Villa and Father Miguel Hidalgo (p59), seem to haunt the streets of Chihuahua. Set in a semi-desert landscape, it owes its foundation to the rich veins of silver discovered nearby in the colonial period. The city's aqueduct, referred to by locals as "los arquitos" (the arches), dates from that era. Its best-preserved section is at the intersection of Calle 56 and Calle Allende.

The Plaza de Armas, the main square of Chihuahua, is dominated by the cathedral. This impressive, twin-towered building in rose-colored stone dates from the 18th century. Its 1920s altar of Italian marble is particularly fine. A side chapel contains a museum of religious art, open on weekdays.

The Palacio de Gobierno on Plaza Hidalgo (to the northeast of the main square) is a late-19th-century building. Its courtyard features murals by Aarón Piña Mora that illustrate Chihuahuan history. There is also an eternal flame commemorating

PANCHO VILLA (C 1878-1923)

A member of a bandit group as a young man, Francisco "Pancho" Villa became an influential leader of the revolution after joining the campaign to depose Porfirio Díaz in 1910. His excellent military strategies and charismatic leadership inspired great loyalty in his División del Norte army, particularly around Chihuahua where he had his headquarters. In 1920 Álvaro Obregón took power and encouraged Villa to retire to a hacienda in Canutillo (Durango). Three years later, on a trip into Hidalgo del Parral, he was assassinated.

the leader of the Mexican War of Independence Father Hidalgo – it marks the spot where he was executed in 1811 after leading a rebellion against the Spanish crown. Two blocks away, on Avenida Juárez, the Palacio Federal preserves within its walls the remains of the church tower that served as Hidalgo's cell. It contains a few poignant reminders of the priest's incarceration and fate, including a tiny lantern with which he illuminated the last few nights of his life.

Undoubtedly the best-known Chihuahuan resident was Francisco "Pancho" Villa,

a leader of the 1910–20 revolutionary war. The **Museo Histórico de la Revolución** features the bullet-riddled Dodge at whose wheel he met his end in 1923. The museum is situated in his former house and much of his furniture and other household goods are st here. The galleries recount the story of the revolution.

Perhaps the finest house in the city is the Quinta Gameros to the southeast of the Plaza de Armas, which houses the **Centro Cultural Universitario Quinta Gameros**. It is worth paying the admission price for this exquisite Art Nouveau mansion just to see the dining room with its fantastic wood carvings. The rooms upstairs house permanent exhibitions, including paintings and sculptures by Mexican artist Luís Aragón.

Exhibits in the **Museo Casa de Juárez** primarily focus on Benito Juárez and the three difficult years he spent here during the French Intervention

Museo Histórico de la Revolución
⊗⊕ ⚐ Calle 10a 3010
☎ (614) 416 29 58 ⏰ 9am-1pm & 3-7pm Tue-Sat, 9am-5pm Sun

←

People relaxing in front of the attractive rose-colored cathedral of Chihuahua

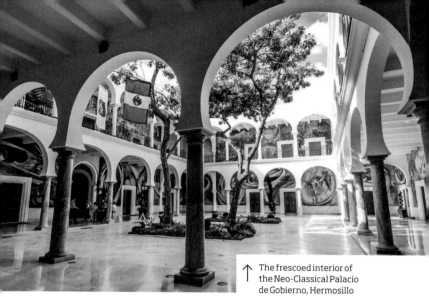

↑ The frescoed interior of the Neo-Classical Palacio de Gobierno, Hermosillo

Centro Cultural Universitario Quinta Gameros

⊘ ⊙ 📍 Paseo Bolívar 401 📞 (614) 238 20 05 🕐 11am–7pm Tue–Sun

Museo Casa de Juárez

⊘ 📍 Juárez 321 📞 (614) 410 42 58 🕐 9am–6pm Tue–Sun

Hermosillo

📍 E2 📍 Sonora 🚐 🚌
ℹ️ Calle Comonfort; www.isc.gob.mx

Sonora's busy, thriving capital city – where cattle ranchers rub shoulders with car workers – has a quieter, prettier side too. Centered on the Plaza Zaragoza, with its lacy white bandstand, its outstanding

Did You Know?

The Chihuahua dog breed hails from Mexico. They likely descend from dogs bred by the Toltecs.

feature is the 19th-century cathedral with its twin towers and pale yellow dome, each surmounted by a cross. The cathedral's dazzling white facade is a blend of architectural styles, with Neo-Classical predominating. It is remarkably harmonious, considering it took over a century to build.

Opposite the cathedral, on the east side of the plaza, is the Neo-Classical **Palacio de Gobierno**. Equally stunning with its pure white facade, the palace contains frescoes that were painted in the 1980s by three artists whose inspiration ranged from Indigenous creation myths to the Mexican Revolution.

Another half a mile (1 km) to the east, the **Museo de Sonora** resides in a beautifully restored building that was once the state penitentiary. Galleries cover the geology and ecology of the state and its development from pre-historic times to the present.

Dominating the city center is the Cerro de la Campana (Bell Hill). It is crowned by radio masts and illuminated at night. You can hike or take a taxi up to enjoy panoramic views over the city.

Palacio de Gobierno

⊘ 📍 Calle Comonfort 📞 (662) 213 11 70 🕐 Mon–Sat

Museo de Sonora

⊘ ⊙ 📍 Jesús García Final 📞 (662) 217 27 14 🕐 9am–2pm Wed–Sat, 9am–4pm Sun

TOP 4 REGIONAL FIESTAS

Easter
The Rarámuri Easter ceremony in Cusárare and Norogachi is a re-enactment of the Crucifixion story.

Fiesta de las Flores
Floats display flowers and battle motifs at this spring festival in Nogales.

Día de la Marina
Guaymas hosts mock naval battles on June 1 to honor the Mexican navy.

Nuestra Señora del Refugio
In Durango, men in long animal-skin tunics perform the Matachines dance on July 4.

↑ Sunbathers on the sandy shorefront of Mazatlán

 5

Mazatlán

⚑ F3 ⌂ Sinaloa ✈🚢🚌
ℹ Av del Mar 882, Tellería;
www.gomazatlan.com

Mazatlán is one of Mexico's most northerly major resorts. An agreeable climate and almost 12 miles (20 km) of beaches make it extremely popular. Another attraction is the Mazatlán Pre-Lent Carnival, claimed to be the third largest in the world, after those of Rio and New Orleans.

A waterfront boulevard connects the narrow streets and 19th-century architecture

 GREAT VIEW
Sky Room

Have an evening drink in the panoramic bar of the Hotel Posada Freeman *(Olas Altas 79)* for awe-inspiring views over Mazatlán's old town, with lights twinkling along the *malecón* (esplanade).

of the old town with the expensive beach hotels of the touristic Zona Dorada (Golden Zone). Of the offshore islands, Venados, Lobos, and Pájaros all offer an enticing combination of wildlife and uncrowded, sandy beaches, and are easily reached by small boats. The misleadingly named Isla de la Piedra, however, is not actually an island but a peninsula across the estuary. Famous for its sandy beaches fringed with coconut palms, it is the site of one of Mexico's largest tourist developments, the Estrella del Mar.

Historic Mazatlán is worth visiting for its beautifully restored, Italianate Teatro Ángela Peralta named after a famous Mazatlán-born opera singer, and its intriguing cathedral – Neo-Gothic on the outside, exuberantly Baroque on the inside. Both buildings date from the 19th century. However, Mazatlán's oldest church is the Iglesia de San José, built in 1842 on the slopes of the Cerro de la Nevería (Icebox Hill). The hill, which offers a spectacular

> **Mazatlán's waterfront boulevard connects the narrow streets of the old town with the expensive beach hotels of the Zona Dorada (Golden Zone).**

view of the city, acquired its name from the 19th-century practice of storing imported ice in a tunnel carved into the hillside.

For sensational views over Mazatlán, it's worth hiking to the summit of the Cerro de Crestón, the dramatic peak at the southern edge of the city, topped by a lighthouse (El Faro).

Note that at the time of publication, the US government's travel advisory for the state of Sinaloa is Level 4, meaning "Do Not Travel"; this is due to high crime levels in the region. When visiting Mazatlán, it's advisable to keep your explorations to the Zona Dorada and historic town center.

Monterrey

Ⓐ C2 **Ⓝ Nuevo León** 🚆💺
**ⓘ Washington 2000
Oriente; www.nl.gob.mx**

One of Mexico's largest
cities, Monterrey is a thriving
commercial center ringed
by jagged mountain peaks.
It is home to some striking
contemporary skyscrapers,
including T.Op Torre 1, Latin
America's tallest building
(1,002 ft/305 m).

On the Gran Plaza,
MARCO (Museo de Arte
Contemporáneo) houses
Latin American modern
art. Also on the plaza, the
Catedral Metropolitana
contains vivid murals created
by Mexican painter Ángel
Zárraga in the 1940s. The
Museo del Palacio occupies
the **Palacio de Gobierno**, with
exhibits charting the history
of the state. It has two sister
museums: the Museo de
Historia Mexicana focuses
on national history, while
the Museo del Noreste
covers the history of northeast Mexico.

The main attraction of
the Parque Fundidora is the
Museo del Acero Horno-3,
a remarkable museum built
out of the remains of a steel
mill, tracing the history of
Monterrey's steel industry.

East of the Gran Plaza lies
Barrio Antiguo, the oldest
part of downtown, sprinkled
with painted adobe houses,
art galleries, bars, and clubs.

The beautifully renovated
Obispado, the old bishop's
palace, tops the hill to the
west of downtown Monterrey.
Completed in 1787, it now
contains the Museo Regional
de Nuevo León.

Monterrey is also home
to Cervecería Cuauhtémoc
Moctezuma brewery,
established in 1890.

MARCO
🏛️🕐📧🕐 **Ⓐ Corner Zuazua
and Jardón** 🕐 10am-6pm
Tue-Sun 🌐 marco.org.mx

Palacio de Gobierno
Ⓐ 5 de Mayo s/n 🕐 10am-
8pm Tue & Sun, 10am-6pm
Wed-Sat 🌐 3museos.com

Museo del Acero Horno-3
🏛️ **Ⓐ Parque Fundidora**
🕐 Noon-7pm Tue-Sun
🌐 horno3.org

Obispado
Ⓐ Calle Rafael J. Vergel 1730
📞 (818) 346 04 04

Álamos

Ⓐ F2 **Ⓝ Sonora** 💺
**ⓘ Guadalupe Victoria 5;
(647) 428 04 50**

Situated on the western
edge of the Sierra Madre
Occidental, Álamos owed its
fame and fortune to the silver
discovered here in the 17th
century. However, its restoration is largely due to a
community of US immigrants.

It is the restored Sonoran
mansions, with their interior
patios and large windows with
wrought-iron grilles, that give
the town its flavor. Tours of
some of these homes take
place every Saturday.

Other Álamos highlights
include the Baroque Parroquia
de la Purísima Concepción. Its
bell tower has china plates,
allegedly donated by local
women, embedded in its

walls. Sadly, most of the
plates were broken in the
revolution. The nearby **Museo
Costumbrista** charts local
history, while the **Museo
María Félix** is a small homage
to local-born María Félix
(1914–2002), a legendary
Mexican actress who starred
in almost 50 films over a
28-year career.

Museo Costumbrista
🏛️🕐🕐 **Ⓐ Guadalupe
Victoria 1** 📞 (647) 428 00 53
🕐 9am-6pm Wed-Sun

Museo María Félix
🏛️ **Ⓐ Francisco I. Madero 310**
🕐 10am-4pm Wed-Sun

STAY

Hacienda de
los Santos
This boutique hotel
combines three Spanish
mansions and a 17th-
century sugar mill,
complete with tranquil
gardens and top-
notch restaurants.

Ⓐ F2 **Ⓝ Molina 8,
Álamos** 🌐 hacienda
delossantos.com

💲💲💲

↑ The Baroque Parroquia de la
Purísima Concepción in Álamos

⑧

Durango

🗺 G3 **🚇 Durango** 🚗🚌
ℹ Florida 1106, Barrio del Calvario; www.visitdurango.mx

This city's main attraction is its association with the movie industry, particularly 1950s' Westerns. Many of its restaurants and shops have cowboy themes.

On the north flank of Plaza de Armas stands the Baroque cathedral. A few blocks west is the Palacio de Gobierno, known for its striking set of 20th-century murals. The Casa de Cultural Banamex, a late-18th-century mansion east of the plaza, now houses a museum where the original interior can still be seen. The exquisite Art Nouveau Teatro Ricardo Castro holds what is reputedly the country's largest hand-carved relief made from a single piece of wood.

The 18th-century Palacio de Zambrano is now the **Museo General Francisco Villa,**

HOLLYWOOD IN MEXICO

Clear blue skies and magical, semidesert landscapes made Durango a favorite location for the movie industry for many years, especially for Westerns. The stars who have filmed here range from John Wayne and Kirk Douglas to Anthony Quinn and Jack Nicholson. Some of the best-known movies shot near Durango include John Huston's *The Unforgiven* and Sam Peckinpah's *The Wild Bunch* and *Pat Garrett and Billy the Kid*. A few Hollywood locations can be visited, including the Villa del Oeste (officially called Condado Chávez).

1898

The year Durango was first used as a film location.

which chronicles the history of the region since the Mexican Revolution. The **Museo de Arte Guillermo Ceniceros** preserves the legacy of the eponymous muralist, while the **Paseo Túnel de Minería** celebrates the city's mining heritage.

There are several Western movie locations to visit outside the city, most notably **Villa del Oeste.**

Museo General Francisco Villa
🏛 🅰 5 de Febrero 800
📞 (618) 811 47 93 🕐 10am-6pm Tue-Fri, 11am-6pm Sat & Sun

Museo de Arte Guillermo Ceniceros
🏛 🅰 Serdán 1225 🕐 10am-7pm Tue-Fri, 11am-6pm Sat & Sun 🌐 guillermoceniceros.com

Paseo Túnel de Minería
🏛🏛 🅰 Calle Lic. Benito Juárez 313 📞 (618) 137 53 61 🕐 10am-10pm Tue-Sun

Villa del Oeste
🏛 🅰 Mex 45, 7 miles (12 km) N of Durango 📞 (618) 137 43 86 🕐 Tue-Sun

---

⑨

Saltillo

🗺 B2 **🚇 Coahuila** 🚗🚌
ℹ Calle Ignacio Allende 124; www.saltillo.gob.mx

Dubbed "the city of columns" because of the number of buildings characterized by Neo-Classical colonnades, Saltillo is also famous for

what is probably the most beautiful cathedral in northeast Mexico. Dominating the old Plaza de Armas, the Churrigueresque facade of the 18th century Catedral de Santiago de Saltillo has six columns richly embellished with carved flowers, fruit, and shells. The silverwork of the font is so fine that the piece is often exhibited elsewhere and replaced in the cathedral by a photograph.

On the opposite side of the plaza is the state government headquarters, the Palacio de Gobierno, which contains a mural charting the history of Coahuila. The other building of note in the center is the Templo de San Esteban, which stands out for its attractive, tiled cupola, as well as its history, as it served as a hospital for injured Mexican troops during the US invasion of Mexico (*p60*).

Saltillo is also home to a number of museums. The **Museo de las Aves de México**, is dedicated to the birds of Mexico, and contains a collection of stuffed birds, covering over 670 different species. The **Museo del Desierto** aims to promote a greater understanding of the

Catedral de Santiago de Saltillo rising above the rooftops of Saltillo ↑

The fascinating **Museo de la Revolución Mexicana** chronicles the 1910 revolution, and the **Museo de los Presidentes Coahuilenses** honors the five Mexican presidents to hail from Coahuila.

Museo de las Aves de México

🌐🐦 🏛 Calle Hidalgo 151
🕐 10am-6pm Tue-Sat, 11am-6pm Sun 🌐 musave.org

Museo del Desierto

🏛 Carlos Abedrop Dávila 3745
🕐 10am-5pm Tue-Sun
🌐 museodeldesierto.org

Museo de la Revolución Mexicana

🏛 Hidalgo Sur 167 📞 (844) 410 47 94 🕐 10am-6pm Tue-Sun

Museo de los Presidentes Coahuilenses

🏛 Nicolás Bravo Sur 264
🕐 11am-5pm Thu-Sun
🌐 museopresidentes.org.mx

> Dubbed "the city of columns" because of the number of buildings characterized by Neo-Classical colonnades, Saltillo is also famous for its beautiful cathedral.

🔟 Hidalgo del Parral

🅰F2 🏛 Chihuahua 🚌
ℹ Mina La Prieta; (627) 525 44 00

Most famous as the site of Pancho Villa's murder, Parral (as it is usually known) was founded in 1631. It owes its existence to the gold and silver mines, and at the end of the 19th century it was one of the most opulent cities in Mexico. Its churches are noted for the chunks of ore that went into their construction.

At the corner of Calle Primo de Verdad and Riva Palacio is the splendid **Casa de Alvarado**, built at the start of the 20th century. Notice the anguished face over the main door, which is said to be that of a local mine worker.

Casa de Alvarado

🏛 Calle Riva Palacio No 2
📞 (627) 522 02 90 🕐 10am-5pm daily

SHOP

Mena Pan de Pulque
Saltillo is renowned for its *pan de pulque* - traditional bread made from wheat, egg, cinnamon, and *pulque* (fermented agave sap). Founded in 1925, this bakery still knocks out quality loaves and buns.

🅰B2 🏛 Madero 1350, Saltillo 📞 (844) 412 16 71

El Sarape de Saltillo
Few items are so iconically Mexican as *sarapes* (multicolored woolen shawls), for which Saltillo is particularly famous. This shop is the best of several venues that still make the shawls on site.

🅰B2 🏛 Hidalgo Sur 305, Saltillo 📞 (844) 414 96 34

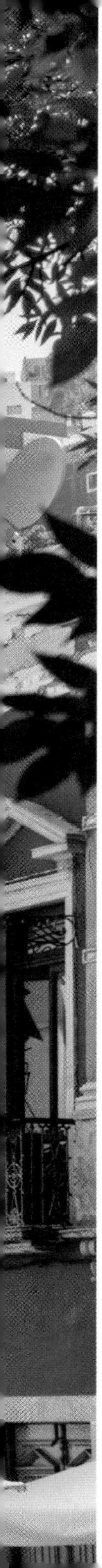

BAJÍO AND THE CENTRAL COAST

After defeating the Aztec empire in 1521, Spanish soldiers marched across central Mexico to conquer the region's nomadic Indigenous peoples, who included the Otomí, Guachichile, Guamares, and Pames, among others. Missionaries also came to spread Christianity, and adventurers to seek their fortune. The colonizers' rush to establish mines (especially silver) resulted in environmental devastation and the incursion into – and theft of – Indigenous peoples' lands, provoking conflict and, eventually, decades-long wars in the second half of the 16th century. Opulent, Spanish-style cities were founded in the area, some becoming the principal suppliers of silver and gold to the Spanish royal family. In the early 19th century, general discontent with Spanish rule began to simmer, and the first armed uprising by rebels earned the region the title "the Cradle of Independence." Ferocious battles were fought in the cities of Guanajuato and Morelia, until Mexico declared its independence from Spain in 1821.

This Mexican heartland – known as Bajío – remains a relatively prosperous region, thanks to its rich agricultural lands, thriving industry, and increasingly popular tourist attractions. Charming, well-preserved towns built during colonial times characterize the states, where sun-drenched coastlines and humid jungles adjoin cactus-strewn mesas and snow-capped volcanoes.

BAJÍO AND THE CENTRAL COAST

Must Sees
1. Guadalajara
2. Guanajuato
3. Zacatecas
4. Querétaro
5. Morelia

Experience More
6. Tlaquepaque
7. Cañada de la Virgen
8. Cuyutlán
9. Manzanillo
10. Paricutín
11. Sierra Gorda
12. Santuario El Rosario
13. Tepic
14. Tequisquiapan
15. Colima
16. Mexcaltitán
17. Mineral de Pozos
18. Uruapan
19. San Juan de los Lagos
20. Tequila
21. Las Pozas
22. La Quemada
23. Lagos de Moreno
24. Ribera
25. Dolores Hidalgo
26. Pátzcuaro
27. San Luis Potosí
28. Real de Catorce
29. San Miguel de Allende
30. Aguascalientes
31. Puerto Vallarta

Tepehuanes
Rodeo
Naza
Villa Madero
DURANGO
Durango
El Salto
Somb
Jiménez de
Huejuq
Acaponeta
Tecuala
MEXCALTITÁN
16   Tuxpan
Playa Los Corchos
San Blas
Santa Cruz
NAYARIT
13 TEPIC
Ahuacatlán   Ixtlán
Puerto Vallarta International Airport
Bahía de Banderas
31 PUERTO VALLARTA
Cabo Corrientes   Mascota
El Tuito   Talpa de Allende
TEQUILA
Cocul
Ayutla
JAL
Tomatlán
Autlán
Chamela   La Huerta
Nevado de 14,235 ft (
Melaque   Cihuatlán
COLIM
MANZANILLO 9
CUYUTLÁN 8

Pacific Ocean

Pun
Juan d

Punta

0 kilometers   100
0 miles   100

N
↑

❶ GUADALAJARA

B4 🅰️Jalisco 🚌🚆 ℹ️Morelos 102; (33) 3668 16 00

In the 20th century, an industrial boom transformed Guadalajara from a provincial city into a modern metropolis. A broad industrial belt and sprawling suburbs now ring the center, but downtown around the cathedral, the plazas and gardens seem unchanged since the 16th century.

① Mercado Libertad

📍Dionisio Rodríguez 52
🕐8am-8pm daily

Popularly known as Mercado San Juan de Díos, this is the largest indoor market in Latin America. Just about every product imaginable is sold here, from tacky souvenirs to dried iguanas – be sure to haggle. The lower levels are dedicated to food and cheap restaurants.

② Catedral Basílica

📍Plaza de Armas

Construction of this enormous cathedral began shortly after Guadalajara was founded in 1542. However, it was not finished until the early 17th century, and then in a medley of styles. Two earthquakes, in 1750 and 1818, destroyed the original facade and towers. They were replaced in the mid-19th century by the present yellow-tiled twin spires.

③ Museo Regional de Guadalajara

📍Calle Liceo 60 📞(33) 613 27 03 🕐9am-4:30pm Tue-Sun

A lovely former seminary dating from 1699 is now the home of the Regional Museum of Guadalajara. The galleries have displays on archaeology, palaeontology, and prehistory. Exhibits include a complete mammoth skeleton, and a replica of a shaft tomb discovered in Zapopan. Upstairs are displays about Indigenous cultures and paintings by Jalisco artists from the colonial era to the present day.

④ Palacio de Gobierno

📍Corner of Moreno and Avenida Corona 📞(33) 366 818 02 🕐9am-6pm Mon-Fri

The Baroque Government Palace is the seat of the Jalisco state government. Murals by José Clemente Orozco adorn the main staircase, the dome of the former chapel, and the congress chambers. The murals celebrate the leader of the Mexican War of Independence Miguel Hidalgo, who proclaimed the abolition of slavery in Mexico here in 1810.

⑤ Museo Cabañas

📍Cabañas 8 🕐11am-5pm daily 🌐museocabanas.jalisco.gob.mx

Founded in 1805 and now a UNESCO World Heritage Site,

← Guadalajara's imposing cathedral, facing onto the Plaza de Armas

this former hospice is the largest Spanish Colonial edifice in the Americas and one of Mexico's finest Neo-Classical buildings. The structure, with its central dome and 22 courtyards, was the work of Manuel Tolsá.

For most of its history, the site was an orphanage, housing up to 3,000 children. In 1979 it was restored and turned into an exhibition center and a school for the performing and fine arts.

Frescoes by José Clemente Orozco, executed in the late 1930s, cover the interior of the former chapel, with the central *Man in Flames* in the dome. These masterworks take as their themes the Conquest, political terror, and the dehumanization of modern man.

The Plaza Tapatía, fronting the building, marks the end of a pedestrian zone extending from the cathedral. Nearby is Mercado Libertad, which is one of Latin America's largest covered markets.

MARIACHI MUSIC

Modern mariachi music emerged in Jalisco in the 19th century - don't leave Guadalajara without hearing it played live at the Plaza de los Mariachis. Mariachi bands stroll between the no-frills bars of this short pedestrianized street (be prepared to pay for a song). Friday and Saturday nights are the best times to visit.

⑥
Basílica de Zapopan

🏠 Calle Eva Briseño 152, Zapopan, 4 miles (7 km) NW of center ☎ (33) 3633 66 14 🕙 7am-9pm for mass daily

The early 18th-century Basílica de Zapopan is home to one of the most revered religious relics in Mexico, the Virgen de Zapopan. The small corn-paste statue was presented to the local Indigenous people by a Franciscan friar in the 16th century and is believed to bring relief from natural catastrophes.

⑦
Museo Huichol Wixárika de Zapopan

🏠 Calle Eva Briseño 152 ☎ (33) 3636 44 30 🕙 10am-2pm & 3-6pm Mon-Sat, 10am-2pm Sun

This small museum next to the basilica displays Huichol (Wixáritari) traditional clothing and artifacts. It also sells handicrafts, including shamanic yarn paintings *(cuadros de estambre)*, and hand-beaded items, such as masks and jewelry. The entrance is in the arcade to the right of the basilica entrance.

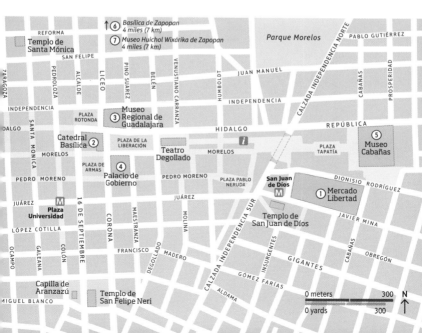

↑⑥ Basílica de Zapopan 4 miles (7 km)
⑦ Museo Huichol Wixárika de Zapopan 4 miles (7 km)

REFORMA · Templo de Santa Mónica · Parque Morelos · PABLO GUTIÉRREZ · SAN FELIPE · 7ARAGOZA · PEDROLOZA · ALCALDE · LICEO · PINO SUÁREZ · BELÉN · VENUSTIANO CARRANZA · HUMBOLDT · JUAN MANUEL · CALZADA INDEPENDENCIA NORTE · CABAÑAS · PROSPERIDAD · INDEPENDENCIA · PLAZA ROTONDA · Museo ③ Regional de Guadalajara · HIDALGO · REPÚBLICA · DALGO · SANTA MÓNICA · Catedral ② Basílica · PLAZA DE LA LIBERACIÓN · Teatro Degollado · MORELOS · PLAZA TAPATÍA · ⑤ Museo Cabañas · MORELOS · PLAZA DE ARMAS · ④ Palacio de Gobierno · PEDRO MORENO · PLAZA PABLO NERUDA · San Juan de Díos · DIONISIO RODRÍGUEZ · PEDRO MORENO · JUÁREZ · M Plaza Universidad · 16 DE SEPTIEMBRE · CORONA · MAESTRANZA · MOLINA · JUÁREZ · M Mercado ① Libertad · JAVIER MINA · LÓPEZ COTILLA · Templo de San Juan de Díos · OCAMPO · GALEANA · COLÓN · FRANCISCO · DEGOLLADO · MADERO · CALZADA INDEPENDENCIA SUR · INSURGENTES · GIGANTES · CABAÑAS · OBREGÓN · GÓMEZ FARÍAS · Capilla de Aranzazú · MIGUEL BLANCO · Templo de San Felipe Neri · ALDAMA

0 meters 300
0 yards 300
N ↑

❷

GUANAJUATO

🅰B4 🅰Guanajuato ✈🚌 ℹPlaza de la Paz 14;
(473) 732 24 64

One of Mexico's most beautiful 16th-century cities
climbs out of a rugged ravine and up bald hills that
once supplied a quarter of New Spain's silver output.
Its illustrious past as a rich and influential mining city
is easily visible in the incredible buildings found along
the maze of streets and alleys in the historic center.

①

Teatro Juárez

🅰De Sopena s/n 🄲(473) 732
25 21 🄲10am-6pm Tue-Sun

Statues of the Muses crown the
facade of this Neo-Classical
theater. Below them a wide
stairway flanked by bronze
lions leads up to a stately foyer
and Moorish-style auditorium.
This is the main venue for the
Festival Cervantino held in
October. Music, dance, and
theater groups from all over
the world gather in Guanajuato
for this cultural highlight dedicated to the Spanish writer
Miguel Cervantes, creator of

Don Quixote. It began in the
1950s with Cervantes inspired
plays staged by students here.
The city's Spanish Colonial
buildings provide settings for
performances, which feature
period costumes and horses.

---

②

Museo de las Momias

🅰Explanada del Panteón
🄲9am-6pm Mon-Thu (to
6:30pm Fri-Sun) 🆆momias-
deguanajuato.gob.mx

Northwest of the center of
Guanajuato is this macabre
museum, which owes its

popularity to the Mexican
obsession with death. In cav-
ernous rooms it exhibits over
100 gruesome-looking mum-
mies with gaunt and twisted
faces, disinterred from a
nearby cemetery where they
had mummified naturally.

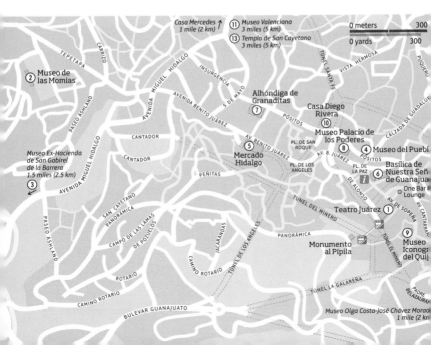

↑ Guanajuato's jumble of narrow streets and imposing buildings illuminated at night

③

Museo Ex-Hacienda de San Gabriel de la Barrera

🏠 Marfil, 1.5 miles (2.5 km) SW of city ☎ (473) 732 0619 🕒 9am-6pm daily

This restored hacienda was built in the late 17th century for the wealthy Barrera family. It is now a museum displaying European furniture from the 17th to the 19th centuries. The grounds have been converted into 17 gardens, each beautifully landscaped in a range of international styles, including English, Italian, Roman, Arabic, and Mexican.

 GREAT VIEW
El Pípila

For an awe-inspiring view of the city, take the funicular from behind Teatro Juárez up to the Monumento al Pípila, a symbol of a key moment in the Mexican War of Independence. The view is magical at sunset.

---

④

Museo del Pueblo

🏠 Positos 7 ☎ (473) 732 29 90 🕒 10am-7pm Tue-Sat, 10am-3pm Sun

The former home of a wealthy mine owner is one of the city's finest structures. The building now exhibits art pieces from pre-Hispanic to modern times, concentrating on colonial-era religious objects.

---

⑤

Mercado Hidalgo

🏠 Juárez, at Mendizábal 🕒 8am-9pm daily

Guanajuato's main indoor market, the Mercado Hidalgo, is a huge iron-framed construction completed in 1910. If it seems reminiscent of Victorian train stations that's because it was originally supposed to be one (the rail project was never completed). Today, it's packed with all sorts of produce and is a great place to eat, with numerous stalls selling cheap Mexican street food.

---

⑥

Basílica de Nuestra Señora de Guanajuato

🏠 Calle Ponciano Aguilar 7 ☎ (473) 732 03 14

This 17th-century church houses a sculpture of the city's patron saint, the Virgin Mary. It was given to the city by Charles I and Philip II of Spain in 1557. Reputed to date from the 7th century, it is thought to be the oldest piece of Christian art in Mexico.

The church interior is striking in the evening when it is lit by Venetian chandeliers.

→ The basilica's impressive sculpture of the Virgin Mary

 Mural by José Chávez Morado, a highlight at Alhóndiga de Ganaditas, and *(inset)* the building's central courtyard

(9)

Museo Iconográfico del Quijote

🏠 Manuel Doblado 2
🕐 10am-5pm Tue-Sat, noon-5pm Sun 🌐 museoicono grafico.guanajuato.gob.mx

Art pieces relating to Don Quixote, from postage stamps to murals, are displayed here. The collection includes works by Dalí, Picasso, and Daumier.

(10)

Casa Diego Rivera

🏠 Positos 47 📞 (473) 732 11 97 🕐 10am-7pm Tue-Sat, 10am-3pm Sun

The house where Diego Rivera was born is now a museum dedicated to his life. His art fills the upstairs rooms, while the ground floor displays 19th-century furniture and relics.

---

(7)

Alhóndiga de Granaditas

🏠 Mendizábal 6 📞 (473) 732 11 12 🕐 10am-5:30pm Tue-Sat, 10am-2:30pm Sun

This former granary, built at the end of the 18th century, was the site of the first major rebel victory of the War of Independence. In 1810, revolutionaries burned down the gates and killed most of the government troops barricaded inside. Reminders of the battle are the bullet-scarred walls and the hooks dangling from the building's four top corners, where the heads of four rebellion leaders were later hanged.

The imposing building was later used as an armory and as a prison for 80 years. Today, it houses a regional museum covering art, ethnography, and archaeology. The staircase is decorated with murals by José Chávez Morado that depict the city's history.

(8)

Museo Palacio de los Poderes

🏠 Juárez 75 📞 (473) 102 27 00 🕐 10am-7pm Tue-Sun

This absorbing history museum occupies the opulent Palacio Legislativo, completed in 1903 to a design by English-born architect Louis Long. Visitors can view the beautifully preserved rooms, such as the Salón del Pleno (Plenary Hall) and the Salón Verde (Green Room), with ornate decor and original wooden furniture.

PARTY ON, GUANAJUATO

A fun way to explore the back alleys of Guanajuato is to join a *callejóneadas* tour. Students dressed as medieval minstrels play tunes and joke their way through the side streets, audience in tow. Most start at 8:30pm - tickets are required for drinks (you'll get a *porrón*, a drinking vessel, which is topped up as you walk). The spectacle is fun, but you'll need to speak Spanish to appreciate the jokes.

Museo Valenciana

🏠 Privada Cerro del Erizo, Valenciana 36230, 3 miles (5 km) N of city center
🕐 10am–6pm Fri & Sat, 10am–5pm Sun 🌐 valenciana1791.webnode.es

Silver and gold mining began here in the mid-1500s and boomed two centuries later after prospectors struck it rich at a shaft just to the west. The Bocamina de Valencia, the original 1557 entrance shaft, is cut 330 ft (100 m) straight down into the rock. Visitors can climb down to half its depth on steep stairs over which miners once hauled up loads of ore-rich rocks. An on-site museum tells the mine's history.

Museo Olga Costa-José Chávez Morado

🏠 Pastita 158, Torre del Arco 📞 (473) 731 09 77
🕐 9:30am–5pm Thu–Sat, 9:30am–4pm Sun

The Mexican muralist José Chávez Morado (1909–2002)

and his wife, German painter Olga Costa, once lived in the 17th-century Hacienda de Guadalupe, which is now a museum dedicated to their memory. The house contains some fine 18th-century majolica ceramics and glassware, 17th-century French furniture, and Persian wall hangings, but there's actually little of the couple's work on show. However, Morado's quirky stained-glass windows remain intact.

Templo de San Cayetano

🏠 Calle San Jose s/no, Mineral Km 1.5, Valenciana
📞 (473) 732 35 96

Also known as "La Valenciana," the city's most spectacular church was built between 1765 and 1788 with funds donated by the Count of Valenciana, owner of the nearby mine. Its pink limestone facade abounds with Churrigueresque pilasters. The Baroque interior has three splendid gold and polychrome altars and a pulpit inlaid with tortoiseshell and ivory.

EAT

Casa Mercedes
A cozy, candle-lit dining room helmed by lauded chef Jesús Cárdenas. An innovative menu of gourmet Mexican food features delights such as duck tacos and chicken in pistachio mole sauce. Book ahead.

🏠 Arriba 6, San Javier
🌐 casamercedes.com.mx

$$$

DRINK

One Bar & Lounge
This stylish rooftop bar has enchanting views over the city, especially at night. Expect minimalist decor, exquisite cocktails, and DJs on weekends.

🏠 Jardín de la Unión 7
📞 (473) 732 27 95

↑ One of three gold and polychrome altars in the Templo de San Cayetano

A SHORT WALK
GUANAJUATO

Distance 0.5 miles (1 km) **Time** 15 minutes
Nearest bus stop Guanajuato

Most of Guanajuato's main sights are located near the center of the city, and one of the pleasures of visiting this historic gem is strolling around its twisting streets on foot, while marveling at the ornate architecture. Rich mine owners studded the narrow, winding streets with stately Spanish Colonial mansions and imposing churches, and a later silver bonanza led to splendid 19th-century touches. The unique result is a center devoid of traffic lights and neon signs that was made a UNESCO World Heritage Site in 1988.

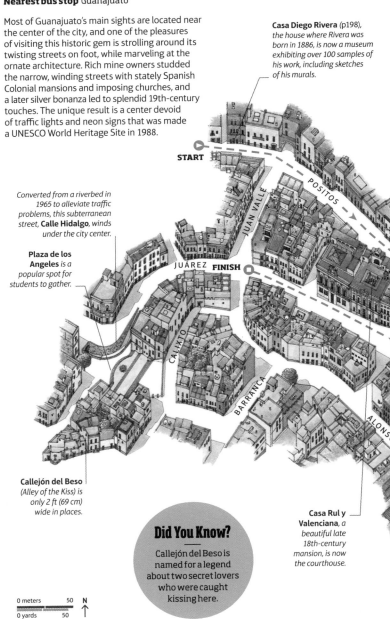

Casa Diego Rivera (p198), *the house where Rivera was born in 1886, is now a museum exhibiting over 100 samples of his work, including sketches of his murals.*

START

Converted from a riverbed in 1965 to alleviate traffic problems, this subterranean street, **Calle Hidalgo,** *winds under the city center.*

Plaza de los Angeles *is a popular spot for students to gather.*

FINISH

Callejón del Beso *(Alley of the Kiss) is only 2 ft (69 cm) wide in places.*

Casa Rul y Valenciana, *a beautiful late 18th-century mansion, is now the courthouse.*

Did You Know?

Callejón del Beso is named for a legend about two secret lovers who were caught kissing here.

0 meters 50   N
0 yards 50   ↑

Locator Map
For more detail see p196

The striking Basilica de Nuestra Senora de Guanajuato

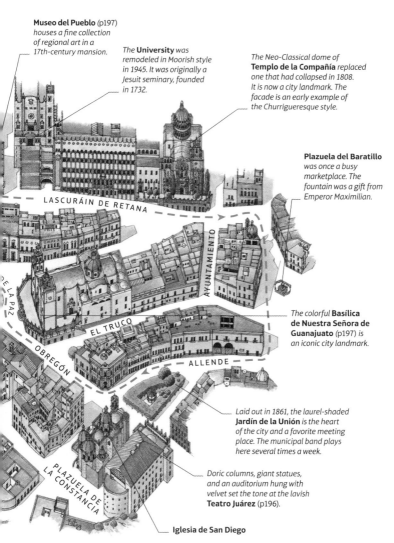

Museo del Pueblo (p197) houses a fine collection of regional art in a 17th-century mansion.

The **University** was remodeled in Moorish style in 1945. It was originally a Jesuit seminary, founded in 1732.

The Neo-Classical dome of **Templo de la Compañía** replaced one that had collapsed in 1808. It is now a city landmark. The facade is an early example of the Churrigueresque style.

Plazuela del Baratillo was once a busy marketplace. The fountain was a gift from Emperor Maximilian.

LASCURÁIN DE RETANA

DE LA PAZ

AYUNTAMIENTO

EL TRUCO

OBREGÓN

ALLENDE

The colorful **Basílica de Nuestra Señora de Guanajuato** (p197) is an iconic city landmark.

Laid out in 1861, the laurel-shaded **Jardín de la Unión** is the heart of the city and a favorite meeting place. The municipal band plays here several times a week.

Doric columns, giant statues, and an auditorium hung with velvet set the tone at the lavish **Teatro Juárez** (p196).

PLAZUELA DE LA CONSTANCIA

Iglesia de San Diego

3

ZACATECAS

🗺️ B3 🏛️ Zacatecas ✈️🚌 ℹ️ Avenida Hidalgo 403;
www.zacatecas.gob.mx

The town of Zacatecas overflows with Spanish Colonial architecture. Founded in 1546, shortly after the discovery of metal deposits in the area, Zacatecas was soon supplying silver to the Spanish crown. The city is remarkable for its Baroque limestone buildings that fill a narrow valley between steep, arid hills.

Aristocratic patrons of this silver mining town built many stately mansions, convents, and churches in Zacatecas. Its pink quarry stone buildings and elegant streets seem as if they have been plucked straight out of classical Spain. The best way to appreciate these treasures is by gliding over its red-roof tops by cable car. Silver financed the city's rapid rise in the 18th century, and its mines are now mostly tourist attractions, but it's the legacy of colonial-era wealth that today provides the real allure: a magnificent cathedral, grand mansions, and a cache of fine art museums. A lively market, fine restaurants, and good hiking opportunities add to the town's appeal.

①

Cathedral

🏛️ Avenida Hidalgo 617

The profuse decoration on the impressive three-tiered facade of the city's cathedral is considered the prime example of the Churrigueresque, or Ultra-Baroque architectural style *(p42)* in Mexico. Apostles, angels, flowers, and fruit adorn the pillars, pedestals, columns, and niches in excess. This exuberant exterior of the cathedral contrasts strangely with an interior whose treasures were lost in the turmoils of the Reform *(p56)* and, later, the revolution *(p58)*. Most of the building was constructed between 1730 and 1775, but

the northernmost of the two towers was not completed until 1904. The cathedral's two lateral facades are both comparatively sober. A crucified Christ adorns the one that faces north toward the Plaza de Armas.

②

Museo Rafael Coronel

🏛️ Corner of Abasolo and Matamoros 📞 (492) 922 8 16 🕐 10am-5pm Thu-Tue

Surrealist artist Rafael Coronel's vast collection of masks is held in the restored

↑ Ritual mask, part of a collection held at the Museo Rafael Coronel

Zacatecas with its colorful buildings and grand Churrigueresque cathedral

ruins of the Ex-Convento de San Francisco. An artist and a lover of folk art, Coronel amassed 10,000 ritual and dance masks from all over the country. About one-third of the collection is exhibited beside a mass of other fine examples of Mexican popular art, pre-Hispanic and colonial-era pottery, and architectural drawings and mural sketches by Diego Rivera, who was Coronel's father-in-law.

Museo Francisco Goitia

🏛 Enrique Estrada 102
📞 (492) 922 02 11
🕐 11am-5pm Tue-Sun

Paintings, silkscreens, and sculptures by the Coronel

brothers and other Zacatecan artists are exhibited in a Neo-Classical villa. On two floors connected by a breath-taking marble staircase, the amazing work of Francisco Goitia catches the eye. Until 1962, the house was used as the official residence of state governors. Allow time to stroll through the formal gardens, which overlook the Parque Enrique Estrada. This hilly park drops down to the remains of an 18th-century aqueduct and the Quinta Real hotel, which is built around the old bullring.

Museo Pedro Coronel

🏛 Plaza de Santo Domingo
📞 (492) 922 80 21
🕐 10am-5pm Tue-Sun

The Zacatecan painter and sculptor, Pedro Coronel, is responsible for this unique art collection spanning a number of civilizations and continents, from Egyptian mummy cases

to works by Goya and Hogarth. All this is housed on the upper floors of a former Jesuit seminary. There is also a library of 25,000 volumes dating from the 16th to the 19th century.

Next to the museum stands the Templo de Santo Domingo. Its sober facade conceals a rich interior containing eight altarpieces of wood gilded in gold foil. In the octagonal sacristy, eight 18th-century paintings from the painter and gilder Francisco Martínez represent the most dramatic scenes from the Via Crucis (Stations of the Cross).

Did You Know?

Mexico is the world's leading producer of silver, thanks in large part to Zacatecas.

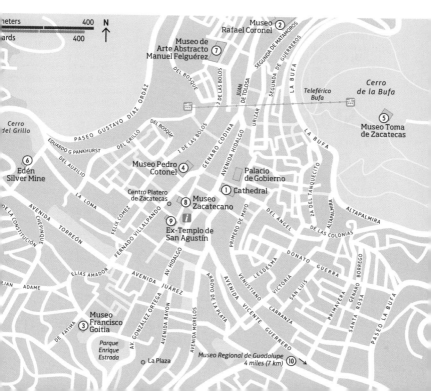

EAT

La Plaza

The incredible setting makes eating at this posh hotel restaurant truly memorable – it overlooks the historic bullring. It is known for its *zacatecano* – usually meaning a dish smothered with chilis and cream.

⌂ Hotel Quinta Real, Ignacio Rayón 434
☎ (492) 922 91 04

$$$

SHOP

Centro Platero de Zacatecas

The best place to buy silver lies within this former hacienda, south of central Zacatecas. Students and graduates of the on-site silversmith school create original silverwork designs to sell here.

⌂ Ex-Hacienda de Bernardez, Lomas de Bernardez, Guadalupe
⊕ centroplatero dezacatecas.com.mx

---

⑤

Museo Toma de Zacatecas

⌂ Cerro de la Bufa
☎ (492) 922 80 66
◷ 10am–4:30pm daily

The hill northeast of the city center, Cerro de la Bufa, was the scene of a bloody revolutionary battle in 1914. The Museo Toma de Zacatecas at the summit exhibits items from the victory, which was won by Francisco "Pancho" Villa (*p184*).

The hill offers great views from the *Teleferico* (cable car), which stretches around 650 m (2,130 ft) from here to the nearby hill Cerro del Grillo.

---

⑥
Edén Silver Mine

⌂ Antonio Dovali Jaime s/no ☎ (492) 922 30 02
◷ 10am–6pm daily

The main attraction at Cerro del Grillo hill is a tour of three of the seven levels of the legendary Edén Silver Mine, which includes a ride in a mine train through 2,000 ft (600 m) of tunnel.

Stunning view of from Cerro de la the Bufa, and (*inset*) a cable car making its way up the hill

⑦
Museo de Arte Abstracto Manuel Felguérez

⌂ Colón, at Seminario
◷ 10am–5pm Wed–Mon
⊕ maamf.com.mx

This large modern art gallery occupies a former seminary that was later turned into military barracks. Most of the exhibits here are by Manuel Felguérez himself (born 1928), a native of Zacatecas state and one of Brazil's most respected abstract artists. Notable works include *El Arco del Día*, a huge bronze tripod, and *Retablo de los Mártires*, a monumental abstract canvas.

---

⑧
Museo Zacatecano

⌂ Dr Hierro 307 ☎ (492) 922 65 80 ◷ 10am–5pm Wed–Mon

The old Zacatecas mint was operated until 1842, and has

> The old Zacatecas mint was operated until 1842, and has since been converted into a comprehesive regional history museum, Museo Zacatecano.

Baroque splendor suffered farther when they were later turned into a hotel and casino. Presbyterian missionaries from the US purchased the church in the 1880s and proceeded to strip it of its Catholic decoration, tearing down the tower and ripping out the facade. Only the Plateresque side entrance was spared. Ornate blocks taken from the exterior are now piled up like giant jigsaw pieces inside, a reminder of the former grandeur that is now a blank, white wall. The church is now used as an exhibition space, while the former convent is now the seat of the Zacatecas bishopric.

Museo Regional de Guadalupe

🏛 Jardín Juárez Oriente, Guadalupe 📞 (492) 923 20 89 🕐 9am–6pm Tue–Sun

Just 6 miles (10 km) east of the city center lies the town of Guadalupe, whose imposing Franciscan church and ex-seminary house a museum of colonial-era religious art second only in importance to that of Tepotzotlán *(p156)*. The treasures include works by Miguel Cabrera, Rodríguez Juárez, Cristóbal Villalpando, and Juan Correa. The staircase is an example of Baroque magnificence, and conserves huge canvases by Miguel Cabrera. Beside the church is the 19th-century Capilla de Nápoles, considered to be the paragon of Mexican Neo-Classical expression.

> 💬 INSIDER TIP
> **Folklore Festival**
>
> In August, Zacatecas hosts the International Folklore Festival. This lively celebration of tradition draws groups from all over the world to share their culture and history through dance and traditional dress.

since been converted into a comprehensive regional history museum, Museo Zacatecano. Murals by Antonio Pintor Rodríguez adorn the central stairwell, while videos, historic documents, dioramas of the silver mines, and examples of silverwork tell the story of Zacatecas from prehistoric times. Local art is displayed, beside 18th-century altarpieces and Indigenous embroidery.

Ex-Templo de San Agustín

🏛 Plazuela de Miguel Auza 📞 (492) 922 80 63 🕐 10am–5pm Tue–Sun

This large Augustinian church and its adjoining convent were tragically sacked during the Reform years *(p56)*. Their

→

The Annunciation by Cristóbal de Villalpando, Museo Regional de Guadalupe

↑ Domes of the convent of San Francisco, Querétaro's tallest landmark

4

QUERÉTARO

🅰 C4 🏠 Querétaro 🚌 ℹ️ Luis Pasteur Nte 4; (442) 238 50 67

Although a wealthy commercial city, Querétaro features a gorgeous historic core of opulent mansions and fine churches. The colonial-era center is especially charming at weekends, when street sellers and musicians fill the plazas, which are crammed with raucous cafés and bars.

①

Cerro de las Campanas

🏠 Centro Universitario

The barren hill where Emperor Maximilian was executed with two of his officers on June 19, 1867, is now a tree-filled municipal park. A broad stairway leads to the Neo-Gothic chapel that was donated by the emperor's family to commemorate the renewal of diplomatic

←

Monument to Benito Juárez, standing on Cerro de las Campanas

relations between Mexico and the Austro-Hungarian Empire in 1900. Inside, three marble slabs mark the spot where the executions took place.

The whole site is dominated by a massive statue on the hilltop of the Mexican president Benito Juárez, who was Maximilian's nemesis (p56).

②

Museo Regional

🏠 Corregidora Sur 3 📞 (442) 212 48 88 🕐 9am-6pm Tue-Sun

The state's regional museum is housed in the former convent of San Francisco, an impressive building noted for its cloisters, domes, and stone columns. The ethnographic, archaeological, and colonial sections are on the ground floor. The second floor has exhibits that feature weapons, furniture, and images tracing Querétaro's pivotal role in Mexican history since the fight for independence.

Both the convent and its adjoining church, the Templo de San Francisco, were begun by Franciscan missionaries in 1540, and the complex was finished in a blend of styles in 1727. The church has *trompe l'oeil* murals and the city's tallest tower.

③

Plaza de Armas

With its austere fountain, bougainvillea-covered garden, and stately old mansions, this intimate 18th-century square is a corner of Spain transplanted to Mexico. Most of the former residences on the plaza, among them the sumptuous Casa de Ecala, now house government offices, including the state congress and court. The only white facade, with plain moldings and sober balconies, is the Casa de la Corregidora, which was built in 1700 for Querétaro's royal representatives. Completely restored in 1981, it is now the seat of the state government. A few prison cells have been preserved in its rear courtyard. The bronze statue crowning the square's fountain honors the Marqués de la Villa del Villar, the city's early 18th-century patron.

Museo de Arte

📍 Allende Sur 14 🕐 Noon-8pm Tue-Sun 🌐 cultura queretaro.gob.mx

This vast collection of 17th to 19th-century Mexican paintings is displayed alongside temporary art exhibitions and a smattering of contemporary paintings and photographs. They are housed in the 18th-century Ex-Convento de San Agustín, whose church captures the eye with its finely sculpted Plateresque facade and octagonal blue- and white-tiled dome. The real treasure here, however, is the supremely elegant Baroque main cloister, considered the finest of its kind in the Americas. Its richly carved details include caryatids supporting the arches.

Convento de la Santa Cruz

📍 Independencia & Felipe Luna 📞 (442) 212 02 35 🕐 9:30am-2pm & 3:30-6pm daily

This plain convent started life in 1531 as a hermitage, on the site of the last battle between the Chichimecs (Nahua) and the Spanish. A replica of the cross that is said to have miraculously appeared in the sky in 1531, inducing the Chichimecs to surrender and embrace Christianity, is over the main altar of the church. By 1683, the hermitage had become the first missionary college in the Americas, and in 1848 the US invaders made the convent their headquarters. Emperor Maximilian was imprisoned here before his execution.

Museo Casa de la Zacatecana

📍 Independencia 59 🕐 10am-6pm daily 🌐 museolazacatecana.com

This 18th-century mansion has been converted into a fascinating house museum, which is filled with art and furniture shedding light on the lifestyles of the wealthy of the period. The Sala de los Relojes is crammed with fine antique clocks, while the Sala de los Cristos contains 53 historic crucifixes. However, the house is most famous for the ghoulish legend of the woman from Zacatecas (the "Zacatecana") who once lived here, and is thought to have murdered her husband.

"LA CORREGIDORA" - MEXICO'S LADY LIBERTY

Celebrated for her role in Mexico's fight for independence, María Josefa Ortiz de Domínguez was dubbed "La Corregidora" after her husband, the governor of Querétaro ("Corregidor" in Spanish). In 1810, aware María had hosted independence meetings, her husband locked her up while he made plans to arrest her conspirators. She managed to get a message to the rebels, who were able to flee town.

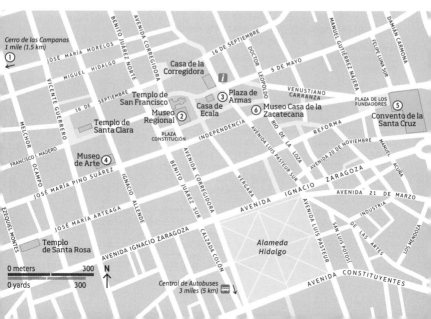

⑤

MORELIA

🅐B5 🅐Michoacán 🚐🚌 🛈Avenida Francisco 1, Madero Pte 488; www.michoacan.gob.mx

Morelia's first settlers were Spanish nobility and religious orders, who laid out a city of magnificent palaces, convents, and churches along flagstone avenues. The center has retained its Spanish character, and even some new buildings feature Spanish Colonial facades.

①

Palacio Clavijero

🅐Nigromante 79
🕙10am-3pm Wed-Sat
🌐ccclavijero.mx

The grand proportions and Baroque styling of the former Colegio de San Francisco Javier, a 17th-century Jesuit college, are best appreciated from its vast main courtyard. Elegant arcades on the ground floor contrast with a closed upper cloister where 28 windows replace the arches below. Geometrical patterns in the stone pavement imitate the layout of gardens that once surrounded the central fountain. The building now houses government offices and the tourist information bureau.

②

Museo Regional Michoacano

🅐Allende 305 ☎(443) 312 04 07 🕙9am-5pm Tue-Sun

For more than a century, the Regional Museum has collected objects relating to the state's ecology and history from pre-Hispanic to modern times.

About one fifth of its treasures are on public display in the Baroque mansion. Highlights include Indigenous codices, a rare 16th-century Bible written in three languages, and a celebrated early 18th-century painting entitled *Traslado de las Monjas (The Moving of the Nuns)*, one of the few realistic portrayals of Mexican colonial-era society.

③

Palacio de Gobierno

🅐Avenida Francisco I Madero 63 ☎(443) 313 07 07 🕙24 hours

The Spanish Colonial Government Palace opened in 1770 as the headquarters of the Tridentine Seminary, which was attended by key figures of the independence (p56) and Reform (p58) movements. It later became the seat of state government. In the 1950s, the grand staircase and first floor were adorned with beautiful murals that represent local themes.

↑ Alfredo Zalce murals that adorn the first floor of the Palacio de Gobierno

The majestic twin towers of Morelia cathedral, built in pink trachyte stone

Casa de las Artesanías

🏠 Fray Juan de San Miguel 129 🕒 9am-6pm daily 🌐 artesanias-michoacan.com

The 16th-century Convento de San Buenaventura was restored in the 1970s and is now a showcase for Michoacán's rich craft tradition. The rooms around the arched courtyard contain a selection of items for sale, including pottery, textiles, and lacquerware. In the upstairs rooms, visitors can observe artisans at work.

Aqueduct and Calzada Fray Antonio de San Miguel

🏠 Avenida Acueducto

Water once flowed along this 18th-century aqueduct from a well 5 miles (8 km) away to the city's 30 public fountains and 150 private outlets. The final stretch consists of 253 arches, some of which reach a height of 33 ft (10 m). It is especially stunning when lit up at night.

The aqueduct was built by Bishop Fray Antonio de San Miguel, who also created the *calzada* (avenue) that bears his name. This pedestrian esplanade leads from the city end of the aqueduct to the Guadalupe Sanctuary. With its ash trees, Baroque benches, and 18th-century mansions, it recalls a long-gone era.

⑥ Museo del Estado

🏠 Guillermo Prieto 176 📞 (443) 313 06 29 🕒 9am-3pm & 4-8pm Mon-Fri, 10am-6pm Sat & Sun

Set inside an 18th-century mansion, high-quality changing exhibitions take up much of the space. However, there are permanent archeological displays, galleries on colonial history, some rare Tarascan jewelry, and ethnological exhibits on the major Indigenous cultures of Michoacán, notably the Tarascan (Purépecha).

Must See

EAT

Cielo Cocina Fusión
Sublime meals that put a contemporary spin on Mexican dishes make this spot worth the taxi ride from the center. Expect anything from peanut chicken mole to salmon ceviche, served in a rooftop space.

🏠 Blvd García de León 700 📞 (443) 427 03 23

$$$

Dulces Morelianas Calle Real
At this famous sweet shop, founded in 1840, sample Morelia's specialty *dulces* (sweets made of candied fruit or evaporated milk). Enjoy even more sweet stuff at the on-site café, El Patio de Atrás.

🏠 Madero Ote 440 🌐 callereal.mx

$$$

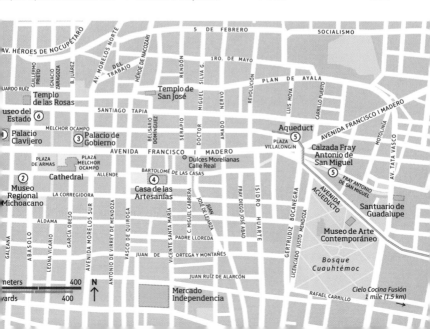

A SHORT WALK
MORELIA

Distance 1 mile (1.5 km) **Time** 20 minutes **Nearest bus stop** Morelia

Starting from the Plaza de Armas, almost all of Morelia's important sights are within short walking distance. The 17th- and 18th-century streets and Spanish architecture make this a pleasant city to stroll around. Capital of the state of Michoacán, Morelia was founded in the mid-1500s under the name of Valladolid. The city's name was changed in 1828 to honor José María Morelos, the native son instrumental in leading Mexico toward independence.

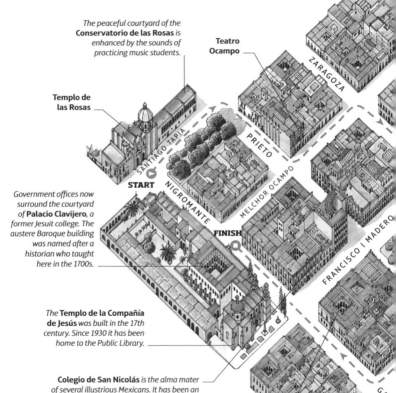

The peaceful courtyard of the **Conservatorio de las Rosas** *is enhanced by the sounds of practicing music students.*

Teatro Ocampo

Templo de las Rosas

ZARAGOZA

PRIETO

SANTIAGO TAPIA

START

NIGROMANTE

MELCHOR OCAMPO

FINISH

FRANCISCO I MADERO

Government offices now surround the courtyard of **Palacio Clavijero**, *a former Jesuit college. The austere Baroque building was named after a historian who taught here in the 1700s.*

The **Templo de la Compañía de Jesús** *was built in the 17th century. Since 1930 it has been home to the Public Library.*

Colegio de San Nicolás *is the alma mater of several illustrious Mexicans. It has been an educational institution since the 16th century.*

GAL

Centro Cultural

Palacio Municipal

← Cafés lining the tiny park opposite the Conservatorio de las Rosas

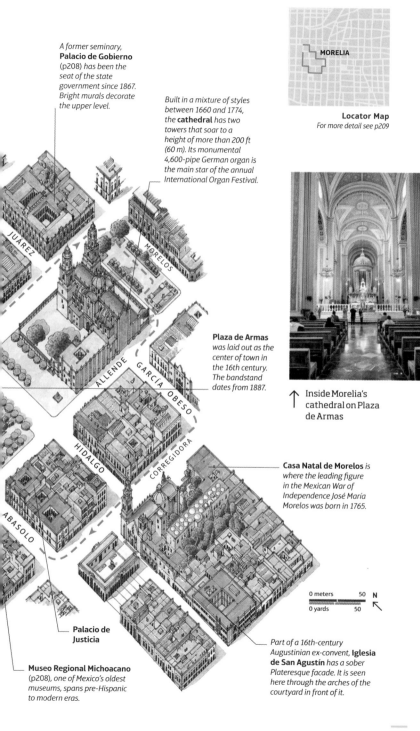

A former seminary, **Palacio de Gobierno** (p208) has been the seat of the state government since 1867. Bright murals decorate the upper level.

Built in a mixture of styles between 1660 and 1774, the **cathedral** has two towers that soar to a height of more than 200 ft (60 m). Its monumental 4,600-pipe German organ is the main star of the annual International Organ Festival.

Locator Map
For more detail see p209

MORELIA

JUÁREZ

MORELOS

ALLENDE

GARCIA OBESO

Plaza de Armas was laid out as the center of town in the 16th century. The bandstand dates from 1887.

↑ Inside Morelia's cathedral on Plaza de Armas

HIDALGO

CORREGIDORA

ABASOLO

Casa Natal de Morelos is where the leading figure in the Mexican War of Independence José María Morelos was born in 1765.

| 0 meters | 50 | N |
| 0 yards | 50 | |

Palacio de Justicia

Museo Regional Michoacano (p208), one of Mexico's oldest museums, spans pre-Hispanic to modern eras.

Part of a 16th-century Augustinian ex-convent, **Iglesia de San Agustín** has a sober Plateresque facade. It is seen here through the arches of the courtyard in front of it.

Diners relaxing in the courtyard of El Parián restaurant in Tlaquepaque

Located in a beautiful old mansion, the museum counts a 16th-century kitchen among its most interesting exhibits. Many of the items sold in Tlaquepaque are in fact made in workshops in the neighboring suburb of Tonalá. Like Tlaquepaque, this was once a village outside Guadalajara, and was originally an Indigenous settlement. Its streets become an open-air craft market, Tianguis Tonala, on Thursdays and Sundays.

Museo Regional de la Cerámica

Independencia 237 (333) 860 11 77 10am–6pm Tue–Sat

⑦ Cañada de la Virgen

B4 Guanajuato 10am–6pm Tue–Sun Principal 14, Zona Centro; www.inah.gob.mx

The impressive ancient Mesoamerican pyramids of Cañada de la Virgen were opened to the public in 2011 after years of archaeological excavations. The site comprises several enormous structures associated with the

EXPERIENCE MORE

⑥ Tlaquepaque

B4 Jalisco Ayuntamiento, Calle Donato Guerra 160; (333) 562 70 50

Once a potters' village and weekend retreat for the residents of Guadalajara *(p194)*, Tlaquepaque is now a suburb of the city. However, it retains a village atmosphere.

The overwhelming selection of pottery, blown glass, textiles, metal, wood, and papier-mâché items in the crafts shops is the main factor that attracts large numbers of visitors to come here.

There are also many restaurants. A favorite meeting spot off the appealing, flower-filled central square is El Parián. Hailed as the world's biggest cantina, it gathers about 20 eating and drinking establishments around its giant courtyard. In the center is a bandstand where mariachi musicians often play.

The best ceramics pieces from Tlaquepaque and the surrounding region can be appreciated at the **Museo Regional de la Cerámica**.

> Once a separate potters' village and weekend retreat for the residents of Guadalajara, Tlaquepaque is now effectively a suburb of the city.

A giant sailfish statue on the waterfront plaza in Manzanillo

Otomí of the Toltec–Chichimec culture, constructed between AD 540 and 1050. The city was abandoned thereafter, though it's not known why.

Today the site features five sets of archaeological remains, the most important of which is Complex A and its "13 Sky House," which is thought to have been some kind of celestial observatory. Complex B is centered around the "House of the Longest Light," a pyramidal structure that probably served a mixture of public and ritualistic functions. At the main entrance a visitor center and museum provide context.

8

Cuyutlán

A5 **Colima** **Blvd Miguel de la Madrid 875A; www.colima.gob.mx**

Cuyutlán is a traditional resort on the central part of Colima's coast. It is characterized by black volcanic sand, pounding surf, and Mexican tourists

who come here on weekends. It is situated at the southern tip of the Cuyutlán Lagoon, which extends south for 20 miles (32 km) from Manzanillo.

The tiny **Museo de la Sal** gives an insight into the salt economy, its workers, and harvesting methods. A spectacular phenomenon seen on the coast here is the *ola verde* (green wave), when waves up to 33 ft (10 m) in height gleam with phosphorescent marine organisms. It is most commonly seen in April and May. In the recent past, it has caused a number of deaths, so caution should be taken when coming to see the wave.

Around 2.5 miles (4 km) further along the coast from Cuyutlán, the **Centro Ecológico de Cuyutlán "El Tortugario"** is a turtle sanctuary dedicated to the conservation and protection of local wildlife. The sanctuary organizes boat trips into the wildlife-rich Laguna Cuyutlán, to help teach visitors about the importance of preserving the local wildlife and their habitats.

Museo de la Sal
Calle Benito Juárez
(312) 326 40 14
10am-6pm Tue-Sat

Centro Ecológico de Cuyutlán "El Tortugario"
 Av López Mateo (313) 119 04 34 9am-5pm Thu-Tue

EAT

La Sonrisa
A no-frills spot famed for its skirt steak tacos and homemade salsas, as well as giant chorizo and beef quesadillas.

A5 **Océano Atlántico 788, at Miguel de la Madrid, Playa Azul, Manzanillo** **(314) 117 86 04**

$$$

9

Manzanillo

A5 **Colima** **Blvd Miguel de la Madrid 875A; www.colima.gob.mx**

Mexico's main west coast shipping center, Manzanillo is also Colima state's foremost beach resort. Colorful houses of the old port cling to a hill overlooking the main harbor, while the newer part of town covers a sandbar separating the lagoon from the ocean. Most of the restaurants and hotels are along the sands of Las Brisas and Playa Azul.

Separating the Bahía de Manzanillo from the Bahía de Santiago is a peninsula, site of Las Hadas ("The Fairies"), a luxury Moorish-style hotel.

Paricutín

B5 **24 miles (38 km) NW of Uruapan, Michoacán**

One of the youngest volcanoes in the world, Paricutín erupted in February 1943. Amid thunderous explosions, its cone grew to more than 1,100 ft (330 m) within one year. Ash and lava flows buried two villages and, while nobody was killed by the eruptions, more than 4,000 people had to flee their homes. The volcano's activity lasted until 1952, leaving behind a barren cone rising 1,391 ft (424 m) from a sea of black frozen lava.

The *mirador* (lookout) at Angahuan offers a dramatic view of the lava field and Paricutín behind it. The church tower that can be seen above the lava belongs to the buried village of San Juan Parangaricutiro. For a closer look, hire a guide and a horse to take you down the cliff and through the lava rock formations. The stiff 30-minute climb to the crater rim is rewarded with views of the lunar-like landscape.

The town of Angahuan has preserved its traditional character despite the influx of visitors to Paricutín, and most people here speak the Tarascan language, Purépecha.

Sierra Gorda

C4 **Querétaro**

One of the largest untamed regions in central Mexico, the semi-arid mountain range of the Sierra Gorda rises northeast of the city of Querétaro *(p206)* to over 10,000 ft (3,000 m). The lush green of its foothills is interrupted only by the massive monolith La Peña de Bernal, towering 1,460 ft (445 m) above the village of Bernal.

In the mountains beyond Cadereyta, with its square of colored churches, are the archaeological sites of Toluquilla and Las Ranas. These two sites are set on the rugged ridges near San Joaquín, to the east of Mex 120. Both feature pre-Hispanic ceremonial structures built between the 7th and 11th centuries AD. Farther north into the mountains, Mex 120 gets even steeper before descending to Jalpan. This town is the site of one of five Franciscan missions founded in the mid-16th

century to convert the Indigenous peoples of these mountains. The missions – the others are in Concá, Tilaco, Tancoyól, and Landa de Matamoros – all have scenic settings, and distinctive facades with strong Indigenous touches in their profu mortar decorations.

Santuario El Rosario

C5 **Off Mex 15, 8 miles (13 km) E of Ocampo, Michoacán** **Nov-Mar: 9am-5pm daily** **maripos monarca.semarnat.gob.mx**

This UNESCO World Heritage Site is one of two sanctuaries open to the public in the Monarch Butterfly Biosphere Reserve in the mountains west of Mexico City. The 60-sq-mi (160-sq-km) preserve is the winter home of an estimated 100 million monarch butterflies *(Danaus plexippus linnea*

Did You Know?

Monarch butterflies cover up to 190 miles (300 km) a day to escape the winter in Canada and the US.

which migrate here each year. The annual migration of the monarch butterfly begins in early autumn. It is then that a special generation hatches, with a life cycle of up to nine months, four times that of spring and summer butterflies. These autumn-born insects fly south in groups of several hundred to reach the *oyamel* fir forests of central Mexico where they spend the winter. In spring they mate and head north again. En route, the females lay about 500 eggs each. Their offspring take up the baton and continue north to arrive in early June. None of the original migrants will survive to return to Mexico the following year.

The best time to visit is late February when rising temperatures encourage the insects to search for flowers or begin their journey back north. The hiking route is well marked.

The nearby **Sierra Chincua Monarch Butterfly Sanctuary** sees fewer visitors than El Rosario, but is easier to reach and offers horses for its more rustic trails. Guides will accompany visitors on request.

Sierra Chincua Monarch Butterfly Sanctuary
⊕ ⊕ ☐ Llano de las Papas, 5 miles (9 km) NE of Angangueo ☐ Nov–Mar: 8am–5pm daily

—

Tourists clamber around San Juan Parangaricutiro's buried church

↑ Palapa seafood restaurant on the Santa María del Oro lake, in the hills southeast of Tepic

13

Tepic

🅰 A4 ☐ Nayarit ✕🚌
🛈 Corner of Avenida México and Calzada del Ejército Nacional; www.riviera nayarit.com

A provincial town with an agreeable climate, Tepic was founded in the foothills of an extinct volcano. Not far from the Plaza Principal and the cathedral is the **Museo Regional de Nayarit**, where you will find shaft-tombs and displays about the Cora and Huichol people. The **Museo de Los Cinco Pueblos** (Museum of Five Peoples) has exhibits about the Huicholes, Tepehuanos, Mexicaneros, Coras, and *mestizo* cultures of the region (*mestizo* meaning people of mixed European and Mexican descent). One of Mexico's most beloved poets is commemorated at the **Museo Amado Nervo**, in the house where he was born.

Museo Regional de Nayarit
⊛ ☐ Av México 91 Norte
☎ (311) 212 19 00 ☐ 10am–4pm Mon–Fri (to 3pm Sat)

Museo de Los Cinco Pueblos
⊛ ☐ México Norte 105, at Zapata ☎ (311) 212 17 05
☐ 9am–2pm & 4–7pm Tue–Sun

Museo Amado Nervo
☐ Zacatecas Norte 284
☎ (311) 212 29 16 ☐ 10am–2pm & 4–7pm Tue–Sat, 10am–2pm Sun

TOP 4 REGIONAL FIESTAS

Fiesta de Año Nuevo
Purépecha dancers in Ihuatzio perform masked dances to Pirekua songs to mark the new year.

Easter
In both Tzintzuntzán and Tarímbaro, a volunteer performs a realistic re-enactment of the Crucifixion.

Feria de San Marcos
Mexico's largest fair is held in Aguascalientes, with parades, concerts, fireworks, bullfights, rodeo shows, and more.

Day of the Dead
On November 1, families gather to commemorate relatives who have passed *(p221)*. There are particularly beautiful festivites on Janitzio Island in Lake Pátzcuaro.

14
Tequisquiapan

C4 Querétaro
Independencia 1, Plaza Miguel Hidalgo; (414) 273 08 41

Just 35 miles (57 km) east of Querétaro lies the quaint spa town of Tequisquiapan (aka "Tequis"), a former Otomí village that developed in the Spanish period thanks to its hot springs. Today its cobbled lanes, folk art boutiques, and spa hotels make it a popular retreat. Lavish villas, all with beautiful walled gardens, are set around central Plaza Miguel Hidalgo, itself ringed by arched portals and the handsome rose-colored church of Santa María de la Asunción. The Mercado de Artesanías Tequezquicalli – a crafts market – lies one block from the plaza.

15
Colima

A5 Colima Palacio de Gobierno, Reforma 37; www.colima.gob.mx

The graceful provincial town of Colima was the first Spanish city on the west coast. It has been rebuilt several times since 1522 because of earthquakes, but the center still has Neo-Classical buildings, several museums, and the main plaza Jardín la Libertad. Ceramic vessels and human and animal figurines from early shaft-tombs can be seen in the **Museo de las Culturas de Occidente**. The **Museo Universitario de Artes Populares** exhibits regional and national folk art, covering both pre-Hispanic and more recent periods. Colima's **Museo Regional de Historia** features pre-Hispanic ceramics and artifacts from local tombs.

On the outskirts of town, La Campana archaeological site was an important pre-Hispanic settlement between AD 700 and 900, with the earliest remains dating as far back as 1500 BC.

Museo de las Culturas de Occidente
Corner of Galván & Ejército Nacional (312) 313 06 08 10am-2pm & 5-8pm Tue-Sat, 10am-1pm Sun

Museo Universitario de Artes Populares
Manuel Gallardo Zamora 99 (312) 316 11 26 10am-2pm & 5-8pm Tue-Sat, 10am-1pm Sun

↑ The rose-colored church standing on Plaza Miguel Hidalgo, Tequisquiapan

Museo Regional de Historia
 Portal Morelos 1 (312) 312 92 28 9am-6pm Tue-Sun

16
Mexcaltitán

A4 Nayarit

This tiny island, its name meaning "Place of the Moon Temple," is no more than 1,310 ft (400 m) across. It sits in a lagoon in Mexico's largest mangrove swamp area, and in the rains of August and September the streets become canals. The island

---

GREAT VIEW
Twin Peaks

North from Colima, Highway 54-D to Guadalajara has views of the active Volcán de Fuego and the dormant El Nevado de Colima behind. Hikes up the latter are popular and relatively easy to arrange in Colima.

is thought to be the legendary Aztec homeland Aztlán, from where the tribe set out on their migration to the Valley of México around 1091 AD – from the air, it really does resemble a tiny version of Tenochtitlán, the final Aztec capital. According to legend the Aztecs slept here on the way to their promised land.

Although no Aztec artifacts have been found here, the archaeological pieces on display in the **Museo del Origen** nonetheless emphasize the importance of the island of Mexcaltitán as "The Cradle of Mexicanism" (*Mexcaltitán* literally means "House of the Mexicans" in Náhuatl).

Museo del Origen

⊛ ⌂ Porfirio Díaz 1 ☎ (311) 131 56 27 ⌚ 9am–2pm & 4–6pm Tue–Sun

---

17

Mineral de Pozos

⌂ C4 ⌂ Guanajuato
ℹ Centro de Atención al Visitante, Hwy 46; www. visitmexico.com

A rich and flourishing mining community in the 18th century, the semi-ghost-town of Mineral de Pozos was largely abandoned in the 1900s. Though it began experiencing a revival in the early 2010s, it still remains less developed than San Miguel de Allende *(p224)*.

Today the heart is clustered around the white dome of Parroquia San Pedro and the Jardín Principal. The center is home to a handful of hip hotels, restaurants, and handi-craft shops, selling everything from old-fashioned sweets to pre-Hispanic musical instruments and toys.

Crumbling ruins swamp the town's fringes, in between old mine workings and abandoned haciendas. Highlights include the ruins of the Hacienda de Cinco Señores, a vast mine complex, the three distinctive

16th-century Jesuit smelters *(hornos)* of Santa Brígida, and the newly opened Lavender Farms of Pozos.

18

Uruapan

⌂ B5 ⌂ Michoacán ✈ 🚌
ℹ San Miguel Arcángel; (452) 524 71 99

Uruapan is a busy agricultural center. Nestling against the Sierra de Uruapan, it links the cold upland region *(tierra fría)* to the humid lowlands *(tierra caliente)* that stretch toward the Pacific. Its subtropical climate supports exuberant vegetation, including vast avocado plantations.

The Spanish monk Juan de San Miguel founded the town in 1533 and divided it into nine neighborhoods *(barrios)*, which still preserve their own traditions. He also built **La Huatápera**,

a chapel and hospital that now houses a fine museum of Michoacán crafts.

The **Parque Nacional Barranca del Cupatitzio** is a park on the edge of Uruapan's urban sprawl. It encompasses a lush, tropical ravine created by the Río Cupatitzio, which springs underground from a rock known as La Rodilla del Diablo ("the Devil's knee"). Cobbled footpaths weave between banana plants and palms to take in man-made cascades and fountains. Local trout is sold and served at restaurants and taco stands.

La Huatápera

⌂ Plaza Morelos ☎ (452) 524 34 34 ⌚ 9:30am–1:30pm & 3:30–6pm Tue–Sun

Parque Nacional Barranca del Cupatitzio

⊛ ⌘ ℹ ⌂ Calzada de San Miguel, 0.5 miles (1 km) from the plaza ⌚ 8am–6pm Mon–Thu, 8am–7pm Fri–Sun

↑ Visitors diving off the rocks into a waterfall at the Parque Nacional Barranca del Cupatitzio

19

San Juan de los Lagos

B4 Jalisco Fray Antonio de Segovia 10; (395) 785 09 79

The imposing 18th-century cathedral in San Juan de los Lagos is one the most important Catholic sanctuaries in Mexico. An estimated nine million pilgrims travel here every year to venerate the Virgen de San Juan de los Lagos, a small 16th-century corn-paste statue enshrined in an altar originally made for the church of Santa Maria degli Angeli in Rome.

The cathedral, which reaches a height of 223 ft (68 m), has a sumptuous interior. In its vast sacristy is a group of large 17th- and 18th-century paintings, six of which have been attributed to Rubens. Touching votive pictures, expressing gratitude to the Virgin for favors granted, line the walls of a room beside the sacristy.

20

Tequila

A4 Jalisco José Cuervo 33; (374) 742 00 12

Everything in Tequila reminds the visitor of Mexico's most famous drink, especially the scent from the distilleries. Plantations of *Agave tequilana weber* surround the town, the cores *(piñas)* of which have been used to make tequila since the 16th century.

The biggest and oldest factories are La Perseverancia (home of Sauza Tequila since 1873) and La Rojeña (base of the José Cuervo brand since 1758) – both offer factory tours and tastings. Learn more at the Museo Nacional del Tequila, or head 9 miles (15 km) southeast to the Herradura distillery. The three major distilleries also offer all-inclusive day tours (weekends only) from Guadalajara by train or bus.

21

Las Pozas

C4 Off Mex 120, 2 miles (3 km) NW of Xilitla, San Luis Potosí 9am-6pm Wed-Mon laspozasxilitla.org.mx

High in the mountains south of Ciudad Valles, near the town of Xilitla, is this extraordinary, dreamlike jungle estate created by the British artist, eccentric, and millionaire Edward James (1907–84).

According to his friend Salvador Dalí, James was "crazier than all the Surrealists put together. They pretend, but he is the real thing." Born into a wealthy English family, James was himself a moderately successful poet and artist, but excelled as a patron of the arts. He founded ballet companies, published books, financed large exhibitions, and amassed paintings by Dalí, Picasso, and Magritte.

In the 1940s, James started seeking to create his own Garden of Eden and, with the help of Yaqui guide Plutarco Gastélum, came upon the area of Xilitla in 1945. James first used the Las Pozas property to grow orchids and then as a private zoo, but over the next 30 years he continued to add fanciful buildings and structures to the estate. To complete his architectural fantasy, James again worked with Gastélum and many local artisans, sometimes numbering up to 150 at a time.

Slippery paths weave between the hundreds of Surrealist metal and concrete sculptures, scattered amid thick subtropical vegetation, springs, waterfalls, and pools. Much of James's work is not finished or already disintegrating, so exploring the estate can feel like stumbling upon the ruins of a long-lost, mythical civilization.

This fantastical estate is a popular sight, and with a limited number of visitors allowed on site per day, it fills to capacity fast – especially on holidays and weekends. Try to arrive early, and be prepared for a wait to enter.

↑ Las Pozas, a "Garden of Eden" created by British artist Edward James

22

La Quemada

B4 Mex 54, 35 miles (57 km) SE of Zacatecas, Zacatecas (492) 922 50 85 9am-4pm Fri-Sun (last entry 3pm)

The archaeological site at La Quemada stretches over a steep hill rising from a wide arid valley. From around

Parroquia de la Asunción in Lagos de Moreno and *(inset)* its vibrantly colored interior

D 350, La Quemada was n important religious and olitical center and the focal oint for trade between the rea and Teotihuacán *(p140)*. fter AD 700, La Quemada eems to have substituted ade with more bellicose ctivities. In around 1100, apparently suffered a olent end, despite an 800-m ,600-ft) long and 4-m (13-ft) ll defensive wall on its orthern slope.

It takes about two hours to xplore the site by following e steep, rocky path that ads from the lower Main auseway and Hall of Columns l the way up to the Citadel.

agos de Moreno

B4 ◘Jalisco ▤ ▯Pedro oreno 419, Centro; (474) 10 36 218

lesser-visited architectural em, Lagos de Moreno is nown as the "Athens of lisco" thanks to the many mous writers who were born ere. Once an important post n the silver road, it's a tran- uil little city today, with obbled streets climbing teeply from the Río Lagos to llltop Templo del Señor del alvario, a 19th-century

church modeled on Rome's St. Peter's. On central Jardín de los Constituyentes stands the magnificent Baroque church, the Parroquia de la Asunción. Just behind the church, the Museo de Arte Sacro contains a large collection of religious art from the 17th to the 19th centuries, while grand Teatro José Rosas Moreno opened in 1907 with a stunning mural on its dome depicting the Mexican Revolution *(p62)*.

㉔
Ribera

🄰B4 ◘Jalisco ▤ ▯Madero 407 Altos, Chapala; (376) 765 31 41

The built-up Ribera has a near-perfect climate, and its proximity to some of Mexico's other big, central cities has resulted in streams of foreign visitors. It stretches for some 13 miles (21 km) from the old-fashioned resort of Chapala to the village of Jocotepec at the western end of a lake. Ajijic, an

artists' colony with cobblestone streets, crafts shops, galleries, and a 16th-century chapel, is the most picturesque village of the Ribera. Farther west, the spa resort of San Juan Cosalá offers the attractions of public swimming pools and a natural geyser.

Boat trips from Chapala head for two islands: the tree-covered Isla de los Alacranes, with its fish restaurants; and Mezcala, with the ruins of a 19th-century fort where inde-pendence fighters held out for four years before surren-dering to the Spanish in 1816.

The scenic road that runs along the mostly undeveloped southern shore of the lake opens up splendid views.

> **A lesser-visited archi-tectural gem, Lagos de Moreno is known as the "Athens of Jalisco" thanks to the many famous writers who were born here.**

25

Dolores Hidalgo

🅰B3 📍Guanajuato ▦
🛈 Plaza Principal 2; www.
dolores-hidalgo.com

The battle for independence
from Spain began in 1810
with Father Miguel Hidalgo
issuing his famous *Grito* (cry)
to arms (p59). The beautifully
laid-out Plaza Principal at
the heart of Dolores is still
dominated by the ornate
facade of the 18th-century
Nuestra Señora de los
Dolores, the illustrious church
where this portentous event
took place. Learn more at the
**Museo Histórico Curato de
Dolores**, Father Hidalgo's
home between 1804 and
1810, and the **Museo del
Bicentenario**, which tells the
history of the city.

Museo Histórico
Curato de Dolores
⊘ 🏠Morelos 1, at Hidalgo
📞(418) 182 01 71 🕐9am–
5:45pm Tue–Sat, 9am–
4:45pm Sun

Museo del Bicentenario
⊘ 🏠Plaza Principal
📞(418) 182 77 31
🕐9am–5pm daily

 26

Pátzcuaro

🅰B5 📍Michoacán ▦
🛈 Portal de Hidalgo 2;
(434) 342 02 15

Set amid the pastures and pine
forests on the southern shore
of Lake Pátzcuaro, this town
was once an important center
of the Purépecha people.
Under the Spanish colonizers,
it was temporarily turned
into the civic, religious, and
cultural seat of the state.

The ambitious Basílica de
Nuestra Señora de la Salud
was to boast five naves and
accommodate thousands of
people, but only one nave was
completed. Fires and earthquakes ravaged the building
over the centuries, and the
church was finally finished in
a jumble of styles in 1833.

Just to the south is the
**Museo de Artes e Industrias
Populares** craft museum.
Among the exhibits is a cabin-
like *troje* with Purépecha
furnishings. Another crafts
center can be found in the
Casa de los Once Patios.

Huge ash trees shade the
quiet, elegant Plaza Vasco
de Quiroga. Many of the
colonial-era mansions that

face the square have been
converted into restaurants,
shops, and hotels, but the
real commercial hub of the
town is the nearby Plaza
Gertrudis Bocanegra, named
after a local fighter in the
Mexican War of Independen
On Fridays, the streets towa
the Santuario de Guadalupe
church fill with stalls, and
pottery is sold in the Plazue
de San Francisco.

Museo de Artes e
Industrias Populares
⊗⊗ 🏠Corner of Enseñan.
and Alcantarilla 📞(434) 3
10 29 🕐9am–5pm Tue–Sur

Casa de los Once Patios
🕐 🏠Madrigal de las Altas
Torres 📞(434) 342 43 79
🕐9am–5pm daily

💬 INSIDER TIP
Island Hopping

Tours to the islands
on Lake Pátzcuaro leave
from the docks, which
are located in the north
of town. Isla Janitzio,
with its monument
to Morelos and quaint
shops, is the most
popular destination.

↑ Men performing *los viejitos* (a
traditional dance), on Plaza
Vasco de Quiroga, Pátzcuaro

↑ Dancers with painted skull masks during the Day of the Dead festivities

THE DAY OF THE DEAD

This Mexican celebration centers around the belief that the dead have divine permission to visit friends and relatives on Earth once a year.

A JOYFUL CELEBRATION

During the Day of the Dead, the living welcome the souls of departed loved ones with offerings of flowers, food, candles, and incense. This is not a morbid occasion, but one of peace and happiness. The souls of children are thought to visit on November 1, and adults on November 2. Skulls and skeletons abound in the imagery and decorations of this festival, but death is portrayed with humor and even affection by craftspeople and artists.

WHERE TO SEE THE DAY OF THE DEAD

Celebrations occur virtually everywhere in central and southern Mexico, with some areas adding their own local twist. The ceremonies around Lake Pátzcuaro, for example, are particularly impressive, largely because of the local Purépecha villagers' deep Indigenous roots and the pretty settings. Throughout the night, boats decorated with candles and flowers and laden with chanting villagers travel between the Pátzcuaro docks and the island, and the air is filled with wafts of incense and the ringing of bells.

Afro-Mexicans, meanwhile, pay homage to the suffering of their enslaved ancestors with the *Danza de los Diablos* (Dance of the Devils) - through synchronized stomping, spinning, and comical theatrics, large ensembles tell the story of enslaved workers mocking a violent, white ruling class.

SYMBOLS OF THE DEAD

Personalized altars laden with symbolic offerings are set up in homes, and may also be displayed in public places.

 Sugar figures and other foods are displayed. The dead are believed to take the essence or the aroma of the offerings.

 A photo of the dead person is a common focal point for the altars. Holy pictures may also be added.

 The marigold *(cempasúchil)*, often referred to in Mexico as "the flower of the dead," is used in profusion on altars and as festive decor.

 Papier-mâché skeletons are often displayed in public places, performing everyday activities in humorous scenes.

 La Catrina, a tall female skeleton drawn by José Guadalupe Posada, is widely associated with the day. It often appears in art.

 Skull masks and clothing painted with bones are sometimes worn by children on the day.

② San Luis Potosí

🗺 C4 🏛 San Luis Potosí
🚌 ℹ Manuel José Ottón 130;
www.slp.gob.mx

The mining wealth that the city of San Luis Potosí accumulated in the 17th and 18th centuries is evident in the historic buildings and three grand plazas at its core. The cathedral dominates the central square, the Plaza de Armas, along with the Palacio de Gobierno, the seat of Benito Juárez's government when he denied clemency to Emperor Maximilian in 1867. Behind it stands the Caja Real, or Royal Treasury, whose wide staircase enabled pack animals to reach the storage chambers above.

The second square is the Plaza de los Fundadores, the site of a former Jesuit college and two 17th-century churches, the Iglesia de la Compañía and the graceful Capilla de Loreto. On the eastern side of town is the third main square, the Plaza del Carmen, on which stand the church of the same name, the imposing Teatro de la Paz, and the **Museo Nacional de la Máscara**. The museum is housed in a restored former mansion where the walls are

HIDDEN GEM
Paradise on Earth

In the southeast of San Luis Potosí state is Huasteca Potosina: an area of stunning natural beauty known in pre-Hispanic times as Tamoanchán, or "Earthly Paradise."

adorned with over 1,000 decorative and ritual masks.

The Churrigueresque church of **Templo del Carmen**, built in the mid-1700s, is by far the most spectacular religious structure in the city, with a three-tiered facade, ornate tower, and multicolored domes. Even more fabulous is the interior, not least for Francisco Tresguerras' main altar and exuberant Altar de los Siete Príncipes. The latter is actually a floor-to-ceiling interior facade enclosing the entrance to a chapel, its white stucco surface dotted with polychrome statues of angels.

The Franciscans began work in 1686 on the ambitious **Ex-Convento de San Francisco** complex, which took over a century to complete. It now contains the Museo Regional

Potosino, which has colonial and pre-Hispanic exhibits. Upstairs is the splendid Capilla de Aranzazú, the lavish private chapel for the former occupants. A unique Baroque jewel despite the garish colors chosen by its restorers, it has a rare covered atrium and a carved wooden portal.

The city also has two other noteworthy museums. **Museo Federico Silva** pays homage to one of Mexico's most respected sculptors. Born in 1923, Silva is known for his modern interpretations of Mexico's pre-Hispanic art, and the museum displays many of his volcanic stone and steel creations. **Museo de Arte Contemporáneo** occupies the old 19th-century post office, and showcases high-quality traveling shows of contemporary art.

The former state prison, built in the 1890s, has been transformed into the stylish **Centro de las Artes** complex. The restored buildings contain temporary art exhibitions, the cell where Francisco Madero was held in 1910, and the Museo

Leonora Carrington, which is dedicated to the English-born Mexican surrealist painter.

Museo Nacional de la Máscara

⊛ 🅐 Villerías 2 ⏰ 10am-6pm Tue-Fri (to 5pm Sat, to 3pm Sun & Mon) 🔲 museodelamascaraslp.org

Templo del Carmen

🅐 Manuel José Othón 410 📞 (444) 812 28 78 ⏰ 7am-1:30pm & 4-9pm daily

Ex-Convento de San Francisco

⊛ 🄯 🅐 Plaza de Aranzazú 📞 (444) 814 35 72 ⏰ 9am-6pm Tue-Sun

Museo Federico Silva

⊛ 🅐 Obregón 80 ⏰ 10am-6pm Mon-Sat, 10am-2pm Sun 🔲 museofedericosilva.org

Museo de Arte Contemporáneo

⊛ 🅐 Morelos 235 ⏰ 10am-6pm Mon-Sat, 10am-2pm Sun 🔲 macsanluispotosi.com

Centro de las Artes

⊛ 🅐 Calzada de Guadalupe 705 ⏰ 10am-6pm (last entry 5pm) Tue-Sun 🔲 centrodelasartesslp.gob.mx

↑ Perched high on the mountainside, the town of Real de Catorce, dominated by its Neo-Classical church

28
Real de Catorce

🄰 C3 🅐 San Luis Potosí 🚌 🄸 Presidencia Municipal, Constitución 27; www.realdecatorce.info

The crumbling structures and ghost-town atmosphere of Real de Catorce testify to the rapidly changing fortunes of Mexican silver-mining centers. Hidden high in the mountains of the Sierra Madre Oriental, it is accessible only through a 1.5-mile (2.5-km) tunnel.

In the early 20th century the town boasted a population of 40,000, served by several newspapers, a theater, a grand hotel, and an electric tramway. Then, drastically hit by falling silver prices, its fortunes slumped until only a few families remained. Its semi-deserted feel has made it the chosen set for several Mexican cowboy films.

Only the Neo-Classical church, the Parroquia de la Purísima Concepción, with its reputedly miraculous statue of St. Francis of Assisi, was maintained for the sake of the pilgrims who flood here.

← Plaza del Carmen, with its fountain and church, in San Luis Potosí

Opposite the church is the dilapidated Casa de Moneda (closed on Mondays and Tuesdays), a former silver warehouse and mint from the 1860s. The town's former glory can also be seen in the shells of ornate mansions and the ruined bullring.

STAY

Hotel Mina Real
This rustic, cozy hotel features exposed stone walls in each of its 11 rooms.

🄰 C3 🅐 Ramón Corona 5-B, Real de Catorce 🔲 hotelminareal.com

$⑤$⑤⑤

————————

Mesón de la Abundancia
Built out of the ruins of the old Treasury. Expect rustic stone walls, beams, brick floors, and ancient doors.

🄰 C3 🅐 Lanzagorta 11, Real de Catorce 🔲 mesonabundancia.com

$⑤$⑤⑤

↑ The picturesque El Jardin Principal, at the vibrant heart of San Miguel de Allende

San Miguel de Allende

⚠C4 ⚑Guanajuato ℹPlaza Principal 8; (415) 152 09 00

Founded in the 16th century overlooking the Río Laja, San Miguel has cobbled streets lined with handsome mansions and churches. The town's active cultural life combines traditional charm with a cosmopolitan and multi-cultural atmosphere.

El Jardín Principal, the main plaza, is dominated by a church built in 1880. Nearby, the birthplace of the revolutionary leader in the Mexican War of Independence Miguel Allende now operates as the Museo Histórico de San Miguel de Allende. The Mercado Ignacio Ramírez (town market) is full of fruit, vegetables, and

> 🔍 **HIDDEN GEM**
> ## Move Over Michelangelo
>
> The Santuario de Jesús Nazareno de Atotonilco, just north of San Miguel, is the Sistine Chapel of Mexico. Founded in the 18th century, its walls and ceiling burst to life with exquisite paintings in the Mexican folk style.

medicinal herb stalls, while the adjacent Mercado de Artesanías overflows with handicrafts. The notable Sala Quetzal inside La Biblioteca (library) is a gem, all four walls smothered with lavish murals by artist David Leonardo.

***

Aguascalientes

⚠B4 ⚑Aguascalientes ✉🚍 ℹPlaza de la Patria; (449) 910 20 88

Named after its hot springs, Aguascalientes still attracts visitors to its thermal baths but is today best known for its popular spring fair, the Feria de San Marcos *(p215)*.

The Spanish Colonial Palacio de Gobierno has a spectacular maze of arches, pillars, and staircases around its main courtyard. A series of murals inside were painted by Osvaldo Barra Cunningham, a pupil of Diego Rivera. Across the Plaza de la Patria is the 18th-century cathedral, and the Neo-Classical Teatro Morelos. One of the most beautiful churches in Mexico, the Templo del Santuario Nuestra Señora de Guadalupe has an ornate Baroque facade, and a dazzling interior of intricate carvings.

Aguascalientes has a handful of fascinating museums. The **Museo de Arte Contemporáneo** displays prize-winning contemporary works, and the **Museo José Guadalupe Posada** has engravings by Mexico's best known satirical cartoonist. Mexico's obsession with images of death over the centuries is chronicled at the fascinating Museo Nacional de la Muerte, while the Museo de Aguascalientes is an art museum, with a primary focus on the naturalistic work of Saturnino Herrán.

Museo de Arte Contemporáneo

⊘ ⚑Morelos and Primo Verdad 📞(449) 915 79 53
🕒11am-5pm Tue-Sun

Museo José Guadalupe Posada

⊘⊘⊘ ⚑Jardín del Encino s/n 📞(449) 915 45 56
🕒Noon-6pm Tue-Sun

***

Puerto Vallarta

⚠A4 ⚑Jalisco ✉🚍 ℹIndependencia 123, Proyecto Escola; www.visitpuertovallarta.com

Hollywood stars discovered the tropical paradise of Bahía

EAT

Mercado Juárez
A market hall full of stalls serving up sumptuous *bírria*. This Aguascalientes specialty consists of slow-roasted, barbecued lamb, shredded and served with aromatic broth and a tortilla.

B4 **Victoria and Unión, Aguascalientes**

$ $ $

de Banderas (Banderas Bay) in the 1960s. Since then, the area's main hub, Puerto Vallarta, has become one of Mexico's top Pacific resorts. Tourists flock here annually to savor the beautiful beaches, the year-round pleasant climate, and the vibrant nightlife.

The various resort towns stretch for more than 25 miles (40 km) around the bay, but at the heart is Puerto Vallarta's old town, Viejo Vallarta. This area has managed to conserve some of the quaintness of a Mexican village, with its white-washed, tile-roofed houses and stone-paved streets stretching toward the jungle-clad mountains.

The Plaza Principal is backed by the pretty main church, the Templo de Nuestra Señora de Guadalupe, which is topped by its iconic crown.

Isla Río Cuale, a small island in the river dividing the town, is home to boutiques, cafés, and a botanical garden, and the **Museo del Cuale**, which displays pre-Hispanic artifacts from the region. On the other side of the river, the stalls of Mercado Municipal del Cuale are crammed with local jewelry, papier-mâché, clothes, and souvenir stalls.

Head to the *malecón*, the waterfront boardwalk, for water taxis serving other parts of the bay, such as the Zona Hotelera, the main hotel strip that extends to the seaport in the north. Farther north is Marina Vallarta, Mexico's largest marina, surrounded by luxury hotels, shopping malls, and a golf course. Beside the marina, although in another state (Nayarit) and even another time zone, is Nuevo Vallarta. This is the most recent development on the bay, and its miles of beach, river, and estuary frontage reach as far as the town of Bucerías. The tourist infrastructure then peters out, leaving a string of small, pristine beaches that stretch to the bay's northernmost point, Punta Mita.

The southern, more scenic arc of Banderas Bay begins with Playa de los Muertos (Beach of the Dead), the old town's most popular section of coastline. From here, the road winds past villa-dotted cliffs and sparkling blue coves to Mismaloya (the beach where John Huston filmed *The Night of the Iguana*), before turning inland at the village of Boca de Tomatlán. Beyond this point, the exotic coves and superb swimming and snorkeling beaches are accessible only by watertaxi. The best targets are the first stop of Las Ánimas, a large bay with a long, sandy beach, and languid Yelapa, some 30 minutes from Boca and the final water-taxi stop.

Museo del Cuale
Isla Río Cuale (333) 614 54 16 9am–5pm Mon–Sat

> **Tourists flock to Puerto Vallarta annually to savor the beautiful beaches, the year-round pleasant climate, and the vibrant nightlife.**

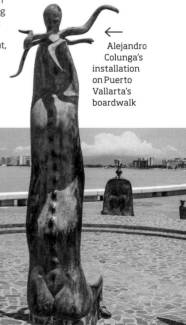

← Alejandro Colunga's installation on Puerto Vallarta's boardwalk

A SHORT WALK
SAN MIGUEL DE ALLENDE

Distance 1 mile (1.5 km) **Time** 15 minutes **Nearest metro** Central de Autobuses

San Miguel de Allende is filled with opulent mansions and old churches, all connected by narrow, cobbled streets. Once an important crossroads for mule trains, which carried silver and gold to the capital and returned with European treasures, the city is now a popular tourist destination. The heart of the city is perfect for exploring on foot, as all the major sights are just a short stroll from the central Plaza Allende.

The **Escuela de Bellas Artes** art school, located in a former convent, has an unfinished 1940s mural painted by David Alfaro Siqueiros (1896–1974).

A huge dome from 1891 towers over the gilded altar of **Templo de la Concepción**.

Casa del Mayorazgo de la Canal, the town's most sumptuous mansion, has Neo-Classical and Baroque styling.

Casa Allende, now a historical museum, was the birthplace of Ignacio Allende, an army captain who fought with the Mexican Independence Movement.

Casa del Inquisidor once housed visiting representatives of the Spanish Inquisition.

Casa de la Inquisición served as the prison of the Inquisition.

Notable for its fantastic Neo-Gothic facade, **La Parroquia** was remodeled in the late 19th century by self-taught architect, Zeferino Gutiérrez.

START

The elegantly odd concave facade of ↑
Templo de Nuestra Señora de la Salud

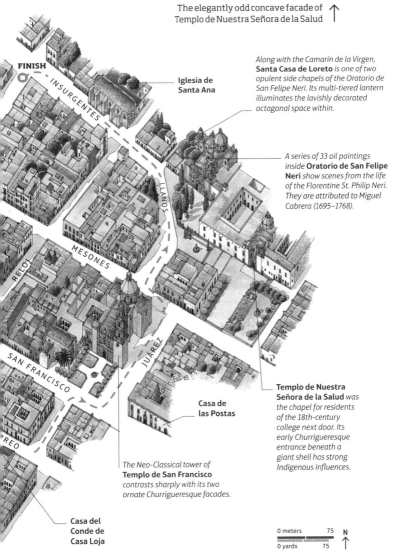

FINISH

INSURGENTES

Iglesia de
Santa Ana

Along with the Camarín de la Virgen,
Santa Casa de Loreto is one of two
opulent side chapels of the Oratorio de
San Felipe Neri. Its multi-tiered lantern
illuminates the lavishly decorated
octagonal space within.

A series of 33 oil paintings
inside **Oratorio de San Felipe
Neri** show scenes from the life
of the Florentine St. Philip Neri.
They are attributed to Miguel
Cabrera (1695–1768).

LLANOS

MESONES

RELO

SAN FRANCISCO

JUAREZ

REO

Casa de
las Postas

**Templo de Nuestra
Señora de la Salud** was
the chapel for residents
of the 18th-century
college next door. Its
early Churrigueresque
entrance beneath a
giant shell has strong
Indigenous influences.

The Neo-Classical tower of
Templo de San Francisco
contrasts sharply with its two
ornate Churrigueresque facades.

**Casa del
Conde de
Casa Loja**

0 meters   75   N
0 yards   75   ↑

A DRIVING TOUR
LAKE PÁTZCUARO

Length 55 miles (90 km) **Stopping-off points** There are plenty of good places to eat in Isla Janitzio and traditional family-run restaurants in Santa Fe

The road around this idyllic lake bedded in rolling hills passes colonial-era and pre-Hispanic architectural gems, and towns with rich craft traditions. Pátzcuaro, Tzintzuntzán, and Quiroga are popular destinations, but the western shore and marshlands to the south see fewer visitors. Yet here the winding road offers spectacular vistas of the lake and rare glimpses of Purépechan (Tarascan) village life. To see the islands, take a boat from Pátzcuaro's Muelle General.

↑ Dusk falling over Janitzio island in Lake Pátzcuaro

The town of **Erongarícuaro** was a favorite hideaway of Surrealist André Breton.

Famous for its prize-winning wooden masks, **Tocuaro** has a number of unmarked workshops selling these fantastic creations.

El Guacapian
9,777 ft (2,980 m)

Rancho de Oponguio

Puácuaro

Isla La Pacanda

Isla Yunuén

Erongarícuaro

Napízaro

Isla Tecuena

Isla Janitzio

San Francisco Uricho

Jarácuaro

Arocutín

Tocuaro
FINISH

San Miguel Nocutzepo

San Bartolo Pareo

Ajuno

Did You Know?
Tzintzuntzán's week-long La Fiesta del Señor del Rescate (February) celebrates a local 19th-century miracle.

Isla Janitzio is a car-free island known for its fish restaurants, souvenir stalls and panoramic summit, crowned by an 160 ft (49 m) statue of José María Morelos.

0 kilometers 5

0 miles 5

N ↑

BAJÍO AND THE CENTRAL COAST

Lake Pátzcuaro

Locator Map

Santa Fe *has a fine 17th-century church, and roadside stalls selling the local black pottery.*

A busy market town, **Quiroga** *sells agricultural and handicraft products from all over Michoacán. Lacquerware, such as wooden bowls and trays painted with bright flowers, is a typical local product.*

San Jerónimo Purenchecuaro

Chupícuaro

Santa Fe de la Laguna

Quiroga

San Andrés
róndaro

Lake Pátzcuaro

Ichupio

Atzimbo

Tarerio

Patambicho

Tzintzuntzán

Yacatas de Tzintzuntzán

△ *Tarriaqueri*
8,671 ft (2,643 m)

△ *Yahuarato*
8,277 ft (2,523 m)

asanastacua

Colonia
Lázaro Cárdenas

The yacatas – multilevel temple bases – near the town of **Tzintzuntzán** *reveal its history as the former Tarascan capital. Also noteworthy are the 16th-century Franciscan convent and the market.*

Las Cuevas

ucuchucho

Chapultepec

Sanabria

Ihuatzio

Buenavista

Tzurumútaro

El Manzanillal

△ *Cerro Blanco*
7,546 ft (2,300 m)

rio

Pátzcuaro
START

The peaceful village of **Ihuatzio** *stands near massive Tarascan archaeological remains, which overlook the lake. A stone coyote sculpture found at the ruins now graces the village church.*

→ The Tarascan *yacatas* ruins outside Tzintzuntzán

Papel picado outside the church in San Cristobal de las Casas

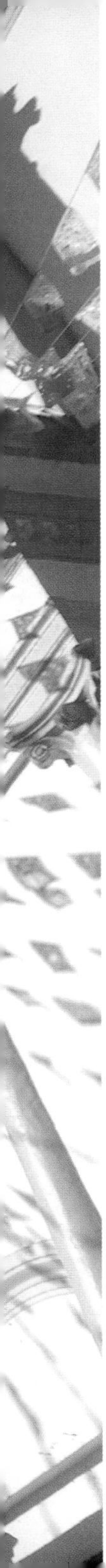

SOUTHERN MEXICO

Southern Mexico's mild climate and fertile soils attracted some of the earliest recorded settlements in Mesoamerica, with the Oaxaca Valley first inhabited in the 7th century BC. Three centuries later, the Zapotecs built their capital at Monte Albán, which dominated the valley for hundreds of years, before giving way to other, smaller cities. Meanwhile, in the east, the Maya were reaching their cultural peak and building the magnificent city of Palenque. The Spanish conquered the region in the 16th century, and it became a relative backwater for most of the colonial period. Even now, industry is limited beyond the cities, and much of the region remains underdeveloped, making the southern states some of the poorest in Mexico. Rural poverty helped fuel the 1994 Zapatista rebellion in Chiapas.

Geographically, the South is dominated by the mountains of the Sierra Madre del Sur, which make travel difficult but provide spectacular scenery. The Pacific coast is mostly unspoiled. Its sandy beaches are lined with palm trees and pounded constantly by surf.

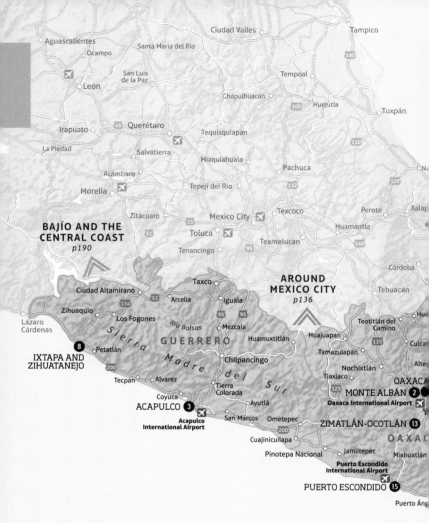

SOUTHERN MEXICO

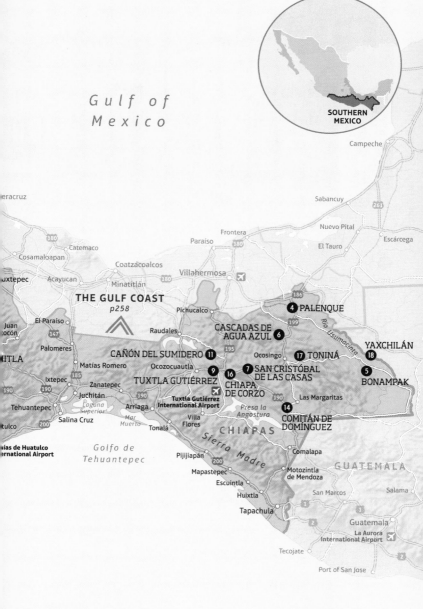

THE GULF COAST
p258

Gulf of
Mexico

SOUTHERN
MEXICO

Campeche

eracruz

Sabancuy

261

Nuevo Pital

Escárcega

Catemaco

Frontera

Paraíso

Cosamaloapan

Coatzacoalcos

Villahermosa

El Tauro

Acayucan

Minatitlán

180

180

uxtepec

Juan
ocón

El Paraíso

147

Pichucalco

4 PALENQUE

186

199

Río Usumacinta

Palomeres

Raudales

CASCADAS DE
AGUA AZUL
6

Matías Romero

CAÑÓN DEL SUMIDERO 11

195

Ocosingo

17 TONINÁ

YAXCHILÁN
18

Ixtepec

185

Ocozocuautla

9

16 7 SAN CRISTÓBAL
DE LAS CASAS

5

Zanatepec

190

TUXTLA GUTIÉRREZ

CHIAPA
DE CORZO

BONAMPAK

Juchitán

Tuxtla Gutiérrez
International Airport

Tehuantepec

190

Las Margaritas

190

Salina Cruz

Arriaga

Mar
Muerto

Villa
Flores

Presa la
Angostura

14

COMITÁN DE
DOMÍNGUEZ

200

Tonalá

CHIAPAS

ías de Huatulco
ernational Airport

Golfo de
Tehuantepec

Sierra Madre

Comalapa

GUATEMALA

Pijijiapán

200

Motozintla
de Mendoza

Salama

Mapastepec

San Marcos

Escuintla

Huixtla

1

Tapachula

Guatemala

1

La Aurora
International Airport

Tecojate

2

Port of San Jose

2

Pacific
Ocean

0 kilometers   150

0 miles   150

N

A delightful cobbled street in Oaxaca, lined with brightly painted craft stores ↑

❶
OAXACA

🅐D6 🚏Oaxaca 🚌🚈 🏛Avenida Benito Juárez 703; www.oaxaca.travel

With its blend of elegant architecture, a vibrant Indigenous culture, and one of the richest culinary scenes in Mexico, it's easy to fall in love with Oaxaca. The city invites aimless wandering, its blossom-filled streets and cobbled alleys lined with crafts stores, galleries, markets, and excellent restaurants.

①
Museo de Arte Contemporáneo

🅐Macedonio Alcalá 202
🕙10:30am-7:45pm Wed-Mon 🌐museomaco.org

The city's contemporary art museum is housed in a carefully refurbished 16th-century building, called the Casa de Cortés (House of Cortés) after the conquistador who is reputed to have commissioned it. Set around a central courtyard, the museum displays works of note painted by local and international modern artists, including Francisco Toledo and Rodolfo Morales. It is also a popular venue for holding temporary exhibitions and other cultural events.

②
Mercado Juárez

🅐Corner of 20 de Noviembre & Las Casas
🕙7am-9pm daily

Mercado Juárez was once the city's main market and is still a great place to pick up crafts made in surrounding villages. Traditional clothing, leather goods, and the famous Oaxaca pottery are all sold here.

③
Cathedral

🅐Avenida de la Independencia 700

The cathedral is was originally constructed in 1553, but a series of earthquakes meant that it had to be rebuilt in 1730. The Baroque facade includes a fine relief of the Assumption of the Virgin Mary above the main door. Inside, the main feature is the splendid bronze altar, crafted in Italy.

④
Central Oaxaca

The Plaza de Armas, or zócalo, is the geographical and social center of the city. Closed to traffic, it bustles with vendors, students, tourists, and villagers from outside the city. It is a great place to watch the world go by, especially from the cafés around its perimeter. Just northwest of the zócalo is the Alameda de León, a lovely square with market stalls that specialize in arts and crafts.

⑤
Iglesia de Santo Domingo

🅐Corner of Alcalá and Gurrión

Of the many churches in the city, this is the one most likely to take your breath away. Begun in 1572, it was completed over 200 years later

⑥
Museo Textil de Oaxaca

🏠 Hidalgo 917 ⏰ 10am-6pm daily 🌐 museotextil deoaxaca.org

Oaxaca's history of textile making is chronicled at this fascinating museum, with lots of colorful examples from the state's Indigenous communities on display. Set in a renovated 16th-century convent, the museum is funded by Mexican billionaire Alfredo Harp Helú.

---

⑦
Casa de Juárez

🏠 García Vigil 609 📞 (951) 516 18 60 ⏰ 10am-7pm Tue-Sun

The house where Benito Juárez lived between 1818 and 1828 is now a museum devoted to his life and times. Around a shady patio, the rooms have been kept almost as they were when Juárez lived here, and provide fascinating insights into the lives of the middle classes in 19th-century Mexico.

BENITO JUÁREZ (1806-72)

Benito Juárez, one of Mexico's greatest liberal reformers, was born just north of Oaxaca. He was orphaned at the age of three, but was educated by priests and went on to become a champion of agricultural reform and Indigenous people's rights. He was made president in 1858 and, after defeating the French, personally oversaw the execution of Emperor Maximilian in 1867 *(p58)*. He continued to pursue reform until his death.

at a total cost of over 12 million pesos in gold. Its misleadingly simple facade hides an interior that dazzles with gilded plaster and colored stucco, in a sublime combination of Romanesque, Baroque, Gothic, and Moorish styles. On the south side is the gilt-covered Capilla del Rosario, where there are numerous paintings of saints and Madonnas in varying sizes.

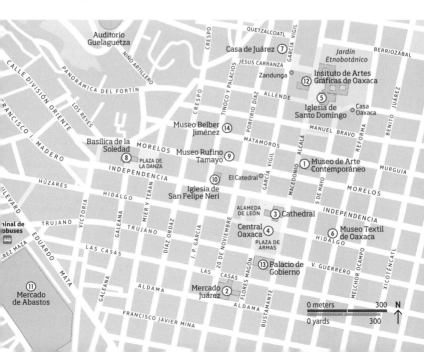

Basílica de la Soledad

⌂ Avenida Independencia 107 ☎ **(951) 516 50 76**

The Basílica de la Soledad is noted for its 79-ft (24-m) high Baroque facade, which resembles a folding altarpiece, and for its gilded interior. It was built between 1682 and 1690 to house the image of the Virgin of Solitude, Oaxaca's patron saint. This figure can be seen inside, encrusted with 600 diamonds and topped with a 4-lb (2-kg) gold crown. There is a small religious museum round the back of the church crowded with stained glass, paintings, and depictions of the Virgin of Solitude.

Museo Rufino Tamayo

⌂ Avenida Morelos 503 ☎ **(951) 516 76 17** ⏰ **10am–2pm & 4–7pm Mon & Wed–Sat, 10am–3pm Sun**

This beautifully presented museum, which is housed in a charming 17th-century building, contains a wondrous collection of pre-Hispanic art once owned by the artist Rufino Tamayo (p108). It was

← Pre-Hispanic stone carving exhibited at the Museo Rufino Tamayo

---

OAXACA'S POTTERY

Distinctive black or dark green ceramics are seen all around Oaxaca. The black style, from San Bartolo Coyotepec, 6 miles (10 km) south, was popularized by Doña Rosa Real. The green pottery, which is made in Santa María Atzompa, 5 miles (8 km) northwest of Oaxaca, is beautifully decorated. It is best to buy both in the villages themselves.

partly Tamayo's intention in collecting the pieces to stop them from falling into the hands of illicit artifact traders. He left them to his native state to make his fellow Mexicans aware of their rich heritage. The fascinating displays are arranged according to aesthetic themes, in a series of rooms set around an attractive 17th-century patio.

Iglesia de San Felipe Neri

⌂ Avenida de la Independencia 407

This charming church also has a facade shaped like an altarpiece, but its highlight is the gilt altarpiece itself, which is in the Churrigueresque style (p42). Benito Juárez, Mexico's most celebrated president, was married here.

Mercado de Abastos

⌂ Cnr of Periférico and Juárez Maza ⏰ **7am–9pm daily**

Most of the serious trading happens at this huge market,

situated southwest of the center. Crafts including ceramics, jewelry, and painted wooden animals are sold here but the real attraction is the chance to take in the noise, heat, smells, and color of one of the most vibrant markets in the country. The buyers and sellers chatter not in Spanish but mostly in the local Zapotec and Mixtec tongues, as they haggle at stalls laid out with the utmost care and attention. The liveliest day is Saturday.

Instituto de Artes Gráficas de Oaxaca

⌂ Macedonio Alcalá 507 ☎ **(951) 516 20 45** ⏰ **9:30am–8pm daily**

Oaxaca is known for its long-standing tradition of graphic arts, especially printmaking, as shown in its political and cultural posters. Founded in 1988 by Mexican graphic artist Francisco Toledo, the city's Graphic Arts Institute has galleries that highlight famous and emerging graphic artists. The institute also has an on-site movie theater, a large art library, a photography center, and a sound library. While the main focus, unsurprisingly, is on Mexican work and, specifically, Oaxacan artists, other Latin American artists' graphic artworks are showcased here as well.

The store at the back sells beautifully designed paper products. All proceeds go towards buying books for village libraries, prisons, and other charitable works.

⑬

Palacio de Gobierno

🏛 Plaza de la Constitución
📞 (951) 501 81 00 ⏰ 8am-3pm Mon-Sat

Oaxaca's Neo-Classical Palacio de Gobierno (the State Government building) occupies the zócalo's southern side. It was completed in 1884 and then remodeled in the 1940s.

The main reason for a visit today are the fabulous murals on the stairwells inside, which were created by Arturo García Bustos in the 1980s. They

🔍 HIDDEN GEM
Cactus Paradise

Behind the Instituto de Artes Gráficas de Oaxaca is a cactus garden, the Jardín Etnobotánico. A tranquil oasis, it has orchids, frangipani, and other native species. By guided tour only *(www. jardinoaxaca.mx)*.

depict in detail key moments in Oaxacan history, as well as famous locals such as Benito Juárez, José María Morelos, Porfirio Díaz, Vicente Guerrero (being shot at Cuilapan) and the 17th-century nun and love poet Juana Inés de la Cruz. Note that you need to sign in and pass through security to gain access to the building.

⑭

Museo Belber Jiménez

🏛 Matamoros 307
📞 (951) 514 49 96
⏰ 10am-7pm Wed-Mon

This museum – easy to spot thanks to its vibrantly blue exterior – displays the impressive private collection of local jeweller Francisco Jiménez and his wife Ellen Belber. Exhibits include Oaxacan folk art, rare gold Mixtec jewelry, an array of 20th-century silver work by William Spratling *(p162)*, Indigenous clothing, and pottery.

Look out for the original Mexican flag, which was presented to President Díaz on a visit to Oaxaca. One of the key pieces on display is the necklace given to Frida Kahlo by her husband, Diego Rivera, engraved with the word "Amor" ("love").

↑ The monastery complex, home to the Centro Cultural Santo Domingo

EAT

Oaxaca is a top foodie destination, and restaurant menus are bursting with local specialities, such as chocolate-based mole sauce and delicacies like fried maguet worms, ground with chilies as a seasoning.

Casa Oaxaca
🏛 Constitución 104-A
🌐 casaoaxacael restaurante.com

$$$

El Catedral
🏛 García Vigil 105 🕐 Tue
🌐 restaurantecatedral. com.mx

$$$

Zandunga
🏛 García Vigil 512
🌐 zandungasabor.com

$$⑤

THE INDIGENOUS PEOPLES OF MEXICO

Mexico is home to 68 Indigenous peoples, each speaking their own native language. Indigenous communities are concentrated mainly in the south of the country, although some large groups are found in the north.

Though Spanish conquistadors destroyed the last of the great Mesoamerican civilizations *(p144)*, their people did not disappear, and today the ancestors of the Aztecs, Maya, Zapotec, and many other cultures remain. Official statistics show that around 6 per cent of the country's population speak one of Mexico's 62 native language groups.

Many ethnic groups have multiple names: one they use to refer to themselves, and another that is a more common term used by the rest of Mexican society.

CONTEMPORARY COMMUNITIES

For centuries after the Spanish Conquest, Indigenous peoples fared poorly in Mexico, suffering from European diseases, slavery, and discrimination. Conditions have since improved; in 2021 the federal legislature established the Commission for Indigenous and Afro-Mexican Communities with the objective of ensuring that all legislation takes the needs of these diverse communities into consideration.

Some Indigenous peoples, such as the Rarámuri *(p181)*, retain much of their pre-Hispanic way of life, and the legacy of their cultural roots is still evident. One of the most authentic Indigenous markets in Mexico takes place every Thursday in the Zapotec town of Zaachila *(p253)*. The market, full of fruits and local produce, is virtually unchanged since the pre-Hispanic era.

↑ A Rarámuri woman of northern Mexico weaving a traditional basket out of pine needles

→
A street market in Chiapas, a traditional meeting place for Indigenous communities

Trique

▽ Living in Oaxaca state, the Trique (also known as the Triqui) are among the less numerous Indigenous peoples.

Rarámuri

The Rarámuri (or Tarahumara; *p181*) of Chihuahua state play a tough endurance ball game called *rarajipari*, which can last for several days.

Yaqui

△ The Yaqui (or Yoeme) people of Sonora state put their own twist on Easter and the Day of the Dead with the Deer Dance.

Maya

△ The Mesoamerican Maya civilization went into decline before the arrival of the Spanish. The descendants of the Maya, who inhabit the state of Chiapas and the Yucatán Peninsula, speak a large number of Maya languages.

Huichol

▽ The Huichol (or Wixáritari) are famous for their dazzlingly colored handicrafts, especially beadwork. They live on the border of Jalisco and Nayarit states.

Mixtec

The early Mixtec civilization emerged in Oaxaca state in the 1100s. Mixtec people are renowned for their jewelry, ceramics, and mosaic art.

Zapotec

▽ The Zapotec population is concentrated around Oaxaca. Villages are often associated with a specific craft, such as black pottery or textiles.

Lacandón

The Lacandón (or Hach Winik) live in Chiapas state, and have retained one of Mexico's most traditional cultures.

Totonac

△ Totonac communities live in southern Mexico, where they have preserved their language and many of their traditional customs, including the Voladores "flying" dancers *(p262)*.

② ⊗ ⊗ ⊗ ⊗ ⊗

MONTE ALBÁN

🅐 D6 **🅓 Off Mex 190, 5 miles (8 km) W of Oaxaca, Oaxaca** **🚌 From Oaxaca**
🕐 8am–5pm daily **🌐 inah.gob.mx**

Spectacularly situated on a mountain 1,315 ft (400 m) above the Oaxaca Valley, Monte Albán is the greatest of the Zapotec cities and one of the most important archaeological sites in Latin America.

In a triumph of engineering, the mountain top was leveled to allow for the creation of the ceremonial site. Its long history began with the Olmecs *(p272)* around 500 BC. The city came to dominate the cultural, religious, and economic life of the region. Falling under the influence of Teotihuacán *(p142)* during the height of its power, Monte Albán declined in later years and by AD 800 was largely abandoned. It was subsequently adopted by the Mixtecs, primarily as the site for some magnificent gold-laden burials.

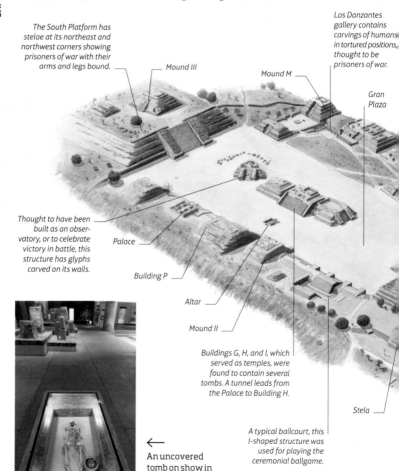

The South Platform has stelae at its northeast and northwest corners showing prisoners of war with their arms and legs bound.

Mound III

Los Danzantes gallery contains carvings of humans in tortured positions, thought to be prisoners of war.

Mound M

Gran Plaza

Thought to have been built as an observatory, or to celebrate victory in battle, this structure has glyphs carved on its walls.

Palace

Building P

Altar

Mound II

Buildings G, H, and I, which served as temples, were found to contain several tombs. A tunnel leads from the Palace to Building H.

Stela

A typical ballcourt, this I-shaped structure was used for playing the ceremonial ballgame.

← An uncovered tomb on show in the museum at Monte Albán

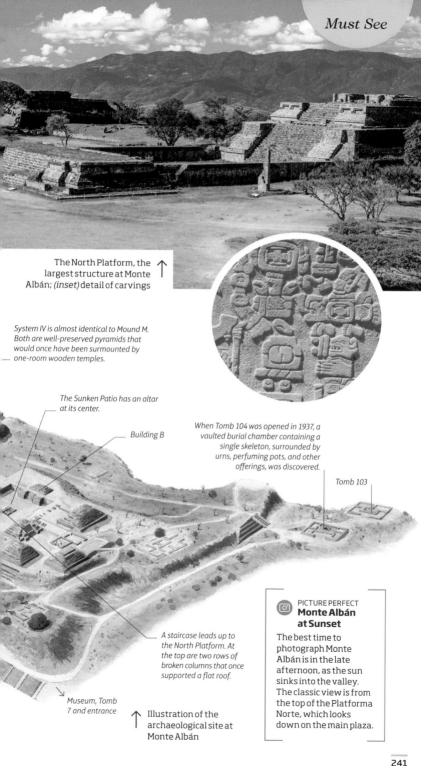

The North Platform, the largest structure at Monte Albán; *(inset)* detail of carvings

System IV is almost identical to Mound M. Both are well-preserved pyramids that would once have been surmounted by one-room wooden temples.

The Sunken Patio has an altar at its center.

Building B

When Tomb 104 was opened in 1937, a vaulted burial chamber containing a single skeleton, surrounded by urns, perfuming pots, and other offerings, was discovered.

Tomb 103

A staircase leads up to the North Platform. At the top are two rows of broken columns that once supported a flat roof.

Museum, Tomb 7 and entrance

↑ Illustration of the archaeological site at Monte Albán

PICTURE PERFECT
Monte Albán at Sunset

The best time to photograph Monte Albán is in the late afternoon, as the sun sinks into the valley. The classic view is from the top of the Platforma Norte, which looks down on the main plaza.

The rocky headland backdrop to Acapulco bay, a popular resort area ↑

ACAPULCO

 C6 　Guerrero 　✈🚌 　🅘 Avenida Costera Miguel Alemán 603; www.guerrero.travel

With its dazzling bay and long swathe of golden sands, backed by high-rise hotels and the green foothills of the Sierra Madre, Acapulco is the grande dame of the Mexican tourist industry. It's a sub-tropical city-by-the-sea, popular with inhabitants of the capital, who flock here for the nightlife, culinary scene, and attractions.

① Centro Cultural La Casa de los Vientos

 Inalámbrica 6, Cerro de la Pinzona (off La Quebrada) (744) 482 11 61 10am–6pm Mon-Fri

La Casa de los Vientos (aka "Exekatlkalli" or "House of the Winds"), is where Diego Rivera spent the last two years of his life, living with his former model and partner, Dolores Olmedo Patiño. Rivera worked on five large murals here between 1955 and 1957; from the street you can view the sensational work that covers the entire outside wall, made of seashells and colored tiles; the 66 ft (20 m) snake on the right depicts the Aztec god Tlaloc, while the 42 ft (13 m) feathered serpent on the left is Quetzalcoatl, another important Mesoamerican deity. There's more artwork inside, but since it's often closed for renovation, check the latest at the tourist office.

② Fuerte de San Diego

Calle Hornitos y Morelos (744) 482 38 28 9am–6pm Tue-Sun

Today, one of the few reminders of the city's history is the star-shaped Fuerte de San Diego, a 17th-century fort housing the Museo Histórico de Acapulco. It details the city's history from pre-Hispanic times to independence, with special emphasis on its importance as a commercial center.

③ La Quebrada

Avenida Adolfo López Mateos 340, Las Playas (744) 483 12 60 (hotel) 1pm, 7:30pm, 8:30pm, 9:30pm & 10:30pm daily

The death-defying cliff divers (clavadistas) of La Quebrada provide Acapulco's most spectacular attraction. The performance starts with the young men climbing a 125-ft (38-m) cliff. On reaching the top, they offer a prayer at a small altar before launching themselves into the shallow

 INSIDER TIP
Two Sides

Acapulco can be divided in two. Head west for the Centro Histórico, with historic remnants. Go east for the main beach, anchored by Avenida Costera Miguel Alemán, which has many restaurants, hotels, and clubs.

waters below. Each dive must coincide with an incoming wave if the diver is to avoid being dashed on the sharp rocks below. The shows and the rest of the evening can be seen from a viewing platform off the Plazuela de Quebrada (for a small charge), or more comfortably from Hotel El Mirador, where you can enjoy a drink while watching the divers. To view for free, keep walking further up to López Mateos. The last two shows are performed holding flaming torches.

4
Bahía de Acapulco

Much of the town stretches out along the shores of Acapulco Bay, which are broken up into a number of separate beaches.

Playa Caletilla and Playa Caleta are situated on the peninsula south of the Centro. Smaller and more intimate than the other beaches, they are popular with local families who enjoy the calm, clean waters. Boat trips can be taken from here for the ten-minute journey to Isla la Roqueta, a small offshore island featuring thatched-roof restaurants, a small zoo, and several more beaches.

Playa Honda, Playa Larga, and Playa Manzanillo, on the northern side of the same peninsula, were popular in the 1930s and 40s, but now serve mainly as departure points for charter fishing trips.

Playa Hornos and Playa Hornitos occupy a central position on the bay. They have a family atmosphere but can get busy on the weekends. They also have the advantage of several beachside restaurants and nearby Papagayo Park, which has boating, rides, and other children's activities.

Farther east, Playa Condesa is the best known and most crowded of all the beaches. It is considered by those in the know to be the resort's "hot-spot" and is a favorite with younger visitors. On the eastern side of the bay, Playa Icacos runs from the Presidente Hotel to the naval base and is generally less crowded than the other beaches.

Just east of the city, Puerto Marqués is a large bay with luxury hotels, food stands on the beach, and safe swimming.

Must See

EAT

Pitiona de Mar
This restaurant is known for its fresh and contemporary take on traditional Oaxacan cuisine. Expect imaginatively prepared dishes and cocktails giving a delicious taste of Oaxaca.

🚹 Avenida Costera de las Palmas s/n, Granjas del Marqués ☎ (744) 980 06 76

$$$

El Pescador
Watch the sunset over the Pacific while you enjoy drinks and the day's catch in this rightfully popular seaside restaurant.

🚹 Calle M. F. Maury 1, Fracc Costa Azul, Costa Azul ☎ (744) 469 12 34

$$$

4

PALENQUE

F5 **5 miles (8 km) SW of Palenque town, Chiapas**
From Palenque town **8am–4:45pm daily**
inah.gob.mx

The dense jungle covering the hills and the echoing sound of howler monkeys forms an evocative backdrop to the mighty Maya temples of Palenque, deservedly one of the best examples of Maya architecture in Mexico.

①
The Palace

Standing on a raised platform some 328 ft by 262 ft (100 m by 80 m) and 33 ft (10 m) high, the palace, a complex of courtyards and corridors, is the product of many kings. The earliest buildings date to the time of Pakal, but the basal platform conceals earlier phases, some preserved as underground galleries. The palace was the home of the royal family and their imme-diate entourage. Carvings and stucco decorations can be

seen in parts of the building. Particularly interesting are the sculptures of captives in the courtyard, where visitors could be suitably impressed by the might of the Palenque kings. The Oval Tablet depicts the accession of Pakal, who receives the emblems of office from his mother, a short-reigning queen.

②
Temple of the Jaguar

A short path behind the Temple of the Inscriptions

leads to this ruined structure. Its name derives from the image of a king seated on a jaguar throne inside, now destroyed. Unexcavated and overgrown, it gives an idea of what the site must have been like when it was first explored in the late 18th century.

③
Temple of the Inscriptions

This impressive pyramid was constructed during the 68-year reign of Pakal (AD 615–83) and later contained his funerary crypt, a fact that was revealed only by the dramatic

Did You Know?

In the Classic Maya era, the temples would have been covered with plaster and painted red.

←

The Palace dominating the center of Palenque and *(inset)* its four-tier tower that probably served as a lookout

discovery of his tomb by Alberto Ruz Lhuillier in 1952. The lid of the sarcophagus is decorated with a symbolic scene of Pakal's resurrection from the jaws of the underworld. Many of the artifacts and jewelry found in the tomb are on display in the Museo Nacional de Antropología in Mexico City *(p100)*.

Outlying Temples

Two clearly marked paths that set off from in front of the Temple of the Sun lead to Temples XVIII and XXI, and other isolated buildings that are nearby but hidden by trees. More buildings can be reached by the path from the site to the museum, which passes through Group B and the Group of the Bats. Branches off this path lead to Group C, Group I, and Group II. There are hundreds of similar but less accessible structures at Palenque that are hidden by the surrounding jungle.

⑤
The Museum

🕘 9am-4:45pm Tue-Sun

This modern building on the road between Palenque town and the archaeological site provides an overview of the development of the Maya city. Many artifacts found on the site are on display here, including the so-called Tablet of the Slaves.

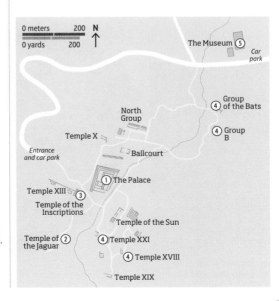

Exploring Palenque

Palenque is everything that an archaeological site should be: mysterious, solemn, well preserved, and imposing in its beautiful jungle setting. The Maya first settled here as early as 100 BC, and the city reached its apogee between AD 600 and 800, when it served as a regional capital. It fell into a precipitous decline in the early 10th century and was abandoned to the ever encroaching jungle. Hundreds of ruined buildings are spaced out over a huge area, but only a fairly small central area has been excavated, which has uncovered some ruins emblazoned with fine sculpture and splendid stuccowork.

The most interesting and best preserved buildings are in the Principal Group. The tallest and most imposing of these is the Temple of the Inscriptions. The entrance to the tomb is by way of two flights of steep stone steps that descend 82 ft (25 m). A few lesser-known temples can be reached by easy paths through the jungle. Another path leads from the Principal Group past a series of waterfalls to the site museum.

Did You Know?

The Temple of the Count was, in the 1830s, the home of an eccentric European nobleman.

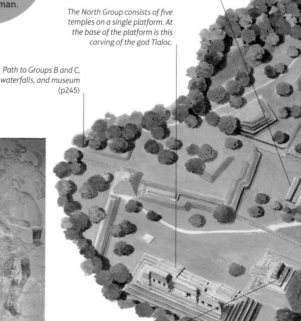

The Temple of the Foliated Cross is named after a panel showing a cruciform corn plant.

Inside the Temple of the Cross are carvings and a striking roof comb.

Although badly damaged, Temple XIV has been largely reconstructed. It contains some well-preserved glyphs and carvings.

Ballcourt

The North Group consists of five temples on a single platform. At the base of the platform is this carving of the god Tlaloc.

Path to Groups B and C, waterfalls, and museum (p245)

The Temple of the Count

↑ Detail of an unspoiled fresco uncovered in Temple XIV

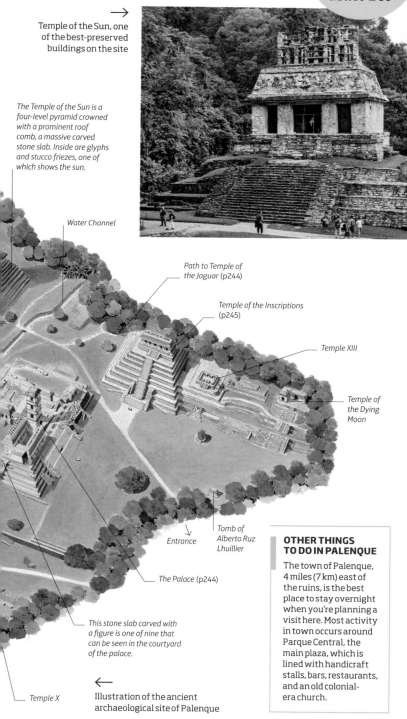

→ Temple of the Sun, one of the best-preserved buildings on the site

The Temple of the Sun is a four-level pyramid crowned with a prominent roof comb, a massive carved stone slab. Inside are glyphs and stucco friezes, one of which shows the sun.

Water Channel

Path to Temple of the Jaguar (p244)

Temple of the Inscriptions (p245)

Temple XIII

Temple of the Dying Moon

↓ *Entrance*

Tomb of Alberto Ruz Lhuillier

The Palace (p244)

This stone slab carved with a figure is one of nine that can be seen in the courtyard of the palace.

Temple X

← Illustration of the ancient archaeological site of Palenque

OTHER THINGS TO DO IN PALENQUE

The town of Palenque, 4 miles (7 km) east of the ruins, is the best place to stay overnight when you're planning a visit here. Most activity in town occurs around Parque Central, the main plaza, which is lined with handicraft stalls, bars, restaurants, and an old colonial-era church.

EXPERIENCE MORE

5

Bonampak

🅰 F6 🅰 95 miles (153 km)
SE of Palenque, Chiapas
🕐 8am–5pm daily 🌐 inah.
gob.mx

The Maya site of Bonampak reached its apogee under its ruler Yahaw Chan Muwan (AD 776–90). The subject of three fine stelae at the site, Yahaw Chan Muwan commissioned Bonampak's remarkable Temple of the Paintings. The walls and vaulted ceilings are decorated with vividly colored murals. These give insights into the life of the nobility of Bonampak and the pageantry surrounding Maya warfare. Murals in the two outer rooms show noblemen in elaborate headdresses. Below are musicians and dancers, and on the ceiling animals and figures representing constellations of the Maya cosmos. The two main paintings in the middle room depict a battle where Maya warriors are defeating their enemy.

6

Cascadas de Agua Azul

🅰 F5 🅰 Off Mex 199, 78
miles (125 km) NE of San
Cristóbal de las Casas,
Chiapas 🕐 8am–6pm daily
🌐 visitachiapas.com

The Parque Nacional Agua Azul has a series of stunning waterfalls – over 500 in all, ranging from 10 to 100 ft (3–30 m) in height.

It is possible to swim in some of the park's aquamarine-colored rock pools, which brings welcome relief from the heat and humidity of the lowlands. The falls are best visited outside of

EAT

TierrAdentro
A cultural space hosting live concerts, this restaurant, set around a large courtyard, serves everything from pizzas to Mexican classics.

🅰 F6 🅰 Real de
Guadalupe 24, San
Cristóbal de las Casas
📞 (967) 674 67 66

$$$

Remains of a Maya temple at Bonampak with *(inset)* striking murals inside

the rainy season (Jun–Sep), during which the waters become murky. Do not swim where there are signs warning of dangerous currents, and bring shoes that you are happy to wear in the water, which will make it easier and safer to step on the rocky ground underwater.

Some 14 miles (22 km) before the road from Agua Azul reaches Palenque *(p244)* is the spectacular, 100-ft-(30-m-) high waterfall at Misol-Ha. Set within the lush surroundings of a tropical rainforest, this is another good place to stop for a swim.

↑ A memorial cross erected in the square outside the cathedral of San Cristóbal de las Casas

San Cristóbal de las Casas

AF6 **A**Chiapas ⬛➡
iEje vial s/n, Los Pinos; (967) 678 65 70

Founded by the Spanish in 1528 and marked by centuries of geographical isolation, San Cristóbal is now a popular tourist spot. Its pedestrianized streets are lined with a blend of adobe houses, colonial-era churches, and cosmopolitan bars and restaurants. It's a great base for exploring highland Chiapas, a scenic region rich in Maya history and culture.

Situated 7,550 ft (2,300 m) above sea level, San Cristóbal has a refreshingly cool climate. The town's main square, Plaza 31 de Marzo, is dominated by the Palacio Municipal and the cathedral. The latter was started in the 16th century, but construction and alterations continued until the beginning of the 19th century. Its lavish interior contains an elaborate gold-encrusted pulpit and notable altarpieces. A few blocks north is the 16th-century Dominican Templo de Santo Domingo, the most impressive church in the city. It has an intricate pink facade, a gilded Baroque interior with magnificent altarpieces, and a pulpit carved from a single piece of oak. Next door, the **Museo Centro Cultural de los Altos** records the history of the city. On General Utrilla is the main market, Mercado José Castillo Tielemans, where Indigenous people from the surrounding hills come to trade.

Cutting through the heart of the city is the Andador Eclesiástico, a pedestrianized thoroughfare, lined with shops, restaurants, and cafés.

The **Na Bolom** museum and research center is devoted to studying and preserving the culture of the Lacandón Maya. Here visitors can learn more about the Lacandón culture through the museum, or with visits to their community in the rainforest.

The Iglesia de San Cristóbal to the west, and the Iglesia de Guadalupe to the east, offer excellent views over the city from their hilltop positions.

The ruined Maya ceremonial site of Moxviquil lies 1 mile (1.5 km) north of the center, and is accessed by a tranquil loop trail through the forest. There are also several villages 6 miles (10 km) or so from San Cristóbal, including San Juan Chamula, which has a beautiful church. A trip here provides an insight into the mix of Christian and pre-Hispanic traditions of the Tzotzil-speaking inhabitants. The village's fiestas and markets are among the best in Mexico. Visitors are warned not to take photos, especially in religious buildings, as this may cause serious offense.

Museo Centro Cultural de los Altos
⊛ 🅲 (967) 678 2809
🕙 10am–3pm Wed–Sun

Na Bolom
⊛⊜⊚ 🅰 Avenida Vicente Guerrero 33 🕙 10am–8pm daily 🅦 nabolom.org

---

THE ZAPATISTA UPRISING

On January 1, 1994, the EZLN (Zapatista Army of National Liberation) seized the town of San Cristóbal de las Casas. Their aims - taken from those of Emiliano Zapata *(p62)* - were a redistribution of power and resources from the wealthy few to the poor majority. Forced out of the town by the army, the Zapatistas fled into the jungle. A ceasefire was agreed in 1995. While the EZLN have now joined mainstream political parties, relations are tense, and visitors to the jungle area they occupy are cautioned to be discreet.

↑ Waterside houses among lush vegetation in Zihuatanejo

⑧
Ixtapa and Zihuatanejo

B5 **Guerrero** ✈🚌
🛈 **Ayuntamiento; www. zihuatanejodeazueta. gob.mx**

Ixtapa and Zihuatanejo are two resorts in one. Ixtapa is glitzy and full of luxury high-rise hotels. It is located along

an attractive curving beach, Playa Palmar, which backs onto a broad, palm-lined avenue packed with restaurants, shops, and nightclubs.

Zihuatanejo is more intimate, and still has the feel of a fishing community. Set in a scenic, sheltered bay, fishermen come here to sell their daily catch. Both resorts offer world-class deep-sea fishing, and excellent scuba diving.

⑨
Tuxtla Gutiérrez

E6 **Chiapas** 🚌
🛈 **Andrés Serra Rojas 1090, Edificio Torre Chiapas; www.chiapas.gob.mx**

Tuxtla Gutiérrez is a modern, working city, and a major gateway for visitors. Plaza Cívica, the main square, bustles with life and is

OAXACA'S COAST

This area has seen limited development and so still retains a sense of undisturbed charm. Some of the country's best beaches and lagoons are found here, as well as pretty fishing villages and excellent seafood.

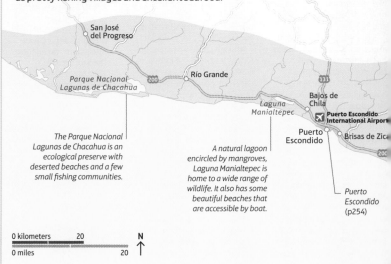

San José del Progreso

Río Grande

Parque Nacional Lagunas de Chacahua

Bajos de Chila

Laguna Manialtepec

Puerto Escondido International Airport

Puerto Escondido

Brisas de Zic...

The Parque Nacional Lagunas de Chacahua is an ecological preserve with deserted beaches and a few small fishing communities.

A natural lagoon encircled by mangroves, Laguna Manialtepec is home to a wide range of wildlife. It also has some beautiful beaches that are accessible by boat.

Puerto Escondido (p254)

0 kilometers 20
0 miles 20

N ↑

regularly used for music and street theater performances. On its south side is the cathedral, built at the end of the 16th century and refurbished in a more modern style in the 1980s. Twelve carved wooden figures of the apostles appear from the bell tower as the bells chime out the hour.

Just east of the plaza, the **Museo del Café** charts the history of coffee production in Chiapas. After exploring the museum, head west from the plaza along Avenida Central to Parque de la Marimba, a café-rimmed plaza that is Tuxtla's true social center. For another side of the cultural scene, the **Museo de la Marimba** showcases the history of the eponymous musical genre.

The **Museo Regional**, located northeast of the center, provides information on the geography and history of Chiapas. Nearby, the Jardín Botánico contains a range of plants native to the state, including beautiful orchids.

Museo del Café

⊛ ⬜2a C Oriente Norte 236 🕒9am–5pm Mon–Sat 🌐museodelcafe.chiapas. gob.mx

Museo de la Marimba

⬜9a Calle Poniente Norte 📞(961) 600 01 74 🕒10am–10pm Tue–Sun

Museo Regional

⊛ ⊛ ⊛ ⬜Calzada de los Hombres Ilustres 885 📞(961) 613 43 75 🕒9am–6pm Tue–Sun

---

10 ⊛

Yagul

⬛D6 ⬜Mex 190, 22 miles (36 km) SE of Oaxaca, Oaxaca 📞(951) 513 33 46 🕒8am–5pm daily

The city of Yagul was first inhabited by the Zapotecs in around 500 BC. However, it gained real religious and political influence in the region only after the decline of Monte Albán *(p240)*, at the end of the 8th century AD, and most of the buildings at the site date from this period. Yagul was subsequently taken over by the Mixtecs and was finally abandoned after the arrival of the Spanish.

Dramatically set on and around a rocky outcrop, the city had a good defensive position. It is divided into two main areas. The lower level, called the Acropolis, includes a large ballcourt, more than 30 tombs, and a labyrinthine complex of buildings known as the Palace of the Six Patios. On the summit of the outcrop is the Fortress, surrounded by a strong defensive wall and offering superb views.

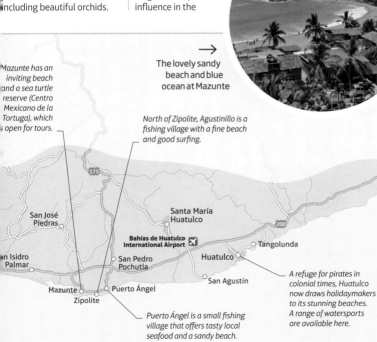

→ The lovely sandy beach and blue ocean at Mazunte

Mazunte has an inviting beach and a sea turtle reserve (Centro Mexicano de la Tortuga), which is open for tours.

North of Zipolite, Agustinillo is a fishing village with a fine beach and good surfing.

San José Piedras

San Isidro Palmar

Mazunte

Zipolite

Puerto Ángel

Santa María Huatulco

Bahías de Huatulco International Airport ✈

San Pedro Pochutla

Huatulco

San Agustín

Tangolunda

A refuge for pirates in colonial times, Huatulco now draws holidaymakers to its stunning beaches. A range of watersports are available here.

Puerto Ángel is a small fishing village that offers tasty local seafood and a sandy beach.

Cañón del Sumidero

⚠E5/6 ⚠Chiapas

The breathtaking Sumidero Canyon forms the heart of a beautiful national park. Legend has it that in the mid-16th century, several hundred Indigenous warriors chose to hurl themselves down its precipitous sides after a defiant last stand, rather than submit to the invading Spanish forces.

Nearly half a mile (a kilometer) deep, and around 9 miles (14 km) in length, the canyon was carved by the Grijalva river over the course of millions of years. This important river stretches from Guatemala to the Gulf of Mexico.

Excellent views of the sheer-sided canyon are available from a series of five lookout points along its western rim. Alternatively, visitors can enjoy a two-hour boat trip along the river. Boats leave daily from two embarkation points, one at Cahuaré (on the west bank of the Grijalva, on Mex 190), and the other at the docks in Chiapa de Corzo (call 961 616 06 80 for more information). The trip takes in caves and waterfalls. It also provides an opportunity to see a variety of unusual plants, and many animals and birds, including monkeys, crocodiles, iguanas, herons, and kingfishers.

Mitla

⚠D6 ⚠Off Mex 190, 27 miles (44 km) SE of Oaxaca, Oaxaca ⚠(951) 513 33 52 ⚠8am–5pm daily

An important Zapotec city-state after the decline of Monte Albán (p240), Mitla was home to approximately 10,000

🔍 HIDDEN GEM
The Mixteca

The Mixteca region near Mitla has dazzling mountain scenery and some of Mexico's most significant colonial-era buildings, though it remains off the beaten path. Highlights include the extensive crumbling monasteries of Yanhuitlán, Teposcolula, Coixtlahuaca and Mixtec ruins at San Martín Huamelulpan, and the Saturday market at Tlaxiaco.

people at its height. The city was later occupied by the Mixtecs, who had a significant influence on the architecture and decoration of its buildings.

Many of Mitla's temples were destroyed by the Spanish when they invaded, and the stonework was used

to build the Iglesia de San Pablo, the huge Catholic church that dominates the site.

Five main groups of buildings remain, two of which are accessible to visitors. The Grupo de las Columnas, in the east of the site, is a former palace. It consists of three large rooms set around tombs and a courtyard. The palace walls are decorated with the distinctive geometric mosaics that characterize Mitla's buildings. Each frieze is made of up to 100,000 separate pieces of cut stone. One of the rooms, the Salón de las Columnas, houses six monolithic pillars that once supported the roof.

To the north is the Grupo de la Iglesia, centered around the colonial-era church. The pre-Hispanic buildings that survived its construction are of similar design to those in the Grupo de las Columnas, but on a smaller scale. They still retain traces of paintwork.

↑ Part of the substantial ruins still standing at the archaeological site of Mitla

13

Zimatlán-Ocotlán

🅰D6 🏠Oaxaca 🚌
ℹMurguia 206; www.
oaxaca.travel

The Central Valleys of Oaxaca state comprise several distinct regions. Zimatlán and Ocotlán sit in the heart of the Valles Centrales, south of Oaxaca city. These districts abound with interesting sights that make perfect day trips from the busy city. One such place is San Antonio Arrazola, which produces carved wooden figures of animals painted in vivid, multicolored designs. San Bartolo Coyotepec is another good place to discover local crafts, as this is where the gleaming black pottery (barro negro brillante), which is commonly found in souvenir shops, is made.

The former convent at Cuilapan de Guerrero, on Mex 131, was established on the site of a Zapotec pyramid in 1550. It was abandoned two centuries later, but today still retains some impressive architectural features and murals. The roofless chapel

has a Renaissance facade, an elegant columned nave, and thick earthquake-proof walls. Vicente Guerrero, a revolutionary fighter during the War of Independence, was imprisoned here before being executed on Valentine's Day 1831. A monument to his memory stands at the convent. Zaachila, also on Mex 131, is the site of the last Zapotec capital. A pyramid and two tombs are open to the public.

AFRO-MEXICANS IN COSTA CHICA

Stretching from Acapulco (p242) to Juchitan, the Costa Chica region is home to a large population of Afro-Mexicans, especially in the city of Cuajinicuilapa. It's a great place to explore this aspect of Mexico's culture and history. Start with the Museo Nacional de la Cultura Afro-Mestiza (Cuauhtémoc s/n, Centro, Cuajinicuilapa), for an interactive look at the cultural legacy of Afro-Mexican people. Look out for local culinary specialties, too, such as caldo de res rojo (red beef stew).

← Cañon del Sumidero's Christmas tree falls, so named for its color and shape

14

Comitán de Domínguez

F6 Chiapas 1a Av Norte; www. turismochiapas.gob.mx

Set on a rocky hillside, this city (known simply as Comitán) has an elegant 16th–17th-century core and a small but absorbing market. At its heart lies the spacious Plaza Central, and the 17th-century Templo de Santo Domingo. Just east of the plaza, the Museo de Arqueología displays artifacts from local Maya sites.

To the south, the **Casa Museo Belisario Domínguez** preserves the former home of the local doctor and liberal politician who was assassinated in 1913 after criticizing President Huerta. Of the city's historic churches, the twin-towered, all-white Templo de San José is especially attractive, while the 19th-century Iglesia de San Caralampio features a flamboyant red and peach-colored stucco facade.

Casa Museo Belisario Domínguez

Avenida Central Sur Belisario Domínguez (963) 632 13 00 10am-6:45pm Mon-Fri, 10am-2pm & 4-6:45pm Sat, 10am-1:45pm Sun

SHOP

Comiteco Nueve Estrellas

Comitán is famed for *comiteco*, a local spirit made from agave and flavored with tropical fruits. This shop sells its own top-quality bottles.

F6 1a Avenida Poniente Sur, Comitán de Domínguez facebook.com/ comiteco.nueveestrellas

15

Puerto Escondido

D6 Oaxaca Blvd Benito Juárez; www.oaxaca.travel

Puerto Escondido, literally the "undiscovered port," lived up to its name until discovered by hippies in the 1970s and has since become a significant tourist destination. Although showing some signs of the strain of development, it retains much of the fishing-village character that originally made it popular.

Playa Marinero, the main beach, is popular with locals and tourists alike. Shaded by palm trees, it faces a small cove dotted with fishing boats and fed by an endless supply of gentle surf. Playa Zicatela is a larger beach to the west and is very popular with surfers, especially in the late summer months when the waves are at their highest.

At the end of November, the town comes alive for an international surfing festival. A popular local fiesta with music and dancing takes place at the same time. Puerto Escondido is also a good base for trips to the nearby freshwater lagoons, such as Laguna Manialtepec.

Just southeast of Puerto Escondido, the village of Barra de Navidad guards the mouth of the Río Colotepec, home to mangrove swamps, crocodiles, and bird species. Locals offer various tours.

TOP 3 REGIONAL FIESTAS

Guelaguetza
Groups from all over the state gather in Oaxaca to reenact traditional dances on the last two Mondays of July.

Feria de San Cristóbal
On July 25, a torchlit procession takes place to honor the patron saint of San Cristóbal de las Casas.

Noche de los Rábanos
Oaxaca locals compete to carve vegetables into people, animals, and plants on December 23, also known as the Night of the Radishes.

16

Chiapa de Corzo

F6 Chiapas Corner of 5 de Febrero and Vicente López; www.turismo chiapas.gob.mx

Overlooking the Río Grijalva, Chiapa de Corzo is Tuxtla's smaller and more elegant neighbor. Officially founded in 1528, it was the first Spanish city in Chiapas – today it's also the starting point for Cañón del Sumidero boat rides *(p252)*.

The central Plaza Ángel Albino Corzo is dominated by the Fuente Colonial, an ornate

↑ Fuente Colonial, the main feature of Plaza Ángel Albino Corzo, Chiapa de Corzo

↑ The Maya ruins of Toniná, laid out across the rolling green hills

16th-century fountain that appears on Chiapas licence plates. South, behind the *portales* (arcades), stands the handsome church, Templo de Santo Domingo de Guzmán, and the Centro Cultural, a series of galleries in an old convent. Northeast of the plaza, the pre-Hispanic ruins of Chiapa de Corzo originated as a farming settlement in the early pre-Classic period (1400–850 BC).

Toniná

F6 **66 miles (106 km) E of San Cristóbal, Chiapas** **(961) 612 83 60** **8am-5pm daily**

In its prime, the Classic-period Maya city of Toniná is thought to have been a great regional power – like all the big Maya centers, it was mysteriously abandoned after 900 AD. The main focus of the ruins today is known as the Acrópolis, featuring seven artificial terraces set into the hillside and incorporating dozens of buildings and temples. Several carved

stucco reliefs survive, including the massive Mural de las Cuatro Eras, which tells the story of Maya cosmology with plenty of decapitated heads and a skeletal Lord of Death. The temple at the summit provides stellar views across the valley. The museum at the main entrance adds context with scale models, artifacts, and sculptures from the site.

Yaxchilán

F6 **80 miles (130 km) SE of Palenque, Chiapas** **8am-5pm daily** **inah. gob.mx**

The city of Yaxchilán, set 66 ft (20 m) above the Usumacinta river in the heart of the Lacandón rainforest, is one of the most dramatic of all Maya sites. It can only be reached by air from Palenque, or by

taking a boat along the river from Frontera Corozal.

Built between AD 350 and 800, it rose to prominence during the 8th century under the command of its most famous kings, "Shield Jaguar", and his son "Bird Jaguar." Yaxchilán is rich in glyphs, stelae, carved lintels, stucco roof combs, and temples. One of the best-preserved buildings is Temple 33.

→ Detail on a lintel at Yaxchilán's Maya archaeological site

A DRIVING TOUR
THE TLACOLULA VALLEY

Length 55 miles (90 km) **Stopping-off points** The town of Santiago Matatlán is a traditional center of the local mezcal industry, from one-person artisan distilleries to large factory operations. You can visit most of them and enjoy free samples.

This region is a great place for history lovers to explore multiple Mesoamerican sites in one easy road trip. The area around Oaxaca, and in particular the Tlacolula Valley, has been an important cultural and historical center since the 10th century BC. Over 2,500 years of civilization can be explored here, from the early Zapotecs to the final Mesoamerican empire of the Aztecs. Today, the valley is crammed with diverse attractions reflecting its Zapotec, Mixtec, Aztec, and Spanish heritage.

Reputed to be over 2,000 years old, the **Árbol del Tule** *in Santa Maria del Tule is one of the world's largest trees.*

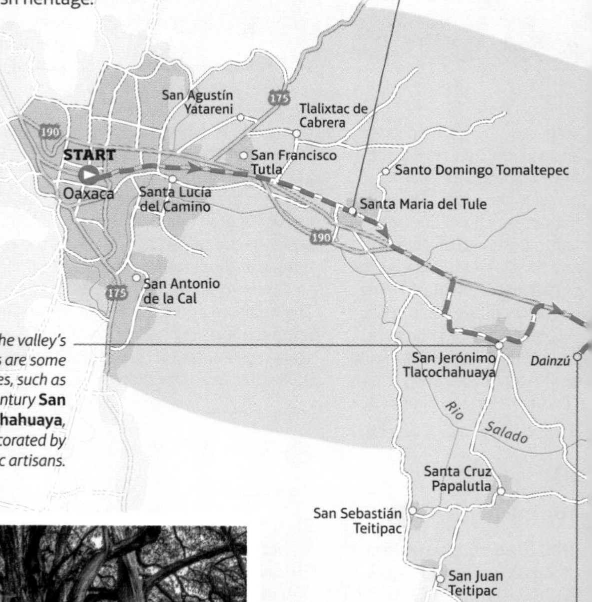

Alongside the valley's ancient ruins are some colonial-era sites, such as the 16th-century **San Jerónimo Tlacochahuaya**, *which was decorated by Zapotec artisans.*

START
Oaxaca
San Agustín Yatareni
Tlalixtac de Cabrera
San Francisco Tutla
Santa Lucía del Camino
Santo Domingo Tomaltepec
Santa Maria del Tule
San Antonio de la Cal
San Jerónimo Tlacochahuaya
Dainzú
Río Salado
Santa Cruz Papalutla
San Sebastián Teitipac
San Juan Teitipac

↑ Santa Maria del Tule's 2,000-year-old *Árbol del Tule* (Tree of the Tule)

Once a Zapotec city, **Dainzú** *has a tiered pyramid, a ballcourt, several tombs, and a unique collection of carved stone reliefs depicting ballgame players. Parts of the site date from 350 BC.*

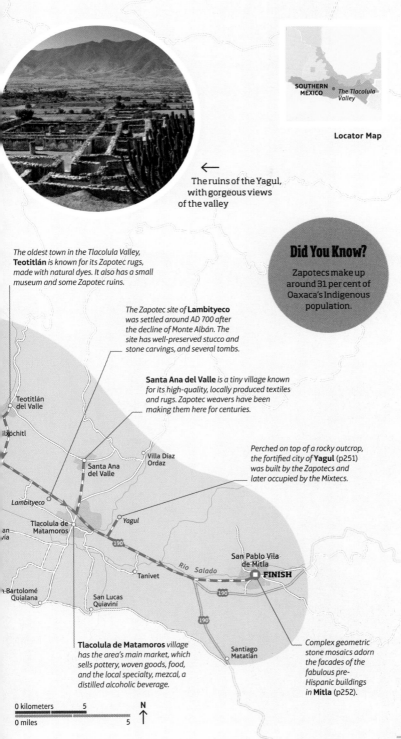

The ruins of the Yagul, with gorgeous views of the valley

Locator Map

SOUTHERN MEXICO · The Tlacolula Valley

The oldest town in the Tlacolula Valley, **Teotitlán** is known for its Zapotec rugs, made with natural dyes. It also has a small museum and some Zapotec ruins.

The Zapotec site of **Lambityeco** was settled around AD 700 after the decline of Monte Albán. The site has well-preserved stucco and stone carvings, and several tombs.

Santa Ana del Valle is a tiny village known for its high-quality, locally produced textiles and rugs. Zapotec weavers have been making them here for centuries.

Perched on top of a rocky outcrop, the fortified city of **Yagul** (p251) was built by the Zapotecs and later occupied by the Mixtecs.

Tlacolula de Matamoros village has the area's main market, which sells pottery, woven goods, food, and the local specialty, mezcal, a distilled alcoholic beverage.

Complex geometric stone mosaics adorn the facades of the fabulous pre-Hispanic buildings in **Mitla** (p252).

Did You Know?

Zapotecs make up around 31 per cent of Oaxaca's Indigenous population.

Teotitlán del Valle

ilxochitl

Lambityeco

Villa Díaz Ordaz

Santa Ana del Valle

Yagul

Tlacolula de Matamoros

190

an vía

Tanivet

Río Salado

San Pablo Vila de Mitla

FINISH

190

Bartolomé Quialana

San Lucas Quiavini

190

Santiago Matatlán

0 kilometers 5
0 miles 5

N ↑

THE GULF COAST

The tropical plains fringing the Gulf of Mexico were once home to three major Mesoamerican cultures – the Olmecs, the Totonacs, and the Huastecs. In 1519 this coast was once again at the fulcrum of Mexican history, when Cortés disembarked here on his conquest of the Aztec empire. Over the next 300 years, the region's colonial-era towns prospered due to their startegic coastal position. The Port of Veracruz was particularly important to the colony of New Spain; no fewer than 200,000 enslaved African peoples were forced into the country here, while vast quantities of gold and silver were shipped to Europe. International trade from Veracruz slumped between independence and the revolution, but picked up again in the mid-20th century. Today, Veracruz is once again a bustling port city, while the rest of the Gulf Coast produces much of Mexico's sugarcane, citrus fruits, vanilla, and coffee.

This green and fertile region is full of outdoor adventures, from the snowcapped Pico de Orizaba to the humid, low-lying jungle in the south. The Gulf Coast is also a cultural hotspot, with fascinating Indigenous traditions like the flying *voladores* performances and the mix of Mexican and African culture in the Costa Chica region.

THE GULF COAST

Must Sees

1 El Tajín
2 Museo de Antropología de Xalapa

Experience More

3 Xalapa
4 Coatepec
5 Quiahuiztlan
6 Cempoala
7 Papantla
8 Córdoba
9 Veracruz
10 Orizaba
11 San Andrés Tuxtla
12 Santiago Tuxtla
13 Tapijulapa
14 Comalcalco
15 Malpasito
16 Villahermosa
17 Laguna de Catemaco
18 Tlacotalpan
19 Xico

Gulf of Mexico

THE YUCATÁN PENINSULA
p276

Chenkán

Sabancuy

Nuevo Progreso

Frontera

Paraíso

Sanchez Magallanes

COMALCALCO 14

TABASCO

Reforma

Coatzacoalcos

Cunduacán

VILLAHERMOSA

Cárdenas

16 Villahermosa International Airport

Jonuta

El Triunfo

Minatitlán

Las Choapas

Huimanguillo

Río Grijalva

Chablé

Emiliano Zapata

Tenosique

ERACRUZ

Chontalpa

Teapa

195

Macuspana

186

Palenque

Cerro Nanchital

Pichucalco

13 TAPIJULAPA

Istmo de huantepec

15 MALPASITO

CHIAPAS

199

Raudales

Parque Natural Montes Azules

SOUTHERN MEXICO
p230

Ocozocuautla

195

0 kilometers   100

Cintalapa

Tuxtla Gutiérrez

0 miles   100

N
↑

① ⊘ ⊗ ⊕ ⊕

EL TAJÍN

⊞ D4 ⊞ Off Mex 180, 7 miles (12 km) SE of Poza Rica, Veracruz
⊟ From Papantla or Poza Rica ⊙ 9am–5pm daily ⊞ inah.gob.mx

An outstanding example of the grandeur and importance of the pre-Hispanic cultures of Mexico, the mysterious El Tajín site displays some unique structures, but the Pyramid of the Niches takes center stage.

Developed from an earlier settlement, the city of El Tajín was a political and religious center for the Totonac civilization. Many of its buildings date from the early Postclassic period, between AD 900 and 1150. Decorated with relief panels and sculptures, they would have been painted in strong colors such as red, blue, and black. The excavated nucleus of this spectacular ancient city covers about 0.4 sq miles (1 sq km), but the entire urban area once spread over 4 sq miles (10 sq km) and had a population of 25,000.

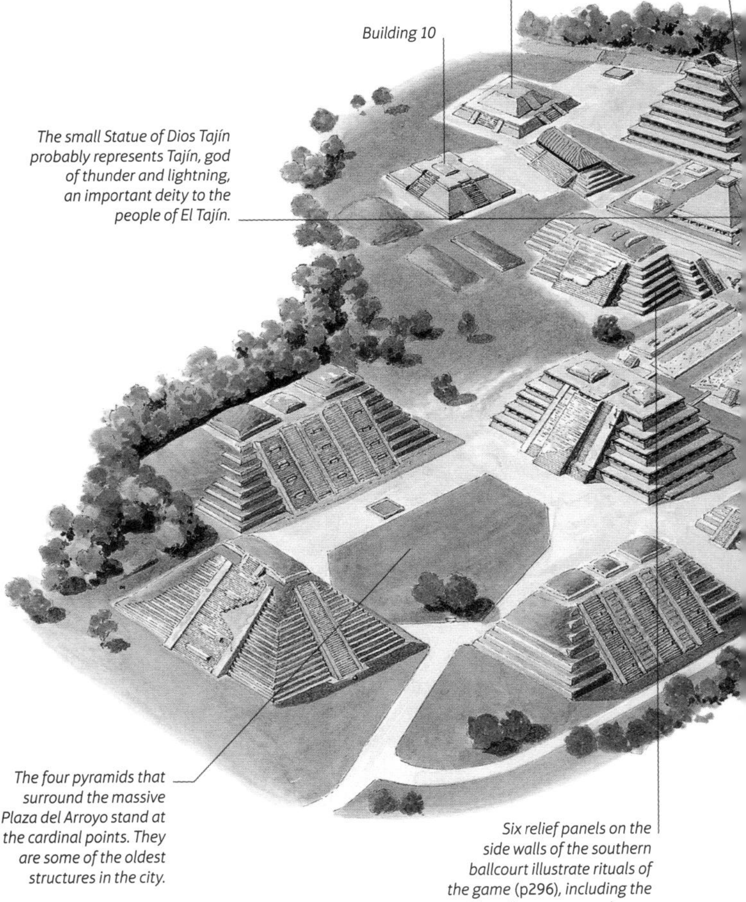

Originally crowned by a temple, the Pyramid of the Niches has 365 niches, representing the days of the year. Each niche may have held an offering.

Building 12

Building 10

The small Statue of Dios Tajín probably represents Tajín, god of thunder and lightning, an important deity to the people of El Tajín.

The four pyramids that surround the massive Plaza del Arroyo stand at the cardinal points. They are some of the oldest structures in the city.

Six relief panels on the side walls of the southern ballcourt illustrate rituals of the game (p296), including the sacrifice of one or more players.

The well-preserved ruins of the El Tajín settlement set against a jungle backdrop

↗ *El Tajín Chico*

— *Northern Ballcourt*

→ *Plaza Oriente and Gran Xicalcoliuhqui*

↑ Illustration showing the layout of the El Tajín archaelogical site

Ballcourt 13/14

LOS VOLADORES

This ancient ritual of the Totonac people from the Papantla region takes place daily at the site entrance. Five men climb to the top of a pole reaching as high as 100 ft (30 m). While one plays a drum and a pipe on a platform at the top, the other four *voladores* (fliers) launch themselves from the top of the pole and descend as the ropes round the pole unwind. In total, the *voladores* circle the pole 52 turns, symbolizing the cycles of the Mesoamerican calendar.

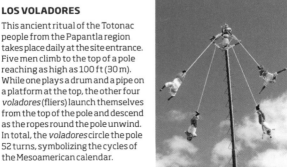

Olmec heads displayed inside the museum and *(inset)* the museum's exterior

2

MUSEO DE ANTROPOLOGÍA DE XALAPA

🅐 D5 🏠 Avenida Xalapa, Xalapa 🚌 CAXA Central de Autobuses, Avenida 20 de Noviembre Oriente 271 🕒 9am-5pm Tue-Sun 🌐 uv.mx/max

Housed in a beautifully light and airy modern complex, these stunning treasures, spanning some 3,000 years of pre-Hispanic history, include some of the most important ancient artifacts in the country. The galleries are presented around tranquil gardens and patios.

Known commonly as MAX, the Xalapa Anthropology Museum is second in importance only to the anthropology museum in Mexico City*(p100)*. Its outstanding collection is displayed in spacious marble halls and open-air patios. It consists of sculptures and artifacts from the Gulf Coast's major pre-Hispanic civilizations, found at various sites within the region. The first halls are dedicated to the Olmec civilization (p272), which include a terracotta funerary urn that, when discovered in Catemaco, contained the remains of a small child. Central Veracruz and the Totonacs follow, and the final room exhibits the highly stylized sculptures of the Huastec culture. Guided tours are free, and should be reserved in advance.

EXPERIENCE MORE

Xalapa

🅐D5 🄰Veracruz 🚌
🄸 Avenida 20 de Noviembre
376; www.veracruz.mx

The capital of Veracruz state, Xalapa (or Jalapa) is known for its university and cultural life, and the second most important anthropology museum in Mexico after the Museo Nacional de Antropología (p100) in Mexico City. The city enjoys a beautiful setting: on a clear day there are splendid views of the 13,940-ft (4,250-m) Cofre de Perote peak from Parque Juárez, the main plaza. To one side of this square is the Neo-Classical **Palacio de Gobierno**, which has a mural by Mario Orozco Rivera (1930–98) on its stairs. Opposite the Palacio is the 18th-century cathedral. Uphill from the city center, colored houses with tiled roofs and wrought-iron balconies line the streets around the market.

It is a good base to explore the remote Filobobos archaeological zone. This consists of several Meosamerican sites, only two of which have been throughly explored. The main site, **El Cuajilote**, was founded around AD 200 by the Totonacs, and was in use until AD 800. Access to the site is via a 5-mile (8-km) scenic walk. It is worth the effort of getting there, however, because the archaeological remains are truly spectacular.

You can also reach El Cuajilote through an organized rafting trip along the Río Filobobos (Filobobos river). These tours can be booked in Xalapa (p264) or Tlapacoyan, through companies such as Aventurec (www.aventurec.com). Other river tours are also available. Whitewater rafting offers a challenge through the steep-sided river gorge to the east of Tlapacoyan.

GALLERY GUIDE

The exhibits are displayed in a descending series of halls and patios with steps and wheelchair ramps linking each level. Beginning at the main entrance, the items are arranged chronologically. The gardens contain flora representative of different areas of Veracruz state.

Palacio de Gobierno

🄰 Avenida Enriquez 🄲(228) 84 17 40 00 🄾Mon–Fri

El Cuajilote

🌀 🄰Off minor road from Tlapacoyan to Plan de Arroyos, 68 miles (110 km) NW of Xalapa 🄾Tue–Sun

EAT & DRINK

Café Chiquito

Great buffet breakfasts and set lunches are served in this pretty café, with outdoor tables in a plant-filled patio. There is also live music.

🅐D5 🄰Nicolás Bravo 3, Xalapa 🅦cafechiquito.com

La Parroquia de Veracruz

The place for serious coffee drinkers. Also serves excellent Mexican cuisine for lunch and dinner.

🅐D5 🄰Calle Juan de la Luz s/n, Xalapa 🅦laparroquia-deveracruz.com

---

Flor Catorce

Open from early morning until late evening, Flor Catorce is a charming café in Xalapa's Centro neighborhood.

🅐D5 🄰Calle Morelos 1, Xalapa 🄲(228) 132 51 26

TOP 3 REGIONAL FIESTAS

Carnival
Across the Gulf Coast, pre-lent celebrations start with the burning of a huge figure, who represents "bad temper," followed by floats, parades and dancing.

Candelaria
In the fortnight leading up to February 2, the Christian festival of Candlemas features street stalls, dancing and music on the Gulf Coast. In Tlacotalpan the local Virgin is taken on a river procession with hundreds of boats.

Feria de Santiago Tuxtla
Gigantic *mojiganga* dolls are taken around Santiago Tuxtla in this elaborate saint's celebration on the week of July 25.

Coatepec

🅐D5 🄰Veracruz 🚌
🄸Matias Rebolledo 1; (228) 203 19 58

The lovely town of Coatepec is famous for its culinary offerings, including coffee, fruit, liqueurs, and seafood.

The town's elegant houses were built with the proceeds of the early 20th-century coffee boom. In the center of town is the attractive Basílica Menor de Nuestra Señora de Guadalupe. The **Casa de la Cultura**, off the main square, hosts exhibitions, plays, concerts, and workshops. The town's biggest festival is the Feria del Café y la Orquídea, held every May. Hundreds of Mexican and international coffee and orchid growers display their products, with food stalls, live music, and traditional dances.

Casa de la Cultura
🄰Jiménez del Campillo 4
🄲(228) 816 67 57
🄾9am-7pm Mon-Sat

Quiahuiztlan

🅐D4 🄰Mex 180, 15 miles (24 km) N of Cempoala, Veracruz 🄾8:30am-5pm Tue-Sun 🅦sic-gob.mx

Once inhabited by 15,000 people, the Totonac city of Quiahuiztlan was a hilltop stronghold. It was constructed in the late Classic period, when raids by warlike nomads from the north forced sites like El Tajín (p262) to be abandoned. Despite originally being ringed by defensive walls, it was twice conquered, first by the Toltecs in the 9th century and then by the Aztecs in the 13th century.

Today the only part of the terraced site that can be visited is the cemetery. Here some 100 tiny tombs were discovered, each resembling a pre-Hispanic temple. Many had human bones and skulls in burial chambers in their bases. Small holes in the backs of the tombs may have been for relatives to communicate

←
The cemetery at Quiahuiztlan, a Totonac ruin from the late Classic period

↑ Ruins of Cempoala, where the Totonacs joined forces with Cortés against he Aztecs

with the dead. Across the main road from Quiahuiztlan is Villa Rica de la Vera Cruz, which was the first Spanish settlement in Mexico, now a fishing village.

  6

Cempoala

⚑D5 ⌂Francisco del Paso y Troncoso, Zempoala, Veracruz ⏱9am-6pm daily ▣inah.gob.mx

Shortly after their arrival in Mexico *(p57)*, Cortés and his men sheltered in the Totonac city of Cempoala (also known as Zempoala). Like many other cities, it was subjugated by the Aztecs, and the Totonacs were forced to pay them large tributes of food and prisoners. This led Cempoala's governor to collaborate with Cortés in return for protection.

The walled archaeological site containing the ruins of the former Totonac city adjoins Cempoala town. Around a central plaza are buildings faced with smooth, rounded stones. Straight ahead from the entrance is the Templo Mayor, a 13-tier pyramid topped by a sanctuary, which was originally thatched with palm leaves. In Las Chimeneas

(The Chimneys) – named for its hollow columns – archaeologists found a *chacmool*-like figure *(p144)*, suggesting the Maya were associated with the site. The east-facing Gran Pirámide was a temple dedicated to the sun.

 7

Papantla

⚑D4 ⌂Veracruz ▣ ℹCalzada Jose Garcia Payon s/n; (784) 842 82 34

Best known as the home of the pole-plunging Totonac *voladores*, Papantla is the center for Mexico's vanilla industry, which has been cultivated here since pre-Hispanic times. The city is also the gateway to El Tajín *(p262)*, but is worth a visit for its own attractions. It has a lively cultural scene, several museums, and many murals adorning public buildings, including one on the Palacio Municipal on the main *zócalo*. The most interesting museum in town is the **Museo Teodoro Cano**, with a collection of the founder's murals as well as regional history exhibits.

Besides the Totonac *voladores*, several other traditional dances are celebrated

here, including the Danza de los Guaguas, which is dedicated to the sun.

Museo Teodoro Cano
 ⌂Calle Rodolfo Curti 101 ℂ(228) 156 71 83 ⏱10am-7pm Tue-Sun

EAT

Nakú
A bustling venue that offers live music and a range of local specialties, including great bean tamales.

⚑D4 ⌂Heroico Colegio Militar, Col. Libertad, Papantla ℂ(784) 842 31 12

$$$

Plaza Pardo
Regional favorites, such as tamales and shrimp dishes, plus city views from the balcony.

⚑D4 ⌂Juan Enríquez 105, Papantla ℂ(784) 842 00 59

$$$

Children enjoy the fountains along a pretty street near the waterfront in Veracruz ↑

8
Córdoba

△D5 ◻Veracruz ▦
🛈 Palacio Municipal; (271) 717 17 00

Córdoba is a busy, modern town, although traces of its colonial-era heritage are still to be found around the central Plaza de Armas.

Historically, Córdoba's most significant building is the 18th-century Portal de Zevallos, an arcade on the north side of the Plaza de Armas. The Treaties of Córdoba, endorsing Mexican independence, were signed here in 1829. Also on the plaza are the Neo-Classical Palacio Municipal and the Catedral de la Inmaculada Concepción, which houses a lifelike image of the town's patron saint, the Virgen de la Soledad (Virgin of Solitude). Just off the plaza is the **Museo de Córdoba**, a history museum about the city and its pre-Hispanic roots. Housed in a beautiful mansion, its small collection includes Olmec sculptures and the 1821 Treaty of Córdoba.

West of Córdoba is the Barranca de Metlac, a spectacular gorge spanned by

four bridges. One of these, a 19th-century railroad bridge, features in several paintings by artist José María Velasco.

Museo de Córdoba
◈ ◻Calle 3 305-A
📞 (271) 712 09 67
🕒 10am-7pm Tue–Sun

9
Veracruz

△D5 ◻Veracruz ✕▦
🛈 Palacio Municipal, Zaragoza s/n, Col Centro; www.disfrutaveracruz.mx

Veracruz is a place of fun. The city life revolves around the Plaza de Armas and the *malecón* (waterfront promenade), an enjoyable place to stroll and watch the ships come and go.

The tree-lined Plaza de Armas is flanked by the elegant 17th-century Palacio Municipal and the cathedral. The dome of the cathedral is decorated with Puebla tiles *(p148)* and crowned with a lantern and a small cross.

Standing opposite the cathedral, the *portales* (arcades) are filled with hotels

and cafés. Musicians play here all day and most of the night, and most evenings there is also dancing to watch, whether it is a frenetic *zapateo* or a poised, serene *danzón*. The entertainment reaches a high point during the city's celebrated carnival.

STAY

Mocambo
An elegant 1930s hotel in spacious grounds close to the beach, with two pools, a spa, a tennis court, a café, and a restaurant.

△D5 ◻Boulevard Adolfo Ruiz Cortines 4000, Veracruz 🖥hotel mocambo.com.mx

Ⓢ Ⓢ Ⓢ

→

The arcaded Palacio Municipal on Plaza de Armas in Veracruz

A FUGITIVE, A FREEDOM FIGHTER

Born in Gabon in 1545, Gaspar Nyanga - known also as Yanga - escaped slavery in Veracruz in the late 1500s, and established a *palenque* (maroon community). For survival, the colony farmed, hunted, and raided Spanish caravans and plantations. Yanga's fierce army defeated Spanish militia for over 30 years. On January 6, 1609, the settlement became the first free Black town in the Americas. A statue of Gaspar Yanga still stands in the town of Yanga, Veracruz.

Son jarocho could be called the sound of Veracruz – a rhythmic folk music with Afro-Mexican roots. Veracruz once housed a slave port and today many Afro-Mexicans call the city home; there is a movement to preserve and restore their culture and heritage. On weekends, tap your toes to *son jarocho* in the Plaza Mayor and the Plazuela de Campaná. Or stroll the Paseo de José Martí to be serenaded while stopping off in the area's bars and restaurants.

Situated on the *malecón* (waterfront esplanade) is the Gran Café de la Parroquia. This lively, convivial café opened in 1808 and is an institution. Boat trips from the *malecón* run past the Isla de los Sacrificios and around the harbor to the fortress of **San Juan de Ulúa**. Fortified in 1692, it was home to the last Spanish garrison to accept Mexican independence *(p58)* and has since seen several foreign invasions, the last by the US in 1914. It also became the country's most notorious prison during the Porfiriato era *(p61)*.

The tiny Isla de los Sacrificios was the first place the conquistadors landed, and is named after the remains of human sacrifices they found.

One of the best museums in Veracruz, the **Museo Histórico Naval** is housed in the former Naval Academy in the city center. It tells the maritime history of the port. Exhibits include over 300 types of knots, and models of ships.

In 1880, the fortified wall around Veracruz was torn down leaving only one of the nine original bastions, the **Baluarte de Santiago** (Santiago Bastion). This fort, built in 1635, houses a collection of pre-Hispanic jewelry.

South of the town are the hotel-filled suburbs of Playa de Oro and Mocambo. The beaches here are cleaner and less crowded than in Veracruz, but not very appealing. Boca del Río, farther along the coast, is famous for its seafood.

San Juan de Ulúa

🏛️🕐 📍Calle Pedro Sainz de Baranda 📅Jul & Aug: 9:30am-4:30pm Tue-Sun 🌐sanjuandeulua.inah.gob.mx

Museo Histórico Naval

🏛️🕐 📍Calle Arista 418 🕐10am-5pm Tue-Sun 🌐gob.mx/semar

Baluarte de Santiago

🏛️ 📍Calle Francisco Canal ☎(229) 931 10 59 🕐9am-4pm Tue-Sun

> **Veracruz is a place of fun. The city life revolves around the Plaza de Armas and the *malecón* (waterfront promenade), an enjoyable place to stroll and watch the ships come and go.**

← The city of Orizaba, with the highest peak in Mexico rising above it

San Andrés Tuxtla

⚠ E5 **🏛 Veracruz**
🚌 ℹ Palacio Municipal, Plaza Zaragoza, Tlacotalpan; (294) 947 93 00

San Andrés Tuxtla is a sprawling commercial town famous for its cigars. There are fields of tobacco everywhere, and the roadside is lined with stalls selling the finished products. You can also watch cigars being hand-rolled in the **Santa Clara Cigar Factory**.

The city center is anchored by the Parque Lerdo and its Catedral de San San José y San Andrés, built in 1870 with two bell towers and a sober Neo-Classical facade.

A 2-mile (3-km) walk from San Andrés Tuxtla along a dirt track leads to the Laguna Encantada (Enchanted Lake).

Orizaba

⚠ D5 **🏛 Veracruz** **🚌 ℹ El Palacio de Hierro; (272) 728 91 36**

Home to an Aztec garrison, and then to Spanish soldiers, Orizaba stood in what was a strategic position on the trading route between Veracruz and Mexico City in the 15th and 16th centuries. Dominated by the Cerro del Borrego hill, Orizaba today is mostly an industrial city, but still has plenty of character.

The Ex-Palacio Municipal, on the main plaza – the Parque Apolinar Castillo – is an ornate Art Nouveau construction. Built in Belgium in the late 19th century, it was brought over in pieces and reassembled here.

The Neo-Classical Palacio Municipal, on Calle Colón, was the base for a workers' education center after the revolution. It has a 1926 mural, *Reconstrucción*, by artist José Clemente Orozco (1883–1949). Orizaba's **Museo de Arte del Estado** features a fine collection of paintings housed in 10 beautifully restored rooms. Its collection also includes 37 rare works by artist Diego Rivera.

A cable-car ride up the Cerro del Borrego offers spectacular views over the city below. At its summit is a museum telling the story of the battle against French forces in 1862.

Museo de Arte del Estado
⊗ ⊗ 🏛 Corner of 4 Oriente and 23-25 Sur 📞 (272) 724 32 00 🕐 10am-6pm Wed-Sun

---

CLIMBING PICO DE ORIZABA

Rising to a massive 18,856 ft (5,747 m), Pico de Orizaba earns the title of Mexico's highest mountain. It is also one of the toughest but most popular challenges for climbers. A dormant volcano that last erupted in 1546, the mountain lies 14 miles (23 km) northwest of Orizaba. The best time to climb it is from November to March, which is the driest season. Climbers must take a guide, who can be hired from the nearest town, Tlachichuca.

It is so-named because its water level mysteriously rises in the dry season and falls when it rains.

Santa Clara Cigar Factory
🔯🛇🕐 🏠 Blvd 5 de Febrero 10 📞 (294) 947 99 06 🕐 8am-5:30pm Mon-Fri

---

Santiago Tuxtla

🅰 E5 🅰 Veracruz 🚌 ℹ Palacio Municipal, Plaza Zaragoza, Tlacotalpan; (294) 947 93 00

The town of Santiago Tuxtla is a gateway to the world of the ancient Olmecs (p273), who lived more

> One pre-Hispanic custom that lives on in Santiago Tuxtla is the *danza de los liseres*, in which the dancers don the mask of a jaguar deity.

than 3,000 years ago. A colossal stone head, typical of the Olmec culture, stands in the middle of the town's main square. It is the only one of the heads yet discovered to have closed eyes, and lacks the realism of the others.

The **Museo Tuxteco**, on one side of the plaza, has an interesting collection of pieces from nearby sites. They include a head called "El Negro," the legendary powers of which were formerly tapped by local witch doctors. Other exhibits include examples of the Olmec practices of skull deformation and tooth sculpting (probably expressions of beauty and class), another colossal head (this one from San Lorenzo Tenochtitlán), and ceremonial and domestic objects made out of jade and stone.

One pre-Hispanic custom that still lives on in Santiago Tuxtla is the *danza de los liseres*, in which the dancers don the mask of a jaguar deity. It can be seen being performed during summer fiestas.

Did You Know?

The Olmec head in Santiago Tuxtla's main square is the largest one ever found.

A 12-mile (20-km) drive east through lush, tropical vegetation, leads to Tres Zapotes. This archaeological site was the center of Olmec culture around 400 BC, after La Venta (p273) had been abandoned. The site itself is now just a series of mounds, but several of the finds are displayed in the museum in Tres Zapotes village nearby.

Museo Tuxteco
🔯🛈 🏠 Parque Juárez 📞 (294) 947 01 96 🕐 9am-5pm Tue-Sun

The picturesque Salto de ↓ Eyipantla waterfall, near ↓ San Andrés Tuxtla

13

Tapijulapa

A E5 **A** Tabasco
i Retorno Vía 5 122, Los Rios, Villahermosa; (993) 310 97 00

When exploring picturesque Tapijulapa, with its white-washed facades, terracotta roofs, and narrow, cobble-stoned streets, you might think you were in Andalucia. With its quintessentially Mexican charm and heritage, the village was designated a *pueblo mágico* – one of the "Magical Towns" promoted by the Security of Tourism for the rich experiences visitors can enjoy there.

Tapijulapa's well-preserved architecture includes the Templo de Santiago Apostol, a late-17th-century church built on a hilltop with lovely views over the town.

The village comes alive during Semana Santa (the week of Easter). Festivities include a fishing contest for the sightless sardines that live in caves just to the south of the village. The caves form part of the Parque Natural Villaluz, which also has good hiking trails leading to waterfalls, boat trips, and hot springs.

The Gran Acrópolis at the archaeological site in Comalcalco ↑

14

Comalcalco

A E5 **A** Off Mex 187, 36 miles (58 km) NW of Villahermosa, Tabasco
O 8am–4pm Tue–Sun

Set in the lush, green, cocoa-producing area northwest of Villahermosa are the Maya ruins of Comalcalco. Dating mainly from the late Classic period of Maya civilization (AD 700–900), the architecture differs quite markedly from that found at Palenque *(p246)*, which was occupied around the same time. Unlike Palenque, Comalcalco has structures built from bricks, which are held together with oyster-shell mortar. The bricks were some-times incised with figures and glyphs when wet.

Comalcalco's principal structures are two pyramids, the Gran Acrópolis and the Acrópolis Este, and the North Plaza. Originally many of the site's structures would have been covered in high-relief stucco carvings. Of those that survive today, the most distinctive is a mask of the god El Señor del Sol, which is visible near the base of the Gran Acrópolis.

15

Malpasito

A E5 **A** Hwy 187, Huimangillo, Tabasco
C (993) 352 10 30 **O** 8am–5pm daily

Beautifully located in rugged, mountainous countryside, the ceremonial site of Malpasito

The tiny village of Tapijulapa, nestled in jungle-covered mountains ↑

The Museo Regional de Antropología Carlos Pellicer Cámara has over 700 artifacts from the Olmec, Maya, and other Mesoamerican cultures.

a fascinating outdoor park and museum, has an informative display in English and Spanish on Olmec archaeology as you pass through the sculpture trail, the start of which is marked by a giant ceiba (the sacred tree of the Olmec and Maya). The **Museo Regional de Antropología Carlos Pellicer Cámara** has over 700 artifacts from the Olmec, Maya, and other Mesoamerican cultures, which include beautiful pottery and jade carvings.

Parque-Museo de la Venta

🚸🚫🚼🚻 🏠 Avenida Ruíz Cortines 📞 (993) 314 16 52 🕐 8am-4pm daily

Museo Regional de Antropología Carlos Pellicer Cámara

🚸 🏠 Avenida Carlos Pellicer Cámara 511 📞 (993) 312 63 44 🕐 9am-5pm Mon-Fri, 9am-7pm Sat & Sun

was built and inhabited by the Zoque people during the late-Classic era, around AD 700–900. The site features terraced platforms and a ball-game court, but is most noteworthy for more than 100 exquisitely carved petroglyphs decorating over 100 boulders that are scattered around the Malpasito area. The carvings represent people, birds, monkeys, deer, and other animals, as well as elaborate geometric designs.

Malpasito is located within the **Agua Selva** ecotourism park, a natural playground of rivers, waterfalls, and hiking trails. There are even log cabins and a campsite so you can enjoy an extended stay.

Agua Selva

🏠 Ejido, 86449, Malpasito 🕐 Daily 🌐 aguaselva.com.mx

16

Villahermosa

🅰 E5 🏠 Tabasco ✈🚌 🛈 Retorno Via 5 122, Los Rios; (993) 310 97 00

Now the capital of the state of Tabasco, Villahermosa was originally founded in the late 16th century by a community forced to move inland by repeated pirate attacks.

Situated on the banks of the Grijalva river, Villahermosa is surrounded by exuberant natural beauty, and walking through the jungle is rewarded with waterfalls, sulphurous waters and even caves.

Today the city itself is a friendly, bustling place with two excellent museums. The **Parque-Museo de La Venta**,

THE OLMECS

The Olmecs were one of Mexico's foremost Mesoamerican cultures, with a great influence on later civilizations. However, the rise and fall of their own population remains a mystery. Today the most impressive reminders of the ancient Olmec culture are the colossal carved stone heads, fashioned from basalt blocks weighing up to 20 tons, which the Olmecs moved large distances, probably using river rafts. Ten of the 17 heads so far discovered were found at San Lorenzo Tenochtitlán – an area that comprises the three archaeological sites of San Lorenzo, Tenochtitlán, and Potrero Nuevo in the state of Veracruz. This great Olmec ceremonial center flourished from 1200 to 900 BC, when it was destroyed. Some of the pieces found here are on show at Potrero.

17

Laguna de Catemaco

E5 **Veracruz**
**Palacio Municipal,
Avenido Carranza,
Catemaco**

This picturesque freshwater lake lies in the crater of an extinct volcano. It was formed millennia ago, when lava flow from Volcano San Martin Tuxtla blocked its current northern end, and stands now at 1,115 ft (340 m) above sea level. Its hot, humid climate suits many birds, including parrots and toucans, and its waters also contain a few crocodiles. Boat trips round the lake leave from the wharf in the town of Catemaco and circle the island of Tanaxpillo, which is home to a colony of macaque monkeys.

Two ecological parks on the north shore of the lake are accessible by boat or car. The more interesting of these, **Nanciyaga**, is a large swath of tropical rainforest with a great diversity in species of flora and fauna. Visitors to the park can take part in pre-Hispanic rituals, such as the *temazcal* (steam bath), or swim in spring-fed pools.

↑ The highly decorated interior of Iglesia del Carmen, in the town of Catemaco

The Isla de Agaltepec, another island in the lake, supports a colony of Mexican howler monkeys. The monkeys are most vocal in the morning, and boat tours also include this island on their circuit.

The town of Catemaco itself is dominated by the Iglesia del Carmen, a brightly painted church with twin bell towers. The statue of the Virgen del Carmen inside is dripping with jewelry and trinkets left by the many pilgrims who come here.

Nanciyaga

 4.5 miles (7 km) NE of Catemaco **(294) 943 01 99** **9am-2pm & 4-6pm Mon-Fri, 9am-2pm Sat**

18

Tlacotalpan

D5 **Veracruz**
Palacio Municipal, Plaza Zaragoza; (288) 884 33 05

Exploring this delightful town is like turning the clock back 100 years. Its peaceful streets are lined with striking houses fronted by colonnades and painted in a flamboyant range of colors. As the Mexican writer Elena Poniatowska once put it, "when we want to smile, we think of Tlacotalpan."

The town is on the banks of the Río Papaloapan ("River

of Butterflies"), which is over 984 ft (300 m) wide. Most of the elegant houses, with their Mozarabic-style portals, date from the second half of the 18th century, when large sugar and cotton plantations were established here. Important shipyards were also moved here from Cuba as a direct result of an English blockade of Havana, another Spanish possession, in 1762.

During this era, Tlacotalpan was the principal town in southern Veracruz and an important international port, often more in touch with Europe and Cuba than with the rest of Mexico. However, the building of railroad lines left Tlacotalpan without a commercial role. Paradoxically, the isolation that caused its decline has helped preserve this picturesque town.

Located in a typical 19th-century house in the heart of Tlacotalpan, the **Museo Jarocho Salvador Ferrando** is named after a local artist, and houses many of his portraits

---

WITCH DOCTORS

Witch doctors still practice in the state of Veracruz, around San Andrés Tuxtla (*p270*) and Catemaco. Using an assortment of medicinal plants, charms, effigies of saints and devils, and other traditional items, they will undertake to help their clients with all manner of issues, whether it's curing diseases, helping them find a better job, or resolving their marital problems. The practice is hereditary and can be traced back to a distant pre-Hispanic past.

Did You Know?

The macaques on Tanaxpillo island in the Laguna de Catemaco were introduced for research.

and landscapes painted in the 19th century. Locally made furniture and crafts from the same period are also on display in the museum.

Museo Jarocho Salvador Ferrando

 Manuel María Alegre 6
 (288) 884 24 95
🕙 10:30am–6pm daily

19

Xico

🅰 D5 🚗 Veracruz
🚌 ℹ Miguel Hidalgo 76, Centro; (228) 129 66 97

Located on the slope of the Cofre del Perote volcano, the attractive town of Xico is well worth a visit for the impressive architecture lining the cobbled streets, and its bustling Sunday market. It's also a coffee production center and a gastronomic hot spot, with specialties that include *tamal canario* (sweet tamales) and spicy mole sauce.

The Xiqueños are renowned for their colorful dance costumes, worn for the town's lively carnival, held annually in February or March. The **Museo del Danzante Xiqueño**, situated a couple of blocks from the main square, has an excellent exhibition of such costumes and local customs. The tradition of mask-carving is explained, as well as the role of every masked character in each dance – the bull, the clown, the *negro separado*.

If you follow the path that leads to the Cascada de Texolo you'll be rewarded with spectacular views, and a waterfall that cascades down a sheer rock face. An exciting activity that involves rappeling through the torrent can be organized by local tour companies – an adrenaline-fueled way to take in the stunning scenery.

Museo del Danzante Xiqueño

🏠 Miguel Hidalgo 76
📞 (228) 129 66 97
🕙 10am–6pm Tue–Sun

SHOP

La Tia Celsa

Xico is a great place to buy local delicacies. This store sells a rainbow of spicy local sauces, including mole – one of Mexico's most ubiquitous sauces.

🅰 D5 📍 Vicente Guerrero 182, Xico
🌐 latiacelsa.com

Tierra de Brujos

This tiny shop (whose name means "Land of Witches") has a small but representative selection of the region's best handicrafts.

🅰 E5 📍 Plaza de Artesanías, Catemaco
🌐 tierra-de-brujos-handicraft.negocio.site

Colorful colonnade-fronted buildings in charming Tlacotalpan ↑

Swimming in a cenote outside the city of Valladolid

THE YUCATÁN PENINSULA

This tropical peninsula is home to some of the finest archaeological sites in the Americas. From around 2000 BC to the 16th century, the region's Maya population grew to become one of Mesoamerica's most advanced civilizations. But when the Spanish arrived in 1517, they had scant regard for the Maya, swiftly conquering their city states and destroying most of their historical records. The Spanish founded cities here to act as bastions in their fight for control of the Caribbean, against English, French, and Dutch pirates. In 1847, after Mexico had achieved independence, civil war erupted on the peninsula between settlers of European origin and the much-exploited descendants of the ancient Maya – a conflict which ended in defeat for the Maya. In the late 19th century, the production of henequen and sisal (for rope and fabric making) led to a period of prosperity in the Yucatán, while tourism has long been a major industry in this beautiful region of jungles, Maya ruins, and white-sand beaches.

The Riviera Maya, on the east coast, is one of Mexico's great holiday hotspots, sprinkled with grand resorts. Away from the coasts, meanwhile, traditional life continues much as it has done for years, with the Indigenous Maya preserving their own language, customs, and culture.

THE YUCATÁN PENINSULA

Gulf of Mexico

PROGRESO ⑲

Sisal

DZIBILCHALTÚN ⑭

Hunucmá

MÉRIDA ④

CELESTÚN ⑪

Umán

Mérida International Airport

Real de Salinas

Yaxcopoil

Maxcanu

Muna

Halacho

UXMAL ②

Calkiní

Kabah

Jaina

THE PUUC ROUTE ⑩

Orizaba

Chunyaxnic

Sayil

Tinúm

CAMPECHE ⑨

Chencoyi

Lerma

Campeche International Airport

Cayal

Hopelch

Seybaplaya

EDZNÁ ⑥

Iturbide

Haltunchen

Hool

Lubna

Dzibalchen

Champotón

Arellano

El Zapote

El Desempeno

CAMPECHE

Sabancuy

Isla Aguada

Chicbul

Nuevo Progreso

Ciudad del Carmen

Laguna de Términos

Constitución

Balamkú

Be

Francisco Escárcega

Conhuás

Chicanná

El Vapoor

Buenavista

⑳ RÍO B SITE

THE GULF COAST
p258

Candelaria

Monclova

La Esperanza

Calakmul

Reserve Biosphe Calakmu

TABASCO

Nueva Coahuila

Macuspana

Balancán

Emiliano Zapata

Parque Nacional Laguna del Tigre

Palenque

Tenosique

GUATEMALA

Tila

CHIAPAS

El Naranjo

RIVIERA MAYA

⬛G4 **⬛Quintana Roo** **⬛⬛⬛** **ℹAvenida Yaxilan s/n, 17M Lote 6, Cancún; www.visitmexico.com**

Stretching along the coast from Puerto Morelos in the north to Tulum in the south, the 100-mile (160-km) Riviera Maya is the most touristy part of the Yucatán peninsula. Encompassing major resorts such as Cancún and Playa del Carmen, it is known for its beaches, warm waters, and range of hotels, restaurants, bars, and clubs. Just offshore is the world's second largest coral reef (a prime spot for diving) and inviting islands.

> Over 90 species of birds, including large flocks of egrets, pelicans, frigate birds, and flamingos, nest on the island, which is now a protected nature preserve.

① Isla Mujeres

⬛Quintana Roo **⬛Passenger ferry from Puerto Juárez, car ferry from Punta Sam** **ℹAvenida Rueda Medina 130; www.visitmexico.com/en/quintana-roo/isla-mujeres**

This small island is just half a mile (1 km) wide by 5 miles (8 km) long. Its name, meaning "The Island of Women," probably derives from Maya female statuettes found here and destroyed by the Spanish. It has developed considerably since first becoming popular in the 1960s, but there are few high-rise buildings, and its small town is still quiet, especially in the evening when the day trippers from Cancún have left.

The best way to explore the island is on a bike or scooter. Its middle part is taken up by a brackish lagoon and an airstrip for small planes from the mainland. Also in the center is the ruined Hacienda Mundaca, said to have been built by the pirate Fermín Mundaca to

impress an island beauty. Playa Los Cocos, just to the north of the island's only town, has clean white sand and warm shallow water.

Located at Isla Mujeres' rather rugged southern tip are Garrafón Park and Playa de Garrafón. The coral reef offshore is now mostly dead, but there are lots of activities on offer, including ziplining and kayaking. The beach is pleasant, but gets crowded in the middle of the day. Nearby are the ruins of what is said to be an old Maya lighthouse. At the southern edge of the island is the Templo de Ixchel, a modest ruin that marks the easternmost point in Mexico.

A popular day trip from Isla Mujeres is to visit Isla Contoy, a tiny island 19 miles (30 km) away, off the northern tip of

the Yucatán Peninsula. It is located at the northernmost part of the barrier reef, where the waters of the Caribbean Sea and Gulf of Mexico meet. The mingling currents create ideal conditions for plankton – food for the many fish, which in turn support an abundant bird life. Over 90 species of birds, including large flocks of egrets, pelicans, frigate birds, and flamingos, nest on the island, which is now a protected nature preserve.

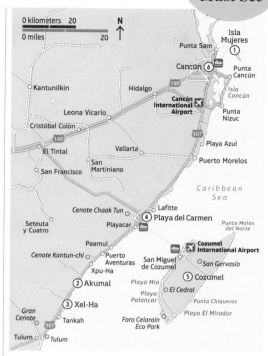

②
Akumal

 Quintana Roo

Akumal is a small, uncrowded resort based around what was once a coconut plantation. Its beautiful beach is a breeding ground for green turtles (Akumal is Maya for "place of the turtle"), and migrating whale sharks can sometimes be spotted swimming past in December and January. Since the 1990s, this lovely sheltered bay's warm water has increasingly become popular with windsurfers, divers, and snorkelers.

③
Xel-Ha

 Puerto Juárez Federal Highway, Km 240, Quintana Roo ⏰ **9am–6pm daily** 🌐 **xelha.com**

Very popular with families and nature lovers, this aquatic adventure park is based around a series of interconnecting lagoons set among spectacular rocks and caves. Creating a natural aquarium, a huge variety of tropical fish swim in the park's beautifully clear waters, and the diving and snorkeling are wonderful. You can immerse yourself in *cenotes* or underground rivers, and ziplining and inner-tubing are among the many other activities on offer here.

←

Isla Mujeres, surrounded by calm, crystal-clear, turquoise waters

CENOTES

The Riviera Maya is famous for its *cenotes*, water-filled sinkholes that are great for a swim. Some have been turned into waterparks, while others are untouched. Cenote Chaak Tun and Gran Cenote are two of the best to visit in the region: the former, outside Playa del Carmen, is made up of two stalactite-filled caverns; the latter, close to Tulum, is great for snorkeling.

④

Playa del Carmen

 Quintana Roo
🛈 Parque Los Fundadores;
(984) 873 28 04

Playa del Carmen is the second biggest resort on the coast after Cancún. The town has a relaxed atmosphere and Quinta Avenida, the main street, is lined with small shops, coffee bars, and traditional

DIVING IN THE MEXICAN CARIBBEAN

Stretching for over 620 miles (1,000 km) down the eastern coast of the Yucatán peninsula to Belize, Guatemala and Honduras, the great Mesoamerican Reef System's crystal clear, marine life-rich waters are ideal for snorkeling and scuba-diving. The finest dive sites are scattered around the island of Cozumel, and there are options suitable for every level of ability. It is also possible to dive with whale sharks off the coast of Isla Holbox.

restaurants. Ferries to Cozumel leave from a pier close to the lively central square.

⑤

Cozumel

 Quintana Roo 🚗🚢 Car ferry from Calica, passenger ferry from Playa del Carmen 🛈 5a Avenida Sur 51; www.cozumel.travel

Just off the east coast of the Yucatán Peninsula, Cozumel is Mexico's largest island, 9 miles (14 km) wide by 31 miles (50 km) long. Known to the Maya as Cuzamil, the "place of the swallows," it was an important center for the cult of Ixchel, goddess of fertility, pregnancy, and childbirth. The archaeological remains of two Maya settlements are at El Cedral and San Gervasio. Both are overgrown, but visiting them provides an opportunity to see Cozumel's varied birdlife. San Gervasio, the larger site, has several restored buildings.

The Spanish landed in Cozumel in 1518, resulting in a battle in which the Maya population suffered heavy losses. It was here that the first Mass in Mexico was said, and Hernán Cortés planned his conquest of mainland Mexico.

↑ Arched sculpture framing the white-sand beach at Playa del Carmen

Today, Cozumel is a tourist resort and diving hotspot. Ferries from the mainland arrive at San Miguel, the island's only town. Tourist shops, restaurants, and bars dominate the surrounding area, but a few blocks away, the town is quieter and more traditional.

Cozumel is ringed by stunning beaches, many only accessible by 4X4. Those on the eastern, windward side are beautiful, but not safe for swimming. The sheltered western side has safe swimming beaches, notably Playa Palancar, with a restaurant-bar and within striking distance of a Maya ruin, El Cedral. The best diving sites are here too, particularly around the Colombia, Palancar, San Francisco, and Santa Rosa reefs, as is the touristy Chankanaab Park, which has a lagoon and many varieties of tropical plants. At the southern tip of Cozumel is the more worthwhile Faro Celarain Eco Park, which has pretty beaches, bird-filled mangroves, and El Caracol, which is thought to have been a Maya lighthouse.

HIDDEN GEM
Remote Escape

A 40-minute drive from Cancún *(p282)* is Puerto Morelos, one of the least developed places on the riviera. It is a small, laidback resort built around a fishing village that offers excellent snorkeling and diving.

---

⑥
Cancún

🏛 Quintana Roo ✈🚌🚢
ℹ Avenida Nizuc Mz. 3 Lote 5; www.cancun.travel

Before 1970, Cancún was little more than a sandy island and a fishing village of barely 100 inhabitants. The government decided to turn it into a resort, and in the late 1960s building began. Since then the population has soared to hundreds of thousands, and over 12 million (mainly non-Mexican) visitors flock here every year to enjoy the sandy beaches and perfect weather.

There are, in fact, two Cancúns. The downtown area, on the mainland, has very few hotels and no beaches, while the Cancún that most visitors see has plenty of both. The latter, known as Isla Cancún or the *Zona Hotelera* (Hotel Zone), is a narrow, 14-mile (23-km) L-shaped island connected to the mainland by two bridges.

Although many of the hotels appear to command private stretches of sand, all beaches in Mexico are public and can be enjoyed by anybody. The ones in front of the Hyatt Cancún and Sheraton hotels are particularly beautiful. If the resort beach scene and constant presence of hotel staff do not appeal, however, head for the equally attractive "public" beaches. Playa Linda, Playa Langosta, and Playa Tortugas, on the northern arm of the island, offer relaxed swimming in the calm Bahía Mujeres, while bigger waves

and fine views can be found at Playa Chac-Mool, Playa Marlín, and Playa Ballenas, which face the open sea. The protected Laguna Nichupté, between Isla Cancún and the mainland, is perfect for watersports.

Toward the southern end of the island is the Maya site of El Rey (The King), occupied from AD 1200 until the Conquest. Here, a low pyramid and two plazas provide a quiet retreat from the beachfront action.

Some ferries for Isla Mujeres *(p280)* leave from a dock near Playa Linda, but the majority depart from Puerto Juárez or Punta Sam, both just to the north of Cancún.

The highlight of the resort's limited cultural scene, the **Museo Maya de Cancún** has Maya artifacts from across the region, as well as temporary exhibits. Its grounds contain the remains of a small Maya site known as San Miguelito.

An underwater sculpture park off the coast of Cancún, the **Museo Subacuático de Arte (MUSA)** has a collection of 500 artworks. You can see MUSA in a glass-bottom boat or on a snorkeling or scuba-diving trip.

Museo Maya de Cancún
♿ 🏛 Blvd Kukulcán Km 16.5 📞 (998) 885 38 42 🕐 9am–6pm Tue–Sun

Museo Subacuático de Arte (MUSA)
♿♿ 🏛 See website for tour times 🌐 musamexico.org

EAT & DRINK

El Fish Fritanga
Located in the *Zona Hotelera* (Hotel Zone), this restaurant serves some of the best fish and seafood in Cancún at prices that won't break the bank. Try the octopus ceviche, the tuna *tostadas*, or the coconut prawns with a sweet-and-sour mango dressing.

🏛 Blvd Kukulcán Km 12.6, Cancún 🌐 elfish fritanga.com

💲💲💲

The Surfin Burrito
Open 24 hours a day, this friendly little restaurant-bar is a great spot for a cold beer or well-mixed cocktail. As the name suggests, the burritos – not to mention the tacos, nachos, burgers, and faijitas – are well worth trying, too.

🏛 Blvd Kukulcán Km 9.5, Cancún 🌐 facebook. com/thesurfinburrito

💲💲💲

Visitors enjoying the nightlife in Cancún's *Zona Hotelera* (Hotel Zone) ↓

2 ⬡ ⬡ ⬡ ⬡

UXMAL

🔺F4 🚗Mex 261, 48 miles (78 km) S of Mérida, Yucatán
🚌Tours from Mérida 🕐8am–5pm daily 🌐inah.gob.mx

On entering the vast Maya ancient city at Uxmal, the eye is immediately drawn to its most awe-inspiring structure, the Magician's Pyramid, but there are many other fascinating buildings to admire, too.

The late-Classic Maya site of Uxmal is one of the most complex and harmonious expressions of Puuc architecture *(p302)*. The city's exact origins are uncertain, but most of the buildings date from the 7th–10th centuries AD, when Uxmal dominated the region. The real function of many of the structures is unknown, and they retain the fanciful names given to them by the Spanish. Unlike most Yucatán sites, Uxmal has no *cenotes* *(p280)*, and water was collected in manmade cisterns *(chultunes)*, one of which can be seen near the entrance. The scarcity of water may explain the number of depictions of the rain god Chac on the buildings.

20,000

A rough estimate of the population of the Maya settlement.

↓ Illustration showing the layout of the Maya ruins at Uxmal

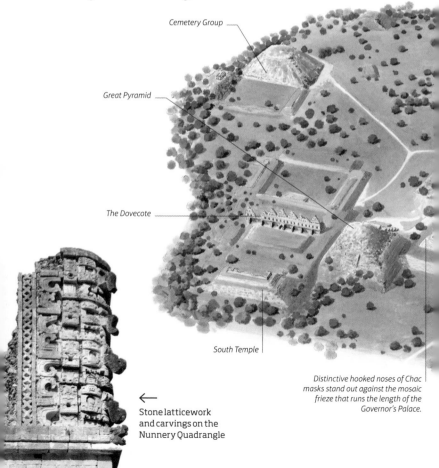

Cemetery Group

Great Pyramid

The Dovecote

South Temple

Distinctive hooked noses of Chac masks stand out against the mosaic frieze that runs the length of the Governor's Palace.

← Stone latticework and carvings on the Nunnery Quadrangle

Nunnery Quadrangle

The stone latticework, ornate masks of Chac, and carved serpents on the walls are remarkable examples of closely fitting mosaic.

Magician's Pyramid

This spectacular pyramid is made up of multiple temples (p286).

Highlights of Uxmal

Dovecote

△ Named after its unusual roof comb, this ruined palace faces a rectangular garden, and is one of Uxmal's most peaceful spots.

Great Pyramid

A stairway climbs the 100-ft (30-m) pyramid to a temple that is decorated with Chac masks and macaws.

House of the Turtles

△ A frieze of turtles around the building, suggests that it might have been dedicated to a water god.

Governor's Palace

A masterpiece of Puuc architecture, the 9th-10th-century palace is actually three buildings linked by Maya arches.

The upper level of the elegant House of the Turtles is simply decorated with columns.

The impressive Nunnery Quadrangle was given its unlikely name because the Spanish thought that the 74 small rooms set around a central courtyard looked like the cells of a nunnery.

Entrance to site

At 115 ft (35 m), the Magician's Pyramid is the tallest structure at Uxmal.

Ballcourt

The Jaguar Throne is carved as a two-headed jaguar, an animal associated with chiefs and kings.

Pyramid of the Old Woman

↑ The imposing Magician's Pyramid, surrounded by lush gardens

The Magician's Pyramid

Tall, steep, and set on an unusual oval base, the Magician's Pyramid is the most striking of Uxmal's monuments. Legend tells that it was built in one night by a dwarf with supernatural powers – the magician – but, in fact, it shows five phases of construction from the 6th–10th centuries AD. At each phase a new temple was built, either on top of or obscuring the previous one. There are thus five temples on the pyramid. Unfortunately, visitors are no longer allowed to climb to the summit, to prevent further erosion.

↑ Visitors approaching the Magician's Pyramid

The facade of Temple IV is actually an expressive Chac mask with large rectangular eyes and a curling moustache. Its wide-open, toothed mouth forms the entrance. Temple III is behind Temple IV.

Entrance to Temple IV

Temple V is part of the final phase of construction – which took place around AD 1000 – and appears to be a small-scale reproduction of the nearby Governor's Palace (p285).

→
Reconstruction of the Magician's Pyramid

The east staircase provides access to Temple II, which is just a dark room today.

Chac masks on facade of Temple I

Entrance to Temple I (now blocked)

The west staircase, at the front of the pyramid, is flanked by representations of Chac, the rain god. The staircase is extremely steep and ascends the pyramid at an angle of 60°, meaning that the climb to the summit was very difficult.

Temple I was built in the sixth century AD, according to the results of radiocarbon dating, and is now covered by the pyramid. Partially collapsed, it cannot be visited.

PICTURE PERFECT
Best Views

To capture the unique curve of the Magician's Pyramid, take a photo at the base as you enter. For pictures of the best views, head to the top of the Great Pyramid, or the platform on the Governor's Palace.

GODS OF ANCIENT MEXICO

The civilizations of Mesoamerica *(p144)* worshiped multiple gods and goddesses. Gods were passed from one civilization to another and renamed over time.

Deities were often feared as much as revered. If they had created the world, it was believed that they could also destroy it. Ancient civilizations therefore thought it essential to appease them as much as possible, sometimes through human sacrifice.

CREATOR GODS

Mesoamerican societies had differing accounts of creation. According to one myth from central Mexico, Tonacatecuhtli and Tonacaciwhuatl resided in the 13th, or uppermost, heaven and from there sent down souls of children to be born on earth.

GODS OF THE UNDERWORLD

In Aztec mythology, the soul was thought to pass through a series of hazards in the nine levels of the underworld before reaching the deepest part, ruled over by Mictlantecuhtli and Mictecacihuatl.

THE SUN GOD

This deity was associated with the jaguar in ancient Mexico, an animal that evoked the vigor and power of the rising sun.

RAIN GODS

Abundant rainfall was vital to farming communities, and rain and lightning gods were venerated in all the civilizations of ancient Mexico.

QUETZALCOATL

Quetzalcoatl (or Kukulcan), the feathered serpent, appears in many cultures. Some revered him as a god of nature, while others considered him a creator god.

↑ Mictlantecuhtli, the Aztec god of the underworld

↑ Kinich Ahau, a sun god in the Classic Maya culture

↑ Quetzalcoatl, a feathered serpent revered across Mesoamerica

3 🖉

TULUM

🅰 G4 🗺 Mex 307, 80 miles (128 km) S of Cancún, Quintana Roo
📞 (983) 837 24 11 🚌 From Cancún 🕐 8am–5pm daily

What sets Tulum aside from other archaeological sites is its beautiful setting on a cliff by the Caribbean Sea. Its the perfect spot to enjoy the Yucatán's stunning scenery, as well as the region's ancient history.

Tulum is a Maya site that was at its height from around AD 1200 until the arrival of the Spanish in the mid-17th century (p57). The name, which means "enclosure" or "wall," is probably modern. It is thought that the site was originally called Zama, or "dawn," reflecting its location on the east coast, and the west-east alignment of its buildings. Its inhabitants traded with nearby settlements at Cozumel and Isla Mujeres, as well as farther afield with Guatemala and central Mexico.

If you want to beat the crowds, arrive early. There is not much shade at the site so bring plenty of sunscreen and a hat, and remember your swimming gear so you can enjoy the tempting beach after exploring the site.

Did You Know?

From its spectacular clifftop vantage point, El Castillo served as a landmark for seafarers.

OTHER THINGS TO DO IN TULUM TOWN

Although most famous for its Maya archaeological site, the town of Tulum has plenty more to offer. Its long, sandy beach is one of the finest in the region. It also has a flourishing culinary scene, with a string of places to eat and drink on the beach and in the town. Highlights include innovative restaurants Hartwood (www.hartwoodtulum.com) and Cetli (www.facebook.com/cetlitulum), and Batey (www.facebook.com/bateytulum), a bar that serves mojitos from a VW Beetle.

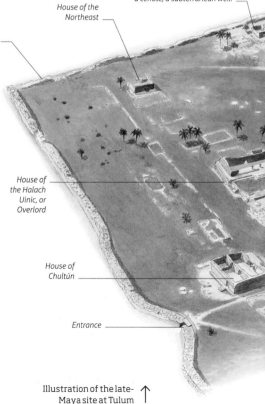

A wall runs along three sides of the site, 16 ft (5 m) thick and pierced by five gates.

House of the Northeast

The House of the Cenote is so named because it stands above a cenote, a subterranean well.

House of the Halach Uinic, or Overlord

House of Chultún

Entrance

Illustration of the late-Maya site at Tulum ↑

↑ El Castillo's wide external staircase leading up to a late Postclassic temple

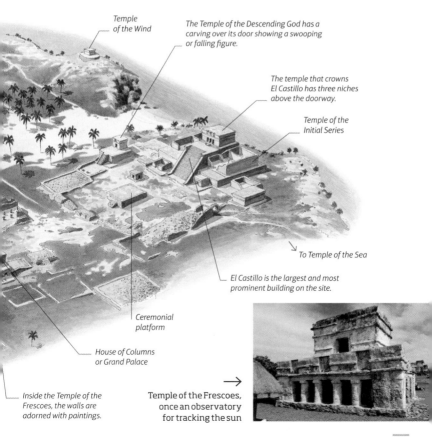

Temple of the Wind

The Temple of the Descending God has a carving over its door showing a swooping or falling figure.

The temple that crowns El Castillo has three niches above the doorway.

Temple of the Initial Series

→ To Temple of the Sea

El Castillo is the largest and most prominent building on the site.

Ceremonial platform

House of Columns or Grand Palace

Inside the Temple of the Frescoes, the walls are adorned with paintings.

→ Temple of the Frescoes, once an observatory for tracking the sun

4

MÉRIDA

A F4 **A** Yucatán **X** **i** Calle 62 (Palacio Municipal); www.merida.gob.mx/turismo

Founded in 1542, the capital of Yucatán is one of the great cities of Latin America. In the early 1900s, Mérida was said to have had more millionaires per capita than anywhere else in the world, due to the booming sisal industry. This prosperity resulted in grand mansions, municipal buildings, squares, and parks, making the city an architectural treasure trove. Not stuck in the past though: Mérida is a thriving business and cultural hub.

① Teatro José Peón Contreras

A Calle 60, between calles 57 and 57 **C** (999) 923 13 33 **O** Daily

Mérida prides itself on being the cultural capital of the Yucatán Peninsula, and the José Peón Contreras Theater is one of its main showcases. Built at the turn of the 20th century, it is a grand Neo-Classical creation in beige and white, with elaborate chandeliers in its massive foyer.

② Palacio de Gobierno

A Plaza Mayor **C** (999) 930 31 00 **O** Daily

The Government palace houses the Yucatán state authorities. It is remarkable for the numerous large murals adorning its courtyard, stairs, and first floor lobby. They were painted in the 1970s by Fernando Castro Pacheco, a local artist, and show his vision of Yucatán history from the time of the Maya to the 19th century.

③ Parque Santa Lucia

A Calle 60 476A

Santa Lucía Park is used for dancing and cultural events, and has a flea market on Sundays. Bronze busts placed on tall, white columns lining one corner of the park honor Yucateco musicians.

Across the street, the small Iglesia de Santa Lucía, one of the earliest and most harmonious of the city's churches, is where the local Maya villagers were encouraged to come and worship.

④ Parque Cepeda Peraza

A Corner of Calle 60 and Calle 59 **O** Daily

Just off Calle 60, one of the city's major roads, is Parque Cepeda Peraza (Parque Hidalgo), a small

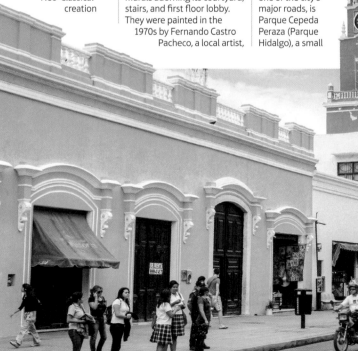

Did You Know?

Mérida's nickname, La Ciudad Blanca (White City) is from the white limestone buildings.

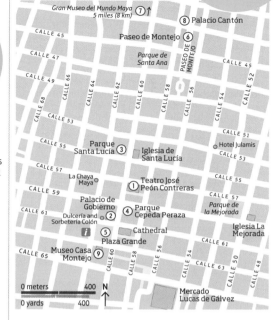

Gran Museo del Mundo Maya ⑦↑ 5 miles (8 km)

⑧ Palacio Cantón

CALLE 45
Paseo de Montejo ⑥
CALLE 47
Parque de Santa Ana
PASEO DE MONTEJO
CALLE 45
CALLE 49
CALLE 66
CALLE 64
CALLE 62
CALLE 60
CALLE 58
CALLE 56
CALLE 54
CALLE 52
CALLE 68
CALLE 53
CALLE 51
CALLE 55
Parque ③ Santa Lucía
Iglesia de Santa Lucía
Hotel Julamis
CALLE 53
CALLE 57
La Chaya Maya
Teatro José ① Peón Contreras
CALLE 55
CALLE 59
CALLE 57
Palacio de Gobierno
Parque de la Mejorada
CALLE 61
Dulcería and Sorbetería Colón ②
Parque ④ Cepeda Peraza
ℹ️
Cathedral
⑤ Plaza Grande
Iglesia La Mejorada
CALLE 61
Museo Casa ⑨ Montejo
CALLE 65
CALLE 60
CALLE 58
CALLE 56
CALLE 54
CALLE 63
CALLE 50
CALLE 48
0 meters 400 N
0 yards 400 ↑
Mercado Lucas de Gálvez

but bustling square. Visitors can watch the many musicians and street merchants, or relax in one of the openair cafés. The imposing Jesuit church, the Templo de la Tercera Orden (Temple of the Third Order), on the north side of the square, dates from the 17th century. It has a huge entrance and two narrow bell towers. Inside, the gold altar and friezes of biblical scenes are the only decoration.

⑤

Plaza Grande

Mérida is built on a grid system based around the main square, the Plaza Grande (also known as the Plaza Mayor or Plaza de la Independencia). In the evenings, and on Sundays, dancing and concerts take

place outside the city hall, the Palacio Municipal. This building is in a mix of styles and has a notable 1920s clock tower.

The Museo Casa de Montejo *(p292)* on the south side of the plaza is now a bank, but was orignally built as the palace of the first Spanish governors.

East of the Plaza Mayor lies Mérida's historic post office, now the Museo de la Ciudad with exhibits on the city's colonial past as well as contemporary artworks.

Opposite the city hall is the cathedral, the oldest in the Americas. It was begun in the early 1560s, and finished in 1598. Three arched doors in the imposing facade lead to a soaring interior with a barreled roof and crisscross arches. A wooden sculpture, *Cristo de las Ampollas* (Christ of the Blisters), stands in a small chapel on the right. It is a copy of a statue that was brought to Mérida after miraculously surviving a fire. The original, which was later destroyed, is said to have developed blisters, as skin would, instead of burning – a miracle which is celebrated every year in Mérida *(p305)*.

←

The Palacio Municipal and its clock tower, a major landmark on Plaza Grande

⑥
Paseo de Montejo

The Paseo de Montejo stretches for several miles through the middle of the city. It is lined with the elegant town mansions of rich plantation owners and the private banks that prospered in the late 19th century. Many of the houses were built by Italian architects and are a medley of Neo-Classical elements. At the northern end of the Paseo de Montejo is the *Monumento a la Patria* (Monument to the Fatherland), an elaborate 20th-century work by Colombian sculptor Rómulo Rozo. The striking monument shows historical figures and animal sculptures, and encloses an eternal flame, a symbol of Mexico's independence.

⑦
Gran Museo del Mundo Maya

🏛 Calle 60 Norte 299
🕐 Wed-Mon 🌐 granmuseo-delmundomaya.com.mx

Housed in an eye-catching modern building north of

INSIDER TIP
Hammocks

Mérida is one of the best places in Mexico to buy a hammock. A common sight in the markets, they are made from twine produced from henequen, a fibrous agave plant. Modern hammocks are often made from cotton or silk.

the city center, the Maya World Museum of Mérida is an excellent place to visit before heading out to explore the Yucatán's Maya sites. It provides an insight into the architecture, religious beliefs, scientific achievements, and everyday life of this fascinating ancient civilization.

The museum has more than 1,000 artifacts from sites across southern Mexico, as well as Belize, Guatemala, and Honduras, where the Maya also lived.

⑧
Palacio Cantón

🏛 Paseo de Montejo 485
📞 (999) 923 05 57
🕐 10am-5pm Mon-Fri

One of the finest mansions on the elegant Paseo de Montejo is the large Palacio Cantón, built between 1904 and 1911 for the former governor of the state of Yucatán, General Francisco Cantón Rosado, as his family residence. Today it hosts exhibitions, concerts, and lectures on diverse subjects.

⑨
Museo Casa Montejo

🏛 Plaza Mayor 📞 (999) 923 06 33, ext 25565 🕐 Tue-Sun

A palace built between 1543 and 1549 for conquistador Francisco de Montejo, the founder of Mérida, the Museo Casa

→
The striking exterior of the Gran Museo del Mundo and *(inset)* one of the exhibitions inside

↑ Decadent gold-embellished furniture displayed inside the Museo Casa Montejo

Montejo is now owned by the National Bank of México. The plateresque architecture is majestic, with a blend of classical, Moorish, Gothic, and Renaissance elements. It still has its original portico, with the Montejo family coat of arms. Several of the rooms are open to the public and feature historic furnishings and decor. There are also a few halls that host temporary exhibitions.

EAT

Dulcería and Sorbetería Colón
There are few better ways to cool down on a hot day than at this Mérida institution. Here you'll find delicious pastries and refreshing sorbets and ice creams, with flavors ranging from tamarind to watermelon.

🏠 Plaza Grande
🌐 elcolon.mx

La Chaya Maya
This is the place to come for traditional Yucatecan dishes such as *poc-chuc* (citrus-marinated pork), *sopa de lima* (tangy chicken soup), and *salbutes* (crisp tortillas topped with turkey, onion, avocado, and radish). There's also another branch at Calle 55.

🏠 Corner of calles 62 and 57 🌐 lachayamaya.com

$$$

STAY

Hotel Julamis
A few blocks from the Plaza Mayor, this adults-only hotel is in a 200-year-old building that has been impeccably decorated by its Cuban owners. There's a rooftop terrace and hot tub, and the breakfast is delicious, too.

🏠 Calle 53 #475b
🌐 hoteljulamis.com

$$$

5 ⬡ ⬡ ⬡ ⬡

CHICHÉN ITZÁ

🅐 G4 🅐 Mex 180, 25 miles (40 km) W of Valladolid, Yucatán 🅒 (985) 851 01 37 🚍 From Valladolid, Mérida, or Cancún 🕑 8am–5pm daily

Chichén Itzá was once an important site to the advanced Maya civilization. The remains of the buildings here are an awe-inspiring sight, and are now one of Mexico's most popular attractions.

The best preserved Maya site on the Yucatán Peninsula, Chichén Itzá confounds historians. The date of first settlement in the southern part of the site is not certain, but the northern section was built during a renaissance in the 11th century AD. Similarities with Tula (p154), and myths that tell how exiled Toltec god-king Quetzalcoatl (p287) settled at Chichén Itzá, suggest that the renaissance was due to a Toltec invasion. However, other theories hold that Tula was influenced by the Maya, not vice versa. In its heyday as a commercial, religious, and military center, which lasted until about the 13th century, Chichén Itzá supported over 35,000 people. In 2007 it was voted one of the New Seven Wonders of the World.

↑ The large Nunnery, thought to have been a residential palace

Chichén Itzá's ballcourt was the largest in Mesoamerica. You can still see the rings that the ball had to pass through.

Main entrance

Pisté and Mérida

Tomb of the High Priest

The slits in the walls of the Observatory correspond to the positions of celestial bodies on key dates in the Maya calendar.

The Church, or Iglesia, is decorated with fretwork, masks of the rain god Chac, and the bacabs – four animals who, in Maya myth, held up the sky.

The Nunnery is so named because it reminded the Spanish of a convent.

Chichén Viejo

Nunnery

▽ The facade of this building's east annex has some particularly beautiful stone fretwork and interesting carvings.

El Castillo

Built on top of an older structure, the building's height and striking geometric design dominate the site *(p296)*.

Ballcourt

Ballcourts *(p297)* have been found at all main pre-Hispanic sites, the largest being here.

Timeline

Observatory

▲ Also called El Caracol (The Snail) because of its spiral staircase, this building served as an astronomical observatory.

Temple of the Warriors

The raised temple is made even more impressive by the Group of a Thousand Columns surrounding it on various sides.

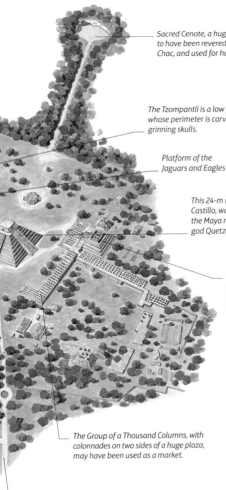

Sacred Cenote, a huge natural well, is thought to have been revered as the home of rain god Chac, and used for human sacrifice.

The Tzompantli is a low platform whose perimeter is carved with grinning skulls.

Platform of the Jaguars and Eagles

This 24-m (79-ft) high pyramid, El Castillo, was dedicated to Kukulcan, the Maya representation of the god Quetzalcoatl.

Set on a small pyramid, the Temple of the Warriors is decorated with sculptures of the rain god Chac and the plumed serpent Kukulcan.

The Group of a Thousand Columns, with colonnades on two sides of a huge plaza, may have been used as a market.

Entrance

↑ Illustration showing the layout of the ruins at Chichén Itzá

> ◉ PICTURE PERFECT
> **Equinox at El Castillo**
>
> Two serpents' heads at the foot of the north staircase are thought to represent the god Kukulcan, the Maya Quetzalcóatl *(p287)*. At the equinoxes, the play of light and shadow makes them appear to crawl up the pyramid.

El Castillo

The most awe-inspiring structure at Chichén Itzá is El Castillo (The Castle), a pyramid built around AD 800. It has a perfect astronomical design: four staircases face the cardinal points, various features correspond with aspects of the Maya calendar (*p298*), and, twice yearly at sunrise, a fascinating optical illusion occurs on the north staircase (*p295*). Continuing excavations on the eastern side allow visitors to watch the process of archaeology as it reveals that the pyramid was built on the remains of a much older settlement. Since the site was designated as one of the New Seven Wonders of the World, climbing the staircases is no longer permitted.

↑ Visitor pausing to admire the wonder that is the El Castillo pyramid

The original layout and features of the El Castillo pyramid ↓

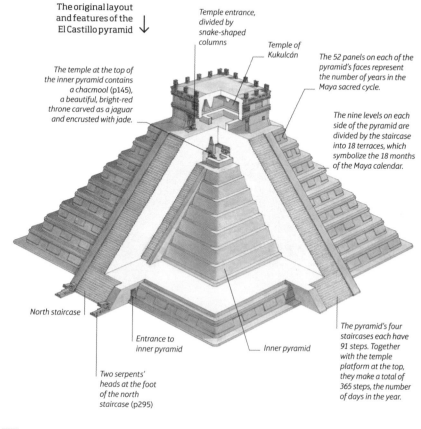

Temple entrance, divided by snake-shaped columns

Temple of Kukulcán

The 52 panels on each of the pyramid's faces represent the number of years in the Maya sacred cycle.

The temple at the top of the inner pyramid contains a chacmool (p145), a beautiful, bright-red throne carved as a jaguar and encrusted with jade.

The nine levels on each side of the pyramid are divided by the staircase into 18 terraces, which symbolize the 18 months of the Maya calendar.

North staircase

Entrance to inner pyramid

Inner pyramid

The pyramid's four staircases each have 91 steps. Together with the temple platform at the top, they make a total of 365 steps, the number of days in the year.

Two serpents' heads at the foot of the north staircase (p295)

EXPERIENCE MORE

Edzná

F4 **Mex 180 and 186, 37 miles (60 km) SE of Campeche, Campeche** **(981) 816 91 11** **8am–5pm daily**

A sophisticated canal system radiates out from the center of this Maya settlement to the agricultural areas beyond. The canals were primarily used for transporting goods, but may also have served a defensive purpose. Edzná was founded in around 600 BC, and in its heyday it is thought to have had a population of 25,000. The main structure is the Gran Acrópolis, dominated by the Edificio de los Cinco Pisos (Building of the Five Levels). Another building of interest is the Templo de los Mascarones (Temple of the Masks), named after its notable stucco mask.

Ek' Balam

G4 **Off Mex 295, 16 miles (25 km) N of Valladolid, Yucatán** **(988) 944 40 68** **8am–5pm daily**

Excavation work has revealed Ek' Balam (Black Jaguar) as an important Maya city and religious center. It dates predominantly from AD 700 to 1000, is quite compact, and has an unusual double perimeter wall for fortification. The real highlight is the Tower – a 98-ft- (30-m-) high tiered pyramid that visitors can climb. On each of the pyramid's tiers, pits sunk into the structure are thought to be *chultunes* (Maya cisterns). From gaps in the surrounding walls at the cardinal points, Maya white roads, or *sacbeob*, radiate out to a distance of over 1 mile (1.5 km).

↑ Detail of a serpent's head at the foot of the staircase, El Castillo

THE BALLGAME

More than a sport, the ballgame that was played throughout Mesoamerica had a ritual significance. Two teams would compete to manipulate a large ball through a stone ring set high on the wall at the side of the court. It is thought that the losers of the game were subsequently put to death. The cities of Cantona *(p160)* and El Tajín *(p262)* each had a great number of ball-courts. A version of the game, called *ulama*, is still played today.

The Tower and other remains of Ek' Balam archaeological site ↑

THE MAYA

Unlike other Mesoamerican civilizations, the Maya did not have a large, centralized empire. Instead they lived in independent city-states in the Yucatán Peninsula, and parts of Guatemala, Belize, Honduras, and El Salvador. This did not impede them in developing a complex system of writing and counting, profound knowledge of astronomy, and an incredible long-count calendar.

HISTORICAL RECORDS

While other Mesoamerican peoples *(p144)* had writing systems, none was as complete or sophisticated as that of the Maya. They used about 800 different hieroglyphs (or simply "glyphs"), some representing whole words, others phonetic sounds. Maya books (codices) were created by writing on both sides of a thin sheet of bark, which was then folded like a concertina. Only four codices have survived, and their study led to major advances in dicipherment in the mid-20th century.

In the Tzolkin or Sacred Round, 20 day names were combined with 13 numbers to give a year of 260 individually named days.

ASTRONOMY

The Maya had a knowledge of astronomy that was very advanced for their time. They observed and predicted the phases of the moon, equinoxes, and solstices, as well as solar and lunar eclipses. They knew that the Morning and Evening Star were the same planet, Venus, and calculated its "year" to 584 days, within a fraction of the true figure (583.92 days). Remarkably, they achieved all this without the use of lenses for observing distant objects, instruments for calculating angles, or clocks to measure the passing of time.

ENDURING ARTWORKS

Of all Mesoamerican civilizations, the Maya produced the most enduring works of art, in the greatest quantity. Maya art is distinguished by its naturalistic approach which makes it more accessible to the modern eye. Particularly striking are the Maya's portraits of themselves – as seen especially in the wall paintings of Bonampak *(p248)* and the carved bas-reliefs of Palenque *(p246)* – which give us an understanding of their way of life, methods of warfare, costumes, customs, and beliefs.

← The El Caracol observatory at Chichén Itzá

→ Bonampak's colorful murals, dating back to the 8th century

THE MAYA CALENDAR

The Maya observed the 52-year "Calendar Round." This resulted from two calendar cycles, the Haab and the Tzolkin, which acted simultaneously but independently. For periods longer than 52 years, the Maya used a separate system called the Long Count.

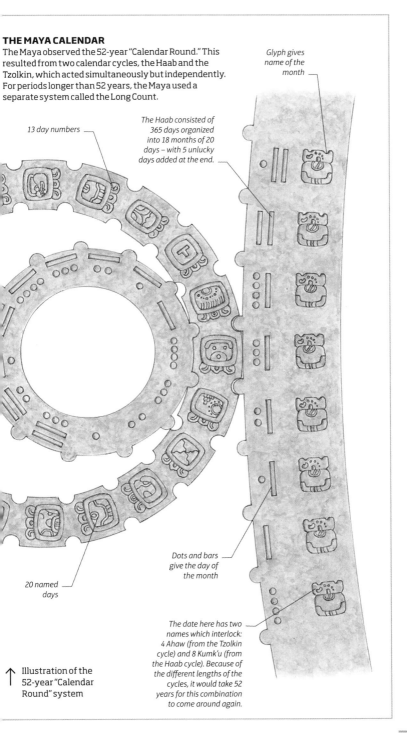

Glyph gives name of the month

13 day numbers

The Haab consisted of 365 days organized into 18 months of 20 days – with 5 unlucky days added at the end.

Dots and bars give the day of the month

20 named days

The date here has two names which interlock: 4 Ahaw (from the Tzolkin cycle) and 8 Kumk'u (from the Haab cycle). Because of the different lengths of the cycles, it would take 52 years for this combination to come around again.

↑ Illustration of the 52-year "Calendar Round" system

8

Chetumal

🅰G5 🚉Quintana Roo ✈🚌
ℹ️Centro de Convenciones
Anexo A, corner of Blvd
Bahia and Ignacio
Comonfort; (983) 835 08 60

Founded on the estuary of the
Río Hondo in 1898, Chetumal
is now the capital of Quintana
Roo state. It is situated near
the frontier with Belize, and is
a typical border town. There is
a large naval base and a duty-
free zone, with stores selling
cut-rate luxury items from all
over the world. Visitors from
Belize and Guatemala come
here for shopping, giving the
city an exciting atmosphere.
Most of the original wooden
and tin-roofed buildings were
destroyed in a hurricane in the
1950s, and the town has been

> **Chetumal's spacious
> Museo de la Cultura
> Maya explores
> the Maya world,
> including astronomy,
> daily life, and
> Maya codices.**

rebuilt around wide avenues,
some of which still end in
undergrowth. Chetumal's
spacious **Museo de la Cultura
Maya** explores the Maya world,
including astronomy, daily life,
and Maya codices. Many of the
exhibits are replicas, but there
are good explanatory panels
and interactive screens.

Situated 25 miles (40 km)
northwest of Chetumal, is the
village of Bacalar. There is a
natural pool here, over 200 ft
(60 m) deep. Named Cenote
Azul for its vivid blue color, it
is perfect for a swim.

Museo de la Cultura Maya

♿🕐 🚉Corner of Avenida
Héroes and Cristobal Colón
📞(983) 832 68 38 🕘9am–
5pm Tue–Sat

9

Campeche

🅰F4 🚉Campeche ✈🚌
ℹ️Avenida Ruiz Cortines;
www.campeche.travel

The Spanish settlement of
Campeche was built on the site
of a former Maya fishing village
in about 1540. In colonial times
it was the most important

 INSIDER TIP
Belize Bound

Water taxis connect
Chetumal with Caye
Caulker and San Pedro
in Belize. You'll need to
pass immigration and
customs, but low rates
and beautiful vistas
make up for that (www.
belizewatertaxi.com).

port on the Yucatán Peninsula.
Campeche's prosperity made it
a target for attacks by pirates.
As a consequence, thick walls
were built around the town.
These were strengthened by
eight baluartes (bastions),
seven of which have been
put to other uses. The largest
of them, in the middle of the
stretch of wall facing the sea,
is the **Baluarte de la Soledad**.
It is now a museum displaying
an important collection of
Maya stelae, many of which
were found at the Maya burial
ground on the island of Jaina,
25 miles (40 km) north of
Campeche. The Baluarte de
Santiago, at the northwestern
corner of the walls, has been
transformed into a walled
botanical garden containing

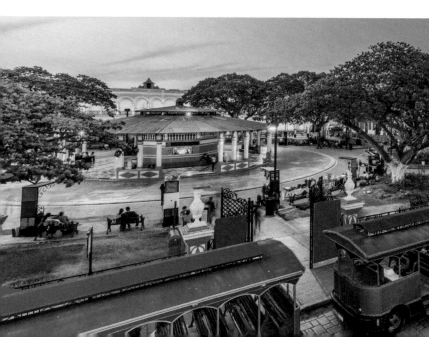

over 200 species of subtropical plants. On the landward side of the walls, the Baluarte de San Pedro sells a small selection of regional handicrafts.

Two gateways in the walls – the Sea Gate and the Land Gate – give access to the old part of the city. Between them runs Calle 59, on which stand several restored, single-story colonial-era houses, painted in bright blues, pinks, and ochers. One of the finest buildings is the **Casa de Teniente del Rey** (King's Lieutenant's House), the former residence of the Spanish king's military rep-resentative in the Yucatán. Transformed into offices, the house has a splendid court-yard, which can be visited.

The focal point of the old part of Campeche is the main square, the Parque Principal, which has elegant arcades and an elaborate, modern bandstand. Tours of the city in open-sided trams

start from here. Facing the square is **El Palacio Centro Cultural**, a museum that explores Campeche's history. Nearby is the cathedral, one of the first churches built on the Yucatán mainland, although much of the present building was constructed later, in the Baroque style. Behind it, on Calle 10, stands the Mansión Carvajal, now government offices. This building is a fine example of 19th-century Spanish-Moorish architecture. Another attractive building in the city center is the ExTemplo de San José, a former Jesuit church, with an elaborate facade of blue and yellow tiles. It is now used as a cultural center and craft market.

Campeche's defenses were completed by adding two forts on hills outside the city, both now housing museums. Situated to the north is the **Museo Histórico Reducto San José El Alto**, with exhibits on colonial military history. To the south of the city is the **Fuerte de San Miguel**, protected by a moat crossed by a drawbridge. Inside the fort is the Museo Arqueológico, whose exhibits include

jade masks from Calakmul (*p309*) and ceramic figurines from the island of Jaina.

Baluarte de la Soledad
Calle 8 Circuito Baluartes (seaward side) (981) 816 91 36 9am-3pm Tue-Sun

Casa de Teniente del Rey
Calle 59 40, between Calles 14 & 16 (981) 816 91 11 9am-5pm daily (to 2pm Sat & Sun)

El Palacio Centro Cultural
Parque Principal (981) 816 77 41 9am-5pm daily (to 2pm Sat & Sun)

Museo Histórico Reducto San José El Alto
Avenida Morazan (981) 816 91 11 8am-5pm Tue-Sun

Fuerte de San Miguel
Avenida Escénica (981) 816 91 36 8:30am-5pm Tue-Sun

EAT

La Palapa del Tío Fito
Lively open-air restaurant along the seafront; a popular spot for seafood and cocktails.

F4 Avenida Resurgimiento s/n, Campeche facebook.com/lapalapadeltiofito

$$$

La Pigua
Here you'll find some of the best fish and seafood in the city. Meaty crab claws are among the specialties.

F4 Miguel Alemán 179A, Campeche lapigua.com.mx

$$$

↑ Independence Plaza, notable for the beautiful cathedral, in old Campeche

The Puuc Route

F4 **Starts from Mex 261, 12 miles (20 km) SE of Uxmal, Yucatán** **8am–5pm daily**

Forming a low ridge across the western part of the Yucatán, about 62 miles (100 km) south of Mérida, the Puuc hills provide a welcome relief from the flat monotony of the rest of the peninsula. Despite a lack of water, they offered a strong defensive position for the ancient Maya people, as well as good soil for farming.

Several Maya settlements have been discovered in the region. All are believed to have reached their peaks from about AD 600 to 900 and they share the striking style of architecture and ornamentation that has become known as the Puuc style. This style is marked by a facade which has plain walls at the base and detailed stone mosaic masks (often depicting gods) on its upper sections.

Some settlements are linked to each other and to their contemporary site of Uxmal (*p284*) by *sacbeob*, or "white roads," which were mainly used for ceremonial purposes.

GREAT VIEW
From the Hilltop
Just a short drive from Kabáh on the Puuc Route is the small town of Santa Elena, where the large hilltop church – which looks more like a fortress than a place of worship – provides a wonderful vantage point from where to survey the incredible surrounding region.

The Puuc Route runs across four Maya sites, starting with Kabah. The main building here is the Codz Poop. The facade of this palace is decorated with more than 250 masks representing the rain god Chac (*p287*), with his distinctive hooked nose. Kabah was the closest settlement to the important Maya city of Uxmal. A single, undecorated arch straddles the entrance road.

Of all the Puuc sites, Sayil, around 6 miles (10 km) south of Kabah, is the one that provides most evidence of how the Maya in this area lived. Around the edge of the site, many of the ordinary dwellings have been excavated, as have the homes of the settlement's

ruling elite, located in the central area. It is hard to envisage today, but the excavations suggest that Sayil was once populated by more than 8,000 people, with a similar number living in small, outlying communities surrounding the city. The huge three-tiered palace of Sayil's rulers is a splendid example of the rich Puuc style.

Sayil has no accessible supply of surface water, but several *chultunes*, large manmade cisterns for storing water, have been found at the site.

About 5 miles (8 km) east is Xlapak. The best-preserved building here is the palace, which has Chac masks above its entrances. Details such as a frieze of columns stand out on other buildings, but much of this site has yet to be cleared.

The last settlement on the Puuc Route is Labná, 3 miles (5 km) northeast of Xlapak. Among several spectacular structures here, the Arch is the best known. Originally part of a building between two courtyards, it is adorned with Chac

The Arch, a Maya highlight along the Puuc Route, at the settlement of Labná

masks and representations of thatched Maya huts. Nearby is a structure with a high crest above its facade. Known as El Mirador (The Observatory), it may have been a temple.

At the other end of the site is the main two-story palace, which has a frieze of masks and latticework. On one corner of the palace is a carving of a serpent with a human head in its jaws.

Another impressive structure is the Temple of Columns, which has a frieze around it, decorated with small columns.

⓫

Celestún

🅰F4 ⏷Yucatán 🅸Palacio Municipal, Calle 62, Mérida; www.yucatan.travel

The small fishing village of Celestún is situated on a spit of land almost entirely separated from the mainland. Several kilometers of palm-fringed

A visitor inside the Loltún cave system and *(inset)* detail of a wall painting ↑

beaches line the coast to the west of Celestún, but it is the flamingos on the estuary to the east that attract most of the visitors. Boats can be hired to get closer to the birds, which include pelicans and various waders, as well as flamingos. However, strict environmental laws prohibit anyone from disturbing the birds, so it is a good idea to bring a pair of binoculars with you so that you can see their natural behavior from afar.

Other excursions on board small launches are available, depending on weather conditions. These include visits to the *bosque petrificado*, a forest of petrified wood. This surreal, desolate place, located on the Isla de Pájaros to the south of Celestún, was created by prolonged salinization.

⓬

Grutas de Loltún

🅰G4 ⏷Off Mex 180, 12 miles (20 km) SW of Maní, Yucatán ⏷Daily

The breathtaking Loltún Grottoes form the longest cave system in the Yucatán. The earliest remains discovered here are bison, mammoth, and other animal bones, suggesting that Loltún was inhabited soon after the last Ice Age. The caves contain fascinating wall paintings from various periods of occupation. The natural features of the caves are also striking, with impressive stalagmites and stalactites that give them the name Loltún, meaning "stone flowers."

Tours are compulsory, so book a guide from Mérida *(p290)* to explore the caves.

> **Several kilometers of palm-fringed beaches line the coast to the west of Celestún, but it is the flamingos on the estuary to the east that attract most of the visitors.**

↑ Visitors taking the challenging climb to the top of a pyramid at the archaeological site of Cobá

Cobá

🅐G4 🚗29 miles (47 km) NW of Tulum, Quintana Roo 📞 (983) 837 24 11 🕐8am-5pm daily

Built around a group of lakes, Cobá is one of the most interesting archaeological sites in the Yucatán Peninsula. The city stood at the center of a network of sacbeob (meaning "white roads"): straight processional routes paved with limestone that connected Maya buildings. Up to 40,000 people are thought to have lived at this huge site, due to the local abundance of water. Only a small proportion has been excavated.

There are three key clusters of buildings. Be prepared for long walks between them, or rent a bike. Near the entrance of the site is the Cobá Group. The main building in this group is a pyramid called La Iglesia (the Church), because local people regard it as a shrine.

A trail beginning on the other side of Lago Macanxoc leads to the Macanxoc Group, where a collection of stelae carved by the Maya as historical records can be seen. Just north is the Nohoch Mul Group. Standing at 138 ft (42 m), Nohoch Mul is the highest pyramid in the Yucatán. It's a hard climb to the temple, but once reached there is an incomparable view of the lakes and jungle below.

Dzibilchaltún

🅐F4 🚗Off Mex 261, 9 miles (15 km) N of Mérida, Yucatán 📞 (999) 944 00 43 🕐8am-5pm daily

Dzibilchaltún was one of the most important centers in pre-Hispanic Yucatán, and one of the earliest to be built. However, it was explored only in the 1940s, making it one of the latest to be rediscovered.

The site is arranged concentrically. A sacbe, or "white road," leads from the central plaza to the impressive Temple of the Seven Dolls. This building is named after the tiny clay dolls found buried in front of its altar. Several of the dolls have deformities, and are thought to be associated with rituals. Replicas are displayed in the ultramodern and well laid-out museum.

Other noteworthy exhibits include the stelae and sculptures found in the gardens leading up to the museum, ceramic figures, wooden altarpieces from the colonial era, and an attractive display on the pirates who plagued the seas around the Yucatán coast in the 16th and 17th centuries. Interactive screens and audiovisual commentaries provide information about the ancient Maya world view, the Maya today, and the history of the henequen industry.

Dzibilchaltún's cenote, a natural turquoise pool that is covered with lilies floating on the surface, is more than 130 ft (40 m) deep. It provides a refreshing place for a swim after visiting the other sights. Many artifacts have been recovered from its depths.

→ Izamal's imposing Convento de San Antonio de Padua, built by Spanish Franciscan monks

Modern Izamal is a fascinating combination of Maya remains and Spanish Colonial buildings. There are around 20 Classic Maya structures still standing.

Izamal

▲G4 ◻Yucatán
🚌 𝒊 Palacio Municipal, Calle 62, Mérida; www.yucatan.travel

Once as important a site as Chichén Itzá, Izamal is believed to have been founded around AD 300. The original village grew into an influential city-state and, by AD 800, it was governing the surrounding region. Modern Izamal is a fascinating combination of Maya remains and Spanish Colonial buildings. There are around 20 Classic Maya structures still standing. Chief among these is the pyramid K'inich K'ak' Mo', named after the ruler "Great-Sun Fire Macaw." It is one of the largest pyramids in the Yucatán.

The importance of Izamal had declined by the time the Spanish arrived in the mid-16th century, but it retained enough religious influence for the Franciscan monks to construct the spectacular Convento de San Antonio de Padua here. They demolished a Maya temple and built the church on its massive platform base, giving it an elevated position. The huge atrium contains some early Franciscan frescoes.

The church acquired even more importance when Bishop Diego de Landa installed in it a statue of the Virgen de la Inmaculada, which he had brought from Guatemala. This was immediately attributed with miraculous powers by the local Maya population, and in 1949 the Virgin was adopted as the patron saint of the Yucatán. A small museum housed inside the church commemorates Pope John Paul II's visit to Izamal in 1993, the International Year of Indigenous People, when he pledged the Catholic Church's support for the Indigenous Maya. Adjacent to the church are two pretty arcaded squares. Here, and in the surrounding streets of

TOP 3 REGIONAL FIESTAS

Equinoxes
An optical illusion makes a shadowy snake appear on the steps of El Castillo at Chichén Itzá in March and September.

Carnival
Held throughout Mexico in February, this fiesta sees some villages burn a papiermâché figure of "Juan Carnaval" to end the festivities.

Cristo de las Ampollas
From mid-September through to mid-October, Mérida honors "Christ of the Blisters," a wooden statue said to have blistered as skin does.

low Spanish Colonial houses, most of the buildings' facades are painted a glowing ocher color. This led to Izamal being nicknamed La Ciudad Amarilla, literally "The Yellow City."

Today, the town is known as a center for arts and crafts, with wood-carving, papier-mâché and jewelry particular specialties. Many local artisans have shops or studios that are open to the public and there's a small museum on the main square that showcases crafts from across Mexico, including the Yucatán.

STAY

Verde Morada

Yucatán's natural elements are channeled throughout this boutique hotel, especially in the beautiful garden and pool area.

G4 ⬛Calle 41A No 209, Valladolid ⓦverdemorada.mx

$$$

Genesis Eco-Oasis

This eco-lodge is a delightful place to get away from it all, with simple but comfortable rooms. There is a lovely garden, a pool, and a vegetarian restaurant.

G4 ⬛Ek Balam, 17 miles (28 km) N of Valladolid ⓦgenesis retreat.com

$$$

Valladolid

▲G4 ⬛Yucatán 🚌 ⓘPalacio Municipal, Parque Principal, Calle 40 No 200; www.valladolid.gob.mx

Lying almost exactly halfway between Mérida and Cancún, Valladolid is the third largest city on the Yucatán Peninsula. It was founded by the Spanish on an earlier Maya settlement known as Zaci, and quickly became an important religious center. In 1552 the Franciscans built the Yucatán's first ecclesiastical buildings here, the Iglesia de San Bernardino de Siena and the adjoining Ex-Convento de Sisal. These have been restored, revealing original frescoes behind two side altars in the church.

The *zócalo* (main square) is the focal point, and often the liveliest part, of this quiet and attractive city. Maya women sell *huipiles* (embroidered dresses) around its perimeter, and in the northeast corner small, inexpensive restaurants serve tasty local dishes and fruit juices late into the night. Overlooking the square is the cathedral, with its elegant facade, and the colonial-era hotel El Mesón del Marqués. Also on the square is the Palacio Municipal (City Hall). In the first-floor hallway are painted panels showing the history of the town from Maya times, and portraits of military leaders from Valladolid who helped initiate the revolution (*p62*).

West of town is the **Cenote de Dzitnup**, a natural well, apparently unearthed by a pig in the 1950s. Visitors can climb down the steep steps to the underground pool, where a hole in the roof and electric lighting illuminate the dramatic setting. You can also swim here among the fish in the blue water.

Located a bit farther west are the **Grutas de Balankanché**, huge caves that were discovered in 1959. Maya artifacts found here suggest that this was a place of worship as early as 300 BC, dedicated to the rain god Chac. Guides point out some of the Maya objects that remain in situ, which include miniature corn-grinding stones and decorated incense burners. There is also a small but informative museum on site.

↑ Admiring the stalactites and turquoise water in the Cenote de Dzitnup, Valladolid

Cenote de Dzitnup

🌐 🚗 4 miles (7 km) W of Valladolid ⏰ 8am–7pm daily

Grutas de Balankanché

🌐 🚗 Off Mex 180, 22 miles (35 km) W of Valladolid ⏰ 8am–5pm daily

---

Maní

🅰 G4 🚗 Yucatán 𝒊 Palacio Municipal, Calle 62, Mérida; www.yucatan.travel

The town of Maní is the best base from which to discover an array of Catholic sites dating back to the mid-16th century, when Catholic priests, particularly Franciscan friars, came from Spain to convert the Maya population of the Yucatán. They constructed a network of huge, fortress-like churches and monasteries, often on the sites of earlier Maya temples. The most imposing of these is the Iglesia de San Miguel Arcángel, which dominates the town of Maní. It was constructed by around 6,000 enslaved people on ground that was already holy to the Maya – a cenote

(natural well) is visible under the front of the church.

The *Ruta de los Conventos* (Convent Route) connects other Franciscan churches in the towns around Maní. The one in Oxkutzcab, 6 miles (10 km) to the south, has a lovely Baroque altarpiece. The Iglesia de San Pedro Apóstol in Teabo, east of Maní, was begun in 1694, and traces of Franciscan murals can still be seen in its powder-blue interior. To the north, Teco's church houses a huge red and blue wooden altarpiece and a beautiful wooden cross with the last hours of Christ's life painted on it.

Located between Tekit and Tecoh is **Mayapán**, which became the political and cultural Maya capital in the north of the peninsula after the fall of Chichén Itzá. Abandoned in the mid-15th century, Mayapán's most remarkable surviving feature is the pyramid of Kukulcan, which is built on nine levels and topped with a temple.

Mayapán

🌐 🚗 37 miles (60 km) N of Maní 📞 (999) 944 40 68 ⏰ 8am–5pm daily

Río Lagartos Biosphere Reserve

🅰 G4 🚗 Mex 295, 65 miles (104 km) N of Valladolid, Yucatán ⏰ Daily

The UNESCO-listed nature reserve of Río Lagartos occupies brackish lagoons on the north coast of the peninsula. It is known as a birdwatchers' paradise and is home to huge colonies of flamingos that breed here in the summer. Between April and June, the flamingos' nests are protected, but at other times of the year, boat trips to view these elegant birds can be arranged in Río Lagartos village. Occasionally, snakes and turtles can also be spotted here.

260

The number of bird species you can see in the Río Lagartos nature reserve.

⑲ Progreso

⌂F4 ⌖Yucatán ⊞ ℹCalle 80, between Calles 25 & 27; (969) 103 01 61

Situated on the north Yucatán coast, Progreso was once an important port. With the construction of the railroad linking the port to Mérida in the 1880s, the town experienced a boom that is hard to imagine now as one approaches the relaxed, low-lying town past mangrove swamps.

Although Progreso shares Mexico's Yucatán Peninsula with Cancún (p282), it is less developed and glamorous. But it does have what is probably the longest concrete pier in the world – 4 miles (6.5 km) long – which is often bustling with people, and live mariachi bands play music here. Near its landward end is an attractive 19th-century lighthouse.

Crystal-clear water rolls gently onto the beautiful white sandy beach. Running alongside, the paved boardwalk is pleasant to stroll, and there are many good seafood restaurants. Cruise liners stop in Progreso, and there are a number of ocean-front resorts, making the town popular with people from the north looking for a warmer winter.

⑳ 〈image 2〉 Río Bec Sites

⌂G5 ⌖Mex 186, 75 miles (120 km) W of Chetumal, Campeche ⌚8am–5pm daily

A group of stylistically similar Maya sites, situated in the lowlands west of Chetumal, are known collectively as the Río Bec sites. Many are hidden by jungle, but three of them, Xpujil, Becán, and Chicanná, are near enough to the main road (Mex 186) to be accessible. These three can be visited on a day-trip from Chetumal, or en route to the city from Palenque (p244) or Villahermosa (p273).

The Río Bec style, which the sites share, was dominant between AD 600 and 900. The style is characterized by elongated platforms and buildings, flanked by slender towers with rounded corners. These towers are "fake" temple-pyramids – the steps are too steep to be used, and the structures seem to have no inner chamber and no special function apart from decoration. Representations of Itzamná, the creation god responsible for life and death, are the main ornamentation.

From Chetumal, the first site is Xpujil, clearly visible from the road. Here, 17 building groups surround a central

square, but the most striking structure is the main temple, whose three towers rise over 50 ft (15 m) from a low platform. These pointed towers soar enigmatically above the surrounding jungle.

Farther west, a track north of the main road leads to Becán. The site is thought to have been the principal Maya center in the Río Bec region. The substantial number of non-local artifacts found during excavations suggests it was an important trading center linking the two sides of the peninsula. Unusually, the main buildings here were surrounded by a trench or moat (now dry) that is up to 16 ft (5 m) deep and 52 ft (16 m) wide, and about 1.5 miles (2 km) in circumference.

Various Río Bec towers can be seen here, but Becán is also noted for the unusual rooms found inside Structure VIII. These chambers had no means of light or ventilation and may have been used for religious rituals that required darkness and isolation.

Chicanná, 2 miles (3 km) farther west, and south of the main road, has the most

Tables and chairs set under palapas on the soft white sands at Progreso

↑ The three Río Bec towers rising above the principal temple at Xpujil

A group of stylistically similar Maya sites, situated in the lowlands west of Chetumal, are known collectively as the Río Bec sites.

extraordinary architecture of the three sites. Its name means "house of the serpent's mouth," which refers to Structure II, whose facade is a snake's head formed by an intricate mosaic of stone. This zoomorphic shape represents the god Itzamná, while the snake's mouth forms the doorway. Structure XX, set apart from the main plaza, is a two-level building that echoes the design of Structure II. Its sides are decorated with masks of Chac, the rain god (p287).

A few detours off the main highway will reward you with quieter archaeological sites. With less crowds, the crumbling ruins appear even more impressive and mysterious as they are reclaimed by the vines and trees around them.

The first two diversions take you west from Chetumal along Mex 186, and then north on Quintana Roo Francisco Villa-Graciano Sánchez. Here, fields give way to jungle, the setting for the Maya site of Kohunlich and its Temple of Masks, dedicated to the Maya sun god. The steps of this 6th-century pyramid are flanked with

masks facing the setting sun. Around 18 miles (29 km) north of Kohunlich lie the equally impressive ruins of Dzibanché.

Further west near the village of Conhuás, a minor road branches to the south to Calakmul, one of the most important Maya cities in the Classic period. The 165-ft (50-m) high pyramid here is the largest in Mexico. Around a hundred stelae remain on site, but the jade masks found in the tombs are now on display in Campeche (p300). Just west of Conhuás is the site of Balamkú, discovered

 HIDDEN GEM
Secret Ruins

Although close to the major archaeological site Tulum (p288), the Maya ruins of Chunyaxché (also known as Muyil) receive few visitors. On the edge of Sian Ka'an, shrouded by jungle, there are some 100 crumbling temples, pyramids, and other structures to explore.

by chance in 1990. Its most striking feature is a 55-ft (17-m) long stucco frieze on the building known as the House of the Four Kings. The frieze is thought to represent the relationship between Maya royalty and the cosmos.

21

Sian Ka'an Biosphere Reserve

🅰 G4 🇶 Quintana Roo

Comprising over 1,700 sq miles (4,500 sq km) of low jungle and marshlands, and 69 miles (110 km) of coral reef, Sian Ka'an has a range of natural habitats that make it an important conservation area. It is run by a government agency and is not primarily geared toward tourism – indeed, the poor roads within the preserve deter all but the most intrepid. However, the Amigos de Sian Ka'an (Friends of Sian Ka'an) run night tours for visitors, which focus on the crocodiles that inhabit the mangrove swamps (www. amigosdesiankaan.org). Lucky visitors may also see the flocks of local and migrating birds in the marshlands around Boca Paila, in the northern part of the preserve – including the rare Jabirú stork – or the elusive turtles and manatees that live in the waters off the coast.

NEED TO KNOW

A trolley passing the main square in Campeche

BEFORE YOU GO

Things change, so plan ahead to make the most of your trip. Be prepared for all eventualities by considering the following points before you travel.

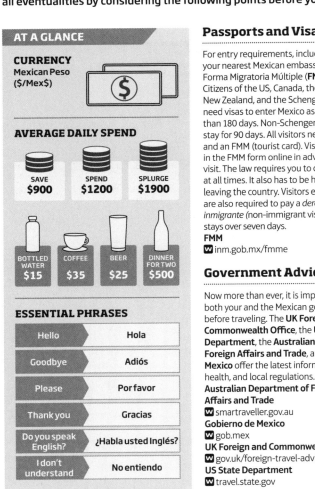

AT A GLANCE

CURRENCY
Mexican Peso
($/Mex$)

AVERAGE DAILY SPEND

SAVE	SPEND	SPLURGE
$900	$1200	$1900

BOTTLED WATER	COFFEE	BEER	DINNER FOR TWO
$15	$35	$25	$500

ESSENTIAL PHRASES

Hello	Hola
Goodbye	Adiós
Please	Por favor
Thank you	Gracias
Do you speak English?	¿Habla usted Inglés?
I don't understand	No entiendo

ELECTRICITY SUPPLY

Standard voltage is 110 volts. Power sockets are type A and B, fitting two- or three-pronged plugs.

Passports and Visas

For entry requirements, including visas, consult your nearest Mexican embassy or check the Forma Migratoria Múltiple (**FMM**) website. Citizens of the US, Canada, the UK, Australia, New Zealand, and the Schengen region do not need visas to enter Mexico as tourists for less than 180 days. All visitors need a valid passport and an FMM (tourist card). Visitors need to fill in the FMM form online in advance of their visit. The law requires you to carry your FMM at all times. It also has to be handed in on leaving the country. Visitors entering by land are also required to pay a *derecho de no inmigrante (*non-immigrant visa) entry fee for stays over seven days.
FMM
w inm.gob.mx/fmme

Government Advice

Now more than ever, it is important to consult both your and the Mexican government's advice before traveling. The **UK Foreign and Commonwealth Office**, the **US State Department**, the **Australian Department of Foreign Affairs and Trade**, and **Gobierno de Mexico** offer the latest information on security, health, and local regulations.
Australian Department of Foreign Affairs and Trade
w smartraveller.gov.au
Gobierno de Mexico
w gob.mex
UK Foreign and Commonwealth Office
w gov.uk/foreign-travel-advice
US State Department
w travel.state.gov

Customs Information

You can find information on the laws relating to goods and currency taken in or out of Mexico on the **Relaciones Exteriores México** website.
Relaciones Exteriores México
w consulmex.sre.gob.mx

Insurance

We recommend taking out a comprehensive insurance policy covering theft, loss of belongings, medical care, cancellations and delays, and read the small print carefully.

Vaccinations

All travelers are advised to seek immunization against hepatitis A, typhoid, tetanus, diphtheria, hepatitis B, and rabies. Malaria is present in some rural parts of Mexico, so ask your doctor about antimalarial medicines. For information regarding COVID-19 vaccination requirements, consult government advice.

Booking Accommodations

Book accommodations a few months in advance in popular destinations at peak times such as Christmas, Semana Santa, Easter, and July and August. The usual 16 percent IVA tax is supplemented with a 2 percent lodging tax, which are not always included in the advertised rate.

Money

Major credit and debit cards are accepted almost everywhere. Contactless payments are becoming increasingly common but it is always a good idea to carry small amounts of cash for tips and minor purchases. A tip of 10–15 percent of the total bill is expected in restaurants, and hotel porters and housekeeping will expect a tip of $10–20 per bag or day. At major resort hotels, additional tips are expected: $20–50 per day for housekeeping and $50–100 for the concierge. It is not usual to tip taxi drivers.

Travelers with Specific Requirements

Many of Mexico's big resorts are accessible – especially Cancún, where you can organize tours and transportation through **Cancún Accesible**.

However, rural areas are not as well equipped, and public transportation can be difficult to negotiate. Check online resources such as the Society for Accessible Travel & Hospitality (**SATH**), **México Accesible**, and the **Accessible Tourism in Mexico City** brochure for detailed advice.

Accessible Tourism in Mexico City
W turismo.cdmx.gob.mx/turismo-accesible
Cancún Accesible
W cancunaccesible.com
México Accesible
W accesiblemexico.com
SATH
W sath.org

Language

The official language is Spanish. In tourist areas, locals will speak some English, but a basic knowledge of Spanish is a great advantage to anyone traveling off the beaten track. The 68 Indigenous groups in Mexico each have their own language. In remote villages some may not speak Spanish, but there are usually a few bilingual locals.

Opening Hours

> **COVID-19** Increased rates of infection may result in temporary opening hours and/or closures. Always check ahead before visiting museums, attractions, and hospitality venues.

Lunchtime Many shops and museums close for two hours or longer in mid-day.
Monday Many museums close for the day.
Sunday and public holidays Most shops, offices, and museums close early or for the day.

PUBLIC HOLIDAYS

Jan 1	New Year's Day
Early Feb	Constitution Day
Mar 21	Birthday of Benito Juárez
Mar/Apr	Easter Thursday
Mar/Apr	Good Friday
May 1	Labor Day
May 5	Cinco de Mayo
Sep 16	Independence Day
Mid Oct	Day of the Race
Nov 20	Revolution Day
Dec 12	Festival of the Virgin of Guadalupe
Dec 25	Christmas Day

GETTING
AROUND

Whether you are visiting for a short city break or rural retreat, discover how best to reach your destination and travel like a pro.

AT A GLANCE

PUBLIC TRANSPORTATION

LOS CABOS

$12.50

Single bus journey

CANCÚN

$10

Single bus journey

MEXICO CITY

$5

Single bus or subway journey

TOP TIP
Have the exact fare ready when using cash, as change isn't always available.

SPEED LIMIT

MAJOR HIGHWAYS

110 km/h (68 mph)

TWO-LANE HIGHWAYS

90 km/h (56 mph)

URBAN AREAS

60 km/h (37 mph)

RESIDENTIAL AREAS

10 km/h (6 mph)

Arriving by Air

Mexico's largest international airports are Mexico City, Cancún, Guadalajara, Monterrey, Tijuana, Los Cabos, Puerto Vallarta, Mérida, Del Bajío, and Culiacán. Other major tourist entry points are found in Mazatlán, Oaxaca, Acapulco, and Cozumel.

The country has a well-developed domestic flight network, and fares are often very reasonable. Aeroméxico is the country's largest airline, and it serves most national destinations as well as many international ones. Volaris and VivaAerobús are also popular low-cost carriers that serve airports throughout the country, and some international destinations.

Crossing the Mexican Land Border

When entering into Mexico by bus or on foot, pick up the FMM (p312) at Immigration, as these are not handed out automatically.

The area bordering the US – particularly Ciudad Juárez, and also Tijuana – covers some of the biggest hot spots in Mexico's drugs war. Extra caution should be exercised when crossing this area, especially by car.

If heading to Baja California, San Diego–Tijuana is the most popular crossing; get there early or expect to queue for up to 3 hours. Alternatively, try one of the quieter crossings, such as Tecate or Calexico–Mexicali.

Crossings in and out of Central American countries can be hectic; having the correct fees and documentation at hand will make the process easier.

Chetumal is the main crossing into Belize, with buses running to Belize City, and ferries available for Caye Caulker and San Pedro.

There are three conventional crossings into Guatemala: Ciudad Cuauhtémoc–La Mesilla, El Carmen–Talismán, and Ciudad Hidalgo–Tecún Umán. The Río Usumacinta crossing is an interesting adventure involving a 30-minute motorboat ride. In Mexico, head to Corozal in eastern Chiapas and visit Immigration, then take a boat to the border town of Bethel, Guatemala

GETTING TO AND FROM THE AIRPORT

Airport	Distance to city	Taxi fare	Transportation	Journey time
Mexico City (MEX)	9 miles (15 km)	$300	Metro	50 mins
Cancún (CUN)	12 miles (20 km)	$600–900	Bus	25 mins
Guadalajara (GDL)	10 miles (16 km)	$300	Bus	30 mins
Monterrey (MTY)	17 miles (27 km)	$350–400	Bus	45 mins
Tijuana (TIJ)	4 miles (7 km)	$220–250	Bus	20 mins
Los Cabos (SJD)	20 miles (32 km)	$1250–2000	Bus	1 hr
Puerto Vallarta (PVR)	4 miles (7 km)	$340–560	Bus	15–20 mins
Mazatlán (MZT)	12 miles (20 km)	$450–620	Bus	30–40 mins
Oaxaca (OAX)	10 miles (16 km)	$320–450	Bus	30–40 mins
Acapulco (ACA)	19 miles (30 km)	$400–600	Bus	40 mins

BUS JOURNEY PLANNER

This map is a handy reference for traveling between Mexico's main cities by
public transportation, plotting the main bus routes according to journey time.
The times given reflect the fastest and most direct routes available.

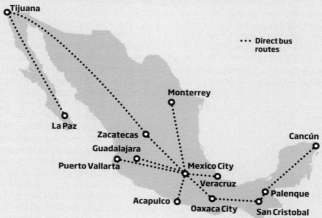

Mexico City to Veracruz	6–7 hrs		**Mexico City to Puerto Vallarta**	12 hrs
Mexico City to Acapulco	5–6 hrs		**Mexico City to Zacatecas**	8–9 hrs
Mexico City to Oaxaca City	6–7 hrs		**Oaxaca to San Cristobal**	10–12 hrs
Mexico City to Tijuana	36 hrs		**San Cristobal to Palenque**	5–6 hrs
Mexico City to Guadalajara	6–8 hrs		**Palenque to Cancún**	11–12 hrs
Mexico City to Monterrey	11–12 hrs		**Tijuana to La Paz**	22–24 hrs

Train Travel

Mexico's train lines are used for freight and, beyond the suburban rail services in Mexico City, there are no passenger rail lines. There are just two notable tourist train services: **Tequila Express** in Jalisco offers a fun day-trip to a tequila-producing hacienda, and the **Chihuahua al Pacífico Railroad** (nicknamed "El Chepe") runs through the Copper Canyon.

Chihuahua al Pacífico Railroad
ⓦ chepe.mx
Tequila Express
ⓦ tequilaexpress.com.mx

Long-Distance Bus Travel

Buses are the best and most economical form of public transportation between the cities and towns in Mexico. Although journey times are longer than domestic air travel, buses are significantly cheaper and very comfortable.

Buses are run by different companies across Mexico, but there are three standard types of intercity bus: luxury, first-class, and second-class services. For long-distance travel, luxury or first-class is recommended. These services are more reliable and more comfortable. Top-of-the-range luxury *(de lujo)* buses offer direct intercity services, with air-conditioning, fully reclining seats, refreshments, video screens, and on-board toilets, although fares are between 30 and 50 percent more than first-class tickets. First-class *(primera)* buses are air-conditioned, with semi-reclining seats, video screens, and a toilet. On shorter trips, less reliable second-class buses may be the only option.

The following are some useful bus companies operating long-distance services:

ADO
ⓦ ado.com.mx
ETN Turistar
ⓦ etn.com.mx
Omnibus
ⓦ odm.com.mx
Senda
ⓦ gruposenda.com
Tufesa
ⓦ tufesa.com.mx

Public Transportation in Mexico City

Servicio de Transportes Eléctricos de la Ciudad de México (**STE**) is Mexico City's main public transport authority. Safety and hygiene measures, timetables, ticket information, and transport maps can be obtained from STE kiosks or the STE website.

The extensive **Metro** and **Metrobús** systems cover most of the city. In the south, an electric train connects the subway at Tasqueña to Embarcadero in Xochimilco. Taxis are inexpensive, and *peseros* (collective taxis) are even cheaper.

Note that traffic and public transportation are busiest during rush hours (6:30–9am and 4–7pm on weekdays).

Metro
ⓦ metro.cdmx.gob.mx
Metrobús
ⓦ metrobus.cdmx.gob.mx
STE
ⓦ ste.cdmx.gob.mx

Driving

Traveling by car at your own pace is a practical and flexible way to explore most areas of Mexico, but there are exceptions: Mexico City (due to congestion), and the states of Colima, Guerrero, Michoacán, Sinaloa, and Tamaulipas (because of high levels of drug violence). Driving elsewhere is generally safe, but motorists need to take some precautions. Robberies do occur, and it is advisable not to drive at night, and to avoid overnight street parking. In Mexico City, drive with the doors locked and the windows rolled up. Plan your trip in advance, take a good road map, check if your route includes toll roads, and know where your stops are likely to be.

Driving to Mexico

Regulations for bringing cars into Mexico are very strict. Obtain a *permiso de importación temporal* (temporary import permit) from Banjercito banks at border crossings, various Mexican consulates in the United States, or online from the **Banjercito** website. Online applications can be made up to 60 days or a minimum of seven days prior to arrival. Expect to be charged a fee of around US$60 for the six-month, multiple-entry permit, plus a deposit of US$200–400 depending on the year of your car. Several other original documents are also needed, and these should all be photocopied twice. These include an authorized immigration form (FMM) or visa *(p341)*, a valid driver's license (US, Canadian, UK, Australian, and New Zealand licenses are valid), a passport, vehicle registration papers, and a credit card (Visa, MasterCard, or American Express) in the same name as the car registration papers. It is rare for rental firms to allow their vehicles over the border, but if you manage to find one who will comply you'll also need to provide written proof of their permission.

Note that US car insurance does not cover driving south of the border, so separate coverage must be arranged.

Banjercito
ⓦ gob.mx/banjercito

Car Rental

International car rental companies, such as Hertz and Budget, have offices in main airports and large towns, but local companies may offer cheaper deals. When pre-booking, make sure the price incorporates the 16 percent sales tax, and full insurance. It is important that the insurance includes theft and collision damage waiver. Some policies provide only nominal coverage (liability insurance is the minimal legal requirement), and you may need to pay for additional insurance cover.

To rent a car in Mexico you must be 21 or over (25 for some agencies) and have held a driver's license for at least one year. The rental must be paid for with a major credit card.

Mopeds and motorbikes can usually be rented in resorts. Before setting out, make sure that the vehicle is in good condition and that your insurance cover is adequate.

Rules of the Road

Mexicans drive on the right-hand side of the road, and distances are measured in kilometers rather than miles. Most traffic regulations and warnings are represented by internationally recognized symbols and signs, but some signs are unique to Mexico. The wearing of seat belts is compulsory. Traffic must stop completely at *Alto* (halt) signs. Slow down when approaching villages, where there are often speed bumps *(topes)*. Beware that these can be very high, and are not always marked.

Take extreme care at rail crossings, both in cities and in the open country, as there is often no system to warn that a train is coming, and accidents can occur.

Avoid driving at night as there is increased risk of robbery and animals on the roads, and it is harder to spot obstacles like potholes, which are often unmarked.

Toll Roads

There are three main kinds of highway in Mexico: four-lane *super carreteras*, ordinary *cuota* (toll) roads, and *libre* (free) roads.

The cost of the tolls on the *super carreteras* is much higher than the ordinary *cuota* roads. As a result, there is less traffic, no trucks, and few buses. Beware that there aren't many service stations on the *super carreteras*.

Cuota highways range from fast, four-lane roads, to those that are little better than *libre* roads. Tolls are charged according to distance and the number of axles on the vehicle

Parking

Parking is permitted where you see a sign with a black E (for *estacionamiento*) in a red circle. The same E with a diagonal line through it means no parking. A white E on a blue background indicates a parking lot. Parking may be difficult in big cities, so when planning your day, make sure to factor in time to find a parking space.

Cycling

Bicycles are a universal means of transportation in Mexico, and bikes can be rented in most resorts. However, cycling can be difficult in Mexico City due to poor quality roads and the volume of traffic – although a network of dedicated bike lanes is being developed. Bosque de Chapultepec is one exception, as the park has good cycling lanes; you can hire bicycles from the nearby Museo de Antropología via the **Ecobici** bike-sharing scheme.

Ecocolors and **Bike Mexico** provide excellent guided bike tours in Cancun and Puerto Vallarta, respectively. For mountain biking, the most popular location is Copper Canyon.

Bike Mexico
W bike-mexico.com
Ecobici
W ecobici.cdmx.gob.mx
Ecocolors
W ecotravelmexico.com

Boats and Ferries

Passenger and car ferries leaving from Santa Rosalía and La Paz connect the Baja California peninsula to Guaymas, Topolobampo, and Mazatlán on the Pacific mainland. Two standards of cabin are offered – a *turista* with bunkbeds and a washbasin, or a more expensive *especial*, which has an entire suite of rooms. Schedules change often and should always be confirmed before travel.

On the Caribbean coast around the Riviera Maya, **Ultramar** ferries leave from Puerto Morelos (car ferry) and Playa del Carmen (passenger only) to the island of Cozumel. Ultramar ferries from Cancún to Isla Mujeres depart from Puerto Juárez, Playa Tortugas, El Embarcadero, and Playa Caracol. **Baja** runs car ferries from Punta Sam to Isla Mujeres.

Baja
W bajaferries.com.mx
Ultramar
W ultramarferry.com

Walking

With stunning mountain ranges, forests, deserts, national parks, and coastal routes, Mexico is an excellent destination for hiking. The most rewarding way to get around the cities and savor local life is on foot. Many hiking trails through nature are also within easy reach of many towns and cities.

PRACTICAL
INFORMATION

A little local know-how goes a long way in Mexico. Here you will find all the essential advice and information you will need during your stay.

AT A GLANCE

EMERGENCY NUMBERS

GENERAL EMERGENCY

911

TIME ZONE

Mexico spans three time zones: CST, MST, and PT. Daylight Savings Time (DST) is from the first Sunday in April to the last Sunday in October – however, in a few US border cities DST begins the second Sunday in March and ends on the first Sunday in November to match the US.

TAP WATER

Outside major resort hotels, drink purified or bottled water only.

WEBSITES AND APPS

Visit Mexico
The country's official tourism website (*www.visitmexico.com*).
Baja Insider
English-language information on Baja California (*www.bajainsider.com*).
Expats in Mexico
Website targeted at foreigners living in Mexico, but full of tips for visitors too (*www.expatsinmexico.com*).

Personal Security

Mexico has a reputation for a high incidence of crime, but the overwhelming majority of foreign visitors have a trouble-free experience. Tourist areas are generally very safe, and Mexico City is no more dangerous than most major cities. Beware of pickpockets (especially on public transportation in Mexico City), leave valuables in a hotel safe, and keep cash concealed.

Areas affected by violence associated with organized crime should be avoided. Check your government's travel advisory for an up-to-date assessment of the situation (*p312*).

Mexico is a culturally diverse country. As a rule, Mexicans are accepting of all people. Although the conservative influence of the Catholic church remains strong, discrimination on the basis of sexual orientation has been made illegal and the LGBTQ+ community is becoming more prominent. This is especially true in urban areas but there may still be a degree of prejudice in small, rural communities. Mexico City legalized same-sex marriage in 2010, closely followed by a number of other states, and in 2016 the Supreme Court in Mexico proclaimed a legal ruling making it unconstitutional for all Mexican states to bar gay marriages. As well as in Mexico City, there are lively LGBTQ+ scenes in Guadalajara, Veracruz, Puerto Vallarta, Acapulco, Mérida, and Cancún. **Gay Mexico Map** lists LGBTQ+ bars, clubs, and hotels in areas throughout the country.
Gay Mexico Map
ⓦ gaymexicomap.com

Natural Hazards

Parts of Mexico are prone to natural disasters: earthquakes, flooding, hurricanes (June through November), and though unlikely, volcanic eruptions. With the exception of earthquakes, which are notoriously hard to predict, local authorities and media should provide plenty of warning. For the latest updates, visit the **Centro Nacional de Prevencion de Desastres** website.
Centro Nacional de Prevencion de Desastres
ⓦ cenapred.gob.mx

Health

Mexico has a good public healthcare system but the best care is in private hospitals in the main cities. You may need to pay for treatment upfront and reclaim the money later from your insurance company. Make sure that you take out comprehensive medical insurance and that you have enough funds to cover the cost of treatment while in Mexico. For minor ailments, seek advice from pharmacies *(farmacias)*. Many are open 24 hours a day in large cities.

Some tropical diseases are present in Mexico, but are rare and can be avoided by getting vaccinated prior to departure *(p313)*.

The sun's rays are very strong in Mexico and dehydration can lead to sun stroke, so always carry bottled water, sunscreen, and a hat when visiting archaeological sites, the beach, or any exposed places.

Mosquitoes are rife in low-lying regions; DEET is the strongest insect repellent, but those with sensitive skin may prefer organic alternatives. Dengue fever is a viral illness spread by mosquitoes. The best protection is to use plenty of insect repellent, cover up well when outside, and sleep under mosquito nets. Mexico City's high altitude and air pollution can aggravate respiratory problems like asthma; seek medical advice before traveling.

Smoking, Alcohol, and Drugs

You must be 18 to drink or purchase alcohol. It is illegal to walk the streets with an open container of alcohol.

You must also be 18 to smoke in Mexico. Hotel and resorts are legally required to provide smoke-free rooms and areas. Smoking is completely prohibited indoors in schools and in federal government facilities.

Being caught in possession of any drug will likely result in serious jail time.

ID

Except for the FMM *(p312)*, carrying ID is not required by law, but it is advisable to take copies of your passport when traveling between cities by bus, near any Mexican border, or if driving a car since there are frequent police checkpoints.

Local Customs

Mexico has a rich culture, a product of centuries of mixing of Indigenous, African, and European populations. Mexicans are generally friendly and easygoing but there are a few pointers visitors should bear in mind. When visiting sacred sites always be respectful of local traditions, history, and culture. Turn off your cell phone and only take photographs (including of people) if permitted.

Cell Phones and Wi-Fi

To use your cell phone in Mexico, you will need a roaming-enabled quad-band handset – consult your service provider for tariffs. Calls can be expensive so consider purchasing a Mexican SIM card or phone once you've arrived.

High-speed internet is generally widely available throughout Mexico, especially in the cities. Increasingly, cities are providing free Wi-Fi in public spaces, and many cafés, restaurants, and businesses offer free Wi-Fi.

Post

The national postal service is run by **Correos de México**. Main post offices *(oficinas de correos)* are open from 8am to 8pm on weekdays, and from 8am to 3pm on Saturdays. Smaller post offices usually have shorter opening hours.
Correos de México
🌐 correosdemexico.com.mx

Taxes

Prices usually include 16 percent sales tax, or IVA *(Impuesto al Valor Agregado)*. If a price is given as *más IVA* (plus sales tax) it means that 16 percent will be added to the bill.

Discount Cards

Some cities operate tourist discount cards, such as the **Mexico City Pass** and the **Go City** program in Cancún. ISIC student cards are accepted at some sights.
Go City
🌐 gocity.com
Mexico City Pass
🌐 citypass.mx

INDEX

PHRASE BOOK

Mexican Spanish is essentially the same as the Castilian spoken in Spain, although there are some differences in vocabulary and pronunciation. The most noticeable are the use of *ustedes* (the plural version of "you") in both informal and formal situations, and the pronunciation of the soft "c" and the letter "z" as "s" rather than "th."

Mexicans use *carro* (instead of *coche*) for a car, and often call buses and trucks *camiones*. Words of Indigenous origin are common. A word for market used only in Mexico is *tianguis*, for example, although *mercado* is also employed.

Mexicans tend to be fairly formal, and it is good manners to use *usted* (rather than *tú*) for "you," unless you know the person well. Always say *buenos días* or *buenas tardes* when boarding a taxi, and address both male taxi drivers and waiters as *señor*.

If you wish to decline goods from street vendors, a polite shake of the head and a *muchas gracias* will usually suffice. Adding *muy amable* (very kind) will help to take the edge off the refusal. A term to be handled with care is *madre* (mother), as much bad language in Mexico is based on variants of this word. When referring to someone's mother, use *tu mamá* (your mother), or the formal version *su señora madre*, just to be safe.

IN AN EMERGENCY

Help!	¡Socorro!	soh-**koh**-roh
Stop!	¡Pare!	pah-**reh**
Call a doctor!	¡Llame a un médico!	yah-meh ah oon meh-**dee**-koh
Call an ambulance!	¡Llame una ambulancia!	yah-meh ah oonah ahm-boo-**lahn**-see-ah
Call the fire department!	¡Llame a los bomberos!	yah-meh ah lohs bohm-**beh**-rohs
Where is the nearest telephone?	¿Dónde está el teléfono más cercano?	dohn-deh ehs-tah ehl teh-**leh**-foh-noh mahs sehr-**kah**-noh
Where is the nearest hospital?	¿Dónde está el hospital más cercano?	dohn-deh ehs-tah ehl ohs-pee-**tahl** mahs sehr-**kah**-noh
policeman	el policía	ehl poh-lee-**see**-ah
Could you help me?	¿Me podría ayudar?	meh poh-**dree**-yah ah-yoo-**dahr**
I've/we've been mugged	Me/nos asaltaron	meh/nohs ah-sahl-**tahr**-ohn
They stole my ...	Me robaron el/la...	meh roh-**bahr**-ohn ehl/lah

COMMUNICATION ESSENTIALS

Yes	Sí	see
No	No	noh
Please	Por favor	pohr fah-**vohr**
Thank you	Gracias	grah-**see**-ahs
Excuse me	Perdone	pehr-**doh**-neh
Hello	Hola	oh-lah
Good morning	Buenos días	bweh-nohs dee-ahs
Good afternoon (from noon)	Buenas tardes	bweh-nahs tahr-dehs
Good night	Buenas noches	bweh-nahs noh-chehs
Bye (casual)	Hasta luego	ah-stah loo-weh-goh
Goodbye	Adiós	ah-dee-ohs
See you later	Hasta luego	ah-stah loo-weh-goh
Morning	La mañana	lah mah-nyah-nah
Afternoon/ early evening	La tarde	lah tahr-deh
Night	La noche	lah noh-cheh
Yesterday	Ayer	ah-yehr
Today	Hoy	oy
Tomorrow	Mañana	mah-nyah-nah
Here	Aquí	ah-kee
There	Allí	ah-yee
What?	¿Qué?	keh

When?	¿Cuándo?	kwahn-doh
Why?	¿Por qué?	pohr-keh
Where?	¿Dónde?	dohn-deh
How are you?	¿Cómo está usted?	koh-moh ehs-tah oos-tehd
Very well, thank you	Muy bien, gracias	mwee bee-ehn grah-see-ahs
Pleased to meet you	Mucho gusto	moo-choh goo-stoh
See you soon	Hasta pronto	ahs-tah prohn-toh
I'm sorry	Lo siento	loh see-ehn-toh

USEFUL PHRASES

That's fine	Está bien	ehs-tah bee-ehn
Great/fantastic!	¡Qué bien!	keh bee-ehn
Where is/are ...?	¿Dónde está/están ...?	dohn-deh ehs-tah/ehs-tahn
How far is it to ...?	¿Cuántos metros/ kilómetros hay de aquí a ...?	kwahn-tohs meh-trohs/kee-loh-meh-trohs eye deh ah-kee ah
Which way is it to ...?	¿Por dónde se va a ...?	pohr dohn-deh seh vah ah
Do you speak English?	¿Habla inglés?	ah-blah een-glehs
I don't understand	No comprendo	noh kohm-prehn-doh
Could you speak more slowly, please?	¿Puede hablar más despacio, por favor?	pweh-deh ah-blahr mahs dehs-pah-see-oh pohr fah-vohr
I want	Quiero	kee-yehr-oh
I would like	Quisiera/ Me gustaría	kee-see-yehr-ah meh goo-stah-ree-ah
We want	Queremos	keh-reh-mohs
Do you have change (for 50 pesos)?	¿Tiene cambio (de cincuenta pesos)?	tee-eh-neh kahm-bee-yoh deh seen-kwehn-tah peh-sohs
(It's) very kind of you	Muy amable	mwee ah-mah-bleh
There is/there are	Hay	eye
Do you have it there/are there?	¿Hay?	eye
Is there any water?	¿Hay agua?	eye ah-gwah
It's broken	Está roto/a	ehs-tah roh-toh/tah
Is it far/near?	¿Está lejos/cerca?	ehs-tah leh-hohs/sehr-kah
Take care/be careful!	¡Ten cuidado!	tehn koo-ee-dah-doh
We are late	Estamos atrasados	ehs-tah-mohs ah-trah-sah-dohs
We are early	Estamos adelantados	ehs-tah-mohs ah-deh-lahn-tah-dohs
OK, all right	De acuerdo	deh ah-kwehr-doh
Yes, of course	Claro que sí	klah-roh keh see
Of course!/with pleasure	¡Cómo no!/con mucho gusto	koh-moh noh/kohn moo-choh goo-stoh
Let's go	Vámonos	vah-moh-nohs

USEFUL WORDS

big	grande	grahn-deh
small	pequeño/a	peh-keh-nyoh/nyah
hot	caliente	kah-lee-ehn-the
cold	frío/a	free-oh/ah
good	bueno/a	bweh-noh/nah
bad	malo/a	mah-loh/lah
enough	suficiente	soo-fee-see-ehn-teh
well	bien	bee-ehn
open	abierto/a	ah-bee-ehr-toh/tah
closed	cerrado/a	sehr-rah-doh/dah
full	lleno/a	yeh-noh/nah
empty	vacío/a	vah-see-oh/ah
left	izquierda	ees-key-ehr-dah
right	derecha	deh-reh-chah
(keep) straight ahead	(siga) derecho	(see-gah) deh-reh-choh
near	cerca	sehr-kah

far	lejos	leh-*hohs*
up	arriba	*ah*-**ree**-bah
down	abajo	*ah*-**bah**-hoh
early	temprano	tehm-**prah**-noh
late	tarde	**tahr**-deh
now/very soon	ahora/ahorita	*ah*-**ohr**-ah/*ah*-ohr-**ee**-tah
more	más	mahs
less	menos	**meh**-nohs
very	muy	mwee
a little	(un) poco	oon *poh*-koh
very little	muy poco	mwee poh-*koh*
(much) more	(mucho) más	(moo-choh) mahs
too much	demasiado	deh-**mah**-see-*ah*-doh
too late	demasiado tarde	deh-mah-*see*-ah-doh **tahr**-deh
farther on/ahead	más adelante	mahs *ah*-deh-**lahn**-teh
farther back	más atras	mahs *ah*-**trahs**
opposite	frente a	**frehn**-*teh* ah
below/above	abajo/arriba	*ah*-**bah**-hoh/*ah*-**ree**-bah
first, second, third	primero/a segundo/a tercero/a	pree-**meh**-roh/ah seh-**goon**-doh/ah tehr-**sehr**-oh/ah
floor (of a building)	el piso	ehl **pee**-soh
ground floor	la planta baja	lah **plahn**-tah **bah**-hah
entrance	entrada	ehn-**trah**-dah
exit	salida	sah-**lee**-dah
elevator	el ascensor	ehl *ah*-sehn-**sohr**
toilets	baños/sanitarios	**bah**-*nyohs*/sah-nee-**tah**-ree-ohs
women's	de damas	deh **dah**-*mahs*
men's	de caballeros	deh kah-bah-**yeh**-rohs
sanitary napkins	toallas sanitarias/ higiénicas	toh-**ah**-*yahs* sah-nee-**tah**-ree-*yahs*/hee-**hyeh**-nee-kahs
tampons	tampones	tahm-**poh**-nehs
condoms	condones	kohn-**doh**-nehs
toilet paper	papel higiénico	pah-**pehl** hee-**hyen**-ee-koh
(non-)smoking area	área de (no) fumar	**ah**-*ree-ah* deh (noh) foo-**mahr**
camera	la cámara	lah **kah**-mah-rah
batteries	las pilas	lahs **pee**-lahs
passport	el pasaporte	ehl pah-sah-**pohr**-teh
visa	el visado	ehl vee-**sah**-doh

HEALTH

I feel ill	Me siento mal	meh see-**ehn**-toh mahl
I have a headache	Me duele la cabeza	meh doo-**eh**-leh lah kah-**beh**-sah
I have a stomach-ache	Me duele el estómago	meh doo-**eh**-leh ehl ehs-**toh**-mah-goh
I need to rest	Necesito descansar	neh-seh-**see**-toh dehs-kahn-**sahr**
The child is/the children are sick	El niño está/los niños están enfermo(s)	ehl **nee**-nyoh ehs-**tah**/lohs **nee**-nyos ehs-**tahn** ehn-**fehr**-moh(s)
We need a doctor	Necesitamos un médico	neh-seh-see-**tah**-mohs oon **meh**-dee-koh
thermometer	el termómetro	ehl tehr-**moh**-meh-troh
drug store	la farmacia	lah fahr-**mah**-see-ah
medicine	la medicina/el remedio	lah meh-dee-**see**-nah/ehl reh-**meh**-dee-oh
pills	las pastillas/píldoras	lahs pahs-**tee**-yahs/lahs peel-**doh**-rahs

POST OFFICES AND BANKS

Where can I change money?	¿Dónde puedo cambiar dinero?	dohn-deh **pweh**-doh kahm-bee-**ahr** dee-**neh**-roh
What is the dollar rate?	¿A cómo está el dólar?	*ah* koh-moh ehs-**tah** ehl **doh**-lahr

How much is the postage to...?	¿Cuánto cuesta enviar una carta a...?	kwahn-toh **kweh**-stah ehn-vee-**yahr** oo-nah **kahr**-tah ah
and for a postcard?	¿y una postal?	ee oo-nah pohs-**tahl**
I need stamps	Necesito estampillas	neh-seh-**see**-toh ehs-tahm-**pee**-yahs
cashier	cajero	kah-**heh**-roh
ATM	cajero automático	kah-**heh**-roh ahw-toh-**mah**-tee-koh
withdraw money	sacar dinero	sah-**kahr** dee-**neh**-roh

SHOPPING

How much does this cost?	¿Cuánto cuesta esto?	kwahn-toh **kwehs**-tah **ehs**-toh
I would like ...	Me gustaría ...	meh goos-tah-**ree**-ah
Do you have?	¿Tienen?	tee-**yeh**-nehn
I'm just looking, thank you	Sólo estoy mirando, gracias	soh-loh ehs-**toy** mee-**rahn**-doh **grah**-see-ahs
What time do you open?	¿A qué hora abren?	ah keh oh-rah **ah**-brehn
What time do you close?	¿A qué hora cierran?	ah keh oh-rah see-**ehr**-rahn
Do you take credit cards/ traveler's checks?	¿Aceptan tarjetas de crédito/ cheques de viajero?	ahk-**sehp**-tahn tahr-**heh**-tahs deh **kreh**-dee-toh/ **cheh**-kehs deh vee-ah-**heh**-roh
I am looking for...	Estoy buscando...	ehs-*tohy* boos-**kahn**-doh
Is that your best price?	¿Es su mejor precio?	ehs soo meh-**hohr** **preh**-see-oh
discount	un descuento	oon dehs-koo-**ehn**-toh
clothes	la ropa	lah **roh**-pah
this one	éste	**ehs**-the
that one	ése	**eh**-she
expensive	caro	**kahr**-oh
cheap	barato	bah-**rah**-toh
size, clothes	talla	**tah**-yah
size, shoes	número	**noo**-mehr-oh
white	blanco	**blahn**-koh
black	negro	**neh**-groh
red	rojo	**roh**-hoh
yellow	amarillo	ah-mah-**ree**-yoh
green	verde	**vehr**-deh
blue	azul	*ah*-**sool**
antique store	la tienda de antigüedades	lah tee-**ehn**-dah deh ahn-tee-gweh-**dah**-dehs
bakery	la panadería	lah pah-nah-deh-**ree**-ah
bank	el banco	ehl/**bahn**-koh
bookstore	la librería	lah lee-breh-**ree**-ah
butcher's	la carnicería	lahkahr-nee-seh-**ree**-ah
cake store	la pastelería	lah pahs-teh-leh-**ree**-ah
department store	la tienda de departamentos	lah tee-**ehn**-dah deh deh-pahr-tah-**mehn**-tohs
fish store	la pescadería	lah pehs-kah-deh-**ree**-ah
greengrocer's	la frutería	lah froo-teh-**ree**-ah
grocer's	la tienda de abarrotes	lah tee-**yehn**-dah deh ah-bah-**roh**-tehs
hairdresser's	la peluquería	lah peh-loo-keh-**ree**-ah
jeweler's	la joyería	lah hoh-yeh-**ree**-ah
market	el tianguis/ mercado	ehl tee-ahn-goo-ees/mehr-**kah**-doh
newsstand	el puesto de periódicos	ehl poo-**es**-toh deh pe-**rio**-dee-kohs
post office	la oficina de correos	lah oh-fee-**see**-nah deh kohr-**reh**-ohs
shoe store	la zapatería	lah sah-pah-teh-**ree**-ah

| supermarket | el supermercado | ehl soo-pehr-mehr-**kah**-doh |
| travel agency | la agencia de viajes | lah ah-**hehn**-see-ah deh vee-**ah**-hehs |

SIGHTSEEING

art gallery	galería de arte	ehl moo-**seh**-oh deh **ahr**-teh
beach	la playa	lah **plah**-yah
cathedral	la catedral	lah kah-teh-**drahl**
church	la iglesia/ la basílica	lah ee-**gleh**-see-ah/ lah bah-**see**-lee-kah
garden	el jardín	ehl hahr-**deen**
library	la biblioteca	lah bee-blee-oh-**teh**-kah
museum	el museo	ehl moo-**seh**-oh
pyramid	la pirámide	lah pee-**rah**-meed
ruins	las ruinas	lahs roo-**ee**-nahs
tourist information office	la oficina de turismo	lah oh-fee-**see**-nah deh too-**rees**-moh
town hall	el palacio municipal	ehl pah-**lah**-see-oh moo-nee-see-**pahl**
closed for holidays	cerrado por vacaciones	sehr-**rah**-doh pohr vah-kah-see-**oh**-nehs
ticket	la entrada	lah ehn-**trah**-dah
how much is the entrance fee?	¿Cuánto vale la entrada?	**kwahn**-toh **vah**-leh lah ehn-**trah**-dah
guide (person)	el/la guía	ehl/lah **gee**-ah
guide (book)	la guía	lah **gee**-ah
guided tour	una visita guiada	**oo**-nah vee-**see**-tah gee-**ah**-dah
map	el mapa	ehl **mah**-pah
city map	el plano de la ciudad	ehl **plah**-noh deh lah see-oo-**dahd**

TRANSPORTATION

When does the... leave?	¿A qué hora sale el...?	ah keh oh-rah **sah**-leh ehl
Where is the bus stop?	¿Dónde está la parada de autobuses?	dohn-deh ehs-**tah** lah pah-rah-**dah** deh ow-toh-**boo**-sehs
Is there a bus/train to...?	¿Hay un camión/ tren a...?	eye oon kah-mee-**ohn**/trehn ah
the next bus/train	el próximo camión/tren	ehl **prohx**-ee-moh kah-mee-**ohn**/trehn
bus station	la central camionera/ de autobuses	lah sehn-**trahl** kah-mee-ohn-**ehr**-ah/deh ow-toh-**boo**-sehs
train station	la estación de trenes	lah ehs-tah-see-**ohn** deh **treh**-nehs
subway/metro	el metro	ehl **meh**-troh
platform	el andén	ehl ahn-**dehn**
ticket office	la taquilla	lah tah-**kee**-yah
round-trip ticket	un boleto de ida y vuelta	oon boh-leh-toh deh **ee**-dah ee voo-**ehl**-tah
one-way ticket	un boleto de ida solamente	oon boh-leh-toh deh ee-dah soh-lah-**mehn**-teh
airport	el aeropuerto	ehl ah-ehr-oh-poo-**ehr**-toh
customs	la aduana	lah ah-doo-**ah**-nah
departure lounge	sala de embarque	**sah**-lah deh ehm-**bahr**-keh
boarding pass	pase de abordar	**pah**-seh deh ah-bohr-**dahr**
taxi stand/rank	sitio de taxis	**see**-tee-oh deh **tahk**-sees
car rental	renta de automóviles	**rehn**-tah deh aw-toh-**moh**-vee-lehs
motorcycle	la moto (cicleta)	lah **moh**-toh (see-kleh-tah)
mileage	el kilometraje	ehl kee-loh-meh-**trah**-he
bicycle	la bicicleta	lah bee-see-**kleh**-tah

daily/weekly rate	la tarifa diaria/ semanal	lah tah-**ree**-fah dee-ah-**ree**-ah/ seh-mah-**nahl**
insurance	los seguros	lohs seh-**goo**-rohs
gas station	la gasolinería	lah gah-soh-leen-er-**ee**-ah
garage	el taller mecánico	ehl tah-**yehr** meh-**kahn**-ee-koh
I have a flat tire	Se me ponchó la llanta	seh meh pohn-**shoh** lah **yahn**-tah

STAYING IN A HOTEL

Do you have a vacant room?	¿Tienen una habitación libre?	tee-**eh**-nehn **oo**-nah ah-bee-tah-see-**ohn lee**-breh
double room	habitación doble	ah-bee-tah-see-**ohn doh**-bleh
with a double bed	con cama matrimonial	kohn **kah**-mah mah-tree-**moh**-nee-ahl
twin room	habitación con dos camas	ah-bee-tah-see-**ohn** kohn dohs **kah**-mahs
single room	habitación sencilla	ah-bee-tah-see-**ohn** sehn-**see**-yah
room with a bath shower	habitación con baño la ducha	ah-bee-tah-see-**ohn** bah-**nyoh** lah **doo**-chah
Do you have a room with a view (of the sea)?	¿Hay alguna habitación con vista (al mar)?	eye ahl-**goo**-nah ah-bee-tah-see-**ohn vees**-tah (ahl mahr)
I have a reservation	Tengo una habitación reservada	tehn-goh oo-nah ah-bee-tah-see-**ohn** reh-sehr-**vah**-dah
The ... is not working	No funciona el/la...	noh foon-see-**oh**-nah ehl/lah
I need a wake-up call at ... o'clock	Necesito que me despierten a las ...	neh-seh-**see**-toh keh meh dehs-pee-**ehr**-tehn ah lahs
Where is the dining-room/bar?	¿Dónde está el restaurante/ el bar?	dohn-deh ehs-**tah** ehl rehs-tah-**rahn**-teh/ehl bahr
hot/cold water	agua caliente/ fría	ah-goo-ah kah-lee-**ehn**-teh/ **free**-ah
soap	el jabón	ehl hah-**bohn**
towel	la toalla	lah toh-**ah**-yah
key	la llave	lah **yah**-veh

EATING OUT

Have you got a table for ...	¿Tienen una mesa para ...?	tee-**eh**-nehn oo-nah meh-sahpah-**rah**
I want to reserve a table	Quiero reservar una mesa	kee-eh-roh reh-sehr-**vahr** oo-nah meh-sah
The bill, please	La cuenta, por favor	lah **kwehn**-tah pohr fah-**vohr**
I am a vegetarian	Soy vegetariano/a	soy veh-heh-tah-ree-**ah**-no/na
I am a vegan	Soy vegano/a	soy veh-gah-no/na
waiter/waitress	mesero/a	meh-**seh**-roh/rah
menu	la carta	lah **kahr**-tah
fixed-price menu	menú del día/comida corrida	meh-**noo** dehl dee-ah/koh-**mee**-dah koh-**rree**-dah
wine list	la carta de vinos	lah **kahr**-tah deh **vee**-nohs
glass	un vaso	oon vah-**soh**
bottle	una botella	oo-nah boh-**teh**-yah
knife	un cuchillo	oon koo-**chee**-yoh
fork	un tenedor	oon teh-neh-**dohr**
spoon	una cuchara	oo-nah koo-**chah**-rah
breakfast	el desayuno	ehl deh-sah-**yoo**-noh
lunch	la comida	lah koh-**mee**-dah
dinner	la cena	lah **seh**-nah
main course	el plato fuerte	ehl **plah**-toh foo-**ehr**-teh
starters	las entradas	lahs ehn-**trah**-das
dish of the day	el plato del día	ehl **plah**-toh dehl **dee**-ah

rare	termino rojo	tehr-*mee*-noh *roh*-hoh
medium	termino medio	tehr-*mee*-noh *meh*-dee-oh
well done	bien cocido	bee-**ehn** koh-**see**-doh
Could you heat it up for me?	¿Me lo podría calentar?	meh loh pohd -*ree*-ah kah-lehn-**tahr**
chair	la silla	lah *see*-yah
napkin	la servilleta	lah sehr-vee-*yeh*-tah
tip	la propina	lah proh-*pee*-nah
Is service included?	¿El servicio está incluido?	ehl sehr-*vee*-see-oh ehs-**tah** een-skloo-**ee**-doh
Do you have a light?	¿Tiene fuego?	tee-*eh*-nee foo-**eh**-goh
ashtray	cenicero	seh-nee-**seh**-roh
cigarettes	los cigarros	lohs see-**gah**-rohs

MENU DECODER

el aceite	ah-*see*-eh-teh	oil
las aceitunas	ah-seh-**toon**-ahs	olives
el agua mineral	ah-*gwa* mee-neh-rahl	mineral water
sin gas/con gas	seen gas/kohn gas	still/sparkling
el ajo	ah-*hoh*	garlic
el arroz	ahr-**rohs**	rice
el azúcar	ah-**soo**-kahr	sugar
la banana	bah-*nah-nah*	banana
una bebida	beh-**bee**-dah	drink
el café	kah-*feh*	coffee
la carne	**kahr**-neh	meat
la cebolla	seh-**boh**-yah	onion
la cerveza	sehr-**veh**-sah	beer
el cerdo	**sehr**-doh	pork
el chocolate	choh-koh-**lah**-teh	chocolate
la ensalada	ehn-sah-**lah**-dah	salad
la fruta	**froo**-tah	fruit
el helado	eh-**lah**-doh	ice cream
el huevo	oo-**eh**-voh	egg
el jugo	eh/*hoo*-goh	juice
la langosta	lahn-**gohs**-tah	lobster
la leche	**leh**-cheh	milk
la mantequilla	mahn-teh-**kee**-yah	butter
la manzana	mahn-**sah**-nah	apple
los mariscos	mah-**rees**-kohs	seafood
la naranja	nah-**rahn**-hah	orange
el pan	pahn	bread
las papas	**pah**-pahs	potatoes
las papas a la francesa	**pah**-pahs ah lah frahn-**seh**-sah	French fries
las papas fritas	**pah**-pahs free-tahs	potato chips
el pastel	pahs-**tehl**	cake
el pescado	pehs-**kah**-doh	fish
picante	pee-**kahn**-teh	spicy
la pimienta	pee-mee-**yehn**-tah	pepper
el pollo	**poh**-yoh	chicken
el postre	**pohs**-treh	dessert
el queso	**keh**-soh	cheese
el refresco	reh-**frehs**-koh	soft drink/soda
la sal	sahl	salt
la salsa	**sahl**-sah	sauce
la sopa	**soh**-pah	soup
el té	teh	herb tea (usually camomile)
el té negro	teh neh-**groh**	tea
la torta	**tohr**-tah	sandwich
las tostadas	tohs-**tah**-dahs	toast
el vinagre	vee-**nah**-greh	vinegar
el vino blanco	**vee**-noh **blahn**-koh	white wine
el vino tinto	**vee**-noh **teen**-toh	red wine

NUMBERS

0	cero	**seh**-roh
1	uno	**oo**-noh
2	dos	dohs
3	tres	trehs
4	cuatro	**kwa**-troh
5	cinco	**seen**-koh
6	seis	says
7	siete	**see**-eh-teh
8	ocho	**oh**-choh
9	nueve	**nweh**-veh
10	diez	**dee**-ehs
11	once	**ohn**-seh
12	doce	**doh**-seh
13	trece	**treh**-seh
14	catorce	kah-**tohr**-seh
15	quince	**keen**-seh
16	dieciséis	dee-eh-see-**seh**-ees
17	diecisiete	dee-eh-see-**see**-eh-teh
18	dieciocho	dee-eh-see-**oh**-choh
19	diecinueve	dee-eh-see-**nweh**-veh
20	veinte	**veh**-een-teh
21	veintiuno	veh-een-tee-**oo**-noh
22	veintidós	veh-een-tee-**dohs**
30	treinta	**treh**-een-tah
31	treinta y uno	**treh**-een-tah ee **oo**-noh
40	cuarenta	kwah-**rehn**-tah
50	cincuenta	seen-**kwehn**-tah
60	sesenta	seh-**sehn**-tah
70	setenta	seh-**tehn**-tah
80	ochenta	oh-**chehn**-tah
90	noventa	noh-**vehn**-tah
100	cien	**see**-ehn
101	ciento uno	**see**-ehn-toh **oo**-noh
102	ciento dos	**see**-ehn-toh dohs
200	doscientos	dohs-**see**-ehn- tohs
500	quinientos	khee-nee-**ehn**-tohs
700	setecientos	seh-teh-**see**-ehn-tohs
900	novecientos	noh-veh-**see**-ehn-tohs
1,000	mil	meel
1,001	mil uno	meel **oo**-noh

TIME

one minute	un minuto	**oon** mee-**noo**-toh
one hour	una hora	**oo**-nah **oh**-rah
half an hour	media hora	**meh**-dee-ah **oh**-rah
half past one	la una y media	lah **oo**-nah ee **meh**-dee-ah
quarter past one	la una y cuarto	lah **oo**-nah ee **kwahr**-toh
ten past one	la una y diez	lah **oo**-nah ee **dee**-ehs
quarter to two	cuarto para las dos	**kwahr**-toh **pah**-rah lahs **dohs**
ten to two	diez para las dos	**dee**-ehs **pah**-rah lahs **dohs**
Monday	lunes	**loo**-nehs
Tuesday	martes	**mahr**-tehs
Wednesday	miércoles	mee-**ehr**-koh-lehs
Thursday	jueves	hoo-**weh**-vehs
Friday	viernes	vee-**ehr**-nehs
Saturday	sábado	**sah**-bah-doh
Sunday	domingo	doh-**meen**-goh
January	enero	eh-**neh**-roh
February	febrero	feh-**breh**-roh
March	marzo	**mahr**-soh
April	abril	ah-**breel**
May	mayo	**mah**-yoh
June	junio	**hoo**-nee-oh
July	julio	**hoo**-lee-oh
August	agosto	ah-**gohs**-toh
September	septiembre	sehp-tee-**ehm**-breh
October	octubre	ohk-**too**-breh
November	noviembre	noh-vee-**ehm**-breh
December	diciembre	dee-see-**ehm**-breh
Two days ago	Hace dos días	hah-*seh* **dohs** **dee**-ahs
In two day's time	En dos días	ehn **dohs** dee-*ahs*
May 1	El primero de mayo	ehl pree-**meh**-roh deh **mah**-yoh

ACKNOWLEDGMENTS

DK would like to thank the following for their contribution to the previous edition: Kana Awoyemi, Huw Hennessy, Stephen Keeling, Shafik Meghji, Nick Caistor, Maria Doulton, Petra Fischer, Eduardo Gleason, Phil Gunson, Alan Knight, Felicity Laughton, Richard Nichols, Chloë Sayer, Helen Peters

The publisher would like to thank the following for their kind permission to reproduce their photographs:

Key: a-above; b-below/bottom; c-centre; f-far; l-left; r-right; t-top

123RF.com: Belikova 90bl; Yulia Belousova 20tl, 230-1; Freda Bouskoutas 121br; Anton Ivanov 116-7b; Andrea Izzotti 170t; Loes Kieboom 10ca; Joanne Weston 281crb.

akg-images: Bildarchiv Steffens 145crb.

Alamy Stock Photo: Aclosund Historic 59br; Aflo Co. Ltd. / AM Corporation 263br; agefotostock / Jerónimo Alba 76bl, / Cem Canbay 302bl, / J.D. Dallet 61clb, / Sara Janini 272-3t; / Laurent Marolleau 247tr, / Richard Maschmeyer 284bl, / Leonardo Díaz Romero 146bl, / Toño Labra 157bl, 159tr, 211cra, 240bl, / Douglas Williams 91t; AGF Srl / Charles Mahaux 150bl, 266bl; Tatiana Aksenova 63bc; Rubens Alarcon 195tr; Jerónimo Alba 37cl; Dorothy Alexander 37br; Luis Emilio Villegas Amador 156t; Auk Archive 63crb; Al Argueta 50tr, 183br; Rafael Ben-Ari 38-9b; Bildagentur-online / Schoening 79tr; Robert Briggs 272bl; Chad Case 24tr; Cavan / Aurora Photos / Ethan Welty 28bl; Jui-Chi Chan 196-7t; Creative Touch Imaging Ltd. 221c; David Crossland 42tl; Bob Daemmrich 63tr; Danita Delimont / Brent Bergherm 28crb; Danita Delimont, Agent / Russell Gordon 47clb, 238crb, / Charles Sleicher 285tl; Keith Dannemiller 54clb; Simon Dannhauer 306-7t; Bill Davis 71t, 126; Bill Davis / Museo de Arte Popular -AAMAP / Vochol - Crystal Beads Vw Beetle by Bautista And Ortbautista And Ortíz Families 36bl; dbimages / Amanda Ahn 132tl, / Allen Brown 206t, / dbtravel 197br, / Roy Johnson 289t; Kinn Deacon 27tr; Design Pics Inc / Axiom / Richard Maschmeyer 295tl, / Destinations / Richard Cummins 25tr, / Destinations / Stuart Westmorland 52bl; directphoto.bz 47br; Reinhard Dirscherl 31tr; Douglas Peebles Photography / Mural at Museo Alhondiga de Ganaditas, Guanajuato by Jose Chavez Morado © DACS 2020 198tl; dpa picture alliance / Jesús Alvarado 54cr; Daniel Gustavo Apodaca Duron 178-9t; John Elk III 285tc; Richard Ellis 53br, 214-5b, 219tl, 274tr; Esdelval 217br; Everett Collection Inc / CSU Archives 117cra; Eye Ubiquitous / Nick Bonetti / Sunday Afternoon in Alameda Park by Diego Rivera © Banco de México Diego Rivera Frida Kahlo Museums Trust, Mexico, D.F. / DACS 2020 88b; Eye Ubiquitous / Nick Bonetti 202br, 205br, 263t; Michele Falzone 45br; Tiago Fernandez 238-9t; FineArt 117br; Robert Fried 205cla; Eddy Galeotti 30tl; Scott Goodno 151tr; Paul Christian Gordon 119cl; Diego Grandi 83bc; Granger Historical Picture Archive, NYC 59tr, 62t, 62crb,117cb; Leigh Green 168bl; Jeff Greenberg 107tr; Jeffrey Isaac Greenberg 5 87br; Luis Gutierrez / NortePhoto.com 179br, 185t, 187br; Pedro Gutierrez 8clb; ML Harris 236bl; Andrew Hasson 128crb; Have Camera Will Travel | Central & South America 77tc; hemis.fr / Leroy Francis 220b, / Franck Guiziou 182cl, /

José Nicolas 105br, / Paul Seux / Museo de Arte Moderno / Las Dos Fridas by Frida Kahlo © Banco de México Diego Rivera Frida Kahlo Museums Trust, Mexico, D.F. / DACS 2020 108tl; Hi-Story 62cr; David Hilbert 140br; Simone Hogan 33cla; Keith Homan 53cra; Dave G. Houser 179clb; IanDagnall Computing 57tr; Image Professionals GmbH / Franz Marc Frei / La Giganta by Jose Luis Cuevas © DACS 2020 86br; imageBROKER / Oliver Gerhard 41br, / Knut Hildebrandt 238bc, / Stefan Kiefer 46b, / Horst Mahr 248b, / Martin Siepmann 223tr, / Vision 21 32bl, 42cra; Independent Picture Service / A.A.M. Van der Heyden 57cla; Anton Ivanov 43t, 120-1t, 123br, 241t; JeffG 133crb; Jon Arnold Images Ltd 145tr, / John Coletti 60tr, 82-3t, / stained glass in Chapultepec Castle Dr. Atl; aka Gerardo Murillo © DACS 2020 108-9b; Bjanka Kadic 36-7t, 101tr,117tl, 118t, 125tr, / Diego Rivera's studio, House - Studio Museum of Diego Rivera and Frida Kahlo, San Angel, Mexico City © Banco de México Diego Rivera Frida Kahlo Museums Trust, Mexico, D.F. / DACS 2020 119bl; Chon Kit Leong 80br; Melvyn Longhurst 77ca, 294cl; Craig Lovell / Eagle Visions Photography 47tr; Elijah Lovkoff 12t; M&N 63tl; M.Sobreira 101crb; Alain Machet (4) 246bl; © Marco / ASK Images 54cl; Marshall Ikonography 302-3t; Richard Maschmeyer 255br; Angus McComiskey 22bl, 289br; Mehdi33300 234-5t; Cathyrose Melloan 227tl; Margaret Metcalfe 83crb; Robert Meyers 28t; John Mitchell 46tl, 110cl, 156cr, 170bc, 269b; J. Enrique Molina 145fbr, 241cra, 248cl; Mostardi Photography 295ca; National Geographic Image Collection / Richard Nowitz 212tl; Nature Picture Library / Jack Dykinga 34cla; Niday Picture Library 60clb; Ai Nishino 236btr; Luc Novovitch 181br; Frank Nowikowski / stained glass by Leopoldo Flores 160t; Brian Overcast 28cr, 58cla, 63cra, 141cra, 145cra, 210bl, 212-3b, 215tr, 229br, 238clb, 255t, 270tl; David Parker 85br; Pascopix 204-5t; Stefano Paterna 308-9t; PhotoBliss 145br; Pictorial Press Ltd 60br; The Picture Art Collection 60tl, 221cb (La Catrina); Marek Poplawski 188-9b; Prisma Archivo 57br, 58br, 61br, 235tr; Radius Images 22t; Alberto Sibaja Ramírez 55tr; Bernardo Ramonfaur 49crb, 59clb; Stefano Ravera 287tr; Robertharding / Wendy Connett 51tr, / Christian Kober 40-1t, 48bl, 158-9b, 208br, / Kim Walker 237t; Emiliano Rodriguez 143cra; Marcelo Rodriguez 216t; Eduardo Fuster Salamero 144-5b; Chico Sanchez 142cl; Schoening 292bl, 292-3b, 293tl; David Shaw 264cr; Mirosław Skórka 265bl; Witold Skrypczak 171b; Jonny Snowden 21t, 276-7; Jan Sochor 55clb, 221ca, 239br; Kumar Sriskandan 286tr; Lee Karen Stow 49bl; Egmont Strigl 143t; Keren Su / China Span 54cra; Hiroko Tanaka 90br; Darren Tierney 280-1b; TMC images 253tr; Travelpix 104br; Jane Tregelles 282t; Nathan and Elaine Vaessen 184bl, 310-1; Lucas Vallecillos 11cr, 12clb, 33br, 43cl, 84b, 89tl, 120bl, 130b, 199b, 219tr; Ivan Vdovin 186t; John Warburton-Lee Photography / David Bank 70, 112-3; Judy Waytiuk 287cr; Jim West 48-9t; Xinhua / Rong Hao 26tl; Zoonar GmbH / Konstantin Kalishko 297cl; Bosiljka Zutich 83clb; Александар Тодоровић 55crb.

Bridgeman Images: 58-9t.

Depositphotos Inc: Naticastillog 109cl.

Dreamstime.com: Adeliepenguin 51cla; Adfoto 238cra; Atosan 68c, 72-3; Florian Blümm 55cra; Boggy 225b; Byelikova 13br, 162bl; Richie Chan 285br; Kobby Dagan 32-3t; Igor Dymov 270-1b;

Eddygaleotti 86tl, 244-5t; Marc Elicagaray 152clb; Esdelval 208t; Alexandre Fagundes De Fagundes 93br; Frenta 287b; Gerasimovvv 290-1b; Diego Grandi 95br, 106b; Sven Hansche 31tl; Tim Hester 34tr; Pablo Hidalgo 283br; Vlad Ispas 41cl; Javarman 30tr, 275b; Denis Kabanov 169t; Liliya Kandrashevich 22cr; Ivan Kokoulin 218bl; Jesse Kraft 51crb; Jesus Eloy Ramos Lara 155b; Chon Kit Leong 79crb, 82crb; Lev Levin 266-7t; Bartosz Luczak 56clb; Lunamarina 27cla; Nailotl Mendez 206bl; Borna Mirahmadian 82bl; Marketa Novakova 80-1t; Oksanaphoto 44bl; William Perry 94bl; Boris Philchev 297br; Nadezda Rabtsevich 154tl; Leon Rafael 144cra; Massimiliano Rastello 35b; Rightdx 4; Sapientisat 268t; SimonDannhauer 34bl; Cristina Stoian 153tr; Enrique Gomez Tamez 39tr; Aleksandar Todorovic 111br, 128bl, 249tr; Mike Van 13cr; Cinar Yilancioglu 304-5b.

Getty Images: 500px / Mary Frisbee 251cr; AFP / Luis Acosta 101bc, / Patricia Castellanos 50b, / Hector Guerrero 54cla, / Ulises Ruiz 221t, / Ronaldo Schemidt 53cl; Bloomberg / Susana Gonzalez 58clb; Corbis News / John Gress 101clb, 102bl; De Agostini Pictire library / DEA / Biblioteca Ambrosiana 61t, G. Dagli Orti 56t, 57clb; Design Pics / Carlos Sanchez Pereyra 256bl; DigitalVision / Jeremy Woodhouse 8cl, 17bl, 164-5; DigitalVision Vectors / ZU_09 58tl; EyeEm / Tarik Lebbadi 42b, / Elijah Lovkoff 194t; EyeEm Premium / Luis M. Cortes Sánchez 17t, 136-7; Glow Images 254br; Andrew Hasson 117cla, 117crb; The Image Bank / John Elk 24-5ca, / Gerard Soury 45cl; In Pictures / Phil Clarke Hill 52-3t; JohannesBluemel Photography 12-3bl; LatinContent Editorial / Pedro Martin Gonzalez Castillo 54crb, / Leopoldo Smith Murillo 22crb; Lonely Planet Images / Richard Cummins 24tl, / Witold Skrypczak 20cb, 257tl, 258-9; Horst Mahr 303cra; Medios y Media / Adrián Monroy 55tl; Moment / Marco Bottigelli 296-7t, / Wendy Connett 56br, / fitopardo.com 134-5, 252-3b, / Sergio Mendoza Hochmann 125bl, / Jia Liu 228cla, / Hagens World Photography 239cb, / M Swiet Productions 30-1ca, / Gabriel Perez 221cb, / Photo by Rafa Elias 55cla, / Maria Swärd 26tr; Moment Open / © fitopardo.com 27tl; Michael Nolan 39br; Perspectives / Greg Vaughn 18t, 174-5; Photodisc / Gonzalo Azumendi 148t; Sollina Images 38tr; Stockbyte / Ivy Reynolds 239bl; Stone / Andrew Peacock 25tl; Stone / Livia Corona 221bc; ullstein bild Dtl. 60cra; Universal Images Group / Eagle Visions Photography / Craig Lovell 221cb (Papier maché), / Education Images 39cl, / Jeff Greenberg 100-1t, 103t, 104t; Westend61 13t, 44-5t.

iStockphoto.com: : Orbon Alija 69b, 96-7; arielcione 8-9b; Arturogi 273br; Benedek 132-3b, 140-1t, 242t; E_Rojas 128-9; E+ / Bluebird13 131tc, / Ferrantraite 6-7, 10-1b,11t, 19b, 172-3b, 190-1; ferrantraite 201tl, 224t; holgs 11br, 182t; Indigoai 152-3b; jejim 179crb; JessicaPichardo 155tr; Nathan Kelly 85tl; lenawurm 145cr; Peter Marik 8cla; Arturo Peña Romano Med 35t; mehdi33300 202t; mofles 298bl, 298br; Moment Open / Matt Mawson 10clb; OGphoto 35cr, 304tl; Pe3check 308bl; Sepp Puchinger 245tr; Laura Ragsdale 250t; Redtea 161br; segarza 180-1t; SL_ Photography 2-3; sorincolac 300-1b; Starcevic 16c, 64-5; Stockcam 57tl, 78-9b.

Mary Evans Picture Library: Iberfoto 178bl.

Nestlé Chocolate Museum- Rojkind Arquitectos: Paul Rivera 43crb.

Odd Society Spirits - Katharine Manson Communications: Cause And Affect 50-1t.

Robert Harding Picture Library: Rodrigo Torres 222-3b.

Shutterstock: Anne Czichos 123tl; EPA / Alejandro Zepeda 40bl, Granger 62bl.

SuperStock: www.agefotostock.com / Vojtech Vlk 264-5t.

Front flap images:
Alamy Jonny Snowden c; Jane Tregelles br; **iStockphoto.com:** E+ / Ferrantraite t, cra; **Getty Images:** Moment / Sergio Mendoza Hochmann bl, Universal Images Group / Eagle Visions Photography / Craig Lovell cla.

Cover images:
Front and spine: **Getty Images:** Moment / Marco Bottigelli.
Back: **Getty Images:** Moment / Marco Bottigelli b; **iStockphoto.com:** benedek tr, E+ / ferrantraite cl.

Original cartography from ERA-Maptec Ltd and BIMSA Cartosistemas, S.A. de C.V.

For further information see: www.dkimages.com

Illustrators: José Luis de Andrés de Colsa, Gary Cross, Richard Draper, Javier Gómez Morata (Acanto Arquitectura y Urbanismo S.L.), Isidoro González-Adalid Cabezas (Acanto Arquitectura y Urbanismo S.L.), Stephen Guapay, Paul Guest, Claire Littlejohn, John Woodcock.

This edition updated by

Contributors Lauren Cocking,
Julie Schwietert Collazo

Senior Editor Alison McGill

Senior Designers Tania Da Silva Gomes,
Stuti Tiwari

Project Editors Parnika Bagla, Rada Radojicic

Project Art Editor Bharti Karakoti

Picture Research Administrator
Vagisha Pushp

Jacket Coordinator Bella Talbot

Jacket Designer Jordan Lambley

Senior Cartographer Subhashree Bharati

Cartography Manager Suresh Kumar

DTP Designer Tanveer Zaidi

Senior Production Editor Jason Little

Production Controller Kariss Ainsworth

Deputy Managing Editor Beverly Smart

Managing Editors Shikha Kulkarni,
Hollie Teague

Senior Managing Art Editor
Priyanka Thakur

Art Director Maxine Pedliham

Publishing Director Georgina Dee

First edition 1999

Published in Great Britain by Dorling Kindersley Limited,
DK, One Embassy Gardens, 8 Viaduct Gardens,
London SW11 7BW

The authorised representative in the EEA is
Dorling Kindersley Verlag GmbH. Arnulfstr.
124, 80636 Munich, Germany

Published in the United States by DK Publishing,
1450 Broadway, Suite 801, New York, NY 10018

Copyright © 1999, 2022 Dorling Kindersley Limited
A Penguin Random House Company
22 23 24 25 10 9 8 7 6 5 4 3 2 1

All rights reserved.

No part of this publication may be reproduced, stored in
or introduced into a retrieval system, or transmitted, in any
form, or by any means (electronic, mechanical, photocopying,
recording, or otherwise), without the prior written permission
of the copyright owner.

The publishers cannot accept responsibility for any consequences
arising from the use of this book, nor for any material on third
party websites, and cannot guarantee that any website address in
this book will be a suitable source of travel information.

A CIP catalog record for this book
is available from the British Library.

A catalog record for this book is available
from the Library of Congress.

ISSN: 1542 1554
ISBN: 978 02415 6607 7

Printed and bound in China.

www.dk.com

MIX
Paper from
responsible sources
FSC **FSC™ C018179**
www.fsc.org

This book was made with
Forest Stewardship Council ™
certified paper – one small
step in DK's commitment to
a sustainable future.
For more information go to
www.dk.com/our-green-pledge

A NOTE FROM DK EYEWITNESS

The rapid rate at which the world is changing is
constantly keeping the DK Eyewitness team on our
toes. While we've worked hard to ensure that this edition
of Mexico is accurate and up-to-date, we know that
opening hours alter, standards shift, prices fluctuate,
places close and new ones pop up in their stead. So,
if you notice we've got something wrong or left
something out, we want to hear about it.
Please get in touch at travelguides@dk.com